Euthanasia and Assisted Suicide

Euthanasia and Assisted Suicide

Global Views on Choosing to End Life

Michael J. Cholbi, PhD, Editor

PRAEGER™

An Imprint of ABC-CLIO, LLC

Santa Barbara, California • Denver, Colorado

Library of Congress Cataloging-in-Publication Data

Names: Cholbi, Michael, editor.
Title: Euthanasia and assisted suicide : global views on choosing to end life / Michael J. Cholbi, PhD, editor.
Description: Santa Barbara, California : Praeger, an imprint of ABC-CLIO, LLC, [2017] | Includes bibliographical references and index.
Identifiers: LCCN 2016033838 (print) | LCCN 2016039716 (ebook) | ISBN 9781440836794 (alk. paper) | ISBN 9781440836800 (ebook)
Subjects: LCSH: Euthanasia. | Assisted suicide.
Classification: LCC R726 .E97 2017 (print) | LCC R726 (ebook) | DDC 179.7—dc23
LC record available at https://lccn.loc.gov/2016033838

ISBN: 978-1-4408-3679-4
EISBN: 978-1-4408-3680-0

21 20 19 18 17   1 2 3 4 5

This book is also available as an eBook.

Praeger
An Imprint of ABC-CLIO, LLC

ABC-CLIO, LLC
130 Cremona Drive, P.O. Box 1911
Santa Barbara, California 93116-1911
www.abc-clio.com

This book is printed on acid-free paper ∞
Manufactured in the United States of America

Contents

Part II   Ethics and Policy

Introduction

Michael J. Cholbi

The modern discipline of medical ethics arose in the 20th century, largely due to increasing interest in three controversial areas of medical practice: medical research, abortion, and end-of-life decisions. End-of-life decisions in particular became an acute ethical issue due to the changing nature of how individuals die in advanced societies. Through the 20th century, dying became a more technological—and often more prolonged—experience. Infectious diseases and injuries as causes of death decreased, and chronic conditions which kill more gradually—such as cancer—became more prominent. Moreover, technologies such as artificial nutrition and ventilation made it possible to extend biological life nearly indefinitely. The result of these developments is that how and when individuals die became a matter of choice to an unprecedented degree. Indeed, many human beings alive today will not die in a way that prior generations would recognize as entirely "natural." Rather, they will die because someone (perhaps the individuals themselves, perhaps their family members or physicians) chooses a course of action that they know full well will hasten death—for example, refusing (or ceasing) a potentially life-extending treatment or opting to remove life-sustaining medical interventions.

The most controversial way for a person to opt to die, however, is through assisted dying. This takes two main forms: euthanasia and assisted suicide. Under euthanasia, an individual dies when someone else (usually, though not necessarily, a physician or other medical professional) brings about the person's death through direct action or intervention and the person benefits from dying. An example of euthanasia is when an individual with a painful and incurable illness knowingly asks a doctor to administer a dose of a lethal sedative. Euthanasia can be voluntary, as in this example, but it need not be. Under assisted suicide, an individual dies after another person (most often a physician or other medical professional) provides material assistance in dying but the patient himself or herself administers the agent or performs the procedure that causes death. An example of assisted suicide is when an individual with a painful and incurable illness asks a doctor to prescribe a lethal dose of a sedative, which the patient later administers with the aim of causing death.

Euthanasia and assisted suicide raise crucial questions regarding the value of life; the goodness of death; and an individual's right to determine the length of his or her life, and the circumstances of his or her death. As even the most cursory review of popular media and academic scholarship indicate, assisted dying is controversial both morally and legally. The sheer volume of literature on the subject can be disorienting to newcomers interested in these controversies. This volume attempts to prevent such disorientation by introducing nonexpert readers to the central legal, political, and ethical issues associated with euthanasia and assisted suicide. Operating from a historical and cross-cultural perspective, the goal of this work is to familiarize readers with the moral, legal, and professional developments that have shaped contemporary debates about euthanasia and assisted suicide.

This book first explains the key concepts used in legal and ethical debates surrounding these practices, and then traces how various global traditions (e.g., Christianity, Asiatic) and societies (e.g., the United States, England, Mexico) have addressed the morality of such practices. It then turns to the key ethical and policy questions concerning euthanasia and assisted suicide. This volume outlines the main ethical arguments both for and against assisted dying, as well as relating assisted dying to other medical practices, such as palliation and advance directives.

The authors of the chapters in this book have striven to present the core issues surrounding euthanasia and assisted suicide in an accessible and nontechnical way. Although these articles only scratch the surface of the numerous complex issues raised by these phenomena, they (along with the chapter bibliographies) nevertheless should leave readers well-positioned to investigate these issues further on their own.

As the discussions in this volume attest, however, the overall global trend with respect to assisted dying is toward general societal acceptance and legal permissiveness. Euthanasia and assisted suicide no longer are purely hypothetical phenomena. To the extent that the moral and legal justifiability of euthanasia and assisted suicide turn on the consequences of social or legal acceptance, we now have far more evidence about these consequences than we did in the past. Yet different communities have responded to the prospect of assisted dying in different ways—colored by their respective ethical and religious commitments. The legal and moral landscape surrounding assisted dying thus is far more diverse than it was just several decades ago.

That said, these communities nevertheless seem to be engaging in the same underlying controversies: Whether assisted dying is ever truly a benefit to a person; how assisted dying fits within various religious outlooks; whether assisted dying should be construed as a right; the role of the medical profession in the provision of assisted dying; and who should be eligible for assisted dying and under what circumstances. The debates ensure that although the moral and legal controversies surrounding assisted dying might dim they are not likely to be fully extinguished in the near future.

PART I

History, Practice, and Law

Physician-Assisted Dying and the Law in the United States: A Perspective on Three Prospective Futures

Arthur G. Svenson

The movement to legalize physician-assisted dying (PAD) in the United States is, at its core, one that focuses on a terminally ill competent adult (TICA) who, because of unbearable pain and suffering, seeks a physician's assistance to hasten death. Consider—one among countless others similarly situated—the declaration of Jane Roe, one of the original litigants in *Glucksberg v. Washington* (1997),[1] the Supreme Court's first of two landmark explorations of PAD and the Constitution delivered on June 26, 1997.

> The pain associated with this cancer is unrelenting. It is a constant, dull pain, interspersed with sharp, severe pain provoked by movement. . . . It is not possible to eliminate my pain and for me to retain an alert state. . . . Chemotherapy caused bone marrow depression, fatigue, severe bladder irritation, diarrhea, and nausea. Radiation caused further bone marrow depression, requiring repeated blood transfusions; severe bleeding; diarrhea; fatigue; severe sore throat; and first-degree skin burns. . . . At the

point at which I can no longer endure the pain and suffering associated with my cancer I want to have drugs available for the purpose of hastening my death. . . . I am mentally competent.

Consider, too, the declaration of George A. Kingsley, one of the original litigants in *Vacco v. Quill* (1997),[2] *Glucksberg's* landmark companion.

At this time I have almost no immune system function. . . . My first major illness associated with AIDS was . . . a parasitic infection which caused me severe fevers and diarrhea and associated pain, suffering and exhaustion. . . . I also suffer from . . . an AIDS-related virus which attacks the retina and causes blindness. . . . I am at risk of losing my sight altogether from this condition. . . . I also suffer from . . . a parasitic infection which has caused lesions to develop on my brain. . . . I inject my leg daily with neupogen to combat the deficit white cell count in my blood. The daily injection of this medication is extremely painful. . . . At this point it is clear to me, based on the advice of my doctors, that I am in the terminal phase of AIDS. . . . It is my desire that my physician prescribe suitable drugs for me to consume for the purpose of hastening my death when and if my suffering becomes intolerable.

For both Roe and Kingsley, and the countless others similarly situated, the movement to legalize PAD in the United States is also about legal end-of-life options that some TICAs find objectionable, primarily (1) to refuse or (2) to remove life-sustaining medical treatment (LSMT) and die, or (3) following drug-induced unconsciousness, to die after food and water have been withdrawn—an option called "terminal sedation." The illegal but unobjectionable alternative for some? Seeking, ultimately, to control the time, place, and manner of one's death. Advocates of PAD aim to legalize a modestly constructed option that allows a physician to prescribe a life-ending drug to a TICA who then self-administers that drug to achieve the "humane and dignified death" the patient desires. The fate of the physician-assisted dying option is determined by state laws that criminalize assisted suicide; however sympathetic the doctor, these legal barriers are unambiguously prohibitive.

In 1997, judicial challenges to those legal barriers arrived before the United States Supreme Court. In *Washington v. Glucksberg* and then in *Vacco v. Quill*, the Court was asked to void assisted-suicide bans as they applied to physicians who agreed to assist qualified patients to hasten an unbearable dying process. In *Glucksberg*, PAD lawyers argued that powerfully inviting language from an opinion written in *Planned Parenthood of Southeastern Pennsylvania v. Casey* (1992)[3] not only reaffirmed a woman's right to an abortion but also, the lawyers argued, invited the Court to recognize physician-assisted dying as a constitutionally protected right. The freedom to make abortion decisions and now PAD choices was embedded in and protected by the *Planned Parenthood* reasoning because—quoting from that opinion—both were among

> the most intimate and personal choices a person may make in a lifetime, choices central to personal dignity and autonomy, and central to the liberty protected by the Fourteenth Amendment. At the heart of liberty is the right to define one's own concept of existence, of meaning, of the universe, and of the mystery of human life. Beliefs about these matters could not define the attributes of personhood were they formed under compulsion of the State.[4]

The Court in *Glucksberg* disagreed, refusing to incorporate PAD within that group of mystery-of-life choices deserving constitutional protection. Surveying the history and tradition of more than 700 years of Anglo-American common law, Chief Justice Rehnquist noted that suicide and suicide assistance had always been prohibited[5]; and a host of valid secular reasons advanced by government to ban assisted suicide, was, for a unanimous court, meaningful and persuasive:[6] First, government's unqualified interest in the preservation of human life; second, government's obligation to protect the integrity and ethics of the medical profession; third, government's need to protect vulnerable groups—those, for example, who were poor, elderly, or disabled—from, in this context, end-of-life abuse; and finally, government's fear that even a modest PAD option would be deconstructed, then immodestly reconstructed to include suffering patients who were not terminally ill, then physician-administered death—"euthanasia"—for patients unable to self-administer life-ending drugs, then, worse, for patients irrespective of their medical condition, mental capacity, or age.

In *Vacco*, the Court was asked to legalize PAD in light of the Constitution's equal protection principle demanding that similar classes of people require similar treatment. Thus, if TICAs tethered to LSMT can choose death by removing that support, a similar group of TICAs not tethered should also have the right to choose death, and in this instance by PAD. The Court disagreed, indicating that the two groups are distinguishable in light of issues relating to intent and causation.[7] The doctor's intent when removing LSMT is "to respect his patient's wishes," and the doctor's intent underlying PAD is to bring about death; the cause of death when life support is removed is the underlying disease, but in PAD the lethal drug causes death. Therefore, the Court reasoned, dissimilar groups can be dissimilarly treated without violating the constitutional principle of equal protection under the law.

Although in *Glucksberg* and *Vacco* the High Court refused to elevate PAD to the status of a protected constitutional right, advocates surely must have been inspired by the closing thoughts of Chief Justice Rehnquist in his *Glucksberg* ruling, "Throughout the Nation, Americans are engaged in an earnest and profound debate about the morality, legality, and practicality of physician-assisted suicide. Our holding permits this debate to continue, as it should in a democratic society."[8] To each state, then, devolved a policymaking green light to legislate over this end-of-life option.

Since the *Glucksberg* and *Vacco* decisions, bills to legalize PAD have been introduced in more than 25 states.[9] As of November 2016, the states of Oregon,[10] Washington,[11] Montana,[12] Vermont,[13] California,[14] and Colorado[15] have legalized PAD. Lawmaking strategies in these states are markedly different. Oregon, Washington, and Colorado relied on voter-approved initiatives; in Vermont and California, state legislatures took center stage; and in Montana, state judges fashioned policy. That California—the most populace state in the union—legalized PAD in 2015, having debated that option for nearly a quarter of a century, is an event of seismic proportions: With the stroke of the governor's pen, 38.8 million Californians have access to this end-of-life choice. Put differently, that equates to one in eight citizens of the United States!

This chapter examines PAD and the law in the United States, with an eye on the past and seeking perspectives on three prospective futures. First, the Oregon model and effect. The first state in the country to legalize PAD, Oregon's law advances three fundamental principles: (1) the law applies to a modest few—only TICAs who can self-administer the death-inducing drug; (2) the law removes all references to suicide from its statutory vocabulary; and (3) to address the fears of PAD opponents, the law codifies a rigorous set of safeguards designed to ensure that its practice will be "safe, legal, and rare." What lessons from Oregon's experience have been learned, and how might those lessons be expected to occupy future PAD debates? What impact might the experience of Oregon—and now California—have on states that might take up the PAD debate? Momentum, perhaps, cascading forward as state after state adopts PAD or, alternatively perhaps, images of Dr. Jack Kevorkian (the "doctor of death") surface as physicians push modest Oregon boundaries to immodest outer boundaries of uncertain acceptability. Might California's as-yet unwritten PAD future lead back to the U.S. Congress where, as before, availing themselves of broad national powers, national representatives debate legislation designed to trump state legislative initiatives legalizing PAD?

Next, the Montana model and effect is examined. The first state to legalize PAD in the courtroom, Montana jurists addressed some of the most fundamental and enduring questions about the exercise of judicial power. Prominent among these questions: Is the courtroom an appropriate forum to make end-of-life policy or are democratic forces better equipped for this task? In this regard and, it should be noted, of enormous consequence is that although Montana jurists legalized PAD, they did so despite their inability to replicate Oregon's rigorously debated regulatory safeguards. Instead, professional best-practice standards—the so-called medical model—were judged to allay fears. About the Montana model, then, will best practices prevent abuse or will PAD practices without publically mandated safeguards slide down a slippery slope into public opprobrium? Finally, with respect to the effect of Montana's model, will other states' jurists be inspired to act independently from—not dependently upon—arguments addressed and resolved by the U.S. Supreme Court? "New Judicial Federalism,"[16] a maturing state judicial trend aiming to expand the scope of state freedoms beyond those minimally protected by the U.S. Supreme Court and the U.S. Constitution, is a prospective future easily imagined from the work of Montana jurists.

The *Lawrence-Obergefell* model and effect is the third prospective future. Are there reasons to believe that the Supreme Court might reconsider its landmark *Glucksberg* and *Vacco* rulings from 1997? Although the unanimous *Glucksberg* and *Vacco* rulings concluded that suicide and suicide assistance were not rights "deeply rooted in this Nation's history and tradition," the High Court since then has recognized fundamental constitutional rights to consensual same-sex sodomy and same-sex marriage, in 2003 and 2015, respectively, and this despite an animas to both that was "deeply rooted in this Nation's history and tradition." Curiously, the very poetic lines from *Planned Parenthood*—"[a]t the heart of liberty is the right to define one's own concept of existence, of meaning, of the universe, and of the mystery of human life"—found not useful to the *Glucksberg* Court were prominently and favorably on display to justify an "emerging awareness" of newfound rights in *Lawrence* and *Obergefell*. An emerging awareness indeed, especially if California's experiences reaffirm Oregon's—that PAD has not been abused—calling into question, as a consequence, government interests to deny TICAs the right to choose a "humane and dignified death."

First, Oregon.

The Oregon Model and Effect

On November 8, 1994, Oregon became the first state to legalize PAD; its Death With Dignity Act (DWDA), a voter-approved initiative, was ratified by a slim 2 percent of the voters. The Act was challenged almost immediately. First, a federal district court enjoined its enforcement, theorizing that the principle of equality required Oregon to protect all citizens from the law banning assisted suicide, not almost all of them—that is, those few TICAs who might choose a hastened death with a physician's assistance. That court order finally was dissolved on October 27, 1997. Next, the Oregon State Legislature required Oregonians to consider repealing their initiative, which, on November 4, 1997, they refused to do—by an overwhelming 20 percent of the vote. Oregon's DWDA, at last, took effect in 1998.

The provisions of Oregon's DWDA are well known. Most significant among them, Oregonians who qualify for a "humane and dignified death" are a narrowly circumscribed group: the patient must be a terminally ill capable adult who could self-administer the prescription drug; mercy killing of any sort remains illegal. Other noteworthy provisions include:

- The patient must be a resident of Oregon and at least 18 years of age;
- The patient must be "capable" of making and communicating health-care decisions, and dying from a terminal illness, that is, a disease that is "incurable and irreversible" and will "within reasonable medical judgment, produce death within six months";
- Attending and consulting physicians must agree on the diagnosis and prognosis;
- The patient's decision to request a lethal prescription must be "informed," requiring the physician to convey "relevant facts" about the diagnosis, the prognosis, possible risks, and, importantly, PAD alternatives such as hospice and palliative care;
- If a doctor suspects a mental disorder, then professional counseling is required;
- The patient's request "to end [his or] her life in a humane and dignified manner" must be made voluntarily, requiring as proof two oral requests for a hastened death separated by no less than 15 days, as well as a written request that is signed, dated, and witnessed by two persons who can attest that "the patient is capable, acting voluntarily, and is not being coerced to sign the request";
- Respecting the written request, the attending physician may not be a witness and one of the two witnesses may not be a relative, or a person who "would be entitled to any portion of the estate of the qualified patient upon death," or "an owner, operator or employee of a health care facility where the qualified patient is receiving medical treatment or is a resident";

- The Act also requires that 48 hours separate the written request and the writing of the prescription.

Lastly, and towering over all other requirements for many PAD sympathizers, the law imposes this interpretive mandate: "Actions taken in accordance with this Act shall not, for any purpose, constitute suicide, assisted suicide, mercy killing or homicide, under the law."

Since 1998, annual reports from Oregon documenting its practice satisfy most observers that PAD is "safe, legal, and rare."[17] The lessons learned from the data are, with small variations, consistent year after year.[18] Although PAD deaths in Oregon have risen incrementally since 1998, no more than 0.3 percent of all deaths in the state are attributable to the Act. Most Oregonians who choose PAD succumb to cancer and die at home; most choose PAD for reasons relating to the loss of autonomy, or dignity, or the "decreasing ability to participate in activities that make life enjoyable." PAD patients are predominately Caucasian, insured, financially comfortable, educated, not disabled, and "were receiving comprehensive pain and symptom management, typically through hospice services."[19] Since 1998, "referrals of patients to hospice increased dramatically as did physician enrollment in continuing education courses on how to treat pain and symptoms associated with terminal illness."[20] As for fears articulated by PAD opponents, no known cases of PAD abuse have been verified to date.[21]

The PAD model that Oregon crafted rests on three foundational principles: (1) qualified patients are modestly limited to only those TICAs who can self-administer a prescription drug; (2) suicide is removed from the law's vocabulary; and (3) a rigorous set of safeguards are codified to prevent PAD abuse. What effect has this model had outside Oregon? On Election Day, November 4, 2008, the State of Washington became the second state to legalize the PAD option. Oregon's model had moved north; Washington's I-1000 replicated the provisions of Oregon's law nearly word for word, including most tellingly the interpretive mandate that "[a]ctions taken in accordance [with the law] shall not, for any purpose, constitute suicide or assisted suicide." On this bedrock issue, during debates preceding Washington's vote, opponents of the measure argued that the initiative would legalize "physician-assisted suicide." Proponents rejected that characterization just as Oregonians had, and for the same reason: Unlike people with suicidal designs, the TICAs who seek PAD are rational and wish to live. Thus, for a small number of TICAs nearing the end of a painful dying process, only "assisted dying" and not "assisted suicide" could accurately describe their choice. On November 8, 2016, Oregon's model moved southeast when Colorado approved its End of Life Options Act, Proposition 106, by a 2-1 vote, making it the third of six states to legalize PAD through an initiative process.[22]

Oregon's model reappeared again in Vermont, but with one enormous exception. Vermont legalized PAD on May 20, 2013, and its provisions, mirroring Oregon's, were effective the moment Governor Peter Shumlin signed the bill into law—Act 39. Vermont—with the second smallest and fastest aging population in the country—had debated PAD for more than a decade and had now become the first state in the nation to legalize this option through the legislative process. An "historic achievement . . . a political breakthrough that will boost death-with-dignity bills nationwide,"[23] observed Barbara Coombs Lee, president of Compassion and Choices, the nation's leading advocate of end-of-life options. As Governor Shumlin observed, "I am grateful that the legislature had such a thoughtful, respectful debate on this deeply personal issue. We will now offer Vermonters who have terminal illness at the end of life a choice to control their destiny and avoid unnecessary suffering."[24]

Vermont's enormous exception to the Oregon model? As originally conceived, Vermont's PAD proposal included provisions that described and regulated the PAD practices in language channeling Oregon's, and with 15 years of data demonstrating that Oregon's practices were not abused, the Vermont bill attracted bipartisan support. The same foundational principles of Oregon's model guided and controlled Vermont's debate. As it turns out, however, an alternative bill that stripped away most Oregon safeguards also was introduced; in this rendering of PAD, the law would merely immunize those physicians from criminal and civil liability who had prescribed death-inducing drugs to TICAs.

The Vermont experience revealed a philosophic divide: legislators who considered public controls like Oregon's absolutely essential as bulwarks against abuse, and legislators who believed burdensome rules and regulations governing the process amounted to an "undue government intervention in what should be a sacred exchange between doctor and patient."[25] Those arguing for public controls predicted that, in their absence, the state could not ensure that "people know what they're doing, they understand the consequences and that we keep records that show us how this is working"[26]; those rejecting "carefully crafted safeguards" held that "the close relations between a doctor and their patients" were safeguards aplenty.[27]

A middle ground of sorts determined Vermont's final version of its PAD measure: the state's PAD practices would be heavily regulated by Oregon-like safeguards until July 1, 2016, when that regulatory scheme with its proven record would be rescinded. As fate would have it, however, no such repeal occurred; in May 2015, choosing Oregon safeguards over best practices, Vermont legislators scuttled their planned 2016 sunset.

Californians have debated a variety of end-of-life options for many years, and with no law to show for it. In 1988, a popular initiative titled "Humane and Dignified Death" failed to generate enough voter interest to qualify for the ballot, probably because of an immodest reach that would have sanctioned euthanasia (or mercy killing) not only for competent adults suffering a terminal illness, but also for incompetent adults who, when competent, had elected in an advanced directive to be euthanized. California's Proposition 161, an initiative appearing on the ballot that did countenance euthanasia was defeated on November 3, 1992.

The California State Legislature also has debated end-of-life measures, but without success. Oregon data demonstrating that PAD is practiced without abuse, and even opinion polls pointing unambiguously to broad bipartisan support among voters in California and elsewhere,[28] could not persuade California lawmakers to act.

Persuasion arrived from an unexpected source, however, and dramatic were its results when Brittany Maynard—age 29, recently married, attractive, passionate, and adventurous—moved from her San Francisco home to establish residence in Portland to avail herself of that state's right to PAD. Diagnosed with brain cancer on January 1, 2014, on January 10 surgeons performed a partial craniotomy of Brittany's temporal lobe hoping to halt the tumor's growth. In April, tragically, the tumor returned. Her doctor's diagnosis and prognosis: stage four glioblastoma; death within six months. Brittany's response was the following:

> Because my tumor is so large, doctors prescribed full brain radiation. I read about the side effects: The hair on my scalp would have been singed off. My scalp would be left covered with first-degree burns. My quality of life, as I knew it, would be gone. After months of research, my family and I reached a heartbreaking conclusion: There is no treatment that would save my life, and the recommended treatments would have destroyed the time I had left.[29]

With that, Brittany and her husband moved to Oregon, established residency, and found new doctors. There Brittany sought to control the time, place, and manner of her dying process. With prescription in hand and her suffering no longer bearable, Brittany would self-administer her lethal potion and "pass peacefully" surrounded by her family and friends. "I am not suicidal," she emphasized, but "who has the right to tell me that I don't deserve this choice? That I deserve to suffer for weeks or months in tremendous amounts of physical and emotional pain? Why should anyone have the right to make that choice for me?"[30]

Brittany shared her story with Compassion and Choices, and on October 5, 2014, a six-minute posting of her story was viewed by millions, prompting bioethicist Arthur Caplan to remark that Brittany

changes the optics of the debate. Now we have a young woman getting people in her generation interested in the issue. Critics are worried about her partly because she's speaking to that new audience, and they know that the younger generation of America has shifted attitudes about gay marriage and the use of marijuana, and maybe they are going to have that same impact in pushing physician-assisted suicide forward.[31]

Compassion and Choices president Barbara Combs Lee put matters this way:

[Brittany Maynard] has changed everything for us in terms of awareness. The general public has sort of an unspoken expectation that this is what old people deal with. [Her] situation is so different. She's young, she's vibrant. She could be my daughter. She could be a granddaughter, a neighbor, a school friend.[32]

As she had planned, Brittany's death arrived on November 1. In a Facebook posting before her passing Brittany wrote:

Goodbye to all my dear friends and family that I love. Today is the day I have chosen to pass away with dignity in the face of my terminal illness, this terrible brain cancer that has taken so much from me. . . . The world is a beautiful place, travel has been my greatest teacher, my close friends and folks are the greatest givers. I even have a ring of support around my bed as I type. . . . Goodbye world. Spread good energy. Pay it forward![33]

Significantly, too, and just before her death, Brittany not only videotaped a plea to California lawmakers to legalize an Oregon-like end-of-life choice, she also spoke with California governor Jerry Brown by phone about her decision and why she believed a law legalizing PAD was necessary and proper.

As if on cue, less than three months after Brittany's passing, Senate Bill 128 was introduced in the California State Legislature; again, modeled after Oregon's, California's End of Life Option Act (ELOA), said one of its sponsors, was introduced in light of the "sea change in public opinion and we think a lot of that has been catalyzed by Brittany Maynard being willing to be public and courageous with her story."[34] Unlike previous attempts in California, the ELOA sailed successfully out of state senate committees and was approved on the Senate floor nearly along party lines, 23 to 15, on June 5, 2015.

Not only was Brittany Maynard's spiritual presence palpably influential, so, too, was an historic shift announced by California's powerful medical association. The first in the nation not to oppose PAD, the California Medical Association (CMA) reasoned that, despite a doctor's obligation to do no harm, "as physicians, we want to provide the best care possible for our patients. However, despite the remarkable medical breakthroughs we've made and the world-class hospice or palliative care we can provide, it isn't always enough. The decision to participate in the End of Life Option Act," explained CMA president Luther Cobb, "is a very personal one between a doctor and their patient, which is why CMA has removed policy that outright objects to physicians aiding terminally ill patients in end of life options. We believe it is up to the individual physician and their patient to decide voluntarily whether the End of Life Option Act is something in which they want to engage."[35]

But the fate of California's ELOA would not only be determined by Brittany Maynard's forceful image, or by the neutrality of California doctors, or by toweringly favorable public opinion polls cutting across political, ethical, and religious lines. In the end, political shenanigans opened a door that had just closed.

In July 2015, ELOA sponsors withdrew their proposal from the Assembly Health Committee convinced, despite a majority of Democrats, that the bill would be resisted by Latino Assembly members lobbied by the Catholic Church. The legislative session ended.

Not to be deterred, however, a special legislative session called by Governor Brown opened in August. According to the governor, this special session was to address pressing issues of public health care financing; reckoning that the ELOA was germane, legislative sponsors reintroduced their PAD initiative. Reconfigured committees and committee assignments during the special legislative session proved beneficial for ELOA advocates. The measure was approved by the Senate and Assembly, and on October 5, 2015, the governor signed the measure into law. In his signing statement, the former Jesuit student ultimately approved the measure on personal grounds no doubt shared by countless numbers of TICAs who sought control over their dying process. Brown wrote, "I do not know what I would do if I were dying in prolonged and excruciating pain. I am certain, however, that it would be a comfort to be able to consider the options afforded by this bill. And I wouldn't deny that right to others."[36]

California's law parrots Oregon's in all crucial ways with one not insignificant exception: ELOA must be reauthorized in 10 years to save it from fading into the sunset. Notably, an attempt to repeal the law with a November 2016 referendum failed to gather requisite signatures.

What will California's PAD experiences reveal? Will Brittany Maynard's young new face have a lasting impact on the movement to legalize PAD? Will other state medical associations follow the lead of their colleagues in California? Having adopted the Oregon model—modest in scope, tightly conceptualized to exclude the vocabulary of suicide, and heavily regulated—might annual reports from California reaffirming the "safe, legal, and rare" practice of PAD fuel successful legislative initiatives across the country? And if data in our largest state indicate otherwise, might the PAD movement itself fade into the sunset along with California's law?

The Montana Model and Effect

Judicial strategies launched in state courts to legalize PAD predictably employ a three-pronged attack on offending state law, one that turns on a statutory argument and two very different constitutional arguments. These strategies rarely are successful, but not for a lack of perseverance, nor a lack of rational and common sense argument. One dramatic victory in Montana continues to stoke interest in courtroom policymaking as a viable remedy for PAD advocates.

The statutory challenge targets a state law that criminalizes assisted suicide; omnipresent throughout the United States, the law makes it a felony for any person to deliberately aid, advise, or encourage another to commit suicide. But does that law apply to a physician who assists in the death of a competent adult dying of a terminal illness? For PAD proponents the answer is emphatically "no." Whether lobbying state legislators, rallying public support, or, in this context, crafting legal arguments for the court, the assisted death of a TICA is not suicide. Returning to a foundational principle of the Oregon model, at the threshold of death the choice is not whether to live or die, but how, when, and where death will occur. A growing number of professional organizations have written legal briefs defending this perspective: the American Academy of Hospice and Palliative Medicine, for example, believes that for TICAs whose pain is unremitting, "a lethal medication that the patient can take by his own hand to end otherwise intolerable suffering" is not suicide.[37]

Underlying the developing popularity of this view is the belief that "profound psychological differences" distinguish suicide from PAD. James Lieberman, an authority often cited on this issue, advances the following list of differences:

(1) "The suicidal patient has no terminal illness but wants to die; the [PAD] patient has a terminal illness and wants to live";

(2) "Typical Suicides bring shock and tragedy to families and friends; [PAD] deaths are peaceful and supported by loved ones";

(3) "Typical suicides are secretive and often impulsive and violent. Death [by PAD] is planned . . . ;"

(4) "Suicide is an expression of despair and futility; [PAD] is a form of affirmation and empowerment."[38]

End-of-life legislation in Oregon, Washington, Vermont, California, and Colorado is evidence of an emerging awareness that distinctions with very compelling differences separate assisted suicide from PAD. In state courtrooms across the country, for these reasons, PAD well-wishers seek statutory clarification from a court that state law against assisted suicide does not apply—and was never intended to apply—to a physician who assists in the death of a TICA. This very line of reasoning might have motivated Michigan jurors who, in three separate trials, acquitted Dr. Jack Kevorkian of unlawful suicide assistance in the 1990s; jurors ultimately convicted Dr. Kevorkian of euthanizing—murdering—a patient otherwise unable to self-administer a lethal drug, circumstances unconnected to the state's law against suicide assistance.

The two state constitutional challenges focus on the most elementary pillars of American civil rights and liberties, namely, that government shall not deny equal protection of the law, nor deprive life, liberty, or property without due process of the law.

Respecting the principle of equal protection, in its landmark decision in *Cruzan v. Director, Missouri Department of Health* (1990)[39]—one that followed approvingly the decision of the New Jersey Supreme Court in *In Re Quinlan* (1976),[40] the Supreme Court unequivocally established that all competent persons enjoy the right to be free from unwanted medical treatment, and in Cruzan's situation, that unwanted life-sustaining medical treatment could be removed. Accordingly, a TICA attached to life support could choose death by removing those devices, or if unattached, the TICA could choose death by refusing treatment. Under the law, death in either case would not be an act of suicide, but rather a death caused by the underlying disease or condition. Based on this established right to refuse or remove LSMT, therefore, PAD advocates stipulate that TICAs not connected to LSMT also deserve a pathway to death, true because similar persons deserve similar treatment as demanded by state and national constitutional principles of equal protection. Thus, in the absence of a meaningful legal distinction between TICAs who seek death by removing LSMT and TICAs not tethered to LSMT who seek death, the equality principle would require the legalization of the PAD option. All TICAs, in short, should have equal access to death! The effect of this legal argument is made even more potentially momentous because, significantly, every state constitution in the Union provides for some form of equal protection guarantee.

The second state constitutional challenge relies on the presence of a due process clause or some alternative reference, perhaps to privacy, dignity, or happiness. Where such language can be located in a state constitution, PAD advocates would ask a state judge to construe those explicit provisions in a way that would embrace a related but unenumerated right to PAD, making a state law that denies the right to PAD null and void. The difficulty here always has been the burden imposed on a judge to validate or justify the discovery of a right not constitutionally enumerated. This PAD strategy is not unprecedented. The U.S. Supreme Court famously discovered the unenumerated right to privacy in *Griswold v. Connecticut* (1965),[41] then, inspired by it, the subsequent discovery of related rights to contraceptive use and abortion, each owing their presence to the penumbras or shadows of the enumerated provisions of the Bill of Rights. Although the Supreme Court refused to include PAD among those penumbral rights in *Glucksberg*, a state judge using analogous state constitutional provisions surely could chart a new legal course and, no doubt, one with historic implications as well. Only a single state supreme court—Montana's—has legalized PAD and both consequential and problematic are its ramifications.

Robert Baxter, dying of cancer, was a 75-year-old retired truck driver from Billings, Montana. Nearing death, this is what he said:

> I have lived a good and a long life, and have no wish to leave this world prematurely. As death approaches from my disease, however, if my suffering becomes unbearable I want the legal option of being able to die in a peaceful and dignified manner by consuming medication prescribed by my doctor for that purpose. Because it will be my suffering, my life, and my death that will be involved, I seek the right and responsibility to make that critical choice for myself if circumstances lead me to do so. I feel strongly that this intensely personal and private decision should be left to me and my conscience . . . and that the government should not have the right to prohibit this choice by criminalizing the aid in dying procedure.[42]

In a Montana trial court, Baxter asserted that the state's ban against assisted suicide as applied to PAD violated the equal protection requirement, as well as the rights to privacy and dignity enumerated in the Montana constitution. In 2008, the trial court dismissed Baxter's equal protection challenge believing that the U.S. Supreme Court had resolved this issue in *Vacco* and that that precedent was controlling in Montana. Again, the *Vacco* court held that the TICAs connected to LSAT and the TICAs who were not are legally distinguishable classes of persons based on notions of causation and intent; Baxter's equal protection challenge was rejected for the same reasons. With respect to enumerated state constitutional guarantees of privacy and dignity, however, the judge found for Baxter.

> [T]he Court concludes that the right of personal autonomy included in the state constitutional right of privacy, and the right to determine "the most fundamental questions of life" inherent in the state constitutional right to dignity, mandate that a competent terminally ill person has a right to choose to end his or her life.[43]

An appeal to the Montana Supreme Court followed, with genuinely innovative results for any court—federal or state.[44] Choosing to avoid a constitutional pronouncement where a statutory remedy would suffice, the Montana Supreme Court engineered a legal justification for PAD that relied upon that state's 1991 Rights of the Terminally Ill Act, a statute that allowed terminally ill competent Montanans attached to life support to suspend such treatment and die. The Montana High Court ruled that this 1991 law should be construed to grant terminally ill competent Montanans not dependent on life support the right to a physician's assistance to hasten death: because both classes were similar, both groups were equally entitled to choose death. The state's judicial innovation is a bold one: Montana's statutory holding contradicts the U.S. Supreme Court's constitutional reasoning in *Vacco*. Comparing the class of TICAs dependent on life support with those similarly situated persons not dependent—the very comparison in *Vacco*—the Montana Supreme Court found distinctions without legally meaningful differences. In both classes the physician makes the terminal prognosis, in both the patient chooses death, and if the "direct act" of removing life support was legal according to the 1991 law, then the "indirect act" of prescribing a drug—"lesser physician involvement"— must be made similarly legal.

Regarding the Montana model, could other state courts replicate its novel equal protection analysis? Absolutely, especially because equal protection principles are sewn into the cloth of every state constitution. Whether other state courts follow the Montana model seems to depend on two factors: (1) the persuasiveness of the argument itself and (2) the willingness of a state court to legalize PAD knowing that the codification of Oregon-like safeguards to prevent abuse is a legislative and not judicial responsibility. Whether state judges trust medical doctors to police themselves was Vermont's very predicament in July 2016. Another consequence of the Montana model: Could its equal protection argument inspire the U.S. Supreme Court to revisit and overrule its *Vacco* precedent, nationalizing as a result a right to PAD on equal protection grounds?

Montana's judicially driven legalization of PAD seemed to have inspired New Mexico courts as well, where lawyers and judges alike engaged in a rigorous and lengthy debate about this end-of-life option. In 2014, a New Mexico trial court held that the state's statutory prohibition against assisted suicide did not exempt physician assistance in the suicide of a TICA. Not unlike the trial court's decision in Montana, however, the New Mexico judge did conclude that the enumerated state constitutional rights "of enjoying and defending life and liberty . . . and of seeking and obtaining safety and happiness" embraced the right to PAD, saying

> This Court cannot envision a right more fundamental, more private or more integral to the liberty, safety and happiness of a New Mexican than the right of a competent, terminally ill patient to choose aid in dying. If decisions made in the shadow of one's imminent death regarding how they and their loved ones will face that death are not fundamental, and at the core of these constitutional guarantees, than [*sic*] what decision[s] are?[45]

As of 2016, trial courts in two states have granted what the U.S. Supreme Court—citing the absence of a supportive history and tradition—refused to do in *Glucksberg*, to wit, to recognize a fundamental constitutional right to PAD. On review, however, a New Mexico appellate court overturned the trial court's holding, arguing that New Mexico courts are obliged to follow *Glucksberg* and that establishing a right to PAD was foreclosed by that precedent. Moreover, the appellate court asserted, on an issue as sensitive as PAD, especially where constitutional language only ambiguously speaks to the right claimed, the democratic forces and not a ruling from a judge should hold sway. That ruling, too, was appealed, whereupon the New Mexico Supreme Court unanimously held that, guided by a "firm legal rationale" articulated in *Glucksberg,* no state constitutional right to PAD could be discovered in enumerated state constitutional rights. Moreover, with language resonating in the Oregon model, the high court opined that the legalization of PAD in New Mexico would "require robust debate in the legislative and executive branches of the government."[46]

In the two cases framed in Montana and New Mexico courts, or by those framed in any other state court system for that matter, a number of issues with uncertain futures are present.

One—and a theme alluded to earlier—if a state court recognizes a state constitutional right to PAD, are prophylactic measures established and proven effective in Oregon automatically enforceable? In those states where PAD has been legalized through a vote of the people or their representatives, rigorous safeguards have been debated and put in place to ensure that the practice of PAD is "safe, legal, and rare." Legislating safeguards is not a judicial power, however; thus, if any state court recognizes PAD as a state right, then the exercise of that right would occur without any statutory safety net modeled after Oregon's. What rules, then, will govern the many hotly debated issues central to PAD? Leading the way in this regard are the criteria to determine patient access to PAD, and whether euthanasia is acceptable for patients not able to self-administer drugs. Ironically, then, when PAD becomes a judicially created right, both opponents and proponents of the right could worry that its practice—minus public safeguards—would not be "safe, legal, and rare."

The trial court in New Mexico, not unlike some legislators in Vermont, took the position that accords great weight to the belief that physicians can and will adopt best-practice protocols to arrest abuse. As Barbara Coombs Lee, president of Compassion and Choices, explains, best practice protocols developed by the medical profession will be enforced through the mechanisms of

> medical peer review, medical licensing and disciplinary proceedings, civil remedies for negligent or reckless acts and police authority and criminal justice systems in every community. . . . Medicine is the most regulated and supervised profession in existence, and the controls in place are able to keep aid in dying as safe as other end-of-life decisions.[47]

Taking judicial notice of this very perspective, the New Mexico trial judge legalized PAD with confidence that Oregon safeguards would be understood and binding. Where "explicit statutory authorization" has legalized PAD, the judge confidently explained, "there is no uncertainty in the law and the practice has developed as one of the standard of care options for [TICAs] at the end of life."[48] In this way, "[a] standard of care for physician aid in dying, informed by clinical practices and authoritative literature, including Clinical Practice Guidelines, has developed."[49]

New Mexico's appellate court was unconvinced, sounding a decidedly pessimistic chord.

> Of yet greater concern would be the dearth of any regulatory framework enforceable by the State to ensure the safety and efficacy of aid in dying

were this judicial body to pronounce its legality. Unlike the three states that have legislatively permitted aid in dying, its practice in New Mexico would occur in a void only minimally filled by externally written and questionably enforceable "professional standards of practice" or some alternatively nebulous "standard of care." In fact, the best examples of why the more capably informed legislative process is the superior means by which aid in dying might achieve legality are the three statutory enactments existing nationally. . . . And it is not the judiciary's place to assume the legislative role necessary to enact some regulatory substitute for that which should accompany and govern any such fundamental transformation in medical caregiving.[50]

An uncertain future indeed. Where PAD operates in an environment without public safeguards, will medical best practices function just as effectively to ensure that PAD is "safe, legal, and rare"?

A second and related uncertainty is this: In the absence of legislatively codified limits, might state judges seize upon valid secular reasons to recognize different, more immodest constructions of the PAD option? Where Oregon safeguards are not present, might asserted valid secular reasons inspire a physician to administer a lethal drug for a TICA not capable of self-administering it? Could a judge find this decision reasonable? Might asserted valid secular reasons inspire a physician to either prescribe or administer a lethal drug for patients not terminally ill but whose life is absorbed with unremitting pain? Could a judge find this decision reasonable? Might asserted valid secular reasons inspire a physician either to prescribe or administer a death-inducing drug to a patient suffering from unbearable psychological grief, or to a patient in the early stages of dementia, or to a patient who is not an adult? Could a judge find any of these decisions reasonable? Professor Yale Kamisar warns of this exact prospect: "Once a right to [PAD] is established, it is difficult to believe it will be confined to the terminally ill for very long."[51] Most especially true, it might seem, when such questions are debated and resolved in a court of law where valid secular reasons abound.

The *Lawrence-Obergefell* Model and Effect

In its 1997 *Glucksberg* ruling, the U.S. Supreme Court settled two matters: (1) although the U.S. Constitution provides no right to PAD for U.S. citizens, (2) each state is invited to debate and, should it approve, to legalize PAD. Oregon, Washington, Montana, Vermont, California, and Colorado have done just that.

But a third and last prospective future for this end-of-life choice could very well reroute the locus of PAD decision making back to Washington,

D.C.! Consider the following. Congress could nationalize a statutory prohibition against PAD, voiding the decision in any state that legalized this option; or the Supreme Court, by overturning *Glucksberg*, could nationalize a constitutional right to PAD—just as it recently has done respecting rights to same-sex sodomy and same-sex marriage.

A return to Congress seems unlikely, not because of a lack of power but because of a lack of will. In fact, in the wake of Oregon's success, the exercise of congressional power aimed at voiding that law was seriously entertained. For congressional critics of Oregon's law, three simple words located in the 1970 Controlled Substances Act (CSA) assumed monumental significance.[52] The CSA regulates the manufacture and distribution of substances thought harmful "to public health and safety." In one of its provisions, the attorney general is authorized to grant prescription licenses to doctors who would dispense drugs for a "legitimate medical purpose." The idea was this: if the attorney general ruled that PAD is an illegitimate purpose, then in a state that had legalized PAD a participating doctor could have his or her prescription license withdrawn, effectively voiding that state's—Oregon's—end-of-life option. On November 9, 2001, Attorney General John Ashcroft did precisely this, with his sights aimed directly at gutting Oregon's law—and the law in any state that might make that option legal. In his "Ashcroft Directive," the attorney general advanced the following proclamation as law: "I hereby determine that assisting suicide is not a 'legitimate medical purpose' . . . and that prescribing, dispensing, or administering federally controlled substances to assist suicide violates the CSA."[53] In *Gonzales v. Oregon*,[54] a 2006 challenge to that interpretive rule, the Supreme Court held that the CSA did not authorize the attorney general's interpretation of it and Oregon's law survived unaffected.

For PAD critics in Congress, defeat illuminated a silver lining: To void the Oregon law, Congress would only have to enact an amendment to the CSA declaring that PAD was not a "legitimate medical purpose," an option made even more effective because it required no questionable proclamation from the executive branch to achieve desired results. Even that option without the will, however, proved impossible to realize as illustrated by two failed congressional attempts in 1999 and 2000 to pass such a law. Vigorously debated, the so-named Pain Relief Promotion Act was approved by the House of Representatives in 1999 and again in 2000, but the measure stalled in the Senate. Make no mistake, however, that although Congress has failed so far to void state law legalizing PAD there is no reason to believe that a Congress differently constituted and motivated might adopt such a measure to trump state initiatives that have legalized PAD.

A return to the U.S. Supreme Court by PAD proponents seeking to nationalize a constitutional right to PAD is gathering very real momentum, particularly in light of the Supreme Court's pronouncements in *Lawrence v. Texas* (2003)[55] establishing a fundamental constitutional right to same-sex sodomy, and in *Obergefell v. Hodges* (2015)[56] recognizing a fundamental constitutional right to same-sex marriage.

Central to the Court's rationale in both *Lawrence* and *Obergefell*—each written by Justice Kennedy, incidentally—was the revelation that "history and tradition" were no longer the exclusive sources for the discovery of unenumerated constitutional rights as had been settled, many scholars believed, in *Glucksberg*; it bears repeating that no evidence existed to demonstrate in that case that the right to PAD was "deeply rooted in the Nation's history and tradition," or that it was "implicit in the concept of ordered liberty." The *Lawrence* and *Obergefell* rulings are difficult to reconcile with *Glucksberg*'s reliance on history, as they seem to chart a new line of constitutional inquiry more sympathetic to the liberty concerns of contemporary American society, and, accordingly, to the existential mission of PAD well-wishers.

In *Lawrence*, acknowledging a long-standing legal history condemnatory of sodomy, the Court's interpretive guide was redirected to an "emerging awareness" within the last 50 years that "liberty gives substantial protection to adult persons in deciding how to conduct their private lives in matters pertaining to sex."[57] For PAD proponents, much of the Court's constitutional analysis in *Lawrence* was inviting and welcoming. For example,

> Had those who drew and ratified the Due Process Clauses of the Fifth Amendment or the Fourteenth Amendment known the components of liberty in its manifold possibilities, they would have been more specific. They did not presume to have this insight. They knew times can bind us to certain truths and later generations can see that laws once thought necessary and proper in fact serve only to oppress. As the Constitution endures, persons in every generation can invoke its principles in their own search for greater freedom.[58]

Even more sympathetic, too, was the Court's insistence that the reasons advanced by the state to prohibit consensual same-sex sodomy could not be "shaped by religious beliefs, conceptions of right and acceptable behavior, and respect for the traditional family."[59] Instead, the Court insisted, "Judeo-Christian moral and ethical standards" must give way to valid secular reasons to sustain such prohibitions. In this way, ultimately, the Court concluded that the "Texas statute furthers no legitimate state interests which can justify its intrusion into the personal and private life of the individual."[60] The *Lawrence* decision overruled *Bowers v. Hardwick* (1986)[61] that had stood for 17 years as a legal justification to criminalize consensual same-sex sodomy; PAD well-wishers might only hope that the *Lawrence* logic would someday inspire a similar consequence for *Glucksberg*.

More momentum still. In *Obergefell*, a holding stunning in its disregard for deeply rooted history and tradition, the Court established a fundamental constitutional right to same-sex marriage in an opinion soaked with *Lawrence* interpretive principles. Noting that marriage had, in "the annals of human history," been exclusively understood as a union between a man and a woman, the Court nevertheless observed that

> [i]f rights were defined by those who exercised them in the past, then received practices could serve as their own continued justification and new groups could not invoke rights once denied. This Court has rejected that approach, both with respect to the right to marry and the rights of gays and lesbians. . . . [R]ights come not from ancient sources alone. They arise, too, from a better informed understanding of how constitutional imperatives define a liberty that remains urgent in our own era.[62]

Additionally, the Court took special care to reiterate a guiding interpretive tenet from *Lawrence*, namely, that when "honorable religious or philosophical premises . . . become enacted law and public policy, the necessary consequence is to put the imprimatur of the State itself on an exclusion that soon demeans or stigmatizes those whose own liberty is then denied."[63] In this way, driven by "reasoned judgment" and "neutral discussions," and applying interpretive methods respecting history "without allowing the past alone to rule the present," the Court was compelled to conclude that "same-sex couples could exercise the right to marry."

"Deeply rooted in this Nation's history and tradition"—the Court's litmus test for announcing fundamental constitutional rights not explicitly enumerated, just how "deeply rooted" was the "emerging awareness" to same-sex intimacies in *Lawrence*? Fifty years by the Court's own calculations. And how "deeply rooted" was the "emerging awareness" to same-sex marriage in *Obergefell*? The decision of the Massachusetts Supreme Court recognizing this right for the first time in our nation's history was delivered in 2003![64] As for physician-assisted dying, will this right find a home in the *Lawrence-Obergefell* model of constitutional interpretation and law?

Epilogue

That a valid secular reason is required to sustain state prohibitions against PAD is abundantly clear from the *Lawrence* and *Obergefell* Courts. On this point, law professor and dean Erwin Chemerinsky has forcefully opined that *Glucksberg* was "tragically wrong."[65] Recounting his time beside the bed of his dying father in 1993, Chemerinsky writes,

> [M]y father was dying of terminal lung cancer. . . . Except when sedated, he was fully conscious and completely rational. . . . He cogently explained to the doctor that either he was awake and in great pain or he was drugged into unconsciousness. He told the doctor that it was his time to go and there was no point in prolonging his life a few more days. No one in our family objected to his choice. . . . The doctor said that the law did not allow that and he would not discuss it further. My father died four days after making that request.[66]

Then, Chemerinsky's lament: "I will never understand what interest the state . . . had in keeping him alive for those few additional days."[67]

Glucksberg is "tragically wrong" for what reasons? In a nutshell, Chemerinsky asks and answers the following questions. Is the state's unqualified interest in the preservation of human life a sufficient reason to sustain the PAD ban? But that interest is not sufficient to disallow TICAs the choice to remove LSMT and die.[68] Less compelling, too, that interest becomes as a TICA approaches death; with the 1996 words from Circuit Judge Stephen Reinhardt as a guide: "When patients are no longer able to pursue liberty or happiness and do not wish to pursue life, the state's interest in forcing them to remain alive is clearly less compelling."[69]

Is the state's obligation to protect the integrity of the medical profession a sufficient reason to sustain the PAD ban? For a TICA, the answer is sadly obvious because no healing is possible,[70] making PAD—for those who choose that option—the only acceptable measure for eliminating suffering. For participating physicians who assist in the patient's death, assisted dying is an essential component of the doctor's role "to make the patient as comfortable as possible."[71]

Is a state's interest in protecting vulnerable groups from PAD abuse a sufficient reason to sustain the PAD ban? Poor women for this reason are not denied the right to choose abortion. Again, persons in vulnerable groups are not prohibited by this interest to die by choosing to remove LSMT.[72]

Finally, what about the state's interest that PAD, once legalized, cannot be effectively closeted—that its presence will lead inevitably down a slippery slope to the nightmare legalization of, at the very bottom, involuntary euthanasia. Is this a sufficient reason to sustain the ban on PAD? Chemerinsky: "[t]he Oregon law gives the lie to the dire predictions" of PAD opponents.[73]

Glucksberg, "tragically wrong" for what reason? One professor's answer: In our day, no valid secular reason justifies a law that denies this option.

Perhaps the arrival of California on this most complex of policy stages will add perspective and clarity in our day to the future debate over government interests advanced to prohibit the PAD choice. Should California—someday flush with data on the practice of PAD—reaffirm the lessons from Oregon, perhaps Oregon's model, or Montana's, or *Lawrence-Obergefell's* will work to legalize PAD's "humane and dignified death" for terminally ill competent adults as government interests that no longer are valid are abandoned. Doing so might remind us all that "[a]t the heart of liberty is the right to define one's own concept of existence, of meaning, of the universe, and of the mystery of human life. Beliefs about these matters could not define the attributes of personhood were they formed under compulsion of the State."[74]

Notes

1. *Washington v. Glucksberg*, 521 U.S. 702 (1997).
2. *Vacco v. Quill*, 521 U.S. 793 (1997).
3. *Planned Parenthood of Southeastern Pennsylvania v. Casey*, 505 U.S. 833 (1992).
4. Ibid., 851.
5. *Glucksberg*, 711.
6. Ibid., 728–33.
7. *Vacco*, 801.
8. *Glucksberg*, 735.
9. "Death-With-Dignity Boom: 26 States Now Considering Laws," *Compassion and Choices,* February 2, 2015, accessed January 15, 2016, https://www.compassionand choices.org/2015/02/03/death-with-dignity-boom-25-states-now-considering-laws/.
10. The Oregon Death with Dignity Act, Or. Rev. Stat. §§ 127.800–127.897.
11. The Washington Death with Dignity Act, Wash. Rev. Code § 70.245.
12. *Baxter v. Montana*, 2009 MT 448.
13. Vermont Patient Choice and Control at the End of Life, Act 39, Vt. Stat. 18 § 5281–5292.
14. California End of Life Option Act, Assembly Bill ABx2-15, Health and Safety Code § 1, Part 1.85.
15. Colorado End of Life Options Act, Proposition 106 (2016), Ballotpedia, accessed November 13, 1016, https://ballotpedia.org/Colorado_End_of_Life_Options _Act,_ Propososition_106_(2016)
16. Robert F. Williams, "Introduction: The Third Stage of the New Judicial Federalism," *N.Y.U. Ann. Surv. Am. L.* 59 (2003): 211.
17. International Task Force on Euthanasia and Assisted Suicide et al., Brief *Amicus Curiae* for Montana, DA 09-0051: 8.
18. Oregon Dep't of Human Services, "Oregon's Death With Dignity Act— 2012," accessed January 28, 2016, http://public.health.oregon.gov/ProviderPartner Resources/EvaluationResearch/DeathwithDignityAct/Documents/year15.pdf.

19. Kathryn L. Tucker, "At the Very End of Life: The Emergence of Policy Supporting Aid in Dying Among Mainstream Medical and Health Policy Associations," *Harvard Health Policy Review* 10 (2009): 45.

20. Ibid.

21. Kathryn L. Tucker, "Aid in Dying: An End of Life-Option Governed by Best Practices," *Journal of Health and Biomedical Law* 8 (2012): 21.

22. Ballotpedia, "Colorado End of Life Options, Proposition 106 (2016).

23. Michael Muskal, "Vermont Governor Signs Death with Dignity Measure," *Los Angeles Times*, May 20, 2013, accessed June 30, 2014, http://articles.latimes .com/2013/may/20/nation/la-na-nn-vermont-governor-signs-death-with-dignity -measure-20130520.

24. Scott Malone, "Vermont Set to Become Third U.S. State to Allow Assisted Suicide," *Reuters*, May 14, 2013, accessed June 30, 2014, http://www.reuters.com /article/2013/05/14/us-usa-vermont-assistedsuicide-idUSBRE94D0NS20130514.

25. Peter Hirschfeld, "Dramatic Vote in Senate Proves Game-Changer for Death with Dignity," *Vermont Press Bureau*, February 13, 2013, accessed June 30, 2014, http://www.vermontpressbureau.com/dramatic-vote-in-senate-proves-game -changer-for-death-with-dignity/.

26. Andrew Stein, "Lieutenant Governor Breaks Tie in Senate, Pushing Drastically Altered Assisted Death Bill to Thursday Vote," *Vermont Digger*, February 13, 2013, accessed June 30, 2014, http://vtdigger.org/2013/02/13/lieutenant -governor-breaks-tie-in-senate-pushing-drastically-altered-assisted-death-bill-to -thursday-vote/.

27. Hirschfeld, "Dramatic Vote in Senate."

28. Justin McCarthy, "Seven in 10 Americans Back Euthanasia: Support Strong for Past Two Decades," *Gallop*, June 18, 2014, accessed January 27, 2016, http:// www.gallup.com/poll/171704/seven-americans-back-euthanasia.aspx.

29. Brittany Maynard, "My Right to Death with Dignity at 29," *CNN*, November 2, 2014, accessed January 26, 2016, http://www.cnn.com/2014/10/07/opinion /maynard-assisted-suicide-cancer-dignity/.

30. Ibid.

31. Arthur L. Caplan, "Terminally Ill Woman Chooses Suicide, May Influence a New Generation," *Medscape*, October 28, 2014, accessed January 26, 2016, http:// www.medscape.com/viewarticle/833603.

32. Sharon Cohen, "Brittany Maynard: New Face of Right-to-Die," *Associated Press*, October 31, 2014, accessed January 26, 2016, http://bigstory.ap.org/article /30a58a58a06046cab8f894ddcc2828e8/young-terminal-new-face-right-die.

33. Lindsey Bever, "Brittany Maynard, as Promised, Ends her Life at 29," *The Washington Post*, November 2, 2014, accessed January 26, 2016, https://www .washingtonpost.com/news/morning-mix/wp/2014/11/02/brittany-maynard-as -promised-ends-her-life-at-29/.

34. Christopher Cadelago, "California Aid-in-Dying Measure Passes First Test Committee," *The Sacramento Bee*, March 25, 2015, accessed January 26, 2016, http:// www.sacbee.com/news/politics-government/capitol-alert/article16295804.html.

35. Tracy Seipel, "Physician 'Aid in Dying': California Medical Association Removes Opposition to Bill," *San Jose Mercury News*, May 21, 2015, accessed January 27, 2016, http://www.mercurynews.com/health/ci_28154975/california-medical-association-removes-opposition-physician-aid-dying.

36. "Jerry Brown Turned to His Own Doctor and Desmond Tutu in Assisted-Suicide Decision," *Los Angeles Times*, October 5, 2015, accessed January 25, 2016, http://www.latimes.com/local/political/la-me-pc-jerry-brown-turned-to-desmond-tutu-doctors-family-of-brittany-maynard-in-assisted-suicide-decision-20151005-story.html.

37. American Academy of Hospice and Palliative Medicine, *Position Statement: Physician-Assisted Death*, February 14, 2007.

38. James Lieberman, "Death with Dignity," *Psychiatric News*, August 4, 2006, accessed January 28, 2016, http://psychnews.psychiatryonline.org/author/Lieberman%2C+E+James.

39. *Cruzan v. Dir. Mo. Dep't of Health*, 497 U.S. 261 (1990).

40. *In Re Quinlan*, 70 N.J. 10, 355 A.2d 647 (1976).

41. *Griswold v. Connecticut*, 381 U.S. 479 (1965).

42. Affidavit, Robert Baxter, June 28, 2008.

43. *Baxter v. Montana*, Case No. ADV 07-781, 18 (2008).

44. *Baxter v. Montana*, 2009 MT 448.

45. *Morris v. Brandenburg*, Case No. D-202-CV 2012-2909, 12–13 (2014).

46. *Morris v. Brandenburg*, Case No. S-1-SC-35478, 2 (2016).

47. Barbara Coombs Lee, "How Montana is Revolutionizing the Movement for End-of-Life Choice," *Huffington Post,* September 15, 2011, accessed June 30, 2014, http://www.huffingtonpost.com/barbara-coombs-lee/aid-in-dying-montana_b_960555.html.

48. *Morris,* 4.

49. Ibid., 5.

50. *Morris v. Brandenburg*, Court of Appeals of the State of New Mexico, No. 33, 630, 60–61 (2015).

51. Yale Kamisar, "Can *Glucksberg* Survive *Lawrence*? Another Look at the End of Life and Personal Autonomy." *Mich. L. Rev.* 106, 8 (2008): 1472.

52. Controlled Substances Act, Public Law No. 91-513, 84 Stat. 1242.

53. Dispensing of Controlled Substances to Assist Suicide, 66 Fed. Reg. 56607, November 9, 2001.

54. *Gonzales v. Oregon*, 546 U.S. 243 (2006).

55. *Lawrence v. Texas*, 539 U.S. 558 (2003).

56. *Obergefell v. Hodges*, 135 S. Ct. 2584 (2015).

57. *Lawrence*, 572.

58. Ibid., 578–79.

59. Ibid., 571.

60. Ibid., 578.

61. *Bowers v. Hardwick*, 478 U.S. 186 (1986).

62. *Obergefell*, 2602.

63. Ibid.

64. *Goodridge v. Dep't of Public Health*, 440 Mass. 309 (2003).

65. Erwin Chemerinsky, "*Washington v. Glucksberg* Was Tragically Wrong." *Mich. L. Rev.* 106, 8 (2008): 1501–16.

66. Ibid., 1501.

67. Ibid., 1501–02.

68. Ibid., 1509.

69. Ibid.

70. Ibid., 1511.

71. Ibid.

72. Ibid., 1512.

73. Ibid., 1514.

74. *Planned Parenthood*, 851.

CHAPTER TWO

The Assisted Dying Bill for England and Wales

Raphael Cohen-Almagor[1]

Preliminaries

In September 2015, the British House of Commons rejected plans for a right-to-die bill in England and Wales in its first vote on the issue in almost 20 years. The results were 118 members of Parliament (MPs) voting in favor and a considerable majority of 330 MPs voting against a bill to enable competent adults who are terminally ill to choose to be provided with medically supervised assistance to end their own lives. In 1997, 72 percent of MPs voted against a similar bill. In 2015, 74 percent of MPs voted against aid-in-dying legislation.[2] This is a massive setback to right-to-die societies in Britain. Many MPs voiced their concern that the bill will fundamentally change the way that society thinks about and deals with the terminally ill, severely disabled people, and the vulnerable, troubled, and elderly. They also feared that the bill will change the medical profession for worse, in a way that does not serve the best interests of patients.[3]

Presently, the British House of Lords is deliberating whether to legislate physician-assisted suicide (PAS), allowing patients who wish to end their lives to seek and secure medical aid-in-dying. The main document under scrutiny is the Assisted Dying Bill, prepared by Lord Falconer of Thoroton.[4]

Alarms have been raised that the law might be manipulated and abused, and that coercion and intimidation in the hands of unscrupulous parties might pressure vulnerable people to choose death over life.[5] These concerns are certainly warranted. They should not be dismissed or ignored. Instead, they should prompt us to think hard and devise a careful list of guidelines for aid-in-dying, if the House of Lords and subsequently the government will decide to pursue this route and admit aid-in-dying into the medical practice.

Over the years, repeated polls have shown that at least 70 percent of the population support physician-assisted suicide.[6] A 2015 Dignity in Dying Poll showed that 82 percent of the public supports such legislation.[7] This extensive opinion poll provides some very interesting findings. It refutes the assumption that legislation of aid-in-dying would decrease trust in physicians and change the culture of medicine for worse. People were asked about their trust in doctors if Lord Falconer Bill would become the law; 37 percent answered that this would "increase trust in doctors," 13 percent "significantly increase trust in doctors," and 25 percent "somewhat increase trust in doctors."[8]

The public also sent a clear message to the politicians. To the question "If your MP was to vote in support of a change in the law to allow assisted dying for terminally ill and mentally competent adults, would you feel more positive or more negative towards them, or would it make no difference to you?" The results were 53 percent "more positive," 19 percent "much more positive," 5 percent "a bit more negative," and 4 percent "much more negative."[9] To the question "Which of the following words and phrases would you most associate with those politicians who are arguing in favour of assisted dying for terminally ill & mentally competent adults?" 65 percent answered "compassionate," 47 percent "caring," 33 percent "in touch," 33 percent "progressive," 32 percent "rational," and 27 percent "responsible."[10] Conversely, to the question "Which of the following words and phrases would you most associate with those politicians arguing against assisted dying for terminally ill & mentally competent adults?" 48 percent answered "lacking compassion," 42 percent "out of touch," 32 percent "religious," 27 percent "backward looking," and 21 percent "cold."[11]

The government needs to address the growing concern about the so-called "death-tourism." Many Britons who wish to decide the time of their death leave their country and their homes, and travel to Switzerland where they receive help to die. Nearly 300 Britons have travelled to Zurich to die with the help of the Swiss aid-in-dying group, Dignitas.[12] The British authorities understand that this "death-tourism" is the result of insufficient legal instruments to enable sick people who are at the end of their lives to seek help at home, permitting them to die peacefully in the company of their family and friends in a warm and loving environment. There is an increasing realization that the time has come for change.[13]

Further, a 2014 poll conducted among British physicians reveals that 37 percent of the 600 UK doctors surveyed thought that health care professionals already help terminally ill patients to die.[14] This poll reveals just how conflicted and unsure British physicians are on this issue. Only 29 percent answered positively the question "Are you in favour of a change in UK law to allow physician-assisted suicide and/or euthanasia?"; 58 percent said "No." A similar percentage of physicians, 29 percent, were asked by a patient to assist them in dying. A greater percentage, 37 percent, believed that there are circumstances where some health care professionals currently assist in the suicide of terminally ill patients. To the question "If physician-assisted suicide were legalised in the UK in defined cases, would you be willing to participate in providing the service?" only a small minority, 19 percent answered "Yes" and 56 percent said "No."[15]

Conversely, to the question "Under what circumstances do you think physician-assisted euthanasia should be permitted?" 54 percent answered "Terminal illness with uncontrollable physical suffering," and 39 percent answered "Under no circumstances." To the question "What system do you think should be in place to safeguard terminally ill patients who want an assisted suicide and safeguard doctors who may be prepared to help them?" 57 percent answered "Legislation to allow the practice within stringent safeguards and national guidelines."[16] Interestingly, the 2015 public opinion poll showed that 44 percent of the public would assist loved ones in their dying although this would amount to breaking the law.[17]

Another study suggests that 51 percent of UK general practitioners (GPs) would be willing to play a role in the assisted-dying process, with a predicted 1,200 new cases each year.[18] An estimated 1,000 people per year die via unregulated voluntary euthanasia.[19] This is taking place behind closed doors, with no safeguards, regulation, or monitoring. The present situation does not serve the patients' best interests.

The practice of ending life should not be left in the gray area. Transparency and regulation are required, but the government is unlikely to move toward legislation as long as the medical profession is officially opposed. At present, the Royal College of Physicians, the Royal College of General Practitioners, and British Geriatrics Society are all officially opposed to a change in the law, along with 82 percent of members of the Association for Palliative Medicine.[20]

The British Supreme Court pleaded with the Parliament to consider changes in the present law. The Supreme Court decision in *Nicklinson and Others* has alerted Parliament to the possibility that the current prohibition against assisted suicide might breach Article 8 of the European Convention in relation to the right to choose how to end one's life. President of the Supreme Court, Lord Neuberger, implored the legislators to consider whether amending the law so as to enable patients to be assisted in ending their lives—subject to regulations and other protective features—might be appropriate.[21]

Existing policies such as the Liverpool Care Pathway for the Dying have attracted criticism. An independent review panel chaired by Baroness Neuberger has identified clear failings in some areas of care, and strongly recommended that use of the Liverpool Care Pathway be replaced within the next 6 to 12 months by an end-of-life care plan for each patient, backed up by condition-specific good practice guidance.[22] It is time for change.

Aim

This chapter aims to suggest an improved set of guidelines for physician-assisted suicide. Thus, it is very practical—based on 25 years of research in eight countries—and it does not expand on the underpinning theoretical basis for the guidelines. This author has been an advocate of physician-assisted suicide and has explained the reasoning elsewhere, primarily in *The Right to Die with Dignity*[23] and *Euthanasia in the Netherlands*.[24] I support the idea that patients should be able to decide the time of their death with the help and support of the medical profession. People have human dignity. At the end of their lives, the medical profession should respect individuals' wishes and help them to the best of their abilities. "Dignity" here means worthiness, merit. The *Oxford English Dictionary* defines it as "the state or quality of being worthy of honour or respect."[25] Immanuel Kant explained that human beings are ends in themselves, and that for something to be an end in itself, "it doesn't have mere relative value (a price) but has intrinsic value (i.e., dignity)."[26] He further elucidated that autonomy is the basis for the dignity of human nature and of every rational nature.[27] Kant calls dignity an unconditional and incomparable worth that admits of no equivalent.[28] All rational creatures have it, by virtue of their reason, and dignity constrains the ways in which we can legitimately interact. In a similar fashion, Ronald Dworkin asserted that individuals have a right to dignity because they are human.[29] I have argued that dignity is both an objective and subjective concept. It is socially constructed and made up of values and feelings that one feels about oneself, about one's self-worth and respect.[30]

Why Physicians Are Irreplaceable

If patients want to continue living, then others should help them in coping with their medical condition. Preserving dignity means helping patients to feel valuable. The preservation of one's dignity involves listening to the patients' complaints, helping patients cure their diseases—or at least assisting them in controlling pain—responding to their distress and anxieties and making an effort to relieve them, demonstrating sensitivity to the physical indignities that occur in severe illnesses, making the patient sense that he or she is a human being and not a mere body—a vessel that consumes resources or a case to be studied for the disease it contains. If patients wish to die, this request should be considered with utmost seriousness. Physicians should not desert patients at a time when they are most needed. Patients ask for help because they fear waking up to an even more dreadful condition if their suicide attempt fails, or because they lack the energies required to commit such an act. Their energies are devoted to cope with the medical condition, often cancer.[31] Patients appeal to those who are expected to provide assistance when one is confronted with severe health problems.

The proposed guidelines for PAS are aimed to empower individuals at the end of their lives. Their formulation is guided by the principles of respect for one's autonomy and dignity, beneficence, anti-coercion, and not harming others. This author believes that people should have a choice to end their lives when they deem life burdensome and coercive. Choosing the moment of death—preferably in one's own bed, surrounded by family and friends—should be an option. At the same time, it is granted that not all physicians would agree to be part of this plan. One physician once told me during a debate: "You do this. You assist patients with suicide. I cannot." He proposed Philosophers-Assisted Suicide instead of Physician-Assisted Suicide. The acronym, PAS, he suggested, could remain. The physician spoke passionately but the recommendation was made half-heartedly, with a healthy dose of cynicism. With all due respect to philosophers, they are incapable of replacing physicians in such circumstances.

Physicians are best equipped in terms of knowledge and expertise to provide aid-in-dying. During the last decades, Western societies have become medicalized with developments such as cosmetic treatments, reproduction, the human genome project, and the rapid increase in pharmaceutical sales in areas such as sex and "anti-aging" medicine.[32] Technology has enabled us to extend life, sometimes beyond what patients themselves want. Technology and knowledge advance at a rapid pace, enabling physicians to sustain the lives of their patients despite challenging medical conditions.

Technology and the diffusion of knowledge also help patients to acquire information about their own conditions and to take better care of themselves. Still, medicine remains the only profession that can help patients in need. The diffusion of knowledge does not make physicians redundant.

The practice of medicine should be deontological rather than utilitarian. Humane and compassionate medicine endorses the values of beneficence, justice, non-maleficence, and enabling patients to make reasoned informed choices where death might be only one of the available choices, and the very last resort after carefully exhausting all other alternatives.[33] Patients' autonomy and preferences should be respected as much as possible. In utilitarian medicine, economy and allocation-of-resources considerations would become paramount in providing medication and treatment; these might not serve the patients' best interests.[34]

Physician-Assisted Suicide Is Not Euthanasia

Although I support physician-assisted suicide, at the same time I am opposed to euthanasia. Initially I supported euthanasia on moral grounds,[35] but I changed my mind on practical, policy grounds, restricting my plea to physician-assisted suicide. This change occurred because of the abuse that has been recorded in the Netherlands and Belgium.[36] A fine line distinguishes moral reasoning and policymaking. I am unable to adhere to abstract moral reasoning while ignoring facts.

In euthanasia, the last act is performed by the doctor. In physician-assisted suicide, the last act is performed by the patient. The difference is crucial, as the control in PAS lies with the patient. The patient must consent to the last act. Possibilities for abuse are reduced.[37] Below is a set of guidelines which should be taken into account. This set integrates Lord Falconer's bill with pertinent guidelines that were adopted in Oregon, where physician-assisted suicide is legal,[38] in the Netherlands[39] and Belgium[40] where euthanasia is legal, in Switzerland where assisted suicide is practiced,[41] and in the Northern Territory of Australia,[42] where physician-assisted suicide was legal for a short period. The proposed set of guidelines also relates to my experience as a member of the public committee that was set up by the Israeli Health Ministry to draft the *Dying Patient Law* (2005).[43] The drafting of the law lasted two years during which we studied all relevant laws across the globe. Thus, the guidelines presented below are the crux of many long deliberations and many years of careful research.

This is a very practical opinion piece; thus it reads more like a bill. In other publications I have explained the reasons for physician-assisted suicide and for the need to support patients who express a wish to die at the last stage of their lives,[44] therefore the guidelines below are proposed rather than analyzed. My aim here is to offer, as much as possible, a coherent set of guidelines for physician-assisted suicide geared to serve the best interests of patients while preventing potential abuse of the practice so as to ensure that a new law will not be detrimental to providing patients with good care at the time when they need it most.[45]

I respect physicians who believe that their profession is to heal and to save lives, and not to end life. Thus, a physician should not be coerced to do something that goes against his or her conscience. My objection to coercion is unequivocal and unqualified. I object to coercing those who do not wish to live to do so, and I object to coercing physicians to do something that goes against their belief systems. From the polls we learn that a significant number of physicians in Britain are willing to engage in physician-assisted suicide, thinking that this would *not* change the nature of the profession for worse. Physicians think that they should provide solace to *all* patients, not just some of them, and for their patients they want the PAD option to be transparent and legal. Making people travel to Switzerland to seek help is not a solution for Britain. Britain should address its challenges and devise appropriate mechanisms. As we are dealing with life and death, the mechanisms should be thorough to prevent potential abuse.

Abuse certainly is a concern and in this context the anti-PAS camp speaks of the slippery slope danger: Once we authorize PAS, many lives might end prematurely. I am not impressed with slippery-slope arguments because they put weight on hypothetical future scenarios and ignore the here and now. Now we have people who need help.

Slippery-slope arguments do not really address the justifications for physician-assisted suicide. All they do is to warn against employing it carelessly.[46] We should help patients to the best of our abilities, addressing their concerns and listening to their reasoning. Speculative fears about something that might happen in the future should not deter us from seeking answers to today's concerns. Not listening to patients because listening might create future abuse is abusive in itself. We have the ability to help patients. We are able to prevent abuse. We are able to introduce changes if and when they are required.

Guidelines for Physician-Assisted Suicide

- A patient may request and lawfully be provided with assistance to end his or her own life. This is provided that:
    a. The patient suffers from an intractable, incurable, irreversible condition that cannot be reversed or remedied and the prognosis is that his or her

life expectancy, even if receiving medical treatment, will not expected to exceed six months;

b.   The diagnosis was confirmed by at least one more expert on the condition from which the patient suffers;

c.   The patient is aged 18 years or older;

d.   The patient expressly wishes to end his or her life and has made a signed declaration to that effect, as is required in Belgium[47] and as is proposed by Lord Falconer (the Oregon statute requires both oral and written declaration);

e.   The patient has been ordinarily resident in England and Wales for at least one year.

- The expressed wish to die should be **voluntary**, made in a **sound mind**, and signed in the presence of a witness who is not related to the patient's family nor to the medical team that treats the patient.

- The decision should not be made by the patient's family or as a result of family pressures. Some families can make the decision to end life because they feel overwhelmed by the patient's illness.[48] Many people cannot cope with the fact that their loved one is dying. For these reasons, the PAS decision must be reached without any pressure.

- Physician-assisted suicide should not be rushed. The patient should state this wish repeatedly over a period of time. It is suggested that a period of not less than 14 days must elapse from the day on which the person's declaration takes effect. This recommendation is similar to that invoked in laws and guidelines in Oregon (15 days), Belgium (one month), and as proposed by Lord Falconer (14 days).

- Social workers must confirm that the request to die is voluntary, and free as much as possible from external pressures.

- **Second opinion**: An expert should examine the patient's medical files, confirm the diagnosis, and verify that the patient's desire to die is genuine and voluntary, and that the attending physician was correct in the diagnosis that he or she made that the patient is, indeed, suffering from an incurable and irreversible disease. The Oregon Death with Dignity Act requires that a consulting physician examine the patient and his or her relevant medical records and subsequently confirm, in writing, the attending physician's diagnosis that "the patient is suffering from a terminal disease." Further, the consulting physician must verify that the patient is capable, is acting voluntarily, and has made an informed decision.[49]

- It is advisable that the identity of the consultant be determined by a committee of specialists who will review the request for physician-assisted suicide. Such is the case in the Netherlands.[50]

- The attending physician and the independent consultant are required to agree that the patient is dying.

- **Palliative care**: Requests to die might be influenced by pain and suffering, both physical and mental; therefore palliative care is mandatory prior to physician-assisted suicide.[51] A palliative care specialist will inform the patient about relevant measures to help the patient cope with pain and suffering, including comfort care, hospice care, and pain control. The Oregon statute requires that the attending physician explore, together with the patient, all feasible alternatives for treatment, including comfort care, hospice care, and pain control. The Australian Northern Territory law held that a medical practitioner shall not assist a patient if there are palliative care options to alleviate suffering to levels acceptable to the patient. The Israeli *Dying Patient Law* stipulates that the responsible physician will make sure that everything possible is done to alleviate the patient's pain and suffering, all in accordance with the principles of palliative care. The proposed British *Assisted Dying Bill* (2014), prepared by Lord Falconer of Thoroton, requires that the patient "has been fully informed of the palliative, hospice and other care which is available to that person."[52]

- The patient must be informed of his or her situation, the limited prognosis for recovery, the expected escalation of his or her disease, and the degree of suffering that might be involved. There must be an exchange of information between physicians and patients. The laws in Belgium and Oregon contain these provisions.

- Requests for PAS should be initiated by the patient. Such a sensitive request should not be initiated by the medical team as such initiative is likely to compromise the voluntariness of the decision.

- The decision-making process should include the patient, his or her loved ones (family and close friends), physicians, a psychologist, and a social worker. Perhaps a lawyer also should be consulted. Section 2 of the Oregon Act requires that the written request for medication to end one's life be signed and dated by the patient and witnessed by at least two individuals who, in the presence of the patient, attest to the best of their knowledge and belief that the patient is capable, is acting voluntarily, and is not being coerced to sign the request.[53]

- Shortly before PAS is performed, the attending physician and a psychiatrist should visit the patient to confirm that the patient wishes to go ahead with the procedure. They should make it clear to the patient that he or she has the right to forfeit the request without any problem. The law of the Northern Territory in Australia and the laws of Oregon and Belgium explicitly accentuate this point. The revocation need not be in writing. Verbal declaration is sufficient.

- Only physicians should perform PAS.[54]

- Nurses are not allowed to perform PAS.[55]

- It is emphasized that physician-assisted suicide is conducted as a **last resort**, after exhausting all treatment options that could potentially bring the patient some relief and reduce his or her suffering.

- Physicians will be allowed to use **only** the lethal medications authorized by the Ministry of Health.

- The physician who performs PAS should not receive a special fee. This is to rule out incentives for PAS at the expense of other procedures.

- The decision-making process leading to death should be documented fully and the happenings on the day of the procedure should be recorded in detail.

- As a control mechanism **pharmacists** should be required to file a report every time lethal medications are sold. This makes it possible to trace the medication to the specific physician, and to keep track of how many times physician-assisted suicide was performed.

- Physicians should not be coerced into taking actions that conflict with their consciences. No coercion should be involved in the process. **Conscientious objection** should be respected as is stipulated in Israeli law and as is proposed by Lord Falconer.

- Physicians who provide aid-in-dying as specified above should not be guilty of an offense.

- A **Monitoring and Control Committee** should be established to review all PAS cases and ensure that they were performed in accordance with the said guidelines.

- **Annual Reports**: Data about all PAS cases will be made public and published annually. In the Netherlands, the Termination of Life on Request and Assisted Suicide (Review Procedures) Act requires that the regional review committees submit annual reports.[56] The reports should be made available to the public. Discussions and debates about their findings should be promoted and encouraged.

Conclusion

Legislation of physician-assisted suicide is a matter of moral necessity and political expediency. It is a matter of moral necessity because the medical profession should not desert patients. It is also a matter of political expediency because politicians are attentive to public sentiments. As a profession, medicine should address the needs and concerns of the entire population, not only the majority. Although the vast majority of the population clings to life no matter what, some patients wish to determine the time of their death. Doctors should examine such requests carefully, and provide patients with treatment options. When medicine fails to provide answers to patients' needs, physicians who feel comfortable with the idea of providing aid-in-dying should be allowed to assist patients in need. Physicians who are providing such assistance should operate under close scrutiny, as issues of life and death are of utmost importance. It is the interest of both patients and physicians to establish careful mechanisms to assure that life is never cut short without ample justifications.

Granted, it is not always possible—far less easy—to produce wise, acceptable, satisfactory legislation to cover all the important facets of human experience. Some people might contest and dispute some of the guidelines offered here. This proposal, based on studying pertinent legislation across the globe for the past three decades, should serve as a springboard for continued debate and discussion aimed at serving the best interests of patients at the end of their lives.

Notes

1. The author is grateful to Kevin Yuill and John Keown for their critical comments and suggestions.

2. Assisted Dying Bill [HL] 2014-15, http://services.parliament.uk/bills/2014 -15/assisteddying.html. See also James Gallagher and Philippa Roxby Health, "Assisted Dying Bill: MPs reject 'right to die' law," BBC (September 11, 2015), http://www.bbc.co.uk/news/health-34208624.

3. Hansard, Assisted Dying (No. 2) Bill, House of Commons (September 11, 2015), http://www.publications.parliament.uk/pa/cm201516/cmhansrd/cm150911/debtext /150911-0001.htm#15091126000003.

4. http://services.parliament.uk/bills/2014-15/assisteddying.html (accessed October 5, 2016).

5. Steve Doughty, "Don't Make Our Mistake: As Assisted Suicide Bill Goes to Lords, Dutch Watchdog Who Once Backed Euthanasia Warns UK of 'Slippery Slope' to Mass Deaths," *Mail Online* (July 9, 2014); Xavier Symons, "Lord Falconer's Assisted Suicide Bill under Attack," *BioEdge* (July 12, 2014), http://www .bioedge.org/index.php/bioethics/bioethics_article/11053.

6. BBC, "Most Support Voluntary Euthanasia" (January 24, 2007), http:// news.bbc.co.uk/1/hi/health/6293695.stm; *Care Not Killing*, "What Does the Public Think?" (June 6, 2008), http://www.carenotkilling.org.uk/public-opinion /opinion-polls/; YouGov UK, "Majority Would Support More Compassionate Euthanasia Legislation" (March 5, 2010), http://yougov.co.uk/news/2010/03/05 /majority-would-support-more-compassionate-euthana/; Chris Davies, The Right to Die—Britain Can Learn the Lessons from Europe, 2012, http://lists.opn.org /pipermail/right-to-die_lists.opn.org/2012-September/005107.html; Ben Clements, "Religion and Attitudes Towards Euthanasia in Britain: Evidence from Opinion Polls and Social Surveys," *British Religion in Numbers* (January 31, 2014), http:// www.brin.ac.uk/news/2014/religion-and-attitudes-towards-euthanasia-in-britain -evidence-from-opinion-polls-and-social-surveys/. For further discussion, see J. Cohen, I. Marcoux, J. Bilsen et al., "Trends in Acceptance of Euthanasia Among the General Public in 12 European Countries (1981–1999)," *Eur. J. Public Health* 16(6) (2006): 663–69.

7. Populus, *Dignity in Dying Poll*, March 11–19, 2015, http://www.populus .co.uk/wp-content/uploads/DIGNITY-IN-DYING-Populus-poll-March-2015-data -tables-with-full-party-crossbreaks.compressed.pdf.

8. Ibid.

9. Ibid.

10. Ibid.

11. Ibid.

12. Fergus Walsh, "The Assisted Dying Debate," *BBC* (May 26, 2015), http:// www.bbc.co.uk/news/health-32893689.

13. J. Shaw, "Fifty Years On: Against the Stigmatising Myths, Taboos and Traditions Embedded Within the Suicide Act 1961 (UK)," *J. Law Med.* 18 (2011): 798–810. For further discussion, see Saskia Gauthier, Julian Mausbach, Thomas Reisch, and Christine Bartsch, "Suicide Tourism: A Pilot Study on the Swiss Phenomenon," *J. Med. Ethics* 41 (2015): 611–17; Silvan Luley, " 'Suicide Tourism': Creating Misleading 'Scientific' News," *J. Med. Ethics* 41 (2015): 618–19.

14. Medix, *Euthanasia & Physician-Assisted Suicide*, Summary of Results, Friday 18th of July–Friday 25th of July 2014.

15. Ibid.

16. Ibid.

17. Populus, Dignity in Dying Poll, March 11–19, 2015, http://www.populus. co.uk/wp-content/uploads/DIGNITY-IN-DYING-Populus-poll-March-2015-data-tables-with-full-party-crossbreaks.compressed.pdf.

18. Jacky Davis and Ilora Finlay, "Would Judicial Consent for Assisted Dying Protect Vulnerable People?" *BMJ* 351 (2015): h4437.

19. C. Seale, "End of Life Decisions in the UK Involving Medical Practitioners," *Palliat. Med.* 23 (2009): 198–204.

20. Michael Cook, "British Doctors Reject Neutrality on Assisted Dying," *BioEdge* (June 25, 2016), http://www.bioedge.org/bioethics/british-doctors-reject -neutrality-on-assisted-dying/11939.

21. R (on the Application of Nicklinson and Another) v. Minister of Justice [2014] UKSC 38. For further discussion, see A. Mullock, "The Assisted Dying Bill and the Role of the Physician," *J. Med. Ethics* 41 (2015): 621–24; Charles Foster, "Suicide Tourism May Change Attitudes to Assisted Suicide, But Not Through the Courts," J. Med. Ethics 41 (2015): 620.

22. J. Neuberger, More Care Less Pathway: A Review of the Liverpool Care Pathway. Crown Copyright (15 July 2013), https://www.gov.uk/government/uploads /system/uploads/attachment_data/file/212450/Liverpool_Care_Pathway.pdf; A. Wrigley, "Ethics and End of Life Care: The Liverpool Care Pathway and the Neuberger Review," *J. Med. Ethics* 41 (2015): 639–43.

23. Raphael Cohen-Almagor, *The Right to Die with Dignity: An Argument in Ethics, Medicine, and Law* (Piscataway, NJ: Rutgers University Press, 2001).

24. Raphael Cohen-Almagor, *Euthanasia in the Netherlands: The Policy and Practice of Mercy Killing* (Dordrecht: Springer-Kluwer, 2004).

25. *Oxford English Dictionary* (Oxford: Oxford University Press, 2002).

26. Immanuel Kant, *Groundwork for the Metaphysic of Morals* (1785), http://www.earlymoderntexts.com/assets/pdfs/kant1785.pdf, chap. 2, p. 33.

27. Immanuel Kant, *Groundwork for the Metaphysic of Morals*, 34.

28. Thomas E. Hill Jr., "Kantian Perspectives on the Rational Basis of Human Dignity," in Marcus Duwell, Jens Braarvig, Roger Brownsword, and Dietmar Mieth, eds., *The Cambridge Handbook of Human Dignity: Inter-Disciplinary Perspectives* (Cambridge: Cambridge University Press, 2014): 215.

29. Ronald Dworkin, *Life's Dominion* (New York: Knopf, 1993). For further discussion, see Matthew C. Jordan, "Bioethics and 'Human Dignity,'" *J. Med. and Philosophy* 35 (2010): 180–96.

30. Raphael Cohen-Almagor, "The Right to Die with Dignity; Should Doctors Suggest Euthanasia to Their Patients? Reflections on Dutch Perspectives," *Theoretical Medicine and Bioethics* 2002; 23(4–5) (2002): 287–303.

31. Studies consistently have shown that the majority of patients who wish to die are cancer patients. See Michael Cook, "15% Rise in Dutch Euthanasia Deaths," *BioEdge* (October 11, 2014), http://www.bioedge.org/index.php/bioethics/bioethics_article/11172; R. Cohen-Almagor, *Euthanasia in the Netherlands*; T. Smets, J. Bilsen, J. Cohen et al., "Legal Euthanasia in Belgium: Characteristics of All Reported Euthanasia Cases," *Medical Care* 48(2) (2910): 187–92; Koen Pardon, Kenneth Chambaere, H. Pasman, W. Roeline et al., "Trends in End-of-Life Decision Making in Patients with and Without Cancer," *J. Clinical Oncology* 31(11) (2013): 1450–57; Oregon's Death with Dignity Act—2013, http://public.health.oregon.gov/ProviderPartnerResources/EvaluationResearch/DeathwithDignityAct/Documents/year16.pdf.

32. Peter Conrad, *The Medicalization of Society: On the Transformation of Human Conditions into Treatable Disorders* (Baltimore: The John Hopkins University Press, 2007).

33. T. L. Beauchamp and J. F. Childress, *Principles of Biomedical Ethics* (NY: Oxford University Press, 2013); Tom L. Beauchamp, "The Autonomy Turn in Physician-Assisted Suicide," in R. Cohen-Almagor (ed.), *Medical Ethics at the Dawn of the 21st Century* (New York: New York Academy of Sciences), Vol. 913 of the Annals: (2000): 111–26.

34. Peter Singer and Helga Kuhse, *Should the Baby Live? The Problem of Handicapped Infants* (Oxford: Oxford University Press, 1985). See also R. Cohen-Almagor, "A Critique of Callahan's Utilitarian Approach to Resource Allocations in Health Care," *Issues in Law and Medicine* 17(3) (Spring 2002): 247–61.

35. R. Cohen-Almagor, "Autonomy, Life as an Intrinsic Value, and Death with Dignity," *Science and Engineering Ethics* 1(3) (1995): 261–72.

36. Carlos F. Gomez, *Regulating Death* (New York: The Free Press, 1991); B. Dierckx de Casterlé, C. Verpoort, N. De Bal et al. "Nurses' Views on Their Involvement in Euthanasia: A Qualitative Study in Flanders (Belgium)," *J. Med. Ethics* 32 (2006): 187–92; J. Bilsen, J. Cohen, K. Chambaere et al., "Medical End-of-Life Practices under the Euthanasia Law in Belgium," *New England Journal of Medicine* 361 (2009): 1119–21; H. Buiting, J. van Delden, B. Onwuteaka-Philipsen

et al., "Reporting of Euthanasia and Physician-Assisted Suicide in The Netherlands: Descriptive Study," *BMC Medical Ethics* 10 (2009): 10–18; B. A. M. Hesselink, B. D. Onwuteaka-Philipsen, A. J. G. M. Jansen et al., "Do Guidelines on Euthanasia and Physician-Assisted Suicide in Dutch Hospitals and Nursing Homes Reflect the Law? A Content Analysis," *J. Med. Ethics* 38 (2012): 35–42; R. Cohen-Almagor, "First Do No Harm: Pressing Concerns Regarding Euthanasia in Belgium," *The International Journal of Law and Psychiatry* 36 (2013): 515–21; P. Walker, "One in Five Dutch Doctors Would Help Physically Healthy Patients Die," *The Guardian* (February 17, 2015), http://www.theguardian.com/society/2015/feb/17/assisted -dying-dutch-doctors-patient-law-netherlands.

37. R. Cohen-Almagor, "An Argument for Physician-Assisted Suicide and Against Euthanasia," *Ethics, Medicine, and Public Health* 1(4) (2015): 431–41.

38. Oregon Death with Dignity Act, https://public.health.oregon.gov/Provider PartnerResources/EvaluationResearch/DeathwithDignityAct/Documents/statute.pdf.

39. Termination of Life on Request and Assisted Suicide (Review Procedures) Act, The Netherlands (April 1, 2002).

40. Belgian Act on Euthanasia, Chapter II, Section 3, no. 1, http://www.ethical -perspectives.be/viewpic.php?LAN=E&TABLE=EP&ID=59 (accessed October 5, 2016).

41. Roberto Andorno, "Nonphysician-Assisted Suicide in Switzerland," *Cambridge Quarterly J. of Healthcare Ethics* 22 (2013): 246–53; G. Bosshard, S. Fischer, and W. Bar, "Open Regulation and Practice in Assisted Dying—How Switzerland Compares with the Netherlands and Oregon," *Swiss Medical Weekly* 132 (October 12, 2002): 527–34; Georg Bosshard, "Assisted Suicide and Euthanasia in Switzerland," *BMJ* 327 (July 5, 2003): 51–52; Stephen J. Ziegler, "Collaborated Death: An Exploration of the Swiss Model of Assisted Suicide for Its Potential to Enhance Oversight and Demedicalize the Dying Process," *Journal of Law, Medicine and Ethics* 37(2) (Summer 2009): 318–30; Nicole Steck, Christoph Junker, Maud Maessen, Thomas Reisch, Marcel Zwahlen, and Matthias Egger, "Suicide Assisted by Right-to-Die Associations: A Population Based Cohort Study," *International Journal of Epidemiology* 43(2) (2014): 614–22.

42. Northern Territory of Australia, Rights of the Terminally Ill Act 1995, http:// www.nt.gov.au/lant/parliamentary-business/committees/rotti/rotti95.pdf (accessed October 5, 2016).

43. Dying Patient Law, Israel (2005), http://98.131.138.124/articles/JME/JMEM12 /JMEM.12.2.asp (accessed October 5, 2016).

44. R. Cohen-Almagor, The Right to Die with Dignity and "Should Doctors Suggest Euthanasia to Their Patients? Reflections on Dutch Perspectives," *Theoretical Medicine and Bioethics* 23(4–5) (2002): 287–303; "Euthanasia Policy and Practice in Belgium: Critical Observations and Suggestions for Improvement," *Issues in Law and Medicine* 24(3) (Spring 2009): 187–218.

45. See R. Cohen-Almagor, "First Do No Harm: Shortening Lives of Patients without Their Explicit Request in Belgium," *J. Med. Ethics* 41 (2015): 625–29.

46. Frederick Schauer, "Slippery Slopes," *Harvard L. Rev.* 99 (1985): 361; Eugene Volokh, "The Mechanisms of the Slippery Slope," *Harvard L. Rev.*116 (2003): 1026.

47. Belgian Act on Euthanasia, Chapter II, Section 3, no. 1, http://www.ethical -perspectives.be/viewpic.php?LAN=E&TABLE=EP&ID=59 (accessed October 5, 2016).

48. John Hardwig, "Families and Futility: Forestalling Demands for Futile Treatment," *J. Clinical Ethics* 16(4) (2005): 328–37; R. Cohen-Almagor, "Fatal Choices and Flawed Decisions at the End-of-Life: Lessons from Israel," *Perspectives in Biology and Medicine* 54(4) (2011): 578–94; Lara Pivodic, Lieve Van den Block, Koen Pardon et al., "Burden on Family Carers and Care-Related Financial Strain at the End of Life: A Cross-National Population-Based Study," *European J. Public Health* 24(5) (October 2014): 819–26.

49. Oregon Death with Dignity Act, Oregon Revised Statutes, Vol. 8 (1998 Supplement), at 981–82; Oregon Death with Dignity Act (1997), Oregon Revised Statutes, http://public.health.oregon.gov/ProviderPartnerResources/Evaluation Research/DeathwithDignityAct/Pages/ors.aspx.

50. M. C. Jansen-van der Weide, B. D. Onwuteaka-Philipsen, and G. Van der Wal, "Implementation of the Project Support and Consultation on Euthanasia in The Netherlands (SCEN)," *Health Policy* 69(3) (2004): 365–73; R. Cohen-Almagor, *Euthanasia in the Netherlands*; KNMG, *The Role of the Physician in the Voluntary Termination of Life* (Amsterdam: Koninklijke Nederlandsche Maatschappij tot bevordering der Geneeskunst [KNMG], 2011); Marianne K. Dees, Myrra J. Vernooij-Dassen, Wim J. Dekkers et al., "Perspectives of Decision-Making in Requests for Euthanasia: A Qualitative Research Among Patients, Relatives and Treating Physicians in the Netherlands," *Palliative Medicine* 27(1) (2012): 27–37. See also Steun en Consultatie bij Euthanasie in Nederland (Support and Consultation for Euthanasia in the Netherlands [SCEN]), a program organized by The Royal Dutch Medical Association (KNMG). SCEN physicians are specially trained and certified by the KNMG. In Belgium, a specialist committee (LEIF) exists only in Flanders, not in Wallonia. Consequently, the euthanasia act does not prescribe that the consultant must be a LEIF physician. Cohen et al. argue for improving the present consultation system in Belgium. J. Cohen, Y. Van Wesemael, T. Smets et al., "Nationwide Survey to Evaluate the Decision-Making Process in Euthanasia Requests in Belgium: Do Specifically Trained 2nd Physicians Improve Quality of Consultation?" *BMC Health Services Research* 14 (2014): 307.

51. M. Laporte Matzo, and D. Witt Sherman, *Palliative Care Nursing—Quality Care to the End of Life* (Dordrecht: Springer-Kluwer, 2001); Arif H. Kamal, Thomas W. LeBlanc, and Diane E. Meier, "Better Palliative Care for All-Improving the Lived Experience with Cancer," *JAMA* (online May 31, 2016).

52. Assisted Dying Bill (2014), Section 3 "Declarations."

53. Oregon Death with Dignity Act (1997), Oregon Revised Statutes, http:// public.health.oregon.gov/ProviderPartnerResources/EvaluationResearch/Deathwith DignityAct/Pages/ors.aspx.

54. In Switzerland, aid-in-dying is commonly provided by lay persons. The law does not insist that only physicians provide this assistance. See Meinrad Schaer, "The Practice of Assisted Suicide in Switzerland," EXIT Report (2010), http://www.finalexit.org/dr_schaer_switzerland_1996-97_report.html; Samia Hurst and Alex Mauron, "Assisted Suicide and Euthanasia in Switzerland: Allowing a Role for Non-Physicians," BMJ 326 (2003): 271–73.

55. In the Netherlands and in Belgium, there were cases in which nurses performed euthanasia. See R. Cohen-Almagor, Euthanasia in the Netherlands; G. G. van Bruchem-van de Scheur, A. J. van der Arend, H. Huijer Abu-Saad et al., "Euthanasia and Assisted Suicide in Dutch Hospitals: The Role of Nurses," *J. Clin. Nurs.* 17(12) (2008): 1618–26; Els Inghelbrecht, Johan Bilsen, Freddy Mortier, Luc Deliens, "The Role of Nurses in Physician-Assisted Deaths in Belgium," *Canadian Medical Association J.* (2010), http://www.sciencedaily.com/releases/2010/05/100517144814.htm (accessed October 5, 2016); J. Bilsen, L. Robijn, K. Chambaere et al., "Nurses' Involvement in Physician-Assisted Dying Under the Euthanasia Law in Belgium," *International J. Nursing Studies* (2014), http://www.sciencedirect.com/science/article/pii/S0020748914001382 (accessed October 5, 2016).

56. In Belgium, the Federal Control and Evaluation Commission is required to submit a report every two years.

CHAPTER THREE

Euthanasia and Assisted Suicide: Attitudes and Policies in Mexico

Asunción Álvarez del Río, Julieta Gómez Ávalos, and Isaac González Huerta

Often, in forums discussing euthanasia or assisted suicide outside of Mexico, resident experts immediately are asked whether a law allowing for such end-of-life options might be enacted in Mexico, given that the majority of the population is Catholic. Such skepticism is certainly well founded.

The Catholic religion is known to have a hierarchy that has radically condemned euthanasia and assisted suicide, comparing these actions to genocide.[1] Nevertheless, Mexico is a secular country with citizens who practice other religions as well as those who profess no religion at all. The problem is that the Catholic Church is not content to influence its members' attitudes alone. Instead, it intervenes in public policies within countries, to promote or prevent laws in keeping with its doctrine without considering that the laws apply to all citizens regardless of whether they are Catholic. This is a concern, because the Catholic Church's power to influence public policy is beyond question; suffice to recall that the largest financial contribution in opposition to the 2014 Death with Dignity initiative in Massachusetts was from Catholic organizations.[2]

Mexico is full of contrasts. One is that within the realm of human rights, some places—such as Mexico City, the nation's capital—have very progressive laws regarding personal issues such as abortion and same-sex marriage, whereas very conservative and restrictive human rights laws predominate throughout most of the states.

In the last few years, participation of the Catholic Church has been decisive in abortion regulation throughout the country. When a law that legalized pregnancy interruption for up to 12 weeks of gestation was passed in Mexico City in 2007, the expected reaction by opposition groups went much further than imagined. To prevent other states in the country from following the example of the capital, legislators in 17 states reformed their constitutions to legally define human life as spanning from the moment of fertilization or conception until *natural death* (italics added). As a result of such reforms, abortion was outlawed, even for reasons that had previously been permitted. This has led to the criminalization of women despite having unintentionally aborted their pregnancies.[3] The aforementioned reforms were made without there being the slightest debate and responded to a dictate of Benedict XVI, the active Pope at the time.[4] Perhaps some politicians acted according to their personal beliefs, forgetting their commitment to a secular state, but others simply yielded to the pressure of the clergy and the promise of being compensated with support during elections.

A large portion of the Mexican population, many Catholics among them, are concerned and outraged that the Catholic hierarchy attempts to impose its dogmas on the laws of the nation, because that hinders people's free choice in paramount issues that should be decided in line with each individual's ethics. Secularism is necessary in plural societies to enable harmony among people with different beliefs and to guarantee that public policies are founded on debate anchored in rational arguments that people can share independent of their religions.

Another major contrast that exists in Mexico is reflected in the distribution of wealth. In other words, 45 percent of the population lives in conditions of poverty or extreme poverty and does not receive adequate health care, so that countless individuals of all ages die from treatable diseases. Alongside such deficient health care, however, is the other extreme—excessive treatment, especially at the end of many patients' lives. This causes enormous suffering that could be prevented if we stopped stubbornly trying to postpone death. The reasons why many doctors continue to apply unnecessary treatments are, on the one hand, fear of legal accusation for the death of a patient whose life could have been prolonged. Conversely there is the conviction of physicians that their professional duty is to combat death, without exception.

Here, then, are two problems that need solving. The first refers to poverty and is beyond the scope of this chapter. It is relevant, however, to mention that this situation has helped make the argument that, in a country whose people have so many needs, euthanasia is not a priority and should not be considered one until health care has become equitable. Nevertheless, the authors believe that concurrently with striving to eradicate the poverty of numerous Mexicans, the end-of-life medical care currently being given must be improved. Treatments that seek to prolong patients' lives indiscriminately should be avoided and palliative care developed and promoted as a way of providing the best possible quality of life to those patients for whom a cure is no longer possible and who should consider their end-of-life choices. After all, working on improving the care given to terminal patients in health institutions within Mexico will solve a problem of social injustice—today, people with financial resources and higher levels of education have more choices and also have the means to receive better palliative care at the final stage of life.

Despite the supposed familiarity of Mexicans with death and the vast number of cultural and artistic expressions dealing with the topic, the reality is that most Mexicans share the same attitudes of denial held by people in other Western countries. Only the communities that identify most strongly with their traditions—mainly indigenous groups—accept finitude as a part of life and know how to prepare to face death. Outside of these communities, the subject is avoided by society in general and regarding medical care in particular. Nevertheless, something is starting to change. As has happened in numerous other countries, many people in Mexico are becoming aware of the importance of dealing opportunely with the subject of the end of life to avoid having to go through very painful experiences that they already have faced during the final stage of a loved one's life. More than death, these people fear the suffering and the undignified conditions in which they could meet death if they passively allow the institutional inertia, at times jointly with the anguish of their family members, to make decisions about care during the final stage of life. In contrast, when the time comes, they would like the medical care to focus on helping the patient live with quality. Fortunately, some legal changes have occurred in this vein. There are people who want to go further, however. They want to have an emergency exit plan ensured should they find themselves in a situation in which speeding up death would be best for them, in which case they would need appropriate assistance to be able die safely and painlessly.

In Mexico, the physician-assisted death (PAD) debate has taken place mainly in the academic and legislative realms. Public opinion also has dealt with the topic intermittently, mainly when bills have come up for laws that would legalize it—and each time the Catholic Church has expressed its clear condemnation.[5] As mentioned, reforms to several state constitutions established that life must be respected until its natural death. Beyond the fact that the concept is ever more difficult to determine because technological breakthroughs are made throughout life, even at the end, it is clear that such rulings sought a position contrary to PAD. Be that as it may, there are people in Mexico who are showing interest in extending the debate on the subject. They believe that euthanasia and physician-assisted suicide (PAS) do not represent the first—but rather the last—solution to the suffering certain patients undergo at the end of their lives. These people want such actions to be allowed as a way of expanding options for individuals who have exhausted the other medical decisions currently permitted. It is necessary to underscore the fact that were euthanasia and PAS to be legalized, they would become options for those people who consider themselves to be in charge of their own life to the point of being able to decide its ending, but there will be others whose beliefs and values make them see things differently, and both positions are equally respectable. That is precisely why there should be laws that uphold the positions of all citizens.

Next, this chapter presents the process that has taken place in Mexico in recent years and led to the regulations that now govern end-of-life medical decisions, followed by an overview of the paths the country could take to allow for PAD.

End-of-Life Medical Decisions, What Is Allowed and What Is Prohibited

Over the last several years, legal changes aimed at improving the care of patients in the final stage of life have taken place in Mexico. They encompass three basic aspects: (1) recognizing a patient's decision not to receive treatments that unnecessarily prolong life, (2) ensuring physicians that in these cases they will not face criminal charges for not preventing the patient's death, and (3) establishing the compulsory nature of providing palliative care to the terminally ill.

The discussion that led to these changes began in 2002, as bills for laws that would legalize PAD started to appear that year, though none were successful. The most complete and well founded was presented to the legislature in 2005 by the Partido de la Revolución Democrática (PRD, Democratic Revolution Party) the strongest left-of-center party at the time. That federal bill (which would have applied throughout the country) sought to regulate the rights of the terminally ill and proposed allowing for euthanasia and PAS.[6] Other bills attempting to regulate PAD followed—some that would have applied solely in Mexico City and others of a federal scope—but they, too, failed. All these bills, however, helped garner the attention of the public and the authorities regarding the importance of addressing the needs and suffering of people with advanced stages of chronic diseases. Cancer, diabetes, hypertension, chronic renal failure, and degenerative neurological disorders are the main causes of mortality in Mexico. Most of the deaths due to these illnesses occur in hospitals, and in many cases in conditions of suffering that could have been prevented.

In 2007, when there was greater awareness of the grim panorama awaiting a good part of the terminally ill population, the centrist Partido Institucional Revolucionario (PRI, Institutional Revolutionary Party) proposed a new bill that would permit euthanasia in Mexico City. The conservative Partido de Acción Nacional (PAN, National Action Party) made a counterproposal that would allow for discontinuation of treatments meant to prolong a patient's life, which was, at the time, still called passive euthanasia. Legislators from the various parties—liberals and conservatives—reached an agreement to take the first step in protecting the rights of patients to make end-of-life decisions. A law was passed allowing patients to discontinue treatments that prolong life under conditions in which they do not want to live (such as measures involving cardiac reanimation, assisted ventilation, and dialysis) and obliging doctors to respect the decision of patients in the knowledge that they would not be accused of homicide. Legislators called this new piece of legislation the Advance Directive Law for the Distrito Federal (Distrito Federal, or Federal District, was the official name of Mexico City before it became a state in January 2016) using a mistaken term. "Advance directive" refers to a living will, a document written by a person in the present stipulating treatments they want and do not want to receive in the future if they are in a situation in which they are no longer able to express their will. The new law mistakenly used the term "advance directive" to refer to a decision made by a conscious and mentally competent patient regarding the present, rather than the future.[7] Later on, the error would be acknowledged, and the law now refers to discontinuation of treatments by terminally ill patients, as well as to writing a living will, which has created confusion and has been an obstacle to adequately stipulating all the specific features of each of the two situations.

A number of similar laws using the same name were introduced after the Advance Directive Law for the Distrito Federal, in different states in the country (Advance Directive Law for Aguascalientes, Advance Directive Law for Nayarit, for a total of 15, fewer than half of the states) and repeating the same confusion. Although the laws have meant progress in terms of protecting the rights of people at the end of life, by copying the errors of the original law they were based upon they are not clear in their scope, and do not adequately specify the two situations they are considering: treatment discontinuation by terminally ill patients and the writing of living wills.

Several elements in all of these laws are worth highlighting. The first is that they state that palliative care must be offered to patients when treatments are discontinued, which the authors see as a major step forward, as long as other changes also guarantee there being palliative care specialists available and that all health personnel who are not specialists in the area are sensitized to patient needs and understand the importance of making timely referrals for such care. Although these changes have begun in Mexico, they clearly are insufficient. This is shown in the evaluation study by *The Economist*, in which Mexico is rated 43 out of 80 in palliative care service.[8] To refer to such care, the term "orthothanasia" was introduced into the laws; it literally means "correct death," and refers to the care given at the end of a patient's life to relieve suffering without speeding up or postponing death. It is not difficult to agree with what the term describes; the problem with it is that Catholic bioethics has been using it in opposition to euthanasia.[9] "Orthothanasia yes, euthanasia no" is repeated as a slogan. Actually, orthothanasia coincides with what is known as palliative care, and introducing a concept steeped in Catholic ideology into the law of a secular country is unjustified. Further related to the use of the term, these laws prohibit actions that seek to intentionally shorten life, in other words—euthanasia and PAS—although they are not mentioned explicitly.

In 2009, the year after the Advance Directive Law for the Distrito Federal was approved, the General Health Law which applies throughout the country was reformed to supporting the right of terminally ill patients to reject useless treatments and mandating palliative care as part of the decision. This reform introduced a hugely important change into the concept of end-of-life medical care: Considering patient needs as a whole, encompassing physical, psychological, social, and spiritual aspects. Conversely, the reform explicitly prohibits actions meant to help a patient accelerate death, in other words, euthanasia and PAS. As discussed, legal breakthroughs in Mexico enable patients to decide how but not when to die.[10]

Although the General Health Law reform was passed in 2009, the standards regulating its application were not published until 2013 and 2014. They legally stipulated that both public and private medical facilities in Mexico must provide palliative care. This includes the possibility of consent by the patient or legal representative for the doctor to apply sedation—including a large and constant dosage until the patient's death—if no other means to relieve the suffering exists. It is understood such sedation will not accelerate the patient's death but it will end his or her active participation in life. For the patient and his or her family, this means it is the time to say their goodbyes because the patient will be in a state of unconsciousness at the time of death. The regulations also point out the importance of preventing patients from being subjected to therapeutic obstinacy (also known as medical futility), and the use of therapeutic or diagnostic measures that do not reflect any patient benefit. For many families, therapeutic obstinacy not only increases the patient's suffering for no reason but also creates a catastrophic economic situation by depleting the family's financial resources.

It should be mentioned that besides prohibiting euthanasia and PAS, the legal changes limit patients' possibilities of choice in another sense, because the changes mandate providing basic care, which includes feeding, hydration, hygiene, and respiratory tract permeability. Understandably, these types of care are essential for patients—except for those who do not want to continue living, in which case food and hydration are types of care that go against their will, whether they are able to express it or have written it in a living will. Such regulations have most likely been influenced by the position of the Catholic Church, in which providing food and water—naturally or artificially—even to patients in a persistent vegetative state, is considered a moral obligation.[11] This obligation, however, contradicts another imposed by the same church: To respect an individual until his or her natural death. Death prevented by artificially feeding a patient who has permanently lost consciousness is clearly not natural.

Possible Paths Toward Legalizing Physician-Assisted Dying in Mexico

Euthanasia, considered homicide in Mexico, and PAS, which is considered suicide assistance, are penalized in Mexico in the Federal Penal Code. The sentence for performing euthanasia can be 12 to 24 years in prison, but the judge could reduce it due to the compassionate reasons behind the action. In the case of PAS, the sentence is 2 to 5 years in prison. As Díaz-Aranda aptly points out,[12] the articles of the Penal Code, dating back to 1931, did not foresee cases of euthanasia or PAS, as they were not topics of discussion at the time. It has taken on importance in the world since the final decades of the 20th century, with strides made in technology and its application to medical care. The author proposes the possibility of modifying articles in the Penal Code that prohibit PAD and legally supporting the right to make decisions about one's own life based on the rights set down in the Mexican Constitution and acknowledgment endorsed by Mexico in the Universal Declaration of Human Rights.

Additionally, it is interesting to note that, with regard to euthanasia, Mexico City has a Penal Code that is more specific and in line with changes in health care and medical breakthroughs. This code establishes a penalty of up to five years of deprivation of freedom for anyone who commits an act of homicide. Although the term itself is not used, the act is understood to mean euthanasia because it is described as an action taken for humanitarian reasons and resulting from a clear, free, and repeated request made by the "victim" who was suffering an incurable illness.

The regulatory text that expressly forbids euthanasia and PAS (though called "assisted suicide," it is understood to refer to help given by a physician), in accordance with the Federal Penal Code, is the General Health Law. This means that to the extent that such law took steps to uphold the right of patients to discontinue treatments, it also ensured explicitly outlawing PAD. For many Mexicans, this meant simultaneous progress and setback on the subject of individual end-of-life freedoms due to imposition of a conservative ideology. That said, the fact that PAD is prohibited does not mean that no patients die through euthanasia or PAS in Mexico, but rather that it is a clandestine practice, thus whether such actions are applied adequately cannot be monitored. Further, continuing to prohibit these end-of-life options adds to discrimination, because patients who choose to die only can do so if the treatment keeping them alive can be discontinued or if they personally know a doctor who is willing to help them put an end to their life.[13]

The Mexican legal system rests on a strict set of principles founded in the Political Constitution of Mexico and international treaties that have been signed over the years. This means that all the laws of the country and sentences passed in the Supreme Court of Justice of the Nation (SCJN) must be based on the principles and rights established therein.[14] The right to life established in the third article of the Universal Declaration of Human Rights has been adopted by Mexican governmental institutions as a higher good with the resulting legal obligation of protecting it using the necessary mechanisms. Up to now, a rigid interpretation of this right—promoted by conservative groups—has hindered approval of bills proposing laws that would legalize PAD. A more promising way to promote this type of legal change, as Díaz-Aranda suggests, is to go around the right-to-life discussion and base the argument on freedom and the individual human right to free development of personality. This assumes acknowledging, on the one hand, patient autonomy to decide and request assistance to end his or her life and, conversely, the authority of a physician who agrees to acquiesce to that request without the fear of committing a crime.

Another possible way to legalize PAD in Mexico is through legal writs of protection known as "*amparos*" presented to the SCJN by individuals requesting authorization to receive help to die, either through euthanasia or PAS, arguing that a negation would be a violation of their constitutional human rights. This situation has not occurred in the country with relation to PAD, but similar *amparo* writs have been granted. One example is the writ recently granted to four individuals for consuming marijuana recreationally. The decision of the SCJN declared the prohibitive articles in the General Health Law as unconstitutional because they oppose the free development of personality, defined as a human right in the Constitution.[15] It is important to note that this *amparo* writ is exclusive to the four individuals involved in the suit until enough other *amparos* are granted to enable establishment of jurisprudence (a resolution by the SCJN that sets a precedent of how to act given a particular issue) and a ruling is made on the recreational use of marijuana to prevent negative public health effects. It is interesting to note that in Colombia—a country with a similar legal system and tutelary rights to those of Mexico and with which there is some cultural identification—euthanasia was decriminalized in 1997, through a Supreme Court decision. The Supreme Court considered that prohibition of merciful homicide was contrary to human rights because it infringed upon human dignity (the first article of the Constitution of Colombia), autonomy, and free development of personality of a terminally ill patient seeking medical help to die.[16]

Currently, a bill proposed and presented to the Mexican Congress by the left-of-center PRD party in April 2015, is being discussed. It proposes legalizing and regulating euthanasia (it does not mention PAS)[17] based on the constitutional right to decide freely about life that is anchored in the human right to free development of personality—including that an individual even may choose when to die in keeping with his will, life project, and intentions. This initiative seeks to reform the articles of the General Health Law and Federal Penal Code that prohibit euthanasia, and to reform other articles to establish the criteria to be followed by physicians who agree to apply euthanasia in accordance with the law. The future of the bill currently being discussed still is unknown. It could suffer the fate of previous unsuccessful attempts, but its existence reflects the fact that a portion of the Mexican population remains interested in the subject and wants to be able to consider all the options and choose the best one given an individual's situation at the end of his or her life.

As shown, according to what the Mexican legal framework allows, much may be done in the country to prevent unnecessary suffering of patients at the end of their lives. Treatments that prolong life may be discontinued; palliative care must be given and can include deep, continuous sedation until death. Ambiguity exists, however, as to the treatments that can be withdrawn, given the lack of agreement as to whether feeding and artificial hydration—both parenteral or through a tube—are to be considered treatments or basic care, and euthanasia and PAS are forbidden. For a significant part of the population it is important to expand the freedom to choose how and when to die. One of the major obstacles to achieving that is not rooted in the functioning of the Mexican legal system but rather comes from social groups that have political and economic power and seek to impose their religious beliefs on discussions that determine public policies that apply to all Mexicans in a secular and plural society.

The next section presents an overview of the attitudes and opinions of Mexicans to PAD over the last 10 years, based on surveys and studies that have explored the subject in Mexico, as well as articles published in the media. It includes a qualitative study carried out in 2015 that is especially interesting because it provides a more in-depth analysis of the outlook of a group of Mexican physicians on the subject.

Attitudes and Opinions of Mexicans About Physician-Assisted Dying

In 2006, the results of a survey carried out by Parametría revealed that 39 percent of respondents agreed with the ending of a patient's life in cases where a group of specialists determined the illness to be incurable, 46 percent disagreed, and the remaining 15 percent was undecided. Taking into account that the questions about euthanasia were not very well worded, findings included that those respondents who agreed were mostly young, between the ages of 18 and 25, had a higher educational level, and were not very interested in religion. Conversely, those who disagreed were mainly older adults, with a low educational level, and religion was a very important part of their lives.[18] In a survey conducted two years later by Parametría and El Colegio de México, when asked whether physicians should be allowed to end the life of a patient who so desires (the question was better phrased), 60 percent of Mexicans agreed, most of these respondents were young, from Mexico City, and do not consider religion important.[19]

This trend toward acceptance of euthanasia already had been detected by Mexican consulting firm Consulta Mitofsky in 2005, when it conducted a national survey of 3,500 people and found that 64 percent of respondents agreed with the regulation on euthanasia. The groups most in agreement were those people between 18 and 49 years of age, university students, and from a middle or high socioeconomic level.[20] In 2007, another national survey, this time including 1,000 individuals, showed that agreement with the regulation on euthanasia remained at 63 percent. This survey showed an increase in the number of people older than age

50 who were in favor of the ruling (an increase from 49 percent in 2005 to 53 percent).[21]

We next examine information on a more specific group: medical doctors. The authors consider it especially important to determine doctors' attitudes and opinions with respect to PAD, not only because of the role they play in deciding and applying it but due to the weight of their opinion in the debate on its legalization. In recent years, several studies have been done that provide pertinent information.

In 2008, Lisker and collaborators published the results of a questionnaire given to 2,097 Mexican doctors from different hospitals in the country, to find out their opinions on euthanasia and on withdrawing and withholding life-sustaining treatment (WD/WH). Forty percent of the doctors agreed with applying euthanasia to a terminally ill patient who requested it due to suffering, 44 percent disagreed, and the remainder was undecided. Further, 48 percent of the doctors agreed on withdrawing treatment from a patient in a permanent vegetative state if the family so requested, 35 percent responded "no," and 17 percent was undecided. In both scenarios, the reasons for agreeing were respect for patient or family autonomy and preventing suffering, whereas the reasons of respondents who answered negatively were mainly ethical and religious considerations (respect for life and defending its sanctity).[22]

A few years later, in 2011, a study was done to explore the psychological significance and attitudes regarding euthanasia in 546 doctors and medical students at different public hospital settings. They were divided into three groups: (1) beginning students, (2) advanced students, and (3) attending physicians, in the specialties of anesthesiology, general surgery, geriatrics, gynecology, psychiatry, urology, and neurology.

The study used the semantic network technique, asking participants to associate terms to the word "euthanasia," which then were analyzed. For advanced students and attending physicians, the psychological significance and attitudes were positive. For the beginning students, the psychological significance was positive as well as negative and attitudes were more ambivalent. This ambivalence toward euthanasia is understandable, because it has to do with an action that involves helping someone through an action that ends his or her life. In other words, the two actions are apparently conflicting, so such ambivalence might also be present in other doctors and medical students whose opinion is explored using questionnaires that are not as appropriate for identifying it.[23]

In 2013, the results of a study carried out in a public hospital in Mexico City were published. The results include opinions of medical students who have had clinical practice (99) and internal medicine residents (140) concerning (1) PAD (both euthanasia and PAS), (2) WD/WH, and (3) PAD for oneself. Fifty percent agreed with PAD and 58 percent with WD/WH, which indicates greater acceptance of these actions within the realm of doctors, which could be due to the age of the participants, possibly because they were younger or have been in practice for fewer years. An important point is that of the 99 students, 46 were at religious schools. This fact was reflected in their opinions, as those students at secular schools agreed significantly more with PAD than the students who went to religious schools (68 percent vs. 33 percent), agreed significantly more with WD/WH (79 percent vs. 39 percent), and agreed more with PAD for oneself (57 percent vs. 48 percent). This difference can be explained by the fact that religious schools convey the values of the Catholic Church for application to medical practice, including opposition to PAD. The same religious school students, however, made exceptions to what they learned; they agreed more on PAD for oneself than if it were applied to a patient.[24]

The following year, 2014, Loria and collaborators conducted a study in two public hospitals in Mexico City to explore the opinions of internal medicine residents (151) and oncology residents (61) regarding PAD and WD/WH. This time, however, instead of asking for their opinion on the actions of others, they were asked if they would carry out PAD and WD/WH. It turned out that beginning residents had a significantly greater proportion of positive responses to PAD than did advanced residents (82 percent vs. 55 percent), which confirms greater acceptance for this action among younger doctors.

It should be noted, however, that the high percentage of agreement resulted when the hypothetical situation of PAD being legalized was posed. The response reflects the interest of participants in there being a legal framework to regulate PAD. Thus, at first, only 16 percent of beginning residents said that they would help in the death of a mentally competent terminally ill patient who had intolerable suffering and requested PAD. The percentage went up to 66 percent if such help was legalized. Of the advanced residents, initially a mere 13 percent said they would help a patient in the same condition to die, but this response increased to 42 percent in the case of PAD being legalized. Moreover, as seen in other studies, participants were more willing to assist death through WD/WH than in giving or applying the means to die (82 percent vs. 18 percent, and 88 percent vs. 12 percent among beginning residents and advanced residents, respectively). Finally, 76 percent of beginning residents and 56 percent of advanced residents responded that they would agree with PAD for themselves.[25]

The results of research carried out by Por el derecho de morir con dignidad (DMD), the only right-to-die association in Mexico, were published in November 2015, at the time the new association was introduced to the media. This study explored the opinion of Mexican physicians regarding different aspects of end-of-life medical care. The qualitative methodology that was used included in-depth interviews of specialists in several fields of medicine (intensive care, oncology, neurosurgery, palliative medicine, general surgery, geriatrics, vascular surgery, and anesthesiology), and focus groups composed of doctors employed by public or private hospitals in Mexico City and the city of Puebla and studying one of these specialties. Besides the physicians' opinions about PAD and WD/WH, the study produced important information for understanding the context within which many doctors work, their available resources, and the conditions in which a large number of patients live.

To begin with, the doctors considered there to be major differences between public and private institutions in the management of patients in the terminal phase, because the saturation of patients in public institutions causes doctors to focus their attention on hospitalized patients who can be cured rather than on relieving the suffering of terminally ill patients. Plus, most public hospitals lack the necessary infrastructure to offer palliative care. These hospitals don't even have opioids for pain management, so doctors feel powerless watching terminally ill patients die in great pain. The way that doctors deal with the situation is to send patients home, sadly without giving them the support they should. Doctors who work in private hospitals have more time, enabling them to have better communication with their patients, although not all the institutions are equipped with palliative care services. What's more, in the interviews the doctors said that unnecessary therapeutic efforts sometimes are made solely for invoicing purposes.

Palliative (also called terminal) sedation is an intervention that some doctors apply to patients who have a short life expectancy and suffer symptoms refractory to treatment, even though certain doctors consider it to be a way to hasten death. Another decision physicians make to prevent a terminally ill patient from further suffering is WD/WH, respecting patient autonomy independently of what the family requests, as in the case of a patient who does not want resuscitation because it would only prolong the suffering. If the patient is unconscious or mentally incompetent— such as a patient with advanced dementia, for example—WD/WH would be performed with the consent of the family. Not all doctors, however, agree with such a decision, arguing that they would not want to face legal problems that could send them to prison or discredit them, which speaks to the lack of knowledge that persists concerning the legality of different end-of-life medical decisions.

When discussing PAD, the doctors had opposing positions. Those in favor thought that terminally ill patients have a right to decide when to end their life if they experience intolerable suffering, an option that the doctors would want for themselves or for a loved one. Some said that PAD should not be limited to the terminally ill but should include patients who consider their life undignified due to their handicaps and dependence. The doctors opposed to PAD said that it goes against the Catholic religion they profess, and that they believe that no individual is master of his or her life, so that nobody has the right to shorten another person's life; moreover, it is an action classified as homicide.

Finally, doctors in favor of PAD gave their opinions on whether it should be legalized, which can be summed up as three positions. One group is clearly in favor, pointing out the importance of having a law that defines the criteria for its application and supervision mechanisms, rather than having it performed clandestinely, as it currently occurs. Another group of physicians is against legalization, arguing that it would be dangerous to permit PAD given the degree of corruption in the country. They claim it would lend itself to application abuses and consider it preferable that it continues to be done clandestinely. The third group wants it to be legalized but believes that the country is not yet prepared to understand and accept PAD. They feel it is first necessary to prepare doctors and the population through education and information on the subject.[26]

Given that the Catholic Church plays an important role in opinion formation among Mexican Catholics, including doctors, the results of a nationwide survey carried out in 2014 are interesting. A total of 2,669 Catholics throughout the country were interviewed about their beliefs and values regarding topics such as sexual and reproductive rights, and the interviews included a question about PAD. Sixty-five percent of the respondents reported agreeing with a doctor helping a person to die who requests it when suffering from an incurable disease and 35 percent disagreed. The data showed a greater trend to agree occurring in urban zones than in rural areas, and 79 percent of the participants in Mexico City were in agreement.[27] It is interesting to note that, according to the results of this survey, ever more Mexican Catholics have been moving away from the moral teachings of their church in terms of contraception and abortion. Thus, for example, 8 out of 10 interviewees support teens having access to modern birth-control methods and knowing in what situations abortion is legal in Mexico. Also, 80 percent of the participants are in favor of a woman being able to interrupt a pregnancy when her life is in danger, and 71 percent are in favor when the pregnancy is the result of rape.[28] It is not surprising that on the subject of end of life there are also many Catholics who do not agree with the limitations on choice imposed by the hierarchy of their church.

Generally speaking, based on the surveys and studies examined here, it can be seen that among both the general population and physicians and future doctors, acceptance of PAD has been on the rise. A survey promoted by the new right-to-die association DMD Mexico currently is being conducted nationally. Expected in late 2016, the results are sure to provide some very important information.

Having discussed the legal situation of PAD in Mexico along with the results of surveys and studies concerning the opinions of the population, the final section of this chapter focuses on the debate that needs to take place leading up to legalizing PAD in Mexico. It also analyzes the challenges that must be met for this end-of-life option to be legalized, as well as the elements that facilitate it.

The Necessary Debate

As happens in many other countries where PAD is banned, a significant portion of the population in Mexico would like people who suffer from a disease or medical condition that cannot be alleviated to be able to have the help of a physician to hasten their death, if they so desire. For some, the reason is that they already are experiencing such a situation. Others who are healthy (or at least think they are), however, realize that the future could bring chronic illnesses or complications of aging under circumstances in which they might prefer death to ongoing suffering. For those individuals, supporting PAD legalization does not necessarily mean that it is an option they are going to use. In fact, few of them will actually do so if they are given appropriate palliative care, but knowing that at the end of life they can choose how and when to die is comforting, as much for patients who know their days are numbered as for people looking forward to many more years of life.

Today, in Mexico as in most countries, solely the wishes of those who do not want the option of PAD are being considered, so it is important to discuss the reasons that currently stand in the way of respecting the wishes of people who support it. Only extremely compelling reasons could justify maintaining the prohibition and ignoring the desire of part of the population. Consequently, it is important to establish ongoing debate in Mexico and examine the reasons for prohibiting PAD, as has been done in other countries that have recently sought to legalize one or both forms of PAD. In Canada, for instance, the reasons for continuing to forbid physicians from helping a patient die were rejected,[29] but in the United Kingdom they were not.[30]

The debate Mexico needs to have must include broad participation of its citizens and agreement as to the meaning of the actions to be analyzed. The authors propose that euthanasia be understood as the action taken by a doctor to cause the death of a patient who has requested such help to put an end to his or her suffering. Euthanasia should no longer be classified as active or passive, because what previously was called "passive euthanasia" now is known as "WD/WH." The same goes for other classifications: Direct and indirect; and voluntary, not voluntary, and involuntary—classifications which only create confusion. Euthanasia is active, direct, and voluntary. In terms of PAS, the authors propose that it be understood as the assistance a physician gives a patient, in response to the latter's request, providing the means for the patient to be the one who carries out the action that leads to death. In Mexico, euthanasia has been discussed much more than PAS, which might be the reason that use of the term "suicide" has not been repudiated as it has in the United States, where supporters of this end-of-life option insist on using the term "aid in dying," instead of PAS. Reasons abound for wanting to avoid using a concept as stigmatized as suicide—which tends to be connected with the image of a violent and avoidable death, an association that could also be made consciously or unconsciously by Mexicans hearing the term "physician-assisted suicide."

It also is important to clearly define what it is that needs to be discussed. Here, we recall the words of Wayne Sumner,[31] who finds it useless to discuss whether euthanasia and PAS are ethical actions given that positions are divided on the subject, with both sides being respectable. Rather than trying to change opinions that are rooted in values and beliefs, we should discuss whether the reasons currently keeping PAD from being an option are valid. Such arguments can be summed up as: Palliative care makes PAD unnecessary, doctors are unable to participate in any action that causes death, and that accepting that PAD might be justified in certain situations opens the door to the inevitable risk of abuses being committed and vulnerable people being harmed if it is allowed.

In a different publication the authors analyzed, reviewed, and rebutted each one of these points. The following is a recap.[32]

• Palliative care and PAD should not be considered mutually exclusive—they actually are complementary. Physician-assisted dying is considered only after every possibility of alleviating the suffering has been exhausted, which involves accepting that such care has limits in terms of helping patients. Further, at times the help offered is unacceptable to patients, because it means practically being under constant sedation or knowing that death will come when they are unconscious. We disagree with the argument that a consequence of legalizing PAD would be the discouraging of development of palliative care because it would be easier to help someone die through PAD than to provide care that would improve his or her quality of life. The experience of countries where PAD is permitted proves just the opposite, as care of patients at the end of their lives actually has improved.

- As for physicians participating in an action that leads to death, doctors' positions are divided. It is easy to understand that being professionals trained to heal people, they would find it very difficult to help a patient die. Clearly, some doctors are categorically opposed to taking part in PAD. In fact, the laws in places where euthanasia or PAS has been accepted address this issue by stating that it is not mandatory for any doctor to respond to and act upon a patient's request for assistance in dying. Some doctors, however, find it difficult to take part in PAD but are willing to do so because they do not want to forsake a patient who they can no longer help any other way. It is questionable, however, to infer loss of faith in the medical profession from this, because what many people want is to be able to count on their doctor helping them die should they need it.

- Finally, regarding abuse and harm to vulnerable individuals, of course legalizing PAD must not lead to such assistance being given to patients who request it under pressure or do so because they mistakenly think they want to die. No one should be coerced by family or society to accelerate his or her own death, feeling they are a burden. It is important to prevent this from happening, and extreme caution would be required in cases where such a situation was suspected. Nonetheless, we must not underestimate the ability of people to decide rationally that they prefer death to continuing to live with the pain that they suffer from a severe disability or illness. In any case, it is unfair and excessive to stand in the way of helping others who unequivocally want to end their life to protect a few individuals who might request PAD for the wrong reasons.

It is important to take into account the risks highlighted in the arguments against PAD that have been discussed so that they can be prevented as much as possible. Which brings us to the next—and possibly the most difficult—topic that must be addressed in Mexico: Determining the criteria for applying PAD and the mechanisms for its supervision. To begin with, the profile of patients who could receive help to die if they so decide must be defined. Previous bills to legalize PAD in Mexico have considered terminally ill patients, yet it is also important to analyze whether this type of assistance should be extended to patients who are not in a terminal phase but suffer from illnesses such as Parkinson's disease, amyotrophic lateral sclerosis, multiple sclerosis, and others that cause some people to feel trapped living in conditions they feel are so miserable that they have no quality of life (although other people in the same situation want to continue living). Further, could minors who are clearly able to decide be helped and patients with Alzheimer's disease who are at an initial stage and still have the mental capacity to decide that they do not want a life that is headed toward the disintegration of their person be included?

Another point that must be explored is how assistance with death would be given. Most of the bills that have been discussed in Mexico refer to euthanasia, but consideration must be given to whether to include PAS, only one of these modalities, or either, as the patient prefers; as well as the way PAD would be overseen, and how to keep abuses from being committed, as far as is possible.

Besides the euthanasia legalization bill that is being discussed in the Mexican Congress, a group of academics from the University Bioethics Program at the Universidad Nacional Autónoma de México (UNAM) and the Colegio de Bióetica A.C. has formed to work on defining the criteria for PAD application and the mechanisms for overseeing it. They also are analyzing the best possible legal procedures to enable Mexicans to be assisted in death by a physician in case the current bill is not approved.

Challenges to Be Met and Favorable Conditions

Perhaps one of the biggest challenges to overcome in Mexico when considering PAD legalization is instilling confidence that it will be applied correctly in a population that has its reasons for not fully trusting institutions or doctors. Patients, family members, and even health personnel report cases of inappropriate medical care, unnecessary procedures being carried out, and, above all a lack of communication of doctors with patients and their families—who often feel neglected, devalued, and even deceived by their doctors, which is a primary cause of their distrust.

This is clearly a problem that affects the practice of medicine in Mexico and first must be acknowledged so that it can be solved, regardless of whether PAD is legalized. If the subject comes up within the context of the debate about PAD, however, then it will be an opportunity to spotlight the need to make changes to improve medical practice and people's confidence in it. This not only will be reflected in PAD being applied correctly but also in better medical care throughout and at the end of life.

Faced with the opinion of those who oppose PAD because it would lend itself to application abuses given the degree of corruption in the country, the authors believe that it is preferable to permit it with very clear regulations on criteria for application, rather than having it continue to be performed clandestinely. This would force transparency and enable having elements to ensure that it is only applied when specific conditions are truly met. Among others, that the physician makes sure that the patient's request is voluntary (not an expression of depression, desperation, or pressure), that the patient endures intolerable suffering that cannot be alleviated, and that the patient has all the information required to make the decision.

The problem of mistrust of health institutions and doctors is inseparable from the need for better professional training to deal with situations that require good communication with patients and making decisions related to the end of life. José Narro, current Minister of Health, has expressed concern about poor use of scientific and technological developments within the medical field and the need to establish clear limits for using them, thereby preventing actions that prolong life unnecessarily at the expense of suffering for the patient and loved ones and excessive, useless, and absurd cost to people or institutions.[33]

Progress toward legalizing PAD must go hand in hand with other changes in medical care. After all, patients and their families deserve to get adequate medical care that provides quality in the final stage of life and enables them to make decisions in keeping with their values. For that to occur, throughout their training, doctors must learn to face death within their practice, a subject that is still not part of the curriculum of Mexican medical schools. The results of research on Mexican physicians who treat terminally ill patients showed that only a small number (28 percent) had had any training for treating this type of patient. Most had learned to handle death through personal experiences and years of practice.[34] We can assume that that is how many doctors learn but, practically speaking, the result of such training is far from optimal. Countless patients die without the care they deserve or the options concerning the end of their life, because their physicians are unaware of the medical decisions that are permitted in the country or because physicians do not know how to establish appropriate communication with a patient so that he or she is well informed about the situation and together with their physician can make the best decisions.

In addition to building society's trust and improving medical training to respond to patient needs, we also must guarantee a secular culture that allows for legal changes to expand the options of Mexicans in the final stage of life. The Pope's recent visit underscores that there are reasons to worry about interference on the part of the Catholic Church in the public policies in Mexico. This is not so much the result of the Pope's words or behavior, as he said what is expected of a religious leader, but rather is a reflection of the attitudes of government officials who are supposedly bound to respect the secularity of the nation but were the first to ignore it by making public statements as if all Mexicans were Catholic, not acknowledging that at least 20 million are not.[35] The huge expenditure of public resources to prepare for the Pope's visit, the excessive blocking of roadways, and extensive interruption of public transportation are examples of the special treatment the government provided the Catholic Church, when there should be impartiality and equal respect for all religions.

Concern with guaranteeing the secular state has been voiced increasingly at various academic forums. Recently, the UNAM Institute of Legal Research celebrated the International Week of Lay Culture by addressing topics such as "Laicism, Reproduction and Diversity," "Laicism, Science and Sexual and Reproductive Rights," and "Laicism, Beginning and End of Life," and concluding with a reflection on the impact on Mexico's secular agenda of the visit of Pope Francis. Academic forums such as this one firmly recognize the need to demand that the government fulfill its duty to respect the secular state and spread the concept of laicism throughout society so that its true meaning is understood: a condition that enables coexistence among people with different beliefs and not an antireligious strategy, as many representatives of the Catholic Church prefer to present it.

As the PAD debate progresses, these same representatives will wield their power and influence to make themselves heard through the media and impose their disapproval, arguing that PAD is used to get rid of vulnerable individuals such as the sick and the elderly.[36] Some Catholics will follow this lead but others will not, and instead will be guided by their conscience, as is the case for numerous women who use contraceptives despite the Vatican's prohibition. They would be backed by the position of Catholic theologians such as Hans Küng, who defends the option of PAD and has said that he himself would resort to it, were it necessary, to die with the same dignity with which he has lived.[37]

Unlike other churches that are opposed to PAD but exclusively address their own members, the Catholic Church wants as its doctrine to apply to all the citizens by means of the law, perhaps because it knows that its members are no longer willing to follow it on some issues. The Catholic population has to decide whether to accept what the Vatican determines, and Mexicans interested in defending the right of individuals to freely make decisions about their own life must keep the Catholic Church from enjoying the support of the Mexican government to attain its objective.

In terms of physicians, it has been shown that their positions regarding PAD are split. The Colegio de Medicina Interna de México, the foremost association in the area, expressed its position on care of the terminally ill and euthanasia during debate on the proposed law in 2007. At that time, it expressed disagreement with euthanasia due to the risk of abuse and loss of trust in doctors who society would view as executioners. Though it has not updated its stance, we might expect a new statement if the euthanasia debate is reactivated in the media with discussion on the latest bill.[38]

As might be expected in a pluralistic country, expressions such as those that oppose euthanasia on the part of physicians are joined by others that support it. For example, María de la Luz Casas has said that the current danger regarding abortion and euthanasia that always has existed is that they be accepted and endorsed by the law, turning murder into a legal act, and the worst part is that there are doctors who support such actions. According to Casas, this is an outcome of ideological pluralism, moral relativism, and excessive promotion of autonomy, repeating the fears mentioned previously. From her viewpoint, permitting euthanasia would put an end to confidence in the physician, as patients would not be able to distinguish whether the doctor's actions were meant to conserve life or promote death.[39] Conversely, Arnoldo Kraus, who is also a physician, has published several opinion pieces encouraging the population to reflect and discuss euthanasia, because he is sure that contemporary modifications on such controversial issues should come mostly from society, less so from doctors, and not at all or nearly so from religious or governmental powers.[40] According to Kraus, defining the limits of life and of medicine when existing has no meaning is a complex task. Between a lifeless life and medicine that at times does not know when to stop, are human beings masters of their most precious possessions, their own life, their own death?[41]

As Kraus says, there is no reason to expect promotion of PAD legalization to come from doctors. After all, if a physician was in a situation in which he or she personally wanted euthanasia or PAS it would not need to be legal—a physician has both the means and the know-how to end his or her own life. It would be up to them to help their patients die, however, which is no easy task, even for medical professionals who are in favor of it.

Conclusion

The drive to promote the debate on PAD legalization in Mexico comes from society. Today we have a bill on euthanasia in the legislature, a group of academics working on a PAD legalization project, another group of academics organized to defend the secular state, and a new right-to-die association, Por el derecho a morir con dignidad, DMD Mexico. The association's main goal is to promote legal and social changes so that Mexicans can opt for dignified death, which includes the option of choosing PAD.[42] Recently, DMD Mexico organized a screening of the movie *Chronic*, produced in

English by Mexican director and screenwriter Michael Franco, one more expression of the interest in the general subject of dignified death and euthanasia in particular.

How close are Mexicans to actually legalizing PAD? This is unknown, but Mexicans definitely are closer to debating what is needed to move forward toward that objective, and forces have come together that allow us to be optimistic that in the not-so-distant future everyone who wants to end intolerable suffering or an undignified existence by ending their lives will be able to do so under conditions that do not endanger the people who assist them.

Notes

1. Juan Pablo II (Pope John Paul II). 1995. "Carta Encíclica Evangelium Vitae." *La Santa Sede*, March 25. http://w2.vatican.va/content/john-paul-ii/es/encyclicals /documents/hf_jp-ii_enc_25031995_evangelium-vitae.html.

2. Span, Paula. 2012. "How the 'Death With Dignity' Initiative Failed in Massachusetts." *New York Times*. December 8. Accessed February 28, 2016. http:// newoldage.blogs.nytimes.com/2012/12/06/how-the-death-with-dignity-law-died -in-massachusetts/?_r=0.

3. Álvarez de Río, Asunción. 2010. "Creencias y Derechos: ¿Podemos Lograr la Necesaria Tolerancia?" *Perspectivas Bioéticas* 15: 94–103.

4. Tapia, Ricardo. 2011. "La Religión y las Leyes Sobre Salud." *Crónica*. June 22. Accessed February 28, 2016. http://www.cronica.com.mx/notas/2011/587145 .html.

5. Barranco, Bernardo. 2007. "Debate Sobre la Eutanasia, Una Nueva Oportunidad." *La Jornada*. June 25. Accessed February 28, 2016. http://www.jornada .unam.mx/2007/06/27/index.php?section=politica&article=021a2pol.

6. Teherán, Jorge. 2005. "Plantea PRD ley para Permitir la Eutanasia." *El Universal*. May 18. Accessed March 1, 2016. http://archivo.eluniversal.com.mx /nacion/125211.html.

7. Colegio de Bioética A.C. 2008. "Voluntad Anticipada." Accessed March 1, 2016. http://colegiodebioetica.org.mx/voluntad-anticipada/voluntad-anticipada/.

8. The Economist. 2015. *The 2015 Quality of Death Index. Ranking Palliative Care Across the World.* United Kingdom: The Economist Intelligence Unit. http:// www.eiuperspectives.economist.com/healthcare/2015-quality-death-index.

9. Valadez, Diego. 2008. "Eutanasia, Régimen Jurídico de la Autonomía Vital." In *Derechos Humanos, Aborto y Eutanasia*, edited by Jorge Carpizo and Diego Valadez, 87. México: Instituto de Investigaciones Jurídicas, UNAM.

10. Gómez Mont, Fernando. 2015. "II. Los Parámetros Legales de la Muerte Digna en México." *Nexos*. June 1. Accessed March 1, 2016. http://www.nexos.com .mx/?p=25090.

11. Levada, William. 2007. "Respuestas a Algunas Preguntas de la Conferencia Episcopal Estadounidense Sobre la Alimentación e Hidratación Artificiales."

Congregación para la Doctrina de la Fe, La Santa Sede. August 1. http://www.vatican .va/roman_curia/congregations/cfaith/documents/rc_con_cfaith_doc_20070801 _risposte-usa_sp.html.

12. Aranda Díaz, Enrique. 2001. "Relatoría: II. Casos Asociados al Termino Eutanasia y Soluciones Jurídicas Tradicionales." *Derecho a Morir Dignamente, Asociación Federal.* http://www.eutanasia.ws/hemeroteca/t273.pdf.

13. Spanzi, Marta. 2013. "The French Euthanasia Debate." *Cambridge Quarterly of Healthcare Ethics* 22: 254–62.

14. Dávalos, José. 1992. "Panorama del Sistema legal Mexicano." *Boletín Mexicano de Derecho Comparado* 25: 485–94.

15. Lelo de Larrea, Arturo. 2014. *Amparo 237/2014 Sobre la Inconstitucionalidad de los Artículos 235, 237, 245, 247 y 248, Todos de la Ley General de Salud, en las Porciones Que Establecen Una Prohibición Para Que la Secretaría de Salud Emita Autorizaciones Para el Consumo Personal Con Fines Recreativos en Relación Únicamente y Exclusivamente con el Estupefaciente Cannabis.* México: Suprema Corte de Justicia de la Nación. Accessed March 2, 2016. http://www2.scjn.gob.mx/Consulta Tematica/PaginasPub/DetallePub.aspx?AsuntoID=164118.

16. Cifuentes Muñoz, Eduardo and Vladimiro Naranjo Mesa. 1997. *Sentencia C-239/97. Sobre el Homicidio por Piedad.* Colombia: Corte Constitucional de Colombia. Accessed March 2, 2016. http://www.corteconstitucional.gov.co /relatoria/1997/c-239-97.htm.

17. Melgar, Ivonne. 2015. "Piden Despenalizar Eutanasia Activa." *Excélsior.* April 23. Accessed March 1, 2016. http://www.excelsior.com.mx/nacional /2015/04/23/1020337#.VtzF5INJhZQ.email.

18. Parametría. 2006. "Eutanasia: Mexicanos Ante la Muerte Asistida." Accessed March 2, 2016. http://www.parametria.com.mx/carta_parametrica.php?cp=4042.

19. Parametría. 2008. "Mexicanos en Favor de la Euthanasia." Accessed March 2, 2016. http://www.parametria.com.mx/carta_parametrica.php?cp=4100.

20. Muñoz, Alma E. 2005. "Más de la Mitad de Mexicanos, en Favor de Aborto y Eutanasia." *La Jornada*, December 30. Accessed March 2, 2016. http://www .jornada.unam.mx/2005/12/30/index.php?section=sociedad&article=034n1soc.

21. Beltrán, Ulises y Asociados. 2007. "Despenalización de la Eutanasia en el Distrito Federal: Acontecer Nacional y Opinión Pública." Accessed March 2, 2016. www.bgc.com.mx.

22. Lisker, Rubén, Asunción Álvarez del Río, A. Villa, and A. Carnevale. 2008. "Physician-Assisted Death. Opinions of a Sample of Mexican Physicians." *Ach. Med. Res.* 39: 452–58. Accessed March 2, 2016. doi: 10.1016/j.arcmed.2008.01.004.

23. Álvarez del Río, Asunción and ML. Marván. 2011. "On Euthanasia: Exploring Psychological Meaning and Attitudes in a Sample of Mexican Physicians and Medical Students." *Dev. World Bioeth.* 11: 146–53. Accessed March 2, 2016. doi: 10.1111/j.1471-8847.2011.00308.x.

24. Loria, A., C. Villarreal-Garza, E. Sifuentes, and Rubén Lisker. 2013. "Opinions of Mexican Medical Students and Residents." *Arch. Med. Res.* 44: 475–78. Accessed March 2, 2016. doi: 10.1016/j.archmed.2013.07.005.

25. Loria, A., C. Villarreal-Garza, E. Sifuentes, and Rubén Lisker. 2014. "Legality and Age Influence End of Life Decisions in Mexican Physicians." *Rev. Invest. Clin.* 66: 59–64.

26. DMD A.C. 2015. "Informe del Estudio de Opinión de los Médicos Sobre el Derecho a Morir con Dignidad." Accessed March 2, 2016. http://www.dmd.org .mx/encuestas.html.

27. Católicas por el Derecho a Decidir. 2014. "Encuesta Nacional de Opinión Católica." Accessed March 2, 2016. http://encuesta.catolicasmexico.org/es /?page_id=2152.

28. Gómez, Carolina. 2015 "Mayoría de Católicos Mexicanos Apoya Información Sobre Aborto Legal: Encuesta." *La Jornada*, May 27. Accessed March 2, 2016. http://www.jornada.unam.mx/ultimas/2015/05/27/mayoria-de-catolicos -mexicanos-apoyan-educacion-sobre-aborto-legal-encuesta-4292.html.

29. Dyer, Owen. 2015. "Canada's Supreme Court Rules in Favour of Physician Assisted Suicide." *BMJ* 350:764. Accessed March 2, 2016. 4 doi: 10.1136/bmj.h764.

30. Mullock, Alexandra. 2015. "The Supreme Court Decision in *Nicklinson*: Human Rights, Criminal Wrongs and the Dilemma of Death." *Journal of Professional Negligence* 2015: 18–28.

31. Álvarez, Asunción, Wayne Sumner. 2012. "Discussing Physician-Assisted Death: Finding Consensus and Agreeing to Differ." Paper presented at the Seminar of the Joint Centre for Bioethics, University of Toronto. Toronto, Canada, September 19.

32. Álvarez del Río, Asunción. 2014. "Eutanasia y Suicidio Médicamente Asistido. ¿Cuál es el Problema?" *Revista de Investigación Clínica* 66: 282–87.

33. Narro Robles, José. 2008. "Los Servicios de Salud ante la Muerte." In *Muerte Digna, una Oportunidad Real*, edited by Guillermo Soberón and Dafna Feinholz, 117–21. México: Comisión Nacional de Bioética.

34. Álvarez del Río, Asunción, Ma. Luisa Marván, Patricio Santillán Doherty, Silvia Delgadillo, and Luis F. Oñate Ocaña. 2013. "Facing Death in Clinical Practice: A View from Physicians in Mexico." *Arch. Med. Res.* 44: 394–400. Accessed March 2, 2016. doi:10.1016/j.arcmed.2013.05.005.

35. Barranco, Bernardo. 2016. "Francisco y la Laicidad del Estado en México." *La Jornada*, February 17. Accessed March 2, 2016. http://www.jornada.unam .mx/2016/02/17/opinion/007a1pol.

36. Zenit Staff. 2016. "Pope's Address to Italian National Committee for Bioethics." *Zenit*, January 28. Accessed March 2, 2016. https://zenit.org/articles/popes -address-to-italian-national-committee-for-bioethics/.

37. Tamayo, Juan José. 2016. "Una Buena Muerte." *El País*, March 14. Accessed March 20, 2016. http://cultura.elpais.com/cultura/2016/03/11/babelia /1457720455_949008.html.

38. Villagómez Ortiz, Asiscio de J. 2008. "Posturas del Colegio de Medicina Interna de México Respecto a la Atención del Enfermo en Estado Terminal y la Eutanasia." *Med. Int. Mex.* 24: 59–64.

39. Casas Martínez, Ma. De la Luz. "Reflexiones Sobre la Práctica de la Eutanasia en el Área Médica." In *La Bioética, un Reto del Tercer Milenio*, edited by Universidad

Panamericana and Universidad Nacional Autónoma de México. 205–12. México: Instituto de Investigaciones Jurídicas.

40. Kraus, Arnoldo. 2013. "Eutanasia Hoy." *El Universal*, March 3. Accessed March 2, 2016. http://www.eluniversalmas.com.mx/editoriales/2013/03/63285 .php.

41. Kraus, Arnoldo. 2015. "III. El Difícil Camino: Eutanasia y Suicidio Asis- tido." *Nexos*, June. Accessed March 2, 2016. http://www.nexos.com.mx/?p=25087.

42. Por el Derecho a Morir con Dignidad A.C. 2015. "Acerca DMD." Accessed March 3, 2016. http://www.dmd.org.mx/acerca-dmd.html.

CHAPTER FOUR

Suffering, Compassion, and Freedom: Mahāyāna Buddhism and East Asian Attitudes Toward Assisted Suicide and Euthanasia

Brett Barleyman

The clarification of life, and the clarification of death, are the one great purpose of Buddhists.[1] Dōgen

> For Shinran . . . *tariki* or other-power was a 'peace beyond ethics'[2]

> When you see [the] cyclical movement [of continual birth and death] clearly then there is no more fear of death. When you have learnt *that* not only have you learnt how to die but you have also learnt how to live.[3] Jacqui James.

The Jacqui James quote and those like it seem to be rather ubiquitous in Buddhist literature. However true the sentiment, and however relevant to the topic of euthanasia and physician-assisted suicide (PAS), the matter seems to pivot on the word "clearly," which means, as James above mentions, Buddhist learning of some form. Even though to a great extent the question of birth and death is a basic existential problem that transcends sectarian boundaries, how to "see" clearly depends greatly on the Buddhist path one takes, be it Theravada, Mahāyāna, or Vajrayana, and then which of the paths or schools within these divisions.

This chapter focuses on Mahāyāna Buddhism as partially representative of the complex of wisdom traditions of East Asia, and its possible role in determining the choices that must be made concerning euthanasia and PAS. It especially focuses on the key Mahāyāna concept of nondualism as it relates to moral freedom, and asks whether in the face of the perhaps more rigid moral interpretations of Thereavada Buddhism, there might be some room for striving toward a compassionate solution to the various situations surrounding euthanasia and PAS from a Mahāyāna point of view.

It also looks at the specific and significant concept of time, again in relation to a Buddhist argument on the importance of time surrounding dying and death, and the time and ethically related doctrine of karma. Related to time is the argument over when a person can be said to have stopped living; not only a critical area when it comes to ethics in Theravada Buddhism over euthanasia and PAS, but more generally when it comes to agreeing on what life and death actually mean for those involved in decision making and communicating those decisions.

The next section looks at the complex but salient issue of compassion, which is, along with wisdom, the key to understanding Mahāyāna Buddhism, as well as being a vitally important issue for those involved with euthanasia and PAS.

Lastly, the chapter brings the above together somewhat, with a concrete look at Japan as an East Asian country that—over a lengthy period—has had some success in negotiating its way (with Mahāyāna values in the background) through to its Organ Transplant Law, an area that has obvious parallels to the debate concerning euthanasia and PAS.

The two quotes at the top of this chapter are from the founder of *Sōtō* Zen in Japan, Dōgen (1200–1253), and about the founder of the True Pure Land (*Jōdo Shinshū*), Shinran (1173–1262), respectively. These two monks are incorporated into the discussion, not only as examples of accomplished Mahāyāna Buddhists, but also as monks that might represent, on the one hand a more monk-orientated Buddhism (Dōgen's so-called self-power Zen), and conversely a more lay-friendly Buddhism (Shinran's "other-power" focus). These two schools remain the most popular in terms of numbers of adherents in Japan even today. The chapter also focuses mainly on the works that are considered more accessible to the lay reader—Dōgen's *Zuimonki* and Shinran's *Mattōshō* and *Tannishō*. Though accessible, these works are—in a way—indicative of Mahāyāna Buddhism itself—often a mix of the everyday and the paradoxical.

Due to space restrictions on what is obviously a massive topic, the focus tends toward key Mahāyāna concepts and their possible general relevance for the euthanasia and PAS debate. For the same reason Japan is singled out from the other East Asian countries both in terms of the two Mahāyāna Buddhists examined, and as a "case study" for how Mahāyāna Buddhism might have relevance in the ongoing decision making over euthanasia and PAS. Obviously, a much more comprehensive study is required to address the situation in China, Korea, and Vietnam (and with specific regard to the debate in Japan), and also how the key concepts presented here might function in specific or individual euthanasia and PAS cases.

Dualism

East Asian Buddhism, rooted in post—Han Dynasty China and influenced by Chinese thought and values, later spread to Korea and Japan where other important schools and movements arose.[4] Compared to Indian Mahāyāna (the "Great Vehicle" Buddhist movement, which became the dominant influence on the Buddhist cultures of Central and East Asia), East Asian Buddhism tended to emphasize non dualism[5] more, applying it more broadly and consistently; nondualism was a general approach applied to various doctrines rather than one particular doctrine.[6]

If we are to think about the topics of euthanasia and physician-assisted suicide (PAS) considering this emphasis on nondualism, one place to start is Lawrence Johnson's look at bioethics seen in an Eastern light. He presents a basic dualism—absolute truth and absolute falsity—and relates that "Asians" understand that life is lived in a world of things and events of "shadowy form" partway between "reality and utter non-being."[7] The following rather long Johnson quote is used as a starting point from which several points are expanded.

> All that we believe and think lies between absolute truth, which cannot be captured by the relatives of thought and word, and absolute falsity, which is nothing at all.[8] Our self, our beliefs, and our experienced world are reality misperceived. So too, everything we do that affects others, and therefore everything within the scope of ethics, lies with us within this realm of intermediate truth and being. Accordingly any effect I might have on another is not really on the illusory self but on that being of which the illusory self is a misperception. The other's fear of suffering or desire for relief from pain

may be a product of ignorance, as what the person really needs is a deeper healing of the soul.[9] So do we all. In the meantime, while we are living this world of illusion, suffering and the need for ethical conduct coexist on the same level of being. The need for compassion and morality will disappear only when suffering disappears.[10]

There are many issues here, including our effect on others, the scope of Buddhist ethics, suffering, compassion, and indeed the question of being. First, however, the dualism presented between absolute truth and absolute falsity needs further examination when it comes to Mahāyāna Buddhism. In Hee-Jin Kim's work on the "greatest religious figure and creative thinker in Japanese history,"[11] the Kamakura period monk Dōgen, dualisms are said not to be annihilated. Tension rather, always exists between two things such as birth and death, yet it remains pure, meaning we can live "from moment to moment in such a way that these moments are the fulfilled moments of moral and spiritual freedom[12] and purity in thusness."[13, 14]

Dōgen expresses this—mixed in with the idea of transcending the ego—succinctly in his well-known *SG* "Genjō Kōan" fascicle.

To learn the Buddha's truth is to learn ourselves.
To learn ourselves is to forget ourselves.
To forget yourself is to be authenticated by all things.
To be experienced by all things is to let our own body-and-mind, and the body-and-mind of the external world, fall away.

The True Pure Land monk Shinran also spoke about this pure tension, but in terms of "belief" (*shinjin*) which had two, seemingly separate aspects: (1) Non-dichotomous identity; the mind of Amida (Buddha) and the mind of the practitioner are identical; (2) A dichotomous relationship; the mind of Amida and the mind of the practitioner are mutually separate and in dynamic interaction.

Again Shinran eloquently presents such an understanding,

Through the benefit of the unhindered light,
We realise *shinjin* of vast, majestic virtues,
And the ice of our blind passions necessarily melts,
Immediately becoming water of enlightenment.

Obstructions of karmic evil turn into virtues;
It is like the relation of ice and water:
The more the ice, the more the water;
The more the obstructions, the more the virtues.[15]

Vietnamese Buddhist monk Nhat Hanh shows us how this "freedom" might play out when looking at the issue of the type of "suicide" known as self-immolation, and in the context of a discussion on nonviolence.

> We do not intend to say that self-immolation is good, or that it is bad. It is neither good nor bad. But nobody can urge another to do such a thing. So such a discussion is not pursued in order to decide whether self-immolation is a good tactic in the nonviolent struggle or not. It is apart from all that. It is done to wake us up.[16]

The last line, perhaps to fully agree[17] with Dōgen, might instead read, "it is done because we are awake."

Nhat Hanh also understands the famous self-immolation of Thich Quang Duc as "[an expression] of the unconditional willingness to suffer for the awakening of others"[18] which sounds likewise, to be an expression of Mahāyāna Buddhist realization, of being awake, or of purity within the tension of duality.

But how does one arrive at such freedom? The realization of freedom ("enlightenment"), is not, according to Dōgen a matter of "one minute I'm ignorant the next free," but is rather a continuous process; in Dōgen's case the state of *zazen* (sitting meditation) is renewed and revitalized at each instant.[19] Thus, from one point of view, nonMonastics (who might find it difficult to meditate in the way monks are able) would have a harder time arriving at such a realization to begin with. In *Zuimonki* (in relation to filial piety) Dōgen notes that only monks can "abandon their debt of gratitude and act freely, like fish swimming in the water, or birds flying in the sky without a trace.[20] However, the more lay-friendly Pure Land Buddhism of Shinran's teacher Hōnen (although not disputing the value of renewing one's realization), would probably see it otherwise.

> Instead of trying to follow difficult teachings, you should follow the easy practice of chanting Amida's name, and thus exit the house of life and death.[21]
>
> Do not worry how heated your passions are, do not bother how grave your sins are, but simply chant *namu Amida butsu*: think how certain salvation is, with your voice.[22]

Of course, euthanasia and PAS involve not only the taking of one's own life, but also head into the ethically more challenging area of helping another to end his or her life. In regard to this many Buddhist scholars mention one of the original stories of the early Mahāyāna School, the *Upāya-kauśalya Sutra* ("Skill in Means Sutra"); a sutra that has long been treated with circumspection because of its liberal attitude toward sexuality and other ethical concerns, and moreover a sutra that is "rarely discussed."[23]

In one story in the sutra, an admittedly ethically complex tale of a protagonist needing to kill an intending mass murderer, self-denying compassion (rather than, for example, anger or righteous indignation) is emphasized as the correct attitude. As Sallie King points out, however, such compassion (or more generally state of mind) is very rare.

> I had a private discussion with a Tibetan lama and Engaged Buddhist about nonviolence in which he brought up [the Upāya-kauśalya] sutra. He emphasized that only a very advanced Bodhisattva—one who could equally choose to consume either a great delicacy or a vile heap of refuse with neither attraction nor revulsion—would be able to generate the state of mind that would be required in order to kill someone without a shred of anger but only out of pure compassion. He indicated that he had never known a person capable of such a thing.[24]

The other side of the story might well be illustrated by what most would agree is a completely misguided interpretation of the message of this sutra by those not "capable."[25] In justifying their attacks on trains in Tokyo, Aum Shinrikyo are said to have believed that killing certain persons would prevent those people from accumulating more bad karma, an idea presented in the Upāya-kauśalya sutra.[26]

We might sum up what we have seen thus far then, by saying that we have a dualism of those capable of pure action, and those who are not. Though we can say that dualisms, soteriologically speaking, are able to be "seen through" and freedom is possible, Johnson's above assertion that suffering and the need for ethical conduct[27] coexist on the same level seems to stand up. However we might better understand the (same) level as one of "understanding" rather than Johnson's level of "being." Also from the viewpoint of these levels of understanding, Johnson's "compassion" and "morality" might not only be applicable in the so-called realm of illusion, but also could be used validly to refer to a pure compassion, and a pure morality[28] which would be enlightened, nondual, and (as usually explained) experienced realities. As William Deal says, "[O]nce enlightenment is attained, dualities expressed in ethical problems cease to exist. Action is not judged not against an absolute moral standard . . . but rather on the basis of its relative merit in leading toward or away from enlightenment."[29]

This "ceasing to exist" might be said to equate with a natural inability to "do evil" which Dōgen understands as the morality of enlightenment.[30]

When understanding this way, we might question the likes of Damien Keown's use of the phrase "[f]rom the perspective of Buddhist ethics," which he frequently uses to introduce an ethical guideline in his exploration of the ethics of the end of life. Although perhaps this stance (which seems to advocate moral criteria for euthanasia based upon so-called "traditional Buddhist views of life and death,"[31] or based upon the necessarily limited sources Keown examined) might be admissible as a type of expedient truth, we must ask further, as Deal says, whether it would lead the person, whoever they might be, toward realization.

Shades of Truth

Above are a couple of rather extreme forms of what might be contingently and variously labeled "suicide" or "compassionate self-sacrifice" (the self-immolation), and secondly "murder" or "compassionate self-other sacrifice" (from the Upāya-kauśalya Sutra). The persons who carried out the acts in question could be thought to have reached a certain level of purity, and those of less capacity considered to have made horrendous decisions (Aum Shinrikyō).

In that we can recognize the more extreme nature of self-immolation as contrasted with a terminal sufferer's suicide, or even the unintentional death of those wanting relief from pain, and also the extreme situation of having to kill a murderer (who wants to live to enjoy the profits of his murder) versus a patient requesting a professional to assist them in dying, we might ask whether there is room for nuance in the interpretation of circumstances within East Asian Buddhism.

Could it be that even as the critical (pure) state of mind is exceedingly difficult to achieve in the case of killing a future murderer, it is less difficult (though perhaps still is somewhat difficult) to achieve in the case of a person wanting to relieve the suffering of an "innocent"? Peter Harvey, for one, argues that one possible way to interpret the Buddhist attitude regarding "mercy-killing" is that "an action is unwholesome [only?] if it is rooted in greed, hatred or delusion"[32] Perhaps the problem here, though, is that however much a person might think that he or she is acting without such root motivations, such motivations might be seen as intrinsic to the "unrealized" position. Harvey mentions (in discussing Theravada Buddhism) that although a doctor's motive to perform a "mercy-killing" is compassionate and good, it is mixed with aversion to the patient's pain, and the risk is that subconsciously the doctor might transfer this aversion to the patient.[33] Also in the same (Theravada) context that for example a mother in severe pain and a son (who is motivated by attachment to his mother[34] and aversion to her pain) who wants to help her, share the delusion that death is the only way out.[35] Does that then leave us with euthanasia as morally unjustifiable which is, for example, a growing consensus in the predominantly Theravada Buddhist country of Thailand?

One possible way through this either "right-or-wrong" thinking is put forth by Sallie King in her discussion on the limits of nonviolence, in which she argues that it is impossible for people (no matter how well-intentioned they are) to be entirely nonviolent, "[Nhat Hanh] proposes that the ethically good thing to do is to strive to become ever more nonviolent. Once we accept this, we realize that it is incorrect to think of the world as composed of two camps."[36]

Of course, that is not to say that these issues (nonviolence and mercy killing) are entirely comparable, but rather that in Buddhism it might be exceedingly difficult to state the case (as in the argument for nonviolence) for either one "camp" (e.g., to perform mercy killing or request assisted suicide) or the other (to not do so). Implied here is that depending on what "camp" one happens to be in, one might progress toward an ideal outcome, the attaining of which—like the outcome of complete nonviolence—perhaps is impossible and might not even necessarily be desirable. As Nhat Hanh says elsewhere,

> [T]he problem is whether we are determined to go in the direction of compassion or not. If we are, then can we reduce the suffering to a minimum? If I lose my direction, I have to look for the North Star, and I go to the north. That does not mean that I expect to arrive at the North Star. I just want to go in that direction.[37]

The Right Time to Die?

We look at time first by bringing up a subject that often is mentioned in Theravada-viewpoint discussions, that of the morality of euthanasia tied to the argument of good or bad future birth. Very simply put, the argument could be that a person shouldn't perform mercy killing or request euthanasia because the person will have to face the same situation in another life, or might end up in worse circumstances in the next life.[38] One difficulty here is that, as C. H. S. Ward points out, not only do "Buddhists usually *ignore* the teaching of their religion that in the next life personal identity and memory will be lost," but also that "all generations of Buddhists down to our own days, have been bewildered by how future life benefit [or indeed punishment] could possibly occur in the face of the non-self doctrine."[39]

Keown, looking at euthanasia from a largely Threavada perspective and positing that Buddhism would oppose the practice of euthanasia, likewise declines to use karma as a grounds for this opposition, saying that "the workings of karma are mysterious."[40] Thus, in keeping with the no-self doctrine, it could be said that rather than worrying about where one might end up in the next life, the incentive for performing or not performing a deed runs much deeper than mere personal gain or loss. As mysterious as they are though, karma and rebirth—least we forget and as Ward importantly says—have played the part of having "saved Buddhism from moral chaos."[41]

From a Mahāyāna perspective however, the duality of either denying or affirming causality (or karma) must itself be transcended; Masao Abe says, "Although karma works deterministically on the horizontal dimension of time, once the vertical,[42]or transtemporal, dimension is opened up as one awakens to the truth of no-self, that person is no longer a slave to karma but becomes its master."[43]

It thus seems to follow that discussions on dying in a "good" state of mind (e.g., before suffering great pain or unconsciousness) might be more applicable to the Theravada context. In the Pure Land branch[44] of Mahāyāna, however, the deathbed did indeed come to take on more and more importance as a final opportunity, especially for "sinful" lay-people, in which an "introspective" death was ideal. This kind of death was "a sobering time when the distractions of a lifetime proved hollow and the heavy karmic bonds of the present were shed, [so one could] attain the Pure Land through Amida's aid."[45] Harvey puts it simply, "[D]ying . . . is a time when a person has to learn to let go, even if she has not yet (through meditation etc.,) done so."[46] David Loy argues that it is a time, ironically, in which the fear of death—which has been repressed throughout our lives with social games and preoccupations—can be faced. This then might force a realization of what authentic life actually is.[47]

Although the deathbed indeed could possess great force, the Kamakura period monk Shinran, came to deemphasize[48, 49] the long-held importance of the deathbed as a soteriological time point in this so-called lay-person's Buddhism. For example, in *Mattōshō* 6, Shinran says,

> I, for my own part, attach no significance to the condition, good or bad, of persons in their final moments. People in whom *shinjin* is determined do not doubt, and so abide among the truly settled. For this reason their end also—even for those ignorant and foolish and lacking in wisdom—is a happy one.

As Dessi says in reference to this specific passage, in Shinran's True Pure Land Buddhism, "equal dignity seems to be conferred to each moment in one's life."[50]

Dessi adds that the importance of this teaching can be seen in the fact that the Bihāra Katsudō (ビハーラ活動) or Vihāra Movement (which provides terminal care to patients in modern Japan) uses this passage to "justify a sympathetic approach towards the patients, which might help them to recover their full dignity during the course of the natural process of illness and dying."[51]

This a situation which shows that life, no matter how close to the end of it one is, might be continued to be deepened at any stage. Ueda puts this into the Mahāyāna framework, "[Shinran] delineates a path of attainment that fully accords with general Mahāyāna thought, in which each step along the way is nondual with the goal of suchness or reality."[52]

Thus, although birth in the Pure Land (after death) was traditionally the goal, Shinran emphasized birth in everyday life (*heizei gōjō*), as being attainable upon understanding the paradoxical nature of fully embodying the truth of impermanence.[53] Further, as Shunshō Terakawa says in terms of ethics, this type of life is one where faith becomes the premise for activity, revealing itself as a dynamic awareness, which orients the practitioner toward "avoiding evil and doing good."[54]

Dōgen, in a complementary way in his *Zuimonki* work, suggests that the correct Buddhist understanding of "dying" is one of a deep attitude of renouncing the ego-self rather than any (merely) physical death. This appears, for example, in *Zuimonki* 2-16, in which Dōgen talks of abandoning our life, if only for a day or a few moments, for the purpose of the buddha-dharma—an action which will result in eternal happiness.[55]

These three Mahāyāna figures of Dōgen, Shinran, and Hōnen (not to mention the historical Buddha) with their journey from a great fear[56] of death, through Buddhist training, and on to Buddhist realization (or ego-death) well before their time came to—in Buddhist terminology—"be released,"[57] and show us that dying is never a straightforward matter of fear of future karma. Thus although the deathbed might carry a force to enable the dying to "recover full dignity," those surviving might be seen as being able to access this force in their continuing lives in striving to "do good."

Life and Death

Time is not only to be considered when thinking in terms of cause and effect, but also about when a person can be said to have stopped living. Harvey, in his discussion on criteria of death draws mainly on Theravada texts, and says that "a case in which an action would be acceptable as no intentional killing occurs would be that in which the action can be seen to occur after the patient has died.[58] This . . . raises the question of the criteria for being 'alive' and being 'dead'."[59]

Shewmon talks about this problem, saying that in the pre-technological era, when the events surrounding death occurred simultaneously, the single word "death" sufficed. That it does not anymore, and

> our insistence on discovering the one correct meaning of death [and I would add "life"] may grow from a[60] "delusion that our concepts of life and death are simply generalized from everyday experience and labeled by linguistic convention with the words 'life' and 'death' when in actuality those very concepts have been shaped by our language, and more importantly constrained by it . . . no wonder that the death-debate is so full of logical inconsistencies and failures to communicate, because people use the same word to express different concepts, not quite realizing that (precisely because of the single word) that the concepts are different."[61]

If people in their everyday experience have problems communicating what they mean by life and death, then the dilemma might be said to be accentuated greatly when an East Asian Mahāyāna Buddhist perspective is added to the mix. It also is worth keeping in mind that perhaps the very purpose of *that* perspective might be to lose the very constraints that have indeed been "shaped by our language."

East Asian Buddhism can be said variously to have taken this questioning of the words "life" "death" and what's more the phrase "life and death" to extremes, with Dōgen being a prime example. Dōgen shakes the "usual" understanding of time, in one particular fascicle denying a before-and-after relationship between firewood and "resultant" ash from "its" burning. "Life" in Dōgen does not *become* "death." Another example of the radicalization of time in Buddhism is the idea of "moment-to-moment life and death"[62] by which our body and mind are said to be born and die split second by split second. These examples might be said to point toward (as mentioned above) a transcendence of commonly debated ethical questions related to thresholds for life and death.

Damien Keown perhaps takes more of a tangible path when he tries to arrive at a definition of death that "Buddhism would endorse."[63] Keown references a debate in which the definition of death falls into three chief schools—the biological, the moral (focus is on the circumstances under which a person ought to be declared dead), and the ontological or metaphysical (focus is on a theory of personal identity)—and says that Buddhism most likely would align itself with the biological. This is because

"Buddhism sees the human individual as constituted by their organic wholeness rather than by their 'personhood'." Keown however admits that if alternative views on how Buddhism understands the living human were taken, then this would mean one of the alternative approaches might be more appropriate.[64]

Although enquiring into the appropriateness of these alternative approaches from more of a Mahāyāna point of view seems of vital necessity, this unfortunately remains too broad a question to be tackled within the confines of this chapter.

Compassion

In contrast to the Theravada emphasis on the *arhat* ("holy one") who has achieved liberation, Mahāyāna focuses on the figure of the *bodhisattva*, who pledges to compassionately assist others to achieve enlightenment. In Dōgen's *Zuimonki*, this compassionate mind is often linked to having no fear of death and a lack of clinging to ego. Dōgen ventures, "In each situation that you are faced with, just consider carefully; do anything which will bring even a little benefit to the person who is before you, without concern for what people will think of you."[65] We might ask: What of compassionately assisting *others* to achieve a better death?

Richard McCormick, in an argument that might resonate with Theravada Buddhists and perhaps some Pure Land Mahāyāna Buddhists, says that the growing emphasis on autonomy and independence means that patients come to understand that dying with dignity (for example with physician-assisted suicide) equals dying "in my way, at my time, by my hand,"[66] and that this equates to a "flight from compassion." McCormick argues, alongside the Anglican Study Group, that (the universal, unconditional love) *agape* demands unlimited caring, and in the recipient absolute trust, asking, "[H]ave we forgotten that dependent old age is a call to cling to a power (God) beyond our control?"[67]

Perhaps, given the emphasis on non-self and interdependence in Buddhism, this might help us to understand why then the act of helping others to die "is condemned (in certain *Vinaya*[68] episodes)"[69] even if the motive is compassion based. In relation to this we also might add a slightly different Dōgen quote, which might then on some level admit to the caution stated above, "In whatever situation, we should choose what is best for the benefit of living beings in the long run and for the *progress of our own practice*"[70] [italics inserted].

Though Peter Harvey admits that a Mahayanist might argue that sometimes "skillful means" implies that it is acceptable to kill if the motive is compassion, the caveat is that "compassion killing" in the scriptures, as discussed above, is always to prevent the victim from committing some evil deed against others.[71] Despite this, Harvey suggests (as mentioned above) that in the face of a lack of specific mercy-killing examples, a better way to interpret the Buddhist attitude to "mercy killing" is that "an action is unwholesome if it is rooted in greed, hatred or delusion."[72] These are the so-called three poisons, which can be simply called the most basic cause of suffering.

Again this seems to bring us back to the dualism mentioned of the "realized (and free from the suffering of the three poisons) viewpoint" versus the many "shades" of the as-yet unrealized (or to whatever degree deluded) viewpoint. It is perhaps with this dualism in mind that Harvey suggests, in a way very similar to McCormick, that wanting to lessen the suffering of a person in pain might come from *not* understanding that the dying person "should use the process of dying as an opportunity for reflection, so as to see clearly the error of attachment to anything which is impermanent."[73] An example is given of a lady with terminal cancer who is, "extremely agitated as a result." "After she was taught a simple meditation, she became happy, and survived for six months rather than the two months that doctors had given her. She then died happy and at peace, making a considerable impression on the doctors and nurses who observed her."[74]

A simple meditation was indeed suggested as an alternative to suicide by the Buddha after a group of Buddhist nuns took their own and each other's lives due to being horrified by their own bodies. "[A] respiration-mindfulness concentration . . . is both peaceful and sublime, unadulterated and of happy life; it suppresses evil and unprofitable thoughts as soon as they arise."[75]

De Silva, however, cautions that there is only a limited amount of material in the *suttas* showing suicidal impulses transformed into dispassion, a dispassion which leads to "insight into the nature of reality."[76] The message remains a ubiquitous one in Buddhism, however, as Sogyal Rinpoche succinctly puts it, "if we can only learn how to face death, then we'll have learned the most important lesson of life: how to face ourselves and so come to terms with ourselves, in the deepest possible sense, as human beings."[77]

Dōgen, in a case closer to a dilemma faced by patients wanting release from pain, also emphasizes the importance of the continuation of practice in a *Zuimonki* talk which laments a layperson's having delayed practice until his recovery from sickness, only to get worse and die before fulfilling his resolve.

> When you are receiving some treatment, but instead of getting better the pain gradually increases, you should practice while the pain is still not too bad.

After the pain has become severe, you should determine to practice before your condition becomes critical. And when your condition has become critical, you should resolve to practice before you die.[78]

Dōgen also gives himself as an example of this kind, when having heard in China of the suitability of *zazen* for learning the Way, he resolved to sit day and night.

At the time, I thought to myself, "I may become sick and die. Still, I should just practice zazen. What is the use of clinging to this body? How can I refrain from practice when I am not sick?" Dying from illness because of practice accords with my original wish (本意 *hon-i*)."[79]

Closer to the present day, Sogyal Rinpoche gives us some insight into what type of practice an accomplished Buddhist might perform when facing death.

I will [when I come to die] invoke all the buddhas and my masters, unite my mind with them, rest in the nature of the mind, and send that love and compassion out to all beings everywhere. I will pray that when I die, my death benefit all; that I may die successfully and, in the future, be reborn to help millions and millions of beings.[80]

This all-important practice during or before dying was for Mahāyāna masters not only an individual but also a collective ritual. The Buddhist master, as Bernard Faure points out, predicting his own death along with giving last words was, "an apotheosis of [the master's] deeds and gestures, a ritualised and collective event, determined in its slightest details by the *imaginarie* of the community. . . ."[81]

Although in the example of the lady with terminal cancer given above we might acknowledge that some experiential understanding was achieved, and recognize expressions of selflessness and interdependence in the Rinpoche quote and Master's death ritual, this is again not to say that one couldn't have such meditative experience, nor think in selfless[82] or interdependent terms well before having to make a decision about one's own impending death.

Ethics of Ambiguity (Japan)

It is shown above that in one understanding of dualism in Mahāyāna Buddhism tension exists between two things yet this tension remains pure, meaning that we may live in moral and spiritual freedom and purity. It also is shown that such purity might be hard to attain, and that without this purity grave misunderstandings leading to varying degrees of "poisonous" action might be committed. It is argued that there might be room for nuance, and that the correct state of mind might be easier to achieve in some circumstances than others, and that we might still strive to seek the ideal. In seeking such an ideal, concepts such as karma that have traditionally prevented Buddhism from falling into "moral chaos" alongside others such as interdependence might help to form our understanding and determine our actions.

Dōgen, for example, although accepting the causal structure of life and practice, would reject, according to David Putney, any rigid interpretation of karma in favor of a "fluid, karmic, interdependent universe that depends upon our actions and understanding as part of its causal structure."[83]

In Shinran's case, although there are a great many interpretations of the value of ethics in the True Pure Land School, some scholars believe its ethical approach aims at the deep participation of the practitioner in the "reflective process of a soteriological quest." This implies that "through ethical involvement one comes to be 'gradually illuminated' by the principles which refer to a 'higher soteriological life,' rather than 'by conventional worldly expectations' and 'self-centred values'."[84]

One contemporary, and collective (rather than individual) East Asian arena in which we might see such striving is in that over an issue closely related to that of assisted dying and euthanasia: the protracted process of the passing of the Japanese Organ Transplant Law. This striving has been interpreted as one of trying to incorporate the idea of an interdependent universe into the decision-making process.

Ronald Nakasone in his chapter "Ethics of Ambiguity: A Buddhist Reflection on the Japanese Organ Transplant Law" talks of more than 30 years of national debate and reflection over the procurement of organs from donors in Japan. Although this 30 years came to an end with the passage of the law, the discussion over the ethics of it, as well as the difficulty of carrying out the procurement, has not ended.

Nakasone says that the law concerning organ procurement has built-in ambiguity and further (with importance in examining euthanasia) does not provide a uniform answer to the question, "What is human death?"[85] What is interesting here is that Nakasone uses the *Huayan* or Flower Garland school[86] of Mahāyāna Buddhism to examine the structure and role of ambiguity in the Organ Transplant Law, saying, "the interdependent and evolving Buddhist vision of reality provides the rationale for ambiguity in decision making and action."[87]

One idea here—the idea of interdependence—can be seen to be an extension and expansion of the law of karma, whereby not only an individual's karmic life, but also the "interaction of conflicting karmic forces and the complexity and multiplicity of causes and conditions that affect an individual's life and the effects it can have on others and the world"[88] are taken into consideration. Thus, in this type of interdependent world, ethical virtues such as fair play, compassion, gratitude, humility, and patience "provide clues to how we should reflect upon such questions as the definition of human death, organ donations and transplants, and decision making."[89]

Nakasone, focusing on the issue the definition of death in relation to organ transplants, says that although the Japanese Ministry of Health and Welfare's final report concluded that brain death is human death, a minority objected which resulted in the current law attempting to accommodate both death as the irreversible loss of consciousness and as cardiopulmonary death. There also is a distinction between a clinical diagnosis and a legal determination of brain death.

In practice, family consultation is undertaken (giving families an opportunity to reflect[90] on the essence of human life) before the physician is allowed to make a legal determination, even if the individual has agreed to be a brain-death donor, and for those who have not agreed, they are considered "alive" until the heart stops.

Although, admittedly, such a scenario plays out within a specific Japanese culture, it does highlight how Buddhism as part of the root system of a particular culture might be seen to play a role in firstly creating and then understanding as well as maneuvering within a workable (if not perfect) guideline for professionals and nonprofessionals alike. Nakasone admits that the decision making is cumbersome, but he thinks that "living and working in ambiguity is often the most productive way of proceeding with ethical reflection and scientific investigation."[91]

Conclusion

The beginning of this chapter looked at Johnson's quote in which he talked about the need for compassion and morality for those who suffer. It then showed that the grounds for a transcendence of that suffering in Mahāyāna Buddhism rested upon a certain experience which can be described as morally free and pure. One key to this experience lies in selflessness and either compassion directed outward, or (in the case of Shinran's True Pure Land Buddhism) in humble thankfulness for Amida's unfathomable compassion. Thus, from one point of view Mahāyāna Buddhism might concur with the likes of Damien Keown that "Buddhism would oppose the practice of euthanasia," but as was shown, perhaps from the point of view of the possibility of the sufferer transcending suffering (the Buddhist goal), than from the necessity of strictly adhering to prescribed doctrine or scripture. As the Dali Lama said, "If a dying person has any chance of having positive, virtuous thoughts, it is important . . . for them to live even just a few minutes longer. . . ."[92]

The chapter also examined the possibility of moving toward the transcendence of suffering from whatever starting point one was at, which might seem to tie in with Dōgen's continuous process of realizing freedom, Shinran's step-by-step progress which is nondual with the goal, and the striving toward being more and more compassionate. This striving is seen by some as having force in the circumstance of the deathbed, but also might be seen as a force that resonates with the survivors and caregivers of those who have passed on.

Lastly, and more concretely, the chapter surveyed how Japanese law reflects ambiguity concerning organ transplantation, and how it seems to endeavor to come to a balance based upon the most fair, compassionate, and patient solution to an extremely complex scenario. It can be asked then whether—considering what is presented above—the same virtues based on interdependence (alongside of emptiness and nonduality) might usefully or practically help to inform the debate on euthanasia and assisted suicide within an East Asian setting, or even beyond.

Notes

1. *Shōbōgenzō* (hereinafter "*SG*") "Shoaku Makusa," Nishijima (1998) vol. 1, p.108. Norman Waddell says that these words from *SG* "Shoaku makusa" ("Not Doing Wrongs"), can be said to form the essence of Dōgen's entire career, and to be the reason for his voluminous literary production as well. Norman A. Waddell and Abe Masao (trans.) (various *Shōbōgenzō* translations) in the *Eastern Buddhist* (Kyoto, Japan): *SG* "Zenki" and *SG* "Shōji", vol. 5, no. 1 (May 1972), 70.

2. Dessi's summation of Ōtani University professor, Kigoshi Yasushi, and Manshi Kiyozawa's take on Shinran's ethical view. See Ugo Dessi (2007), *Ethics and Society in Contemporary Shin Buddhism* (Berlin: Münster Lit.) 81.

3. Jacqui James, *The Many Faces of Death, An Inward Journey Book* (Inward Path, P.O. Box 1034, 10830 Penang, Malaysia). From the book *Modern Buddhism* by Alan & Jacqui James, published by Aukana Trust (1993).

4. David Barnhill, "East Asian Buddhism and Nature," Nov. 21, 2010. University of Wisconsin–Oshkosh. Accessed February 1, 2016. https://www.uwosh.edu/facstaff/barnhill/244-intro/buddhism-ern.

5. Also, relatedly emptiness and faith are paramount. Nonduality is specifically based on emptiness (*sunyata*), which is, an extension of "no-self" thinking. Everything is contingent upon everything else, and all things are empty of an

independent self-subsisting existence. Even (or especially) *nirvana* (enlightenment) and *samsara* (cycle of existence) are the same thing. As for faith, the Zen master Dōgen likens it to "being free from confusions, delusions, and disarray, as well as from judgements of superiority or inferiority, good or bad" and "Faith is so called when the entire body becomes faith itself (*konshin-jishin*). Faith is one with the fruit of enlightenment; the fruit of enlightenment is one with faith" *SG* "Sanjū shichibon bodai bunpō" (Kim trans.). This points to a transcendent ethic.

6. Ibid.; Barnhill (2010).

7. Lawrence E Johnson, *A Life-Centered Approach to Bioethics: Biocentric Ethics* (2011), 343.

8. What the author means here by "nothing at all" is unclear.

9. This author understands "soul" here to actually be an example of the very duality which needs to be worked through. That is, although one aspect of Buddhism admits that there is no soul, the doctrine of karma often seems imply some sort of "surviving" personality.

10. Johnson (2011) at 343–44.

11. Reiho Masunaga, *A Soto Approach to Zen* (Tokyo: Layman Buddhist Society Press, 1958).

12. Dōgen scholar Steven Heine calls this "transcendental awareness," an unfettered free activity described as a "leaping" into nondifferentiablity, an exploration of "creative tension," and an interplay of forms and formless, subjectivity and objectivity. See Steven Heine, *A Blade of Grass: Japanese Poetry and Aesthetics in Dōgen Zen* (New York: P. Lang, 1989), 36.

13. Thusness; all things just as they are in themselves.

14. Hee-Jin Kim, *Eihei Dōgen Mystical Realist* (Somerville, MA: Wisdom Publications, 2004) 285.

15. *Hymns of the Pure Land Masters*.

16. Nhat Hanh, *The Raft is Not the Shore*, 62, in Sally B. King, *Being Benevolence: The Social Ethics of Engaged Buddhism*, 193.

17. This is not to say that Dōgen would necessarily agree with self-immolation.

18. Nhat Hanh, "Love in Action," p. 43, in Gowans, *Buddhist Moral Philosophy: An Introduction* (2015), 274.

19. Thomas P. Kasulis, *Zen Action, Zen Person* (Hawaii: University Press of Hawaii, 1981), 91. Also compare with Haneda, in a True Pure Land Buddhist context, "A Buddha is a constant seeker and learner . . . one with the very freshness of life itself. This is what 'Dharma' means. A Buddha embodies this dynamic truth. . . . A Buddha's desire is to be 'life itself,' this is the 'innermost aspiration'." Nobuo Haneda, "Shakyamuni and Shinran; Is Jodō Shinshū Really Buddhism?" (2001), *The Living Dharma Library* (presented Nov. 11, 2001), Living Dharma (May 24, 2005). http://www.livingdharma.org/Living.Dharma.Articles /L.D.Seminar2-01.html.

20. See Okumura, Shōhaku (trans). *Shōbōgenzō-zuimonki—Sayings of Eihei Dōgen Zenji Recorded by Koun Ejō* (Kyōto, Japan: Kyōto Zen Center, 1987) p. 98, note 3.

21. 昭和新修法然上人全集 *Shōwa shinshū Hōnen Shōnin zenshū* (HSZ), pp. 681–82.

22. HSZ, 495.

23. King (2005), 190.

24. Ibid.

25. De Silva says of the possibility of going astray, "as a way of liberation from suffering, the difficult problem emerges, as the struggle for liberation and disgust with the world may not always be blended with dispassion and equanimity." Padmasiri De Silva. "Suicide and Emotional Ambivalence: An Early Buddhist Perspective," *Pali Buddhism* (Curzon Press, 1996), 132.

26. King (2005), 190.

27. De Silva says "ethics are merely a stage on the path to liberation." Padmasiri De Silva, *Buddhism, Ethics, and Society: The Conflicts and Dilemmas of Our Times* (Clayton, Vic.: Monash Asia Institute, 2002), 94.

28. Dōgen in *SG* "Shoaku-Makusa" ("Not Doing Evils") says "not doing evils is unlike what commoners first construe in their moral deliberations" and that 'not to commit any evil" is . . . the direct expression of supreme enlightenment itself.

29. William E. Deal, "Buddhism, Bioethics in," *Bioethics* Jennings (ed.), 460.

30. See *SG* "Shoaku-Makusa" ("Not Doing Evils").

31. Damien Keown, *Buddhism & bioethics* (New York: St. Martin's Press, 1995), 185.

32. Peter Harvey, *An Introduction to Buddhist Ethics: Foundations, Values, and Issues* (Cambridge: Cambridge University Press, 2000), 296.

33. Harvey (2000), 297.

34. Compare this to Shinran's talking about his parents in *Tannishō*.

35. Harvey (2000), 297.

36. King (2005), 199.

37. Thich Nhat Hahn (1987), *Being Peace*, Arnold Kotler (ed.) (Berkeley, CA), 98; Ronald Y. Nakasone, "Ethics of Ambiguity: A Buddhist Reflection on the Japanese Organ Transplant Law," *Handbook of Bioethics and Religion,* ed. David E. Guinn (Oxford: Oxford University Press, 2006), 301.

38. See, for example, Harvey (2000) at 303, in relation to a Thai doctor and the Dali Lama.

39. Ward, C. H. S., *Early Buddhism: Doctrine and Discipline* (Delhi, India: Caxton Publications (reprint 1988), 94.

40. Keown (1995), 185.

41. Ward (reprint 1988), 94.

42. To illustrate this, Abe gives an interesting example from Christianity of how, in the present, if we give our will over to God we are "forgiven" our previous (on the horizontal dimension) sins. In examining how this happens, however, we can say that "something changed" affecting how the sin *comes to be thought of* in the present. This is the vertical dimension, that the time has somehow gone backward, or that the past has been affected.

43. Abe, Masao, *A Study of Dōgen; His Philosophy and Religion* (Albany: State University of New York Press, 1992), 103.

44. Which promised nonmonastic practice that would lead to salvation.

45. Yoshifumi Ueda and Dennis Hirota, *Shinran: An Introduction to His Thought* (Kyoto: Hongwanji International Center, 1989), 138.

46. Harvey (2000), 302.

47. Loy says that if anxiety is experienced by us in the "right" or skillful way (under conducive circumstances), it "schools" us to root out everything *finite* and petty. See David Loy (1990), "The Nonduality of Life and Death: A Buddhist View of Repression," *Philosophy East and West*, Vol. 40 No. 2 (1990), 151–74.

48. Havelock Coates (ibid.) 153.

49. Shinran's teacher Hōnen had espoused that if one repeats the *nenbutsu* chant in the right spirit at any time in one's life it has the same value as if said in one's dying hour.

50. Dessi (2007), 186.

51. Ibid.

52. Ueda (1989), 139.

53. See Nobuo Haneda, "Shinran's View of the Two Types of Birth," *The Living Dharma Library.* Living Dharma. (Accessed September 2007), 211.

54. Shunshō Terakawa, "Life in the Vow: Dynamics of Faith in Jōdo Shinshū." *The Pure Land* (New Series 10–11, 1994), 20–21.

55. See *Zuimonki* 2–16 (Okumura trans.).

56. Steven Heine says that Dōgen's repeated highlighting of the imminence and universality of death was an "ecclesiastesean moral admonition to awaken to the need for genuine self-reflection and emancipation from petty ambitions and vain desires." Steven Heine "From Rice Cultivation to Mind Contemplation: The Meaning of Impermanence in Japanese Religion," *History of Religions*, Vol. 30, No. 4 (May 1991), 388.

57. A release from Saṃsāra, karma and rebirth as well as the dissolution of the skandhas. The term "parinirvana" refers to this nirvana-after-death.

58. The example Harvey gives is of a person in a "persistent vegetative state." He asks "if someone is permanently without any sign of conscious awareness and the ability to make decisions . . . (1) is the patient still a 'person' with value? And (2) is the patient alive?" Keown (1995) seems to agree that "killing a dead person" is acceptable, however he uses brain death as the criterion.

59. Harvey (2000), 305.

60. First part of quote: Stuart J. Youngner, "The Definition of Death," *The Oxford Handbook of Bioethics*, 300.

61. D. Alan Shewmon and Elisabeth Seitz Shewmon, "The Semiotics of Death and Its Medical Implications," *Brain Death and Disorders of Consciousness,* D. Alan Shewmon (ed.) (Calixto Machado, 2004), 91

62. 刹那生死 *setsuna-shoji.*

63. Buddhism's "endorsement" might be taken very broadly. In the first case endorsing does not necessarily mean "recommending," and secondly "Buddhism"

is, as is mentioned above in relation to Keown, an exceedingly broad term in its own right. Roy Perret for instance criticizes both Damien and John Keown for presenting the Theravada tradition as representative of the Buddhist position, in an article discussing euthanasia in Buddhism and Christianity. See Roy. W. Perrett, "Buddhism, Euthanasia and the Sanctity of Life," *Journal of Medical Ethics* (1996), 310.

64. Keown (1995), 141–42.

65. *SG Zuimonki* 1–19 (Okumura trans.).

66. Compare this to Shinran's belief, for example, that the ultimate reality of Buddhism is not to be identified in any way with the domain of human intellect or will.

67. Richard A. McCormick, "Physician-Assisted Suicide: Flight from Compassion." Stephen E. Lammers and Allen Verhey, *On Moral Medicine: Theological Perspectives in Medical Ethics* (Grand Rapids, MI: Eerdmans, 1987), 1083.

68. The regulatory framework for the monastic community of Buddhism.

69. Harvey (2000), 295.

70. *SG Zuimonki* 1–20 (Okumura trans.).

71. Harvey (2000), 296.

72. Ibid.

73. Ibid.

74. Mettanando Bhikkhu, "Buddhist Ethics in the Practice of Medicine," in Fu and Wawrythko (1991): 195–213; in Harvey (2000), 302–3.

75. Nanamoli, Bhikkhu (trans.), *Mindfulness of Breathing (Anapanasati): Buddhist Texts from the Pali Canon and Extracts from the Pali Commentaries*, 68.

76. De Silva (2002), 931.

77. Sogyal Rinpocehe, "The Art of Dying," in D. Wolter, *Losing the Clouds, Gaining the Sky: Buddhism and the Natural Mind* (Boston: Wisdom Publications, 2007), 231.

78. *SG Zuimonki* 6–8 (Okumura trans.).

79. *SG Zuimonki* 1–14 (Okumura trans.).

80. Sogyal Rinpocehe, "The Art of Dying," in D. Wolter, *Losing the Clouds, Gaining the Sky: Buddhism and the Natural Mind*, 234.

81. Bernard Faure, *Visions of Power: Imagining Medieval Japanese Buddhism* (Princeton, NJ: Princeton University Press, 1996), 148.

82. For a Theravada example of "selfless" death, see also Padmasiri De Silva's discussion of the story of the monk Channa. This monk in great pain committed suicide, but incurred "no blame" as (according to De Silva) his action transcended the existential ambiguity of craving to live or craving to die. The suicidal impulse is "tamed" and there is a "sense of equanimity with which death . . . is faced." De Silva (2002), 88–89.

83. David Putney, "Some Problems of Interpretation: The Early and Late Writings of Dōgen," *Philosophy East and West*, Vol. 46, No. 4 (1996), 512.

84. Dessi 99, after Kenneth Tanaka's "Ethics in American Jodo-Shinshu: Trans-Ethical Responsibility," *The Pure Land (New Series)* 6: (91–116) (2007), 107–8.

85. Ronald Y. Nakasone (2006), 292.

86. The name Flower Garland is meant to suggest the crowning glory of profound understanding.

87. Nakasone (2006), 292.

88. Ibid., 293.

89. Ibid.

90. Nakasone says of this reflection, "[they] recall deeply ingrained, if only vaguely understood, notions of life and death, and reactions are emotional rather than rational." Ibid., 296–97.

91. Ibid., 302.

92. See Harvey (2000), 304.

Selected Bibliography

Abe, Masao (1992). *A Study of Dōgen; His Philosophy and Religion*. Albany: State University of New York Press.

De Silva, Padmasiri (2002). *Buddhism, Ethics, and Society: The Conflicts and Dilemmas of Our Times*. Clayton, Vic.: Monash Asia Institute.

De Silva, Padmasiri (1996). "Suicide and Emotional Ambivalence: An Early Buddhist Perspective." *Pali Buddhism*. Curzon Press.

Dessi, Ugo (2007). *Ethics and Society in Contemporary Shin Buddhism*. Berlin: Münster Lit.

Gowans, Christopher W. (2015). *Buddhist Moral Philosophy: An Introduction*. New York; London: Routledge.

Haneda, Nobuo (2001). "Shakyamuni and Shinran; Is Jodō Shinshū Really Buddhism?" *The Living Dharma Library*. November 11, 2001(presented). Living Dharma. May 24, 2005.

Harvey, Peter (2000). *An Introduction to Buddhist Ethics: Foundations, Values, and Issues*. Cambridge: Cambridge University Press.

Heine, Steven (1989). *A Blade of Grass: Japanese Poetry and Aesthetics in Dōgen Zen*. New York: P. Lang.

Heine, Steven (1991). "From Rice Cultivation to Mind Contemplation: The Meaning of Impermanence in Japanese Religion." *History of Religions*, Vol. 30, No. 4 (May 1991), 373–403.

Johnson, Lawrence E. (2011). *A Life-Centered Approach to Bioethics: Biocentric Ethics*. Cambridge: Cambridge University Press.

Kasulis, Thomas P. (1981). *Zen Action, Zen Person*, Hawaii: University Press of Hawaii.

Keown, Damien (1995). *Buddhism & Bioethics*. New York: St. Martin's Press.

Kim, Hee-Jin (2004). *Eihei Dōgen Mystical Realist*. Somerville, MA: Wisdom Publications.

King, Sally B. (2005). *Being Benevolence: The Social Ethics of Engaged Buddhism*. Honolulu: University of Hawaii Press.

McCormick, Richard A. (1987). "Physician-Assisted Suicide: Flight from Compassion." In *On Moral Medicine: Theological Perspectives in Medical Ethics*, eds. Stephen E. Lammers and Allen Verhey. Grand Rapids, MI: Eerdmans.

Nakasone, Ronald Y. (2006) "Ethics of Ambiguity: A Buddhist Reflection on the Japanese Organ Transplant Law." In *Handbook of Bioethics and Religion,* ed. David E. Guinn. Oxford: Oxford University Press.

Okumura, Shōhaku (trans.) (1987). *Shōbōgenzō-zuimonki—Sayings of Eihei Dōgen Zenji Recorded by Koun Ejō.* Kyōto, Japan: Kyōto Zen Center.

Perrett, Roy W. (1996). "Buddhism, Euthanasia and the Sanctity of Life." *Journal of Medical Ethics.*

Rinpocehe, Sogyal (2007). "The Art of Dying." In *Losing the Clouds, Gaining the Sky: Buddhism and the Natural Mind,* ed. D. Wolter. Boston: Wisdom Publications.

CHAPTER FIVE

The Continental Perspective on Assisted Suicide and Euthanasia

Jack Simmons

Traditionally, continental philosophers have not addressed specific ethical problems, such as assisted suicide and euthanasia, and instead have focused on hermeneutics and metaphysics which in the 20th century led to the development of phenomenology, existentialism, and postmodernism. In discourse on these subjects, the question of ethics generally takes the form of metaethics and a questioning of the relationship between the individual and universal ethical principles. When continental thinkers take up specific ethical problems, such as suicide and euthanasia, these problems typically are used as examples to demonstrate a metaethical or existential claim.

When it comes to the question of death, virtually all continental thinkers have waded into the argument, wondering if death might point to something unique about human existence. It is from this direction that this chapter examines the question of assisted suicide and euthanasia: not as a direct effort to answer the question of whether specific approaches to suicide and euthanasia are ethical, but how we might think of these approaches within the larger question of the individual's relationship to death.

The distinction between the analytic tradition of philosophy and the continental tradition of philosophy might best be illuminated in the comparison of two great fictional detectives: Edgar Allen Poe's Dupin and Sir Arthur Conan Doyle's Sherlock Holmes. Holmes is the epitome of scientific reasoning. His sidekick Watson explains that, "Of contemporary literature, philosophy and politics he appeared to know next to nothing. . . . He said that he would acquire no knowledge which did not bear upon his object. Therefore all the knowledge which he possessed was such as would be useful to him."[1] Watson is flabbergasted that Holmes is "ignorant of the Copernican Theory and of the composition of the Solar System" and what's more, doesn't care and chooses to forget as soon as he learns of it. Holmes explains, "What the deuce is it to me?" Holmes says. "If we went round the moon it would not make a pennyworth of difference to me or my work."[2]

Dupin, on the other hand, thinks of himself as a whist player who

> makes . . . a host of observations and inferences . . . and the difference . . . lies not so much in the validity of the inference as in the quality of the observation. The necessary knowledge is that of *what* to observe. Our player confines himself not at all; nor . . . does he reject deductions from things external to the game.[3]

Dupin encourages "comprehension of *all* the sources whence legitimate advantage may be derived" to *disentangle* the truth.[4]

Without preference for one sleuth or the other, we might characterize Doyle's Holmes as scientific and analytic, and Poe's Dupin as hermeneutic and phenomenologically oriented. Philosophers in the phenomenological tradition often claim to study the "lived world" and take seriously the history of philosophy, to the extent that it connects us to past lived worlds, which presents a picture of the world that demands greater disentangling and a wider search for sources of legitimate advantage.

The reader will suspect that this brief characterization of continental and analytic philosophy must necessarily fall short and that the analogy with these two famous sleuths will, like all analogies, fail under close scrutiny. However feeble, this author offers this characterization as an introduction to the following investigation of assisted suicide and euthanasia—an investigation that attempts to approach the subject from the perspective of continental philosophy. This task presents a second danger, namely, that the chapter will offer a unified interpretation of the problem, as if the philosophers within this tradition agree on the subject. This is simply not the case. However, all of the thinkers discussed here approach the problem of death from a common, phenomenological perspective:

- Life has no pre-given value.
- Life has the value we give it in living. *If you live a life without value, then your life is valueless.*
- My death transcends any external ethic or morality.

This chapter explains the grounds for this perspective and shows why it calls for an existential ethic that generates a paradox: allowing for ethical judgment and a radical relativism, simultaneously. The reader will note, however, that this paradoxical outcome is the product of the enigmatic character of death and, at least for the purpose of this chapter, is intended to apply only to the question of assisted suicide and death. The conclusion is not intended as a general conclusion about all ethical questions.

The Idiot by Dostoyevsky

In *The Idiot*, Dostoyevsky introduces us to a foolish young man, Hippolite, who, suffering from tuberculosis and having only two weeks left in which to live, decides to kill himself at a party, among his friends. As a prelude to his suicide, Hippolite reads a carefully written letter titled "My Essential Statement," to the party guests. In this lengthy statement, Dostoyevsky introduces four ideas critical to continental thought and the discussion of suicide and euthanasia:

1. Most people do not know how to live,
2. The knowledge of my own death may inspire my desire to begin truly living,
3. My death transcends morality and religion, and finally,
4. I should have the right to dispose of my life, when facing imminent death, as I wish.[5]

At the conclusion of his reading, the sun rises, Hippolite steps out on the veranda, puts a small pocket pistol to his head, and pulls the trigger. There is a click, but the pistol does not go off, and his effort misfires. Although Hippolite attempts to convince the partygoers that he had intended to kill himself and simply mislaid the firing cap, Dostoyevsky leaves us unsure as how to interpret the character—sage or idiot. With this tale, Dostoyevsky sets the stage for the continental dialogue on death, and a sophisticated discussion of assisted suicide and euthanasia, taken from the standpoint not of religion or morality, as we might expect, but rather from the standpoint of the lived-world and a character attempting to manage his own mortality.

The notion of the lived-world has its philosophical origins in the work of Wilhelm Dilthey, Edmund Husserl, and Martin Heidegger, and suggests that life itself is not a given fact. We are not simply alive or dead, but rather, we live *our* life, and although it has universal features, our essential situation is ours alone. Dostoyevsky recognized this, and recognized that most people fail to recognize it. In other words, most people live lives dictated by the objective, socially structured conditions in which they find themselves. Dostoyevsky asks, "Whose fault is it that they don't know how to live?"[6] Heidegger describes this as the problem of "*everydayness.*"

> In utilizing public means of transport and in making use of information services such as the newspaper, every Other is like the next. This Being-with-one-another dissolves one's own Dasein completely into the kind of Being of "the Others," in such a way, indeed, that the Others, as distinguishable and explicit, vanish more and more. In this inconspicuousness and unascertainability, the real dictatorship of the "they" is unfolded. We take pleasure and enjoy ourselves as *they* take pleasure; we read, see and judge about literature and art as *they* see and judge; likewise we shrink back from the "great mass" as *they* shrink back, we find "shocking" what *they* find shocking. The "they," which is nothing definite, and which all are, though not as the sum, prescribes the kind of Being of everydayness.[7]

We fall easily into the forms of life presented to us in everyday life by the "*they.*" We enjoy our lives according to the public standards for enjoyment, and we resist the public standards according to the public standards for resistance. We are left with few other options, and when new options are discovered—by bold, enterprising individuals—those new options are quickly assessed, categorized, and absorbed into everydayness so that we can participate in them according to the carefully prescribed modes of participation. Theodore Adorno points to the example of camping to demonstrate how culture absorbs and prescribes the modes of *everydayness* to us. Camping, which began as a youth movement, allowing young people to escape the confines of everyday, bourgeois life, quickly gives rise to the hobby of camping, involving the development of camp grounds, camp sites, camping stores, camping equipment, camping seasons, camping styles, and eventually people who describe themselves as campers and those who dislike camping.[8] Here we see the dictatorship of the *they* unfolded; camping is part of everyday life, and why Dostoyevsky describes us as, "scurrying, bustling people, forever anxious, gloomy, restless, darting all around . . . unhappy," because consumed with everydayness, we remain unaware of *our* lives.[9] We know that objectively, we are alive, and that objectively, we are individuals, but within the confines of the life we live, our lived-world, we encounter little in our lives that would distinguish us from anyone else in any significant fashion. Walter Kaufmann describes Dostoyevsky's concern as an existential one: the quest for authentic existence, the scorn of the inauthentic, the problem of how to meet death, and the experience of time [which brings us nearer to death].[10]

Writing Death with a Hammer

Frederick Nietzsche describes his writing as philosophizing with a hammer, because he intends to strike at the eternal idols as with a tuning fork, to determine whether they are hollow.[11] In *Thus Spoke Zarathustra*, Nietzsche aims his hammer at the everyday idea of death, and finds it the hollowest nut wanting to be cracked.[12] Nietzsche begins from Dostoyevsky's suggestion that few truly know how to live, describing the *they* as a "*herd*," which involves a life-negating morality, generally producing the same consequences as those described above: an inauthentic life. Nietzsche sees a free death as an important strategy for avoiding the herd mentality, and to this end admonishes us to "Die at the right time!"[13] And yet, he immediately recognizes that this advice is useless because most people don't know how to live, "Of course, how could those who never live at the right time die at the right time?"[14]

For Nietzsche, the question of how to die remains generally part of the problem of how to live. Nietzsche laments that even though few know how and when to live, they, "still make a fuss about their dying. . . . Everybody considers dying important; but as yet death is no festival. As yet men have not learned how one hallows the most beautiful festivals."[15] Here, Nietzsche acknowledges that we consider death important, but that our approach to death fails to reflect an authentic concern. Instead, we die in factory fashion, as Rainer Maria Rilke describes in *The Notes of Malte Laurids Brigge*, in 1910.

> This excellent *hôtel* is very old: even in King Clovis' times one died there in a few beds. Now one dies in 559 beds. Factory fashion, of course. In view of this enormous production rate, the individual death is not so well executed; but that is beside the point. It is the quantity that counts. Who, today, would still give anything for a well-executed death? No one. Even the rich, who could after all afford to die elaborately, are beginning to become negligent and indifferent; the wish to have a death of one's own is becoming rarer and rarer. A little while yet, and it will be as rare as a life of one's own. God, it's all there. One comes along, one finds a life, ready-made, one only has to put it on. One wants to go or is forced to go: well, no trouble at all: voilà votre mort, monsieur. One dies at random; one dies whatever

death belongs to the disease one happens to have: for since one knows
all diseases, one also knows that the different lethal conclusions belong to
the diseases and not to the human beings; and the sick person, as it were,
doesn't have anything to do.[16]

The hospitals define our demise for us, typically in the form of disease. The disease will then predict our future well-being or the time and
fashion of our demise. We are offered therapies to stave off the disease or,
if it is incurable and fatal, to reduce our pain and suffering; all of these
therapies follow carefully outlined protocols for managing the medical and
ethical concerns that arise. These protocols are developed by professionals
representing their profession. Physicians, hospital administrators, hospital
attorneys, insurance providers, risk analysts, medical ethicists, in short,
professionals that we never meet, work out the details of the protocols
that will govern our dying or recovery. In many cases, these protocols have
the weight of the law behind them. For example, after the evacuation of
Memorial Hospital following Hurricane Katrina in which doctors were
accused of ordering the lethal overdosing of patients, new protocols were
developed regarding emergency evacuations and laws were passed to grant
physicians greater immunity from legal liability in emergencies, so that
doctors could act with greater autonomy and less responsibility to their
patients.[17] The protocols are so complete that even in the case of temporary
social collapse, your death will follow standard guidelines and procedures.
    Now, fully in the grip of everydayness, Rilke points out that just as
everyone now seeks a ready-made life, so too do we seek a ready-made
death, as dictated to us by the professionals. There must be great debates
and discourses on how to die, books and essays on the subject, legal briefs,
judicial decisions and legislative action, and despite the best intentions to
educate people and invite them into reflection that might allow for the
possibility of an authentic death, most of the discourse ultimately produces further protocols and laws that more fully dictate the manner of
our dying. In turning our death over to these professionals, we become
consumers of death. We participate in our own death in the same way we
might participate in a holiday on a cruise ship. As with all industries that
provide products and services, the industry generates a standard of care
and this standard dictates the attitudes and expectations of both the provider and the customer. Rikle explains,

In hospitals, where people die so agreeably and with so much gratitude
toward doctors and nurses, one dies a death prepared by the institution:
they like it that way. If, however, one dies at home, one chooses as a matter

of course that polite death of the better circles with which, so to say, the funeral first class and the whole sequence of its touching customs begin. In front of such a house the poor stand and stare to their heart's content. Their death, of course, is trite, without all fuss. They are well satisfied if they find one that fits approximately. No matter if it is too big: one is always apt to grow a little more. But if it does not close over the chest or if it chokes, that is bad.[18]

Rilke describes the consumer of death as being like a customer at a fine hotel, someone seeking satisfaction and a good fit, whether at home or away. Should customers find themselves upgraded to a suite, so much the better, but only if the bed is not too small or hard.

The same institutions provide data and statistics regarding their success and failures in regard to the management of death, such that our own death is absorbed by the industry and expressed in charts and figures along with everyone else's death. This is perhaps the greatest indignation—that regardless of our legacy to our friends and family, whether we wish to be remembered or forgotten, our death will be counted and categorized in the service of the industry that manages death for everyone. Even in death we are drawn back into everyday life.

It is perfectly reasonable to ask how an authentic death might compare to an inauthentic death, or whether the notion of an authentic death holds meaning at all. Nietzsche offers us something of an Aristotelian solution to this question, invoking the notion of a complete life, defined by a timely death. In *The Twilight of the Idols*, Nietzsche recommends that those who have a true goal and a true heir, should die at the right time for that goal and heir.[19]

I show you the death that consummates—a spur and a promise to the survivors. He that consummates his life dies his death victoriously, surrounded by those who hope and promise. Thus should one learn to die; and there should be no festival where one dying thus does not hallow the oaths of the living.[20]

Readers familiar with the *Nichomachean Ethics* are likely to see the similarity to Aristotle's description of the good life. Aristotle explains that the good life involves activity of the soul in accordance with virtue, surrounded by parents, children, wife, friends, and citizens, and consummating itself in a complete life.[21]

Nietzsche's "goal," echoes Aristotle's assertion that human good involves activity, motivated to some end. The "truth" of Nietzsche's goal reflects Aristotle's claim that the end should be in accordance with virtue. We see Aristotle's recognition that the good life naturally involves our family, friends, and citizens in Nietzsche's call for an "heir, and a promise to survivors," and finally, Nietzsche's death that consummates is one that finalizes a complete, goal-oriented life. Nietzsche includes death in the formation of a purposeful life, however, whereas Aristotle considers death an accident that, with luck, comes after the completion of a good life. In this way, Nietzsche tries to remove the accidental, making death part of life's purpose. For Nietzsche, death consummates the true goal and heir. He warns us that many people cling to life long beyond what their goals require, and he calls for a great storm to shake the rotten wood from the trees. Others, like Jesus, die too soon, before they can learn to love the earth.[22] Death then is no accident, but must come at the right time. Unlike Jesus, we must live long enough to identify the true goal (in Jesus' case, love of the earth rather than a desire for heaven), and die before we advance to an age that no longer allows for vigorous activity toward our true goal (such that we become rotten wood on the tree and useless to our purpose). We might therefore read Nietzsche as holding to a very strict Aristotelianism which demands that our life span match up with our purpose. We should live long enough to complete the purpose, but no longer or else we become purposeless. Of course, accidental death cannot be ruled out, but we should no more relinquish our death to accident than we should our lives.

Nietzsche uses the term "free death" rings of a good death (euthanasia), and on this matter Nietzsche is quite clear: "the free death which comes to me because I want it."[23] He admonishes us to "die at the right time!" in support of Dostoyevsky's critique of everyday life and in support of Hippolite's final statement.[24]

> I am not dying for lack of strength to endure those three weeks. Oh, I would have had strength enough, and if I wished I would have drawn sufficient consolation just from the awareness of the wrong done to me; but I am no French poet and I don't want such consolation. Finally, there is a temptation; nature has so limited by activity by its three-week sentence that suicide is perhaps the only thing I still have time to begin and bring to a conclusion of my own free will. Well, why shouldn't I take advantage of the last possibility to *act*? A protest is sometimes no small matter.[25]

Hippolite's final act, a free action, consummating a goal, and a small resistance to the herd—which judges his effort as unseemly—offers us a glimpse of how the want of death might manifest itself. Notice that it is not represented as a lack of strength for the life that remains, but rather a desire to exhibit vitality of life one last time.

For Dostoyevsky, Nietzsche, and Rilke, a good death should be sought to the extent that it helps us avoid an extended, accidental, meaningless life. If we were to conclude the present study here, we would argue that in the pursuit of an authentic existence we ought to be allowed control over the timing of our death. This does not, however, provide us with any guarantee that the purpose to which we put our life will be authentic, and if that purpose proves to be inauthentic, then there is a danger that our decision regarding our death might also be inauthentically chosen. Given that all three philosophers acknowledge that the vast majority of people live inauthentic lives, we might very well conclude that a person should not be given the liberty to determine the end of his or her life, for fear that the individual would make the decision in error.

Death As the Archimedean Lever Against Everydayness

Existential philosophy strives to open the possibility to authentic, human existence, which naturally begs the questions: What is authentic and inauthentic existence and how might we distinguish them so as to pursue an authentic life? Although this chapter cannot provide a full analysis of the question, a brief description clarifies the discussion of authentic death.

José Ortega and John Paul Sartre, suggest that the human essence is distinguished from the essences of stone, for example, by its duality—having both a natural and extra-natural part.[26] John Paul Sartre would have referred to a factual and a transcendent self. In either case, the natural part of us is that which is objectively given, realized by itself: we are carbon-based life forms that possess opposable thumbs and are capable of walking upright. This fact presents no problems, except to the extent to which we might possess some natural handicap. John Paul Sartre was born with a lazy eye, but this feature realizes itself. It required no effort on his part. Sartre did not choose to have a lazy eye.

The anti-natural refers to the sort of person Sartre wishes to be, what Ortega calls his life project. The anti-natural is not given, but instead, chosen, which means that

> I am free. But . . . I am free by compulsion, whether I wish to be or not. . . .
> To be free means to be lacking a constitute identity, not to have subscribed to a determined being, to be able to be other than what one was, to be unable to install oneself once and for all in any given being.[27]

A person must select who they wish to be. Inauthentic existence occurs when a person takes his or her essential being as a natural fact, and makes choices as if from a menu—occupation, residence, marriage, retirement. People trapped in an inauthentic existence are almost universally unaware of it, and so Kierkegaard concludes in *Sickness Unto Death*, that, "the specific character of despair is precisely this: it is unaware of being in despair."[28] An authentic existence would express the individuality of human subjectivity, of the anti-natural character of the individual's life.

Swallowed by everydayness, which dictates the objective reality in which we find ourselves and prescribes ready-made lives, it is difficult to know where we might start the search for authentic existence. Martin Heidegger suggests in *Being and Time* that death offers us a lever with which we might shift everydayness and create room for our own, authentic existence. His argument is famously esoteric, involving a vocabulary of its own. This section refers to that vocabulary when necessary, but presents Heidegger's perspective on death in the most neutral terminology possible.

For Heidegger, "everydayness" is precisely that Being which is "between" birth and death.[29] This "Being" is distinct from "being" in that "being" refers to the manner in which objects exist, and "Being" represents the world that human beings encounter, full of meaning, purpose, and urgency—the extra-natural aspect of human existence. Heidegger describes the entity that encounters Being as *Dasein*, which translates from German as "being-there." For Heidegger, Dasein means the entity that is thrown into Being. This "throwness" could be experienced as one's own, or as the generic existence of everyday life. In "everydayness" our birth and death are presented as objective facts. We are born naturally, or via cesarean, after a long and difficult or brief and eventless labor. We arrived early or late, and were small or large, jaundiced, or with any number of other conditions. These objective facts are recorded in the medical records that situate us neatly within the institutions of childbirth. This chapter already has examined how Rilke and Nietzsche discuss the way in which *everydayness* captures the objective fact of a person's death. Although it might be difficult to know how your death will occur, that you ultimately will die is an objective certainty. This is the ontic, objective, or natural character of human existence from birth to death.

The *they* defines the ontic character of death in the way it talks about death. Heidegger explains that we obtain data and statistics about the longevity of plants, animals, and men by ascertaining them ontically (as objects).[30] "People who are no acquaintances of ours are 'dying' daily and hourly. . . . 'Death' is encountered as a well-known event occurring within-the-world. As such it remains in the inconspicuousness characteristic of what is encountered in an everyday fashion. The *they* has already stowed away an interpretation for this event."[31] To the extent to which the *they* defines death publicaly, and *everyone* dies, then in dying we are in no case ourselves, but rather we die like everyone else. Heidegger concludes that in *everydayness* death belongs to nobody in particular, and therefore in dying we become like everyone else; we become nobody.[32] Echoing Rilke's concern, we experience an inauthentic death when we die in this everyday, objective fashion.

This is the unique, ontological character of Dasein's vulnerability to *everydayness*: that Dasein has a birth and death

> of the kind appropriate to anything that lives; and it has it, not in ontical isolation, but as codetermined by its primordial kind of Being. In so far as this is the case, Dasein too can end without authentically dying, though on the other hand, *qua* Dasein, it does not simply perish.[33]

Here Heidegger suggests that even though we can die in the same way that plants and animals die, there is also something about our death that is different. To perish is to move from living to nonliving, to demonstrate the characteristics of life, and then cease demonstrating those characteristics, while still existing. This description of death, however, is the description of some other's death. This is not the death that Dasein will experience. Rather, death presents Dasein with a unique hermeneutic problem: How to understand our lives.

We attempt to understand the world (as opposed to objectively occupying it) and we attempt to understand ourselves (our own being is an issue for interpretation). We are constituted of a past, present, and future, all of which require interpretation. The interpretation of our past, present, and future constitutes our lived-world. Interpreting the future poses particular challenges, in that it has not yet occurred. I can try to understand how I will feel upon the birth of an expected child, but cannot know for sure until the child arrives. I again could try to understand how I will feel upon the birth of a second child, perhaps with greater accuracy, but will not be sure until the second child arrives. The ultimate hermeneutic is the anticipation of death. Ontically, I know that I will die, but I can know nothing of my death until I die. In this way, my own death outstrips the everyday interpretation of death.

Hermeneutic philosophy addresses the possibility of arriving at the final, accurate interpretation of any phenomenon (proposition, object, and event). Philosophers in the continental tradition typically question whether interpretation ever can be final or accurate. The hermeneutic double-bind, or hermeneutic circle, is the realization that we cannot escape our role of interpreter. When trying to deduce whether Hippolite intended to kill himself or instead intentionally mislaid the firing cap, we cannot escape our role as interpreter because *The Idiot* provides us with no answer.

Kierkegaard famously captures the hermeneutic double bind in his recounting of the story of Adam of Eve in the Garden of Eden, and God's instructing them that they should not eat from the Tree of Knowledge of Good and Evil. Kierkegaard reminds us that we generally interpret this allegory in reverse, assuming Adam's knowledge of good and evil prior to his eating from the tree, which is, of course, impossible. Prior to eating from the tree, Adam would have no knowledge of good or evil, and so God's prohibition could not mean to Adam what it means to us, that eating from the tree would be bad. Rather, Kierkegaard points out that the prohibition can only be experienced as the possibility of *being able*.[34] Of what he is able to do, Adam can have no idea, and so this possibility presents itself as a pure possibility, as a pure hermeneutic, in which Adam is completely alone, must make the decision out of nothing, and must bear the entire responsibility for the decision, for he cannot refer to any preestablished norm for behavior, or any objective analysis of the possible outcome. Kierkegaard suggests that such a decision inspires dread. Heidegger calls this anxiety.

The hermeneutic double bind endangers our access to the absolute truth of intentions, objects, and events, and presents the danger of relativism. If understood correctly, however, it can be a relativism of meaning rather than a relativism of nihilism. Philosophers in the continental tradition typically conclude that the assertion of absolute meaning is best expressed by *everydayness* and is the source of nihilism, for it renders the individual irrelevant. Faced with the hermeneutic double bind, and the impossibility of objective truth, we experience anxiety: the realization of one's own, nonrelational being. In this anxiety the possibility of meaning falls away and we are left essentially alone in the world.[35]

The universal source for this anxiety is forged in the anticipation of one's own death because, as already noted, everyone dies. This anxiety in anticipation of death can serve as a lever against *everydayness* and pry open the possibility for freedom, a true freedom, in which a person authentically choses his or her own life. The hermeneutic of death generates the purest, most profound anxiety, because one's own death so clearly resists *everyday* interpretation: No one can experience death and live to report on it. Knowing that our death is an objective certainty, and a subjective impossibility (it can never be lived), Heidegger concludes that, "death reveals itself as that *possibility which is one's ownmost, which is non-relational, and which is not to be outstripped.*"[36] It cannot be outstripped because it cannot be avoided (we all will die) and it is nonrelational because no one else can live it and report it to us.

Heidegger concludes that when we consider death this way—subjectively rather than objectively—the potential for authentic existence arises.

> If Dasein stands before itself as this possibility [of no-longer-being-able-to-be-there] it has been fully assigned to its ownmost potentiality for Being. When it stands before itself in this way, all its relations to any other Dasein have been undone. This ownmost non-relational possibility is at the same time the uttermost one.[37]

The possibility of Dasien (being there) no-longer-being-able-to-be-there is a paradox. This paradox is the possibility of an impossibility. Furthermore, this paradox is nonrelational, in that no other person's death presents the possibility of my no-longer-being-able-to-be-there. This paradox mirrors Kierkegaard's description of the possibility of *being-able*, expressed in the story of Adam and Eve. Heidegger describes "Being-towards-death as a *Being towards a possibility*."[38] That possibility is the possibility of recognizing our inauthentic existence in *everydayness* (the *they-self*), which leaves open the possibility of authentic existence in anticipation of our own death.

> Being-towards-death as we have projected it existentially: *anticipation reveals to Dasein its lostness in the they-self, and brings it face to face with the possibility of being itself, primarily unsupported by concernful solicitude, but of being itself, rather in an impassioned freedom towards death—a freedom which has been released from the illusions of the "they," and which is factical, certain of itself, and anxious.*[39]

The anticipation of death, the ultimate hermeneutic double-bind, provides the lever by which we might neutralize the *everyday* notions of death, because no other's death can be one's own.

> One becomes free *for* one's own death, one is liberated from one's lostness in those possibilities which may accidentally thrust them-selves upon one: and one is liberated in such a way that for the first time one can authentically understand and choose among the factual possibilities lying ahead of that possibility which is not to be outstripped.[40]

For Heidegger, the anticipation of death forces upon us the freedom Rilke spoke of, a freedom of compulsion emerging from the dissolution of an identity constituted by *everydayness*, which enables us to be someone different than we were before: an authentic individual.

Although it is perilous to attempt a simplification of Heidegger's thought, we might understand Heidegger as asserting that our entire life is predetermined by the mode of everyday existence, and that this *everydayness* obviates our ability to live free, self-determined lives because *everydayness* constitutes the conditions of our birth, our life, and our death. In *everydayness*, every person is like the next. I can be replaced in my job, in my marriage, someone else could raise my children, others play chess better than I, cook better than I, and make love better than I, but no one can die my death for me. The unique character of death is that it cannot be played out for us. Death is the possibility of the impossibility of existence. This is a formal discovery utterly lacking content. It is precisely this lack of content that makes it impossible for *everydayness* to seize it. When we consider our own death, our own nonexistence, we are confronted with the impossibility of *everydayness* to constitute that death meaningfully for us, and that everyday objective conception of death collapses. The collapsing of the objective conception of death is like a domino. In falling, it might knock down all of the everyday, objective conceptions of our existence, leaving us alone in the world.[41] Suddenly finding ourselves alone in the world we experience anxiety (dread). Dread can cause us to rush back to everydayness and blindly reaffirm its validity, or we might allow our suspense to range where it will, leaving us free to determine our life and death for ourselves. Heidegger calls this state freedom toward death. As Thomas Tierney explains in "Death, Medicine and the Right to Die: An Engagement with Heidegger, Bauman and Baudrillard," Heidegger, "pointed out that to some degree, but not completely, death was concealed through its appropriation by culture, and that a certain degree of liberation could be provided by the fleeting recovery of an authentic experience of death."[42] Hence, our death serves as a lever against inauthentic existence.

Death as the Foundation for Absolute Ethics

Like Heidegger, Jacques Derrida sees in death something unreachable, something that defies our efforts to capture and understand it: for indeed, what can be said of nonexistence? Facing death is for Heidegger the possibility of an impossibility: the possibility of an existing being (Dasein) facing its own nonexistence.[43] For Derrida, it is possibility as impossibility—that what is impossible (an existing being facing nonexistence) is made possible when that existing being authentically confronts its own nonexistence.[44] Derrida describes this as "aporia": impossibility or contradiction manifest in the human condition. Because contemplation of our own death is an aporia, this phenomenon resists traditional efforts to understand it. Derrida follows a long history of continental thinkers who conclude that death offers a final assault on reason and science.

This section focuses on Derrida's notion of aporia and how this generates a foundation for what might be seen as transcendental ethics or a rejection of ethics. There are, as this author sees it, two ways to approach Derrida's conception of aporia. The first is to untangle Derrida's argument and follow it to its conclusion. The second is to use Kierkegaard's characterization of the absurd in the story of Abraham, which is far easier. It should be noted that after a long struggle with his own argument, Derrida ultimately references Kierkegaard's characterization of the absurd, so it would seem that even Derrida is pointing us in that direction.[45] Readers keen to fully engage with Derrida's prose on this matter might consider *Aporias* and *The Gift of Death*, both by Derrida.

Abraham, having heard the command from an angel to sacrifice his son Isaac, must decide whether the command is divine. He must decide whether to follow a command that runs contrary to every ethical, moral, cultural, and religious norm that Abraham knows. Recall that God had told Abraham he would be the father of many nations, and Isaac is Abraham's only legitimate son. Abraham must choose, and Kierkegaard explains that he must choose out of nothing. He must decide whether the command is truly from God and, if it is, whether it must be followed. The message could have any number of sources. Abraham could be dreaming, drunk, deluded, duped by a friend, duped by the devil, or truly in the presence of God. But how could he know? What interpretative technique will tease out the truth of the message? What could ever count as evidence of the veracity of the message? Jean Paul Sartre characterizes this existential dilemma by suggesting that "anyone in such a case would wonder, first, whether it was indeed an angel and secondly, whether I am really Abraham. Where are the proofs?"[46] In other words, how could God prove to Abraham that he was God? Any message or miracle would require further interpretation, and could again be a product of a dream, drunkenness, or delusion.

Abraham cannot escape the role of interpreter—the hermeneutic double-bind—and ultimately must decide for himself whether the message is from God or from some other source. In this decision, Abraham is necessarily alone. Any word of advice from another also would be subject to the same interpretative dilemma. If his wife advises him that the message expresses divine intent, then he must decide whether he has dreamed up her advice, or whether she too might not be dreaming, drunk, or deluded. In interpreting God's command, Abraham faces the possibility of an impossibility: following a moral commandment that is immoral. Abraham can reference no external norm to justify his decision. Facing this choice is a confrontation with the absurd, which Heidegger sees in death. It is a choice that requires a commitment from Abraham, and a decision for which Abraham is solely responsible.

Rather than creating nihilism and meaninglessness, Kierkegaard contends that the hermeneutic creates the need for a leap of faith, which allows us to assert truth as a subjective act. Abraham's decision to accept the message as divine generates the meaning that gives the story its significance. Had Abraham known for sure that the message was divine, the act would have been of no consequence, as commonplace and insignificant as heeding the announcement that his train had arrived at the station.

Derrida sees in this choice an aporia. Abraham must choose from nothing, nonetheless a choice is made. We know how the story ends, but the end is immaterial. At that moment Abraham must make a leap of faith, transgress ethical duty, and make the ultimate sacrifice—to kill his son. Out of this paradox a new, absolute ethic is created, based on individual conscience. In most decisions choice is determined by social convention— mores, ethics, and laws—but in this situation, Abraham comes face to face with aporia, a situation that defies all conventional thinking. Abraham's example is the most popular among continental thinkers, but we have heard of others: Adam's decision to eat the apple and Sophie's choice to save her son Jan over saving her daughter Eva from the concentration camp.[47] What guidance is possible in these cases? In confronting the impossible, the impossible becomes possible. This new possibility is the possibility for responsibility; I must make a decision, but in making this decision I can find guidance from no other person or conventional standard. The decision inspires a profound inwardness that Derrida describes as conscience. This conscience is absolute in that it transcends all conventional, ethical authority.

Derrida argues that the hermeneutic of death reduces all established social order to chaos and reveals aporia at its core.[48] From this deconstruction of social order and ethics he concludes that absolute conscience is the self-evident authority in all personal decisions. Derrida explains that in confronting the aporia of my own death, I am like Abraham in that, "God is in me, he is the absolute 'me' or 'self,' he is that structure of invisible interiority that is called, in Keirkegaaard's sense, subjectivity."[49] Following Heidegger's lead, Derrida accepts the claim that no one can live my death for me, and so no convention can authentically capture it. The result is ethical relativism stemming from the aporia of death. Whether he succeeds in this deconstruction of ethics is a question for another time, but Derrida's assertion that the aporia of death exceeds all attempts to rationalize it is fairly straightforward. My conscience becomes the self-evident authority in personal decisions regarding my death because I cannot accurately allude to anything outside of myself for an explanation of the unexplainable: my death, my nonexistence. This impossibility opens up the possibility of my taking responsibility for myself, my life, my death. For Derrida, this responsibility is meaningful, as it is my own.

Suicide Is Absurd

Until this point, the continental perspective on death seems to suggest that in anticipation of my own death, no external morality holds sway. Jean Paul Sartre undermines this argument by reminding us that if death is not part of our life, then we can know nothing of it, never live it, and it therefore can offer us no basis for life decisions. In keeping with the tradition of existentialism, Sartre argues that we are creatures whose being is determined after our actions. This coincides nicely with Nietzsche's notion that we have goals and heirs, and that our victories in our goals determine the meaning and value of our life, what we are, and when we should die.

Death, however, cannot be a goal or a pursuit because death provides no meaning to life. Death is the annihilation of our future, the end of all possibilities, a denial of the future, which is the source of human meaning. If we die, then our life has no meaning, our problems and goals receive no solution that we can experience. Sartre concludes, therefore, that death is not part of our ontological being. Rather, death is an ontic fact but a fact that we will never experience, for it involves our nonexistence. Suicide, or the deliberate ending of one's own life, cannot be part of an authentic choice because it has no conclusion, no result for life. To the extent to which we determine our unique essence through our choices, suicide is absurd and is a contradiction because nonexistence cannot be part of our essence; we are condemned to freedom and we must live to experience this freedom. Choosing death is committing myself to an ontic, natural, or objective fact about myself: that I will die. This natural fact cannot be the basis of an authentic mode of existence.

Sartre has understood the ontology of what it is to be human differently than Heidegger and Derrida. For Sartre, death cannot be part of my ontological being because I cannot experience it. Heidegger would answer to the contrary, that I cannot experience it means that it cannot be part of my ontic being, but that I must live in anticipation of it as an objective fact. For Heidegger, it is the anticipation of death, rather than death itself, that informs one's being at all times: hence, it is a structural component of one's existence. I will not attempt to settle this difference here, but rather point out that the difference depends upon how we understand death: as an ontic or ontological feature of human existence.

The Iron Cage of Irony

In his essay "Death, Medicine and the Right to Die: An engagement with Heidegger, Bauman, Baudrillard," Thomas Tierney uses Zygmunt Bauman and Jean Baudrillard in an effort to bring Heidegger's analysis on death to bear on the specific question of assisted suicide and euthanasia, and provide some guidance to the matter from a continental perspective. In this insightful work, Tierney concludes that the contemporary social conditions make an ironic approach toward death the only possible path to a personal freedom and authenticity. The following develops the basis of Tierney's argument and clarifies what an ironic approach to death might mean.

Whereas Heidegger asserts that *everydayness* conceals our death from us by focusing on the objective fact of our death, Tierney suggests that the question of death is resurfacing within the medical field, such that individuals must think about death in terms of medical choices: the disposition of organs, the limitations of extensive life-saving techniques, the writing of living wills, and participation in experimental treatments.[50] Tierney uses Bauman's argument to support his claim that modern culture exposes us to death, making it ever present, rather than concealing it as Heidegger suggests.[51] In *Mortality, Immortality and Other Life Strategies*, Bauman argues that humans self-consciously know of their own mortality, and that culture has developed largely to suppress this awareness. He goes on to argue that all human institutions, rituals, and beliefs demonstrate the presence of death as either a conscious or repressed human knowledge.[52] In this way, death is ever present in our lives, built into every aspect of human culture. For Tierney, this ever-present death materializes in the medical and legal acts that take death out of the hands of the individual and place it firmly within grips of the medical and legal community. Of course, many human acts are defined legally and medically, but this is remarkable for Tierney because Tierney accepts Heidegger's assertion that death remains ontologically my own—unique and individual.

Tierney sees Bauman's argument regarding culture as support for the claim that the assimilation of death into the realm of medicine forces death upon us. He sees the move by Bauman as something of a rebuke of Heidegger's suggestion that *everydayness* conceals our death from us. This conclusion might result from Tierney's mistaking the ontic (objective) features of death from the ontological (essential) features of death. Bauman's assertion that culture always has been a device for the suppression of death remains in almost perfect accord with Heidegger's claim that in *everydayness* (culture), death is treated as an objective fact, designed to conceal knowledge of our mortality.[53] This misunderstanding does not diminish Tierney's conclusion, but instead situates the medical and legal acts governing our relationship to death neatly within the realm of *everydayness*.

Modern medical and legal acts express a tendency in modern science committed to delivering us from natural limitations and dependencies. We see how modern inventions such as automobiles and ovens free us from walking and cooking over a fire, and modern democracies free us from tyranny. In medicine, modern practices and pharmaceuticals strive to free us from illness. Ultimately, modern medicine attempts to free us from death itself, but the paradoxical character of death makes it an anathema to modern science, which nonetheless must endeavor to free us from this natural limitation to our lives.[54] Consequently, Bauman concludes that modern science and reason must see in death an absurdity, an irrationality, an offense, that manifests itself in what can only be described as paradoxical descriptions of mortality.

> All deaths have causes, each death has a cause, each particular death has its particular cause. Corpses are cut open, explored, scanned, and tested until the cause is found: a blood clot, kidney failure, hemorrhage, heart arrest, lung collapse. We do not hear of people dying of mortality. They die only of individual causes, they die because there was an individual cause.[55]

The science of cause and effect cannot allow for an event (death) to have no cause, and yet death must come for all living creatures at some point. The assignation of a cause conceals our mortality and replaces it with a medical condition. No one dies of mortality, and yet everyone dies of mortality.

Treating death as a limitation to life, modern science and reason must understand death as an accident that has an external cause and should be avoided. This sets up a challenge for modern science and reason: How to avoid death. Tierney points out that Heidegger's analysis of death eliminated the traditional spiritual hedge against death by making death an end of human existence.[56] As such, we could no longer count on a life after death, because no one could know what our death would entail. Tierney concludes that removing the spiritual hedge against death forced us to emphasize our bodies in relation to death. That is, instead of thinking of death in terms of spiritual preparation, we now think to avoid death by maintaining the health of our bodies. Although it seems unlikely that

Heidegger's analysis of death is responsible for the cultural shift from a spiritual approach toward death to a focus on bodily health, there is plenty of evidence to support Tierney's claim that we now primarily think of death in terms of the health care and fitness culture.[57]

By shifting the location of the struggle against death from the mind (spirit) to the body, modern culture objectifies the body and objectifies our approach toward death. The struggle against death manifests itself in the physical fitness industry, the health care industry, and the risk-management industry. In each case we are compelled to avoid risky behaviors and encouraged to participate in safe, health-sustaining behaviors. Tierney points out that Baudrillard locates death in the body, stressing a mortality that is determined by health care management, seeing to extend life to the normal or proper term. To this end, the health care industry establishes quantifiable norms (i.e., life expectancy, standard blood pressure, body mass index) providing targets for the fitness industry, the health care industry, and the risk-management industry. Baudrillard concludes that the concept of a natural death "issues from the possibility of pushing back the limits of life: living becomes a process of accumulation, and science and technology start to play a role in this quantitative strategy."[58] As the cultural struggle with death focuses on pushing back the limits of life, Bauman concludes, in an apparent response to Heidegger, that "[t]he existential worry [about death] can be now all but forgotten in the daily bustle about *health*."[59]

In the struggle against death, the meaning of life becomes survival. The struggle for survival is waged on the battlefield of the body. This is where the meaning of one's life will be settled, and it will be settled quantitatively, in the accumulation of years. When we speak of "safe sex" we mean sexual activity that is safe for our bodies. We think little of the emotional dangers that sex possess. Even arguments for abstinence until marriage quantify sexuality by demanding that we have zero sexual partners until we are married, at which point we may have one partner. The purpose of "safe sex" is to keep us healthy, to avoid AIDS and other dangerous diseases, for the sake of a long life. In the same way that Christianity once predicated the meaning of life (immortality) focusing on control of the spirit, now the health industry predicates the meaning of life (survival) focusing on control of the body. Historically, the effort to control the spirit crept into control of the body, and we see the same mission creep in with the health industry's control of the body, influencing the human spirit. In focusing on control of the spirit, the body was controlled for the sake of the human spirit; in focusing on the body, the human spirit is controlled for the sake of the body. The body, as object, belongs to the health industry that deploys medical techniques to achieve proper cholesterol levels and other standard measures of health. In this way, the body belongs less and less to the individual who inhabits it, such that the medical and legal communities feel perfectly comfortable forbidding pregnant women from drinking, smoking, or consuming recreational drugs.

Tierney points out that, for Baudrillard, this new cultural security created by the health care industry generates a social control that is required to ensure long, safe lives and natural deaths for individuals, and ends up producing a dead culture.[60]

> Thus came safety: mummified in his helmet, his seatbelt, all the paraphernalia of security, wrapped up in the security myth, the driver is nothing but a corpse, closed up in another, non-mythic, death as neutral and objective as technology, noiseless and expertly crafted. Riveted to his machine, glued to the spot in it, he no longer runs the risk of dying, since he is already dead. This is the secret of security, like a steak under cellophane: *to surround you with a sarcophagus in order to prevent you from dying.*[61]

The health industry spins the myth of security by constantly providing new techniques and technologies for improving safety—baby seats, new airport screening protocols, and healthier diets. All of these security measures transform your body into the steak in the cellophane, objectified, protected, and utterly in the grasp of the health industry: the *They*. The death Baudrillard speaks of is an ironic death, in that the individual is far less likely to die, but also is far less likely to live his or her own, authentic life.

We might respond to this cultural analysis of the fitness, health care, and risk-management industries by simply asking, "What is wrong with staying healthy and fit? What is wrong with avoiding danger? Should we not wish to live long, healthy lives so that we might pursue those things in our lives that are meaningful? How is the pursuit of a long, healthy life contrary to a meaningful life?" Surely we cannot find authentic existence if we engage in risky behaviors and die. Any utilitarian analysis would conclude that maintaining a healthy body is more likely to help us achieve our life goals. As obvious as this response may seem, however, there lurks here a paradox—namely that, in neatly conforming to the health industry, we objectify ourselves to ensure our subjectivity. Once objectified, we cannot easily find subjective meaning in our lives because our lives are the same lives everyone lives.

We see the paradox in the health industry itself. The company that sells the sports drink Gatorade—designed to enhance athletic performance—is the same company that that uses the slogan "Coke Adds Life," to sell a soft drink recognized by the health care industry as unhealthy.[62] The fitness, health care, and risk-management industries advertise their products in the same way that other commodities are advertised: always with the promise of improving the quality of life for the buyer. The cultural objectification of our bodies for the sake of health is almost indistinguishable from the cultural objectification of our lives. Both follow the same culturally established rules and regulations for advertising, and both create the same consumer culture that offers us pharmaceuticals, diet books, exercise equipment, and low-carb beer, and by their nature, these products must be designed for general consumption, for everyone, and never for a unique individual.

The famous medieval school of medicine in Salerno, Italy, offers an alternative vision for an approach to health that leaves more autonomy regarding individual death. The Salerno school represented no single medical authority, but rather was a community of medical practitioners who produced patient-specific cures based on the Aristotelian principle of moderation. After leaving the care of the physicians in Salerno, patients were advised that the best medicine is good humor, rest, and sobriety.[63] This generic prescription for health intends to promote a long, healthy life, but it differs from the contemporary health industry in three important ways.

First, like Aristotle, the School of Salerno acknowledges that what counts as moderate for one person might not be moderate for another. Aristotle uses the example of the wrestler Milo who eats 10 pounds of meat a day. He points out that although this is a moderate amount of meat for Milo, who trains all day long, it would not be a moderate amount of meat for most other people.[64] In the same vein, the School of Salerno acknowledges that different customs have value in and of themselves. Patients are recommended not to abandon their customs, even if those customs appear strange, because "long use is a second nature taken."[65] Here we see an approach to health that recognizes and supports diverse modes of life.

Second, the prescription of moderation concerns virtues of the mind and the body. The School regularly considers the relationship between individual temper and health, and discusses the advantages of good humor and rest against the disadvantageous of overindulgence, pride, and dishonesty.[66] Finally, the Salerno School offers no quantification of the health of our bodies. Instead of being advised to ask our doctor if we are healthy enough for sex, we are told that "Venus recreation doth no harm, yet may too much thereof turne to a scourge."[67] The patient is warned that the behavior can be both beneficial and detrimental, but it is the patient, not the physician, who is left to determine the beneficial course, based upon his or her own goals and interests.

We might argue that sophisticated, modern health care products tailor to individual needs, that modern physicians remain sensitive to the specific individual needs of their patients, and that physicians respect diverse ways of life. The guiding principles of modern bioethics are autonomy, beneficence, non-maleficence, and justice, suggesting that the modern health industry places the interests of the patient first. These are reasonable defenses of modern medicine over its medieval counterpart, but no such defense is necessary. The purpose of the Salerno example is not to recommend a return to pre-modern techniques. Rather, the Salerno example demonstrates that it is possible to conceive of health care that does not quantify our lives from birth to death and cause us to fall victim to the curious paradox Bauman identifies. What the Bauman paradox demonstrates is that the modern approach to medicine vitiates precisely the thing that the continental thinkers would have us most concerned with: the individual.

Tierney sees the same paradox in questions regarding euthanasia and assisted suicide. Both generally have been championed as techniques for providing greater autonomy to the individual in making end-of-life decisions. The general fear regarding euthanasia and assisted suicide is that the health industry might establish protocols that designate certain groups of people as not only having a right to die, but rather an obligation to die.[68] Tierney points out that in Holland experience with assisted suicide produced neither effect. Instead, even though the Dutch adopted measures to allow for euthanasia and assisted suicide on the basis of enhancing patient autonomy and self-determination, the result actually increased the paternalistic power of the medical profession above its last limit, the law.[69] Similarly, in the United States, the matter primarily is being discussed in the courts, where the legal and medical authorities are finding consensus that the physician should decide whether a suicide request is rational or emotional—thus leaving the fate of the individual in the hands of the medical industry.[70] Although there is little doubt that the situation in Holland and the United States remains more nuanced than Tierney's characterization, Tierney does neatly capture the concern that begins with Dostoyevsky's Idiot and is crystalized in the work of Rilke: The institutionalization of end-of-life choices rarely produces greater individual autonomy.

For this reason, Tierney concludes that we should understand the question of euthanasia and assisted suicide ironically. Based on his analysis of Heidegger's analysis of death, and the input of Bauman and Baudrillard, Tierney argues that we find ourselves in a cultural position that makes any public-policy approach unlikely to enhance the individual's ability to retain authentic control over his or her own death. Because Heidegger's "anxiety in the face of death" might have supported the modern project of evading death through medicine, anxiety about the possibility of a prolonged existence in oblivion, or the fear of a long and painful death, might only serve to expand medicine's normalizing power in the realm of suicide.[71] Although he does not acknowledge it, Tierney's conclusion reflects Derrida's conclusion that the aporia of death necessarily deconstructs conventional ethical authority and gives way to a transcendental, absolute conscience. Tierney describes this move as a shift from ethics to irony.

> For if any freedom is to be gleaned from late modernity's engagement with death, I think it will emerge not out of anxiety or fear, but rather from a sense of irony about the extent to which modernity has gone in its attempt to order death. Irony appears to be the least dangerous stance to take towards death today . . . not just in the idea that the right to assisted suicide is becoming an important element of personal freedom, but also in the realization that one of the greatest threats to this freedom may be the medical and legal recognition of suicide as a right.[72]

Tierney echoes Dostoyevsky's initial concern that our ability to take our lives and deaths into our own hands remains precarious. No matter how seriously we attempt this, our efforts must necessarily fall into the hands of those who will judge whether we are sane and whether we are serious, and that judgment invariably will be informed by *everydayness*, the very thing the continental philosophers hoped to avoid. As has been shown, the ironic, aporic, or anxious approach to death does not dictate whether one should or should not consider suicide as part of an authentic approach to life, but only demonstrates that a conventional medical or legal policy, no matter how well intended, is unlikely to produce personal autonomy toward death. Rather, this autonomy must be arrived at on our own, even if that means bringing a pistol to a dinner party.

Notes

1. Arthur Conan Doyle, *A Study in Scarlet and the Sign of Four* (Mineola, NY: Dover Publications, 2003), 9.

2. Conan Doyle, 9.

3. Edgar Allan Poe, "The Murders in the Rue Morgue," in *Ten Great Mysteries by Edgar Allan Poe*, ed. Groff Conklin (New York: Scholastic, 1989), 6 (emphasis original).

4. Poe, "The Murders in the Rue Morgue," 3–5 (emphasis original).

5. Fyodor Dostoyevsky, *The Idiot*, trans. Henry Carlisle and Olga Carlisle (New York: New American Library, 1969), 407–14.

6. Dostoyevsky, 413.

7. Martin Heidegger, *Being and Time*, trans. John Macquarrie and Edward Robinson (New York: Harper and Row, 1962), 164.

8. Theodore Adorno, *The Culture Industry* (New York: Routledge, 1999), 190.

9. Dostoyevsky, 412–13.

10. Walter Kaufmann, *Existentialism from Dostoevsky to Sartre* (New York: New American Library, 1975), 135.

11. Friedrich Nietzsche, *The Twilight of the Idols*, trans. Anthony Ludovici (New York: Macmillan, 1927), xviii.

12. Friedrich Nietzsche, *Thus Spoke Zarathustra*, trans. Thomas Common (London: George Allen & Unwin, 1967), 125.

13. Nietzsche, 128.

14. Ibid.

15. Ibid.

16. Rainer Maria Rilke, *The Notes of Malte Laurids Brigge,* trans. M. D. Herter Norton (New York: W. W. Norton, 1949), 17–18.

17. Ryan Bailey, "The Case of Doctor Anna Pou—Physician Liability in Emergency Situations," in *AMA Journal of Ethics*, accessed December13, 2015. http://journalofethics.ama-assn.org/2010/09/hlaw1-1009.html.

18. Rilke, 135.

19. Nietzsche, 129.

20. Ibid., 128–29.

21. Aristotle, "The Nicomachean Ethics," in *The Internet Classics Archive*, accessed December 13, 2015. http://classics.mit.edu/Aristotle/nicomachaen.1.i.html.

22. Nietzsche, 129–30.

23. Ibid., 129.

24. Ibid., 128.

25. Dostoyevsky, 434.

26. Jose Ortega, "Man Has No Nature," in *Existentialism from Dostoevsky to Sartre*, ed. Walter Kaufmann (New York: New American Library, 1975), 154.

27. Ortega, 155.

28. Søren Kierkegaard, *Sickness Unto Death* (Princeton, NJ: Princeton University Press, 1941), 48, accessed December 8, 2015, http://www.naturalthinker.net/trl/texts/Kierkegaard,Soren/TheSicknessUntoDeath.pdf.

29. Heidegger, 276.

30. Ibid., 290.

31. Ibid., 297.

32. Ibid.

33. Ibid., 291.

34. Kierkegaard, 104.

35. Heidegger, 294.

36. Ibid.

37. Ibid.

38. Ibid., 305.

39. Ibid., 311.

40. Ibid., 308.

41. Ibid., 294.

42. Tierney, Thomas, "Death, Medicine and the Right to Die: An Engagement with Heidegger, Bauman and Baudrillard," in *Body and Society,* vol. 3, issue 4 (1997), 51.

43. Jacques Derrida, *Aporias* trans. Thomas Dutoit (Stanford, CA: Stanford University Press, 1993), 68.

44. Derrida, *Aporias,* 76. Analysis of Aporias by Megan Neatherland.

45. Jacques Derrida, *Gift of Death,* trans. David Wills (Chicago: The University of Chicago Press, 1995).

46. Jean Paul Sartre, "Existentialism is a Humanism," ed. Walter Kaufmann (New York: New American Library, 1975), 351.

47. William Styron, *Sophie's Choice* (New York: Random House, 1979).

48. Scott David Foutz, "Jacques Derrida's *The Gift of Death,*" trans. David Wills (Univ. Chicago Press, 1995), accessed November 15, 2015, http://www.quodlibet.net/gift.shtml.

49. Derrida, *The Gift of Death,* 109.

50. Tierney, 52.

51. Ibid., 57.

52. Zygmunt Bauman, *Mortality, Immortality and Other Life Strategies,* in "Death, Medicine and the Right to Die: An Engagement with Heidegger, Bauman and Baudrillard," in *Body and Society,* vol. 3, no. 4, 1997, 57.

53. Bauman, 57.

54. Tierney, 58.

55. Bauman, 59.

56. Tierney, 61.

57. Ibid., 60.

58. Ibid., 67.

59. Ibid., 60.

60. Tierney, 69.

61. Ibid.

62. "Soda Health Facts: Are Soft Drinks Really Bad for You?" WebMD, accessed December 15, 2015. http://www.webmd.com/diet/sodas-and-your-health-risks-debated?page=4.

63. *The School of Salernum,* trans. Sir John Harington (Salerno: Ente Provinciale Per Il Turismo, 2006), 17.

64. Aristotle, *Nicomachean Ethics,* in *The Internet Classics Archive,* accessed December 15, 2015. http://classics.mit.edu/Aristotle/nicomachaen.2.ii.html.

65. *The School of Salernum,* 50.

66. Ibid., 75.

67. Ibid., 70.

68. Tierney, 70.

69. Ibid., 71.

70. Ibid., 72.

71. Ibid., 74.

72. Ibid.

CHAPTER SIX

Christian Perspectives on Assisted Dying: An Issue for Religious Ethics

Lloyd Steffen

The purpose of this chapter is to address the issue of assisted dying from a Christian perspective. Understanding this issue requires first grasping how a religious ethic differs from those philosophical ethical perspectives such as virtue ethics or utilitarianism that address moral meaning outside the boundaries of religion and specific religious traditions. This general concern with religious ethics provokes a question specific to Christian ethics, namely, "Is diversity in ethical thinking possible within the context of Christian faith affirmations?" Put another way, "How can Christians disagree with one another over ethical matters?"

The third section of this chapter provides a formal response to the issue under consideration—Christian perspectives on assisted dying. The task in this section is to provide some indication as to how Christian bodies rather than individual thinkers arrive at ethical conclusions on the topic of assisted dying based on Christian texts, Christian moral traditions, and Christian beliefs and practices. Individual Christian thinkers—theological ethicists in particular—often address ethics issues to influence how the church or other religious bodies in the church will provide guidance on ethical matters for their followers. Thus, this chapter focuses on church directives rather than on the individual Christian voices seeking to influence the church's ethical deliberations.

The fourth and final issue addressed is a constructive argument that follows from the view that Christian ethics might be more flexible on this and other life-and-death issues than those outside the faith suspect. This chapter argues that there is room for diverse views on difficult ethics topics, including assisted dying, just as there can be diverse or contrary views when relying on utilitarianism or virtue ethics as an access point to moral meaning. That Christian ethics necessarily imposes a single response on moral questions or that ethical diversity is lacking due to the impact of Christian values on moral thinking are views held in large part because of the strong ethical stances of Roman Catholicism and evangelical Christianity. Roman Catholicism—which claims the largest Christian body of believers—speaks with a commanding and seemingly unified voice due to its status as a powerful global religious-political institution; and evangelical Christianity often shares moral conclusions with the Catholic perspective even if it arrives at those conclusions by alternative routes. An overarching point that is emphasized in this chapter is that Christianity is complex and variegated. From this understanding, the chapter concludes with a natural law–based ethical proposal that is consistent with a Christian perspective on the issue of assisted dying in some theological particulars; and it will both oppose active assistance to the dying in general but allow for it in specific cases.

With the direction of this chapter now laid out, let us address the first question, "How does an ethic grounded in religion differ from more philosophical ethics approaches with which we might be familiar in a nonreligious or secular context?"

Religious Ethics

Religious ethics function as any secular ethic would to guide behavior and provide tools and resources for assessing the best way to realize action that is good, right, and fitting. The question is reasonably asked, however, "Compared to a secular and more philosophically neutral perspective, does a religious ethic lead to different moral conclusions, or is a religious ethic distinct in how it stresses motives and intentions—reasons for acting one way rather than another—rather than ethical conclusions?"

If religious perspectives claim to have moral insight on ethics issues such as euthanasia or physician-assisted suicide, then clarifying how a religious ethic functions as an ethic is important to a moral analysis of the issue. How seriously is one to take the religious contribution to such an analysis if one is not religious? How should one go about settling a disagreement between differing ethical perspectives among different religious viewpoints? Is a religious ethic by definition a sectarian perspective that makes no sense except for those who avow the tenets of a specific religion or the specific form of a particular religion?

Ethics essentially is a philosophical enterprise that addresses question of goodness, value, character, and right action. Ethics asks the questions, "Why do people do what they do?" and "Why should a person do one thing rather than another?" Ethics holds that practical reason is able to discern goodness with most ethical theories holding that human beings seek to use practical reason to act in ways that reason itself recognizes as good, right, and fitting. Inquiring into how religious ethics work reminds us that an enduring issue in ethics is that of authority. On what basis and by what—or whose—authority does one decide how best to act? Philosophical ethics and religious ethics both seek to serve the ethical aim of realizing what is good, right, and fitting, but in their appeal to authority to determine how one action is preferable to another differences arise.

In the West, the ancient Greeks established that good action arose from a good character; the aim of a meaningful life was the realization of happiness, and happiness was derived from being a person who pursued excellence of character. Virtue therefore was the source of ethical norms. Although the focus of ethics was on character and on the question "What kind of person should I be?" rather than "What should I do?", virtuous character was itself a product of using reason in ways that helped to discern goodness and thus instill good behaviors. Reason directed that persons seek happiness by avoiding excess and deficiency in their behaviors and instead follow a temperate "middle way." The aim of ethical life—human happiness—was achieved through virtuous living in accordance with reason. Reason supported and sustained the ancient Greek approach to the moral life, and one can find similar approaches to ethics in Asian culture, especially in Confucianism, where the cultivation of honored traits of character dear to Chinese society and the Chinese understanding of the "way of Heaven" were held up for emulation. Confucianism identified various virtues that prevailed as guides to character development and right action and influenced the lives of Chinese people for millennia.

In the West, the Enlightenment era emphasized a new and commanding role for reason in the formulation of ethical theory. The foundation authority for ethics in the work of Immanuel Kant, whose work in ethics is still read and is still influential—many university departments of philosophy have teachers committed to the Kantian ethical perspective—was, again, reason. Kant articulated formal rational principles that if followed would, by reason's command, determine how to act to realize right action. In articulating the Categorical Imperative, Kant found a grounding for ethics in a rational principle that states that if an action is right for me to do it is right for all to do and, conversely, any action that is wrong for me is also wrong for anyone. Kant's appeal to this principle of universalizability established the authoritative basis for determining moral meaning in reason and in rational principles conformed to reason. In another run at reason-based ethical imperatives, Kant articulated a "respect for persons" principle, which recognizes unrestricted moral worth in the rational agent, whose status as "person" is such as to bestow upon all persons moral worth due to the possession of reason. Persons defined as rational agents must not be treated merely as a means to any end but must be respected as possessing intrinsic moral worth because they possess reason. Kant's ethic states that rational agents have a duty to do what reason bids them do, which is to obey the principles of universalizability and respect for persons; and thus it is considered a duty-based or a "deontological" ethic, which captures out of the Greek the idea of ethics as a science of duty ("deon" meaning "duty" and "logos" meaning "study of" or "science of").

Utilitarianism is another perspective that arose from Enlightenment thinking, with Jeremy Bentham and John Stuart Mill as its main proponents. This ethic also appeals to the authority of reason, embodying the Enlightenment confidence in reason as the source of knowledge and the authority for ethical understanding. The utilitarian ethic holds that the action is good, right, and fitting that produces the most utility for the greatest number. The "utility" could be pleasure, as it was for Bentham, or happiness, as it was for Mill. The idea is that one runs a calculus, tries to foresee the consequences of various options for action, then opts for that action that maximizes utility for the greatest number. This is a rational determination of the "best" action and this means "best" in the moral sense, as in "the most ethically appropriate" action. A person determines outcomes and consequences to establish moral meaning. Kant's ethic focused on intention and the good will, and paid no attention to consequences. Utilitarians moved in the opposite direction, basing moral meaning on reason's ability to calculate benefits over burdens (utility over disutility) in projected outcomes and reasonably foreseen consequences. Both ethical approaches—different as they are—appeal to reason as the arbiter of moral truth. Reason, then, holds the authority to determine moral meaning.

Religious ethics recognize a different foundational authority for establishing action that is good, right, and fitting. That authority is not reason, but a transcendental source of meaning and value. In Western religions that affirm theism—and that is the context at present given this chapter's topic—that source authority is God. No Western religion claims that human persons have direct access to the mind of God and know God's will directly, but Western traditions affirm the goodness of God and hold that God—being omniscient—knows in every situation which action would be the good, right, and fitting action. Practitioners of a religious faith who seek ethical guidance within the context of their tradition believe that God has revealed the divine will in matters that include moral matters; and they thus turn to those points of access to God's will that reveal what God would have the faithful do to align themselves with the divine understanding of what is good, right, and fitting. Thus, to understand the divine will in moral matters, the faithful turn to the conveyances of divine revelation, including symbols, sacred texts, interpreters, traditions of interpretation, and practices that comprise ethical perspectives grounded in religious understanding. Religious persons also can vest revelatory authority in such matters as religious experiences, corporate membership and community life, rituals, and any other response to revelation that could be considered appropriate to what is believed about the divine will in a particular tradition. Religious traditions articulate expectations for human behavior on the belief that God wants people to act in ways that align human behavior with divine intention and purpose; and thus is achieved the foundation of religious ethics as an ethic.

Religious ethics as a normative ethic concerned with what people do and how they act for certain reasons is, like any other ethic, concerned with goodness and right action. What distinguishes a religious ethic from a secular philosophical ethic grounded in reason is the foundational authority for ethical understanding. In "divine command" ethics, philosophical ethics actually recognizes religious ethics as a legitimate philosophical ethics perspective, for if ethics asks "Why do people do what they do?" then a person who acts out of religious justification for action and under direction of a "divine command" ethics could respond meaningfully, coherently, and reasonably saying, "I do what I do because an infallible arbiter of moral truth, God, has directed me to act this way rather than that."

Is a divine command ethic a weak sister to those imposing the reason-based Enlightenment ethics we have received from intellectual giants such as Kant and Mill? No. A religious ethic has two potentially fatal flaws. The first is that believers could be wrong about the transcendent reality they accept as authoritative, for such an authority might not in actuality exist (i.e., there is no God). The second is that believers could be mistaken in how they interpret the divine will because it is not communicated directly but rather through revelation—meaning that human beings have to interpret the divine communications as they come to human beings through texts, experiences, and traditions. Neither of these potential problems with a divine command ethic is a minor problem. Having acknowledged these issues, however, it also can be said that a divine command ethic—which is grounded in confidence that the divine will has been revealed and correctly received—provides a very strong basis for action. Some religions, such as Judaism, identify very specific divine commands as their ethical foundation. In Judaism it is the 613 commands or *mitzvoth* in the Torah. Christianity grounds ethical direction in certain stories, parables, sermonic commands, and virtues that reflect a vision of life with God believed to be inspired by God through revelation of the divine will in the life and work of Jesus of Nazareth and leaders like St. Paul—for example the Sermon on the Mount, or the virtues and attitudes of love, joy, peace, patience, kindness, and others that St. Paul announces in Galatians (Galatians 5.22–25). Divine command as an ethic is a philosophically valid ethic even if many people would question its soundness, but to be able to say that "I do what I do because God, the infallible and all-knowing source of moral knowledge, directs me to do this rather than that" is to act on the basis of moral certainty few other ethical perspectives can generate.

Religious ethics often can yield to absolutism in ethical matters—so can Kantian ethics for that matter—because of the degree of confidence people have that the revelation of the divine will has been issued actually and received without error. Although such ethical absolutism is not an ethical stance characteristic of all (perhaps not even many) religious believers, it is a possibility given the transcendent source of ethical directives. To possess confidence that one has ethical direction from God, that such direction has been clearly communicated and accurately received, creates a very strong place to stand ethically. Religious ethics are not monolithic and can differ from tradition to tradition, from community to community, and even from individual to individual within a tradition, and differences can arise because of the degree of confidence believers and communities have in the ability of human beings to receive ethical directives from the divine will with accuracy. Religious believers might not doubt that God knows with certainty the good, right, and fitting thing to do, but they could exhibit humility and refuse to claim that a transmission of the divine will has come to fallible human beings purely and without interpretation and absent misunderstanding. Religious believers inclined to humility could reference such factors as sin or the capacity of human beings to act perversely, knowing the good and choosing not to do it; and in the face of difficult ethical situations they might reference teachings about human frailty and fallenness, which is a comment on the limitations of human volition and of reason itself.

Religious ethics as a type of ethics is not inherently irrational or even necessarily nonrational, and the results of following a religious ethic often yield actions indistinguishable from those grounded in a reason-based ethic. A Christian, a Muslim, and a Jew will all hold that lying is a moral offense, and so will a philosophical Kantian and a secular utilitarian. The reasons for action will differ for each of these adherents to a particular moral or moral-religious viewpoint, but the behavior will be the same, which is important when considering ethics as an enterprise that deals with universals. It is worth remembering that both Kant and Mill believed that in formulating ethics in accord with reason they were providing contemporary justification for prescriptions found in religious ethics, altering the foundation of justification toward reason but endorsing the religious vision for good action. As Mill said, "In the golden rule of Jesus of Nazareth, we read the complete spirit of the ethics of utilitarianism. To do as you are done by, and to love your neighbor as yourself, constitute the ideal perfection of utilitarian morality."[1]

Religious ethics could, in following a religious vision, move in directions contrary to the dictates of prudential or practical reason. When Jesus encourages followers to turn the other cheek and give up self-defense (Matthew 5.39), when the Hebrew Bible imposes the death penalty for a child striking a parent (Exodus 21.15), or when Islamic Penal Code imposes death for adultery (Article 102—"An adulterous man shall be buried in a ditch up to near his waist and an adulterous woman up to near her chest and then stoned to death"),[2] these violate ordinary moral sensibilities even if some religious adherents still endorse them. Religious ethics might move in directions that violate the moral sensibilities of those conformed to secular ethical and cultural norms, and for this reason religious ethics are subject to moral evaluation, just as modern secular or reason-based ethical norms are subject the same way from the point of view of religious ethics. The essential ethical task concerning religion and ethics is that religious people have to make decisions about how they want to be religious, and thus is religion in the sense of choosing to be religious subject to ethical critique. In light of that critique, religious people might act in ways deemed irrational, and certain actions endorsed by religion could defy modern moral sensibilities whatever their justification might have been at a previous time. To legitimate actions that were at one time justifiable but now seem no longer to withstand critical moral scrutiny, however, is to invoke the very ethical relativism that many who espouse religious ethics wish to condemn.

People trying to align their actions with their avowed religious interpretations might act in ways that appear irrational, but this is not confined

to religious ethics. Kant's stance on bodily integrity that would today prohibit organ donation to save a life also could appear irrational.[3] In the
end, religious ethics should be approached as ethics based on a distinctive
notion of authority; religious ethics also can be evaluated as supporting
actions that reasonable people would recognize as reasonable. When *any*
ethic is employed to endorse actions that can be evaluated as irrational
or harmful to persons, that ethical stance ought to be subject to critique.
Such actions—when held up against standards of reasonableness—can be
shown to be inadequate, falling short of the vision of goodness to which
any and all ethical perspectives aspire.

We can now note a few things about Christian ethics.

Christian Ethics

Another question worth asking concerns the specific contribution of a
religious ethic grounded in Christianity and what a Christian ethic thus
conceived would have to offer. Is there a view on assisted dying—or on
any ethical issue—that is clearly and indisputably identifiable as Christian,
so that believers are bound to acting consistently with that ethic at the risk
of violating their allegiance to, or acceptance by, the faith? Christianity as
a religion sponsors ethical outlooks for the faithful, but the problem that
one confronts in talking about a "Christian ethic" on assisted dying and
euthanasia (or on any number of other ethical issues) is that there are different perspectives offered from within the Christian context, specifically
within the context of Christian communities, namely, the church; and all
of these communities, different as they might be from one another, claim
continuity with Christian practice and belief and what could be called a
Christian worldview. "How can this be?" one might reasonably ask. Good
question.

An adequate response to this question would open us to a deep historical study not possible here. Suffice it to say, however, that that ethical diversity is a hallmark of that religious ethic we call "Christian." How
has such diversity arisen within the world's largest religion? History has
so transpired since the founding of Christianity in the first century of
the common era, that we now have three Christianities generally housed
under the headings of Catholic, Protestant, and Orthodox—but that is
just the start. Roman Catholicism is a huge religion with more than 1.2
billion members,[4] but there are other forms of Catholicism with 21 different traditional rites in communion with Rome. Denominationalism
marks Protestant Christianity and there are literally thousands of forms of
Protestant Christianity around the world. Orthodoxy is a communion of

14 regional churches located traditionally in Eastern Europe, Russia, and Greece. Christianity is a fragmented religion in many ways, so it should not be a surprise that ethical viewpoints can vary widely, especially in light of the Protestant move to leave to individual conscience interpretation of Scripture, which could have a marked effect on Christians determining ethical direction.

How Christians go about making ethical determinations thus can vary widely. Natural Law plays a large role in Roman Catholic ethical determinations, but in Protestantism there is appeal to such ethical viewpoints as utilitarianism and virtue ethics, as in Joseph Fletcher's widely read book, *Situation Ethics.*[5] This influential book interpreted Christian ethics through application of act utilitarianism with "love"—Christian love, *agape*—supplying content to the principle of utility: That act is right which maximizes love for the greatest number. There also are even ideas that different forms of Christianity emphasize particular aspects of the Trinity, so Roman Catholics and Reformed Protestants are associated with God as Father/Creator and emphasize Law; pietistic Christians, Franciscan Catholics, or Protestant Anabaptists who reflect lives seeking to emulate the life of Jesus as the Christ, stress the pacifism and purity of Christ's life and teaching; and Pentecostals reflect a Christianity under the dominating influence of the Holy Spirit.

Recognizing the diversity of theological orientations is prelude to any effort to comment on the idea of a Christian ethic on such difficult and divisive topics as assisted suicide and euthanasia. Differing Christian ethical perspectives are possible—which is also to say that there is no one "Christian" perspective on any ethical issue, whether it is euthanasia, assisted dying, abortion, war, peace, or any other ethics topic. Like-minded people of faith will join communities and denominations or church bodies with which they share a theological orientation and understanding, and some of these bodies will in deliberation as a body take stances on issues. It must be remembered, however, that whereas the direction of a papal encyclical might prove all important to many Catholics, Protestants often disagree with any effort of their own denomination to speak to such issues on their behalf. In Protestantism, statements directed to ethics issues often come with an implicit disclaimer that the body issuing the statement is speaking for itself and not for any particular church in the denomination or on behalf of individual members or even for the denomination itself.

The diversity of opinion on ethical issues within the religion of Christianity cannot be overemphasized, and the differences will be grounded in Church teaching, in scriptural interpretation, and in the application of values held to be important for Christian belief and practice. Different forms of Christianity—churches, church bodies, and denominations—will rely to greater or lesser degree on how these interpretations and values are to be applied and used for purposes of ethical evaluation. Ethical justification for a position on an issue will appeal to Christian values and can invoke sacred Scriptures, the work of councils, or theologians of high standing in the community. Seen from afar, however, Christianity provides a religious ethic that is open to differing interpretation based on the tradition, the particular form of Christianity, including the denomination or church body, and the conscience of individual believers. Widespread agreement can often be found among Christians, but reasons for holding certain views can differ based upon a use of distinct aspects of the faith tradition. Protestants by tradition have relied upon interpretation of Scripture in accordance with Martin Luther's dictum of *sola scriptura* and his notion that "everyone is his or her own priest." Conversely, Roman Catholics rely on local priests, bishops, councils, and popes to deliberate on issues in light of Scripture and then invoke their authority within the tradition of interpretation to direct moral attention and adherence to ethical stances. Protestants and Catholics can wind up in the same place advocating similar actions, but each relies on a different process of reasoning and application of Christian values.

Christian Views of Assisted Suicide and Euthanasia

Having now claimed that ethical diversity can be expected among Christians in the practice of their faith and in their ethical determinations, we can turn to the topic of euthanasia and assisted suicide. The first thing that must be said might appear to negate everything just argued, for a discussion of how Christian ethics would approach the issue of assisted dying can proceed on this proposition, namely, that in general Christians oppose active euthanasia and assisted suicide, including physician-assisted suicide. Christians (again, in general) would hold this position for reasons related to their understanding of core values upheld in the faith tradition, interpretations of sacred texts, and long-standing biblically grounded faith-based traditions of moral interpretation.

In reference to the discussion above about religious ethics as a reasonable way of approaching the task of ethics and the assertion made that conclusions about moral meaning drawn in the context of a religious ethic often can reach conclusions similar to reason-based ethical directives, we should note that euthanasia and assisted suicide are widely opposed in secular, nonreligious ethical perspectives. Active euthanasia and assisted suicide are troubling issues for ethics in general—religious and nonreligious—because these activities involve killing, and killing a person is the most serious moral issue on the ethics agenda. Some killings might be morally justifiable, but there is a presumption in ethics that killing is wrong, and to justify a killing requires serious moral deliberation.

The ethical opposition to assisted dying that Christians will offer does not appeal to a violation of a principle of respect for persons or the harmful consequences to the medical profession if doctors are seen as agents who end life directly or assist in a suicide—these could be arguments a deontologist or a utilitarian might offer, respectively. The Christian as ethical thinker, rather, will vest opposition in religiously relevant values and ideas, especially in scriptural warrants and ethical directives from the tradition itself. Assisted death is rather easy to oppose from both a religious and a nonreligious or secular ethical perspective, and it even could be said that there is a general moral agreement among all persons of goodwill that ordinarily a physician ought not to be about the work of euthanizing patients or helping them to commit suicide. Christians, non-Christian religious people, and those who hold secular or nonreligious theories of ethics can share conclusions about moral meaning, and although those conclusions are derived from different systems of justification, the moral conclusions to be drawn from differing systems of justification can lead to a similar action outcome, in this case, opposition to assisted dying. There is nothing unreasonable in opposing assisted dying on religious grounds, morally speaking, but advocates for the different routes to that conclusion of opposition to assisted dying—religious on the one hand, secular and reason-based on the other—would not agree on the adequacy of the reasons the other perspectives would advance in support of their conclusion.

Christian Scriptures do not address in any explicit way the topic of assisted dying, euthanasia, or physician-assisted suicide, but the values Christians affirm relevant to the issue are scripturally based and also involve traditions of ethical thought within various forms of Christianity. A spectrum of views on the topic of assisted dying can be identified, with some Christian perspectives taking an absolutist stance of opposition to assisted dying, as was expressed in a 2009 statement on euthanasia posted on an evangelical Protestant Christian website.

> The Christian perspective on the subject of "assisted suicide" is simple. We believe in the sanctity of life from the moment of conception until natural death. There are over 60 passages of Scripture in the Bible that relate to the sanctity of life, beginning with "Thou Shalt Not Kill." Ultimately, we believe that God is the giver and taker of life and that His will in such matters takes precedence over man's [sic] will.[6]

The statement goes on to give support to the idea that God wants humans to experience all that life has to offer, even suffering, and because God has a reason "for everything under heaven," God has a reason for allowing people to suffer. Moreover, modern medical intervention can eliminate or diminish pain, so the statement goes on to support palliative care in terminal situations if such care "does not seek to lengthen or shorten the days of a dying person." "The purpose is never to take direct action to cause death."[7]

Worth noting in this statement is how close it is in its conclusion to a Roman Catholic perspective, especially in its claim (which is identical to what one would expect on this issue from the Roman Catholic hierarchy) that "we believe in the sanctity of life from the moment of conception until natural death." What distinguishes this statement from a Catholic perspective is its direct appeal to the Bible and the 60 passages that the writers of the statement rely on to back up their interpretation, including the "divine command," namely, "Thou shalt not kill."

At the other end of the Christian ethics spectrum on this issue are statements from certain liberal and mainline Protestant denominations that do not explicitly endorse the idea of active euthanasia, but do respect individual conscience in making a choice for assisted dying as an expression of autonomy and freedom. The United Church of Christ, for example, although not endorsing assisted dying per se, did pass a resolution at its Twenty Sixth General Synod in 2007, calling on church members to study the issue and report back to the denomination views on the following proposition:

> that on the grounds of compassion and choice, if strict safeguards to prevent abuse are followed, a terminally ill and mentally competent adult should have a legal right to request and receive medication from a willing physician to hasten death if the patient finds his or her suffering to be unbearable.[8]

Like the "absolute opposition" statement quoted above, the United Church of Christ resolution is grounded in a declaration of Christian values, namely, that "life is both a sacred and perishable gift from God"; it quotes Scripture in support of its positions, Luke 10:25–37 ("compassion—love acted out—flows from the heart of God") and Psalm 139:7–12 ("God leads us, sustains us and is always with us"); then launches into specific issues relevant to resolution.[9] The resolution discussion arose because of several relevant factors: the recent enactment of the Oregon "Death with Dignity Law;" the lack of any evidence of abuse once the law took effect; the U.S. Supreme Court's decision that the state of Oregon had a right to pass such a law; and then the statement quoted above, preceded by this "Whereas": "Many physicians, religious leaders, dying patients and family members strongly support physician aid in dying with strong safeguards to prevent abuse."[10]

This statement reflects the views of those Protestant Christians who affirm by appeal to conscience and as a matter of faith the right of persons to make decisions about life and death and the right of physicians to assist in the dying process. The statement stops short of endorsing active euthanasia, but it does reject the idea that assisted dying violates Christian sanctity-of-life principles. The statement does not valorize suffering or attach suffering to an expression of God's will for human beings, but sees assisted dying as an act of compassion toward the suffering and a means of showing respect for the dignity of persons if related to compassion; and it affirms a Protestant affirmation of self-determination. As it had done on the abortion issue, the United Church of Christ affirmed that a person's right to make a decision for ending life in the face of difficult dying was a legitimate Christian option on a troubling moral issue.[11]

These two ends of the spectrum show that Christians can approach the issue of assisted dying in different ways and also reflect within the context of religious ethics the very range of opinions nonreligious ethical views would advance, from absolute prohibition to a permissibility for assisted dying for reasons of compassion for the suffering. Those Christians who oppose assisted dying do share certain values with those who support such assistance, and those similar beliefs would include the following: that life is a gift of God; that a person's value in the sight of God is not diminished due to illness or nearness to death; that handicapped or otherwise-abled persons who exhibit vulnerability, mentally or physically, should not be diminished in value compared to other persons and certainly not made a target for assisted dying or euthanasia by proxy; and that there are situations of medical futility where continued attempts to seek cures for illness or injury should not be aggressively pursued.

Those who oppose assisted dying might turn from these common values shared with those who support choice in dying to add other considerations believed to be grounded in Christian values. For example, opponents of assisted dying affirm that human beings bear the image of God and that the value of a human life is sacred due to that image; that the physician's role is to relieve suffering and affirm the value of human life, but that relieving suffering does not extend to producing death in pursuit of that aim. The Christian Medical and Dental Associations (CMDA) in its 2009, "Euthanasia Ethics Statement" put it this way:

[W]e oppose active intervention with the intent to produce death for the relief of suffering, economic considerations or convenience of patient, family or society. We do not oppose withdrawal or failure to institute artificial means of support in patients who are clearly and irreversibly deteriorating, in whom death appears imminent beyond reasonable hope of recovery. . . . The Christian physician, above, all, should be obedient to biblical teaching and sensitive to the counsel of the Christian community.[12]

The statement supports physicians who would refuse on grounds of conscience to be involved in assisted dying, rejecting euthanasia yet encouraging alternatives such as palliative care and interventions to "provide companionship, and give opportunity for spiritual support and counseling."[13] In a separate statement on "Physician Assisted Suicide and Euthanasia," this Christian organization of medical and dental professionals advanced the view that physician-assisted dying is "dangerous for physicians and healthcare workers, but it is also dangerous for our country, our health care system and for every patient." The statement concludes by quoting the American Medical Association's Code of Ethics, which states, "Physician-assisted suicide is fundamentally incompatible with the physician's role as healer, would be difficult to control and would pose serious societal risks."[14]

Individual decision making in matters of assisted dying have been supported by Episcopalians, although in England the Anglican Archbishop of Canterbury, Rowan Williams, was unequivocally opposed to right-to-die legislation being debated in Parliament even as his adviser, Professor and Canon Robin Gill, said, "'There is a very strong compassionate case for voluntary euthanasia" and in some cases "there is an overwhelming case for it."[15]

Support for individual conscience to make a free and thus licit decision for assisted death has been advanced by the some regional conferences of the Methodist Church that have endorsed the legalization of physician-assisted dying; and Presbyterians and the United Church of Christ, along with Unitarians and Quakers, have also joined in this perspective.[16] The Evangelical Lutheran Church declared in a 1992 statement its opposition to euthanasia but acknowledged that sometimes inactions that hasten death could constitute "the lesser evil in ambiguous borderline situations—for example when pain becomes so unmanageable that life is indistinguishable from torture," adding that "[h]ealth care professionals are not required to use all available medical treatment in all circumstances. Medical treatment may be limited in some instances, and death allowed to occur."[17] Pain management is thus a physician responsibility, but the church, according to the Lutheran statement, does not accede to the view that death is a solution to suffering because suffering instead can be an opportunity for Christians to practice faith through acts of caring.[18] The Presbyterian Church has concluded that the withdrawing or withholding of care with foreseen death a consequence—what many would term "passive euthanasia"—can be dissociated from euthanasia and deemed allowable. The Orthodox Church, including the Russian Orthodox Church and the Eastern Orthodox Church, has held consistently to the view that assisted dying and euthanasia are impermissible acts of "moral alienation" that violate the sanctity of human life and are thus impermissible moral violations not to be sanctioned.[19]

The Roman Catholic opposition to assisted dying and euthanasia is deserving of some special attention for reasons including that the Roman Catholic Church influences an enormous number of persons worldwide on ethical issues, and the church takes care to pronounce on issues with a consistent ethical perspective grounded in Scripture, in natural law ethics, which implies appeal to reason, as well as in the teachings and traditions of the Catholic Church.

The Roman Catholic Church opposes euthanasia and assisted suicide on the grounds that human life, the basis of all goods, is a "gift of God's love" and "No one can make an attempt on the life of an innocent person without opposing God's love."[20] As the church's *Declaration on Euthanasia* states, "Intentionally causing one's own death, or suicide, is therefore equally wrong as murder." To assist a person in dying arises from an error in judgment and even if done "perhaps in good faith, [it] does not change the nature of this act of killing, which will always be in itself something to be rejected."[21]

The Roman Catholic Church in its *Catechism* acknowledges that

> Discontinuing medical procedures that are burdensome, dangerous, extraordinary, or disproportionate to the expected outcome can be legitimate; it is the refusal of "over-zealous" treatment, . . . [and] the use of painkillers to alleviate the sufferings of the dying, even at the risk of shortening their days, can be morally in conformity with human dignity if death is not willed as either an end or a means, but only foreseen and tolerated as inevitable.[22]

The church recognizes that

> palliative care is a special form of disinterested charity. As such it should be encouraged. Here one does not will to cause death; one's inability to impede it is merely accepted. The decisions should be made by the patient if he is competent and able or, if not, by those legally entitled to act for the patient, whose reasonable will and legitimate interests must always be respected.[23]

"Direct euthanasia," however, which "consists in putting an end to the lives of handicapped, sick, or dying persons" is a grave wrong. The *Catechism* declares: "It is morally unacceptable."[24]

The Roman Catholic Church also is concerned for those who would seek assistance in suicide because "suicide contradicts the natural inclination of the human being to preserve and perpetuate his life," and although acknowledging that cooperating with a suicide is "contrary to the moral law" and that "grave psychological disturbances, or grave fear of hardship, suffering, or torture can diminish the responsibility of the one committing suicide," suicide is contrary to the "just love of self. It likewise offends love of neighbor because it unjustly breaks the ties of solidarity with family, nation, and other human societies to which we continue to have obligations."[25] Suicide is "contrary to love for the living God" although, recognizing that those suicidal persons who suffer mental disturbance and thus can be adjudged as suffering diminished capacity, the *Catechism* goes on to say, "We should not despair of the eternal salvation of persons who have taken their own lives. By ways known to him alone, God can provide the opportunity for salutary repentance."[26]

Assisted dying raises the issue of care for the dying, allowing the gravely ill to die by withholding care or acting in a way that avoids interference with the natural dying process. Not all agree that it is reasonable to term a refusal of medical intervention that then leads to death as being passive euthanasia, for some would view such active inaction as simply allowing nature to take its course. Some of these issues were faced in a speech Pope Pius XII gave before a conference of anesthesiologists on November 24, 1957, in which he addressed the question about keeping a patient alive by means of treatment deemed "extraordinary" (artificial respiration via ventilator) "even against the will of the family."[27] The pope distinguished between "ordinary" and "extraordinary" means and between active euthanasia (a direct and intentional killing) and letting an individual die naturally.

- In ordinary cases the doctor has the right to act in this manner [that is, using the extraordinary means of artificial respiration], but is not bound to do so unless this is the only way of fulfilling another certain moral duty.
- The doctor, however, has no right independent of the patient. He can act only if the patient explicitly or implicitly, directly or indirectly gives him the permission.
- The treatment as described in the question constitutes extraordinary means of preserving life and so there is no obligation to use them or to give the doctor permission to use them.

- The rights and the duties of the family depend on the presumed will of the unconscious patient if he or she is of legal age, and the family, too, is bound to use only ordinary means.

- This case is not to be considered euthanasia in any way; that would never be licit. The interruption of attempts at resuscitation, even when it causes the arrest of circulation, is not more than an indirect cause of the cessation of life, and we must apply in this case the principle of double effect.[28]

The pope's analysis condemns a direct killing of the patient, that is, euthanasia, which is "never licit," and although withholding "extraordinary means" is not euthanasia "in any way," the idea of passive euthanasia or death resulting from nonintervention (i.e., refusal or decision not to resuscitate) seems to be applicable even if justified by invoking the double-effect principle. Double effect refers to good, well-intended actions that have a negative secondary consequence. The principle allows a good action to proceed even if there is a secondary negative effect as long as the unwanted secondary consequence (the double effect) is not intended, even if foreseen.[29] Physicians who provide morphine to patients for the good end of pain management even if the dosage suppresses respiration and leads to death are able to administer such a dose because of the double-effect principle. Pope Pius XII appeals to double effect to withhold or withdraw treatment and allow a person to die in accordance with ordinary and natural means, and his argument is consistent with natural law ethics. The pope condemns euthanasia in absolute terms, yet he allows that physicians may help a patient die "naturally" by appealing to double effect. Physician assistance that prevents an unnatural prolongation of life does not seem to be absolutely restricted, especially because the inaction or passive euthanasia also can be seen as positive well-intentioned action in relation to patient care. The withholding of medical intervention results from decision making that foresees but does not intend the negative consequence of patient death.

The Roman Catholic hierarchy has held that action to avoid needless suffering could be licit when such suffering is created by "extraordinary" technological means that interfere with the natural dying process. Thus is the view advanced that death is a natural part of human life and should be respected as a normal or "ordinary" event, and the dying need to receive care. The medieval hospital was a creation of the Catholic Church, and because the hospital since its founding was a place to care for the sick and dying, the idea of palliation is consistent with Roman Catholic—and Christian—religious values and commitments of care. Christians in general would subscribe to the idea of tending the dying while acting to alleviate unnecessary suffering. Active assistance in dying is condemned, but that is because such assistance is action directed intentionally at causing death. What is not condemned is assisting the dying in proceeding toward death under the guise of direct care and management of pain to alleviate suffering.[30]

A Proposal for a Reason-Based Christian Ethic on Assisted Dying

The approach of Christian ethics to the issue of assisted dying laid out thus far has emphasized that euthanasia is widely condemned as a prohibited killing, as is physician-assisted suicide, which as a form of suicide also is deemed illicit. Many—if not most—Christians believe that these actions violate Christian affirmations that life is a good of life and that it is a gift given to human beings by God, who entrusts human beings with its care. On this theological foundation, Christians in general hold that human life should not be destroyed, certainly not willfully and intentionally, and thus euthanasia and physician-assisted suicide are in general prohibited. Even those Christians who support the right of persons to exercise conscience and request assistance in dying do not take the step of endorsing such actions as good and desirable for all dying persons, but rather as allowable only in those particular medical circumstances when, tragically, individuals are facing intractable pain or loss of dignity in a difficult dying process. These ethical views are consistent with similar conclusions that could be drawn from secular philosophical ethics such as Kantian ethics, which would prohibit such assistance actions, and utilitarianism, which might allow for some exceptions but could easily conclude from a calculation of "greatest good for the greatest number" that such assistance should be disallowed. For consequentialist utilitarians, turning physicians into agents of procured death could be calculated to cause greater harm to society and to the delivery of medical care than would come from assisting in the death of a limited number of individuals for whom palliation might be a reasonable alternative to such assistance in dying. This logic could sway the utilitarian to oppose assistance in dying due to the overriding burden of negative consequences.

The natural law tradition of ethics, however, holds open some possibilities for thinking about the ethics of assisted dying that avoid the absolute prohibitions that can be found in some religious ethics and in some versions of philosophical Kantianism. This chapter concludes by considering possible contributions from natural law ethics. This approach has the advantage of falling on both the side of religious ethics, Christian ethics in particular for purposes here, and on the side of more broadly conceived secular-philosophical ethics.

Natural law ethics holds the "constant assertion that there are objective moral principles which depend upon the nature of the universe"[31] and it asserts reason's capacity and ability to discern such principles and moral meaning. Natural law provides the Roman Catholic moral tradition with a serious philosophical grounding for ethics. Natural law also is the basis for a theological ethics within Catholicism, because God is believed to be the creator of both nature and the human capacity to discern moral meaning through reason, which also is a gift of God. Yet natural law ethics constitute a form of "reason-based" ethics due to the idea that natural law ethics can be construed this way: The image of God—the *imago Dei*—is, in fact, reason itself, and that reason is sufficient unto itself to bring human being to a recognition of a divine reality even if it does not suffice to lead reason to the specific revelation of God's will expressed in Christianity as the Christ event. Ethics, however, in this kind of natural law construction, understands that ethical vision and moral meaning are available through reason, thus rendering natural law ethics reason-based. Natural law as reason-based connects to religious ethics, then, in the sense that reason—which is itself a good of life and a gift of God—can function to conform human life to the ethical injunctions that express the will of God. Not all natural law theorists would affirm this particular view, and some proponents of natural-law thinking might bracket out the question of God but still recognize the objective moral principles that depend upon the nature of the universe. For the moment, however, let us avow that the religious connection in the Roman Catholic treatment in natural law ethics is vital to the religious ethics avowed and affirmed by the church.

Having connected natural law ethics to religion through reason—a good of life and a gift of God—this final section of the chapter calls attention to the possibility of constructing a reason-based Christian ethic that can then be applied to the specific issue of assisted dying. This move depends upon recognizing that a natural law ethic can be considered a religious ethic on Aquinas' view that natural law participates in the eternal law[32] and expresses God's providence as it provides the rational plan according to which all of the natural universe is ordered. Natural law thus can be looped into religious ethics by the Thomistic move of grounding principles of moral meaning in the natural order, which then itself is understood to be an expression of the divine mind. A Christian natural law ethicist working from such a theologically based premise would conclude that good actions are those that are consistent with Christian values, as those values are themselves grounded in natural law, "those objective moral principles which depend upon the nature of the universe."[33]

From this understanding we can move to consider that assisted dying could be configured differently from the rather strict, even absolutist, natural law moral prohibitions on assisted dying drawn by the Roman Catholic hierarchy. The church has, in some of its pronouncements, taken such an absolutist stance, such as on the issue of abortion, with assisted dying appearing to reflect a similar strictness in application of natural law. In proposing to defend natural law as an ethic that appeals to religious ethics, and specifically to Christian ethics (at least in its Roman Catholic configuration), and also to secular ethics, because natural law is built upon reason's recognition of various goods of life that must be preserved and promoted in moral decision making, I seek to moderate the Roman Catholic natural law view that gravitates toward absolutism in its prohibition on euthanasia and assisted suicide. This author would offer the contrary view that "nature" in "natural law" indeed might be more flexible in what it models for human reason. In calling moral absolutism into question, I am yet holding natural law to its anchor in human reason as the means by which the ordering of nature is discerned and incorporated into ethical thinking and moral assessment.

An alternative to the "absolutism" of the Roman Catholic view might proceed along an alternate route, one based on the model of just war thinking, which is another natural law ethical frame preserved and followed by Roman Catholic moral theology. On this alternative moderated view, reason discerns a common moral agreement concerning assisted dying, just as it recognizes such an agreement undergirding just war thinking, which can be articulated thusly: Ordinarily human beings should not use force to settle conflicts. The just war criteria—just cause, last resort, legitimate authority, and the others—provide moral guidance for evaluating whether lifting the common agreement that reasonable people hold against using force can, indeed, be justified. Likewise on assisted dying. We can on this issue articulate a common agreement. This chapter states consistently that, in Christian ethical views and in philosophical views as well, physicians ought not help patients kill themselves or assume the role of agents who help dispatch persons to their deaths, even if requested to do so by suffering people. To extract this view from moral absolutism, simply qualify it by saying "ordinarily"—physicians *ordinarily* ought not actively assist patients in the dying process. Reasonable people could be expected to agree with this common agreement, be they deontologists, utilitarians, virtue ethicists, or religious persons, including people seeking to follow a specifically Christian ethical viewpoint.

As the criteria of just war can be invoked and used to guide moral reasoning to an exception of our common agreement that ordinarily force ought not be used to settle conflicts, a similar move can be made with the issue of assisted dying. Ordinarily, physicians should not kill a patient directly or indirectly, and patients ought not to commit suicide in the face of dying. If an exception is to be considered, however, then what criteria would be used to guide moral reasoning?

This author's suggestion on the issue of physician-assisted suicide (PAS) is the following, which closely reflect central features of Oregon's "Death with Dignity Law."

- The patient makes the request fully informed of his or her situation and prospects.
- The patient's condition is terminal and death is imminent, with six months prospect of life being a generally accepted medical time frame for defining "terminal."
- The patient's request is not prompted by depression, thus a psychological evaluation is necessary.
- The resources of palliative care will prove to be limited and not provide a dignified death or prove fully efficacious in the final period of the end stage.
- The patient's autonomy is to be respected throughout and patients can withdraw the request for PAS at any point in the process.
- The physician who participates must be willing to participate and have no mental reservations about involvement. There must be no coercion placed on the physician or patient by relevant or interested parties, including family, the state, other medical authorities, and insurance companies.
- The actual means of dispatch must be swiftly acting and painless.
- Laws must exempt the physician who follows these guidelines from any prosecution for wrongful death, and the family of the patient must be protected from those who would seek to benefit from PAS, for example an insurance company that seeks to renege on a death benefit due to the patient's suicide.
- Physician-assisted suicide must be approached as a "last resort" that is designed to preserve the value of physician beneficence and autonomous patient decision making in the face of imminent and intractably painful death.
- Actual use of PAS must be publically reported in a timely and regular manner so that any statistical trends showing abuse or discrimination against particular groups because of race, age, sex, or class status can be subjected to investigation and the practice of PAS be halted if evidence of abuse becomes apparent.[34]

Deriving an ethical conclusion from this mode of ethical analysis grounded in natural law can be reasonably understood in secular philosophical ethics—the idea of articulating a reason-based common agreement and considering actual situations in light of justice-related criteria to guide ethical evaluation and decision making. It also has background in those religious ethics that are natural law ethics, however, and which make the Thomistic move of connecting natural law to God's ordering of the universe and to reason's capacity (also a gift of God) to discern moral meaning. Such an ethical approach would not allow ethics to yield to blanket permissions or prohibitions (i.e., absolutist responses). Ethics, rather, becomes the arena where practical reason seeks to discern which actions are morally permissible and which are not. If it were always clear what our duty was, then there would be no need for moral judgment.

This is an ethical proposal that might be of help to broader Christian ethics. This type of natural law ethic could be understood as a means for eschewing absolutes to allow compassion and other Christian values to enter into as factors that help determine moral meaning in assisted-dying issues. What is happening with the dying? What responsibility does the moral community have toward patients when pain itself cannot be adequately regulated or the dignity of persons is undermined by illness or injury?

Christian ethics in general opposes assisted dying, as does this natural law proposal. The question facing Christian ethics is one facing other ethical approaches as well, namely, "What exceptions to our moral rules and our traditional moral understanding—our common agreements on such issues—are possible when modern technologies have made dying difficult and have interfered with natural death?" This question will continue to be significant for Christian ethics as well as for religious ethics grounded in other traditions and secular-philosophical ethics. Christians can avow certain general moral agreements that conform to the same common agreements to be found in nonreligious, secular, and philosophically framed ethical perspectives, but the critical issue facing Christians is how to formulate possible exceptions in accordance with values affirmed within the Christian community—compassion, care for the suffering, love, kindness, hope, and faith itself. It is in the answers to that issue's questions that we see a diversity of opinion on issues such as assisted dying, even in that broad community of believers who identify as Christian.

Notes

1. John Stuart Mill, "Utilitarianism," in John Stuart Mill, *Utilitarianism, On Liberty, Essay on Bentham*, edited and introduction by Mary Warnock (Cleveland, NY: World Publishing, a Meridian Book, 1962), 268.

2. "Iran: Code of Punishment for Adultery in Iran," *Women Living Under Muslim Laws*, http://www.wluml.org/node/3908 (accessed January 13, 2016).

3. Gregory Pence, *The Elements of Bioethics* (New York: McGraw-Hill, 2007), 52–80.

4. BBC News (2013), "How Many Roman Catholics Are There in the World?" http://www.bbc.com/news/world-21443313 (accessed August 3, 2016).

5. Joseph Fletcher, *Situation Ethics: The New Morality* (Louisville, KY: Westminster-John Knox Press, 1966).

6. "Euthanasia—How Do Christians Respond?" *Faith Facts: Finding Facts for Life's Tough Questions*, http://www.faithfacts.org/christ-and-the-culture/euthanasia (accessed January 3, 2016).

7. Ibid.

8. United Church of Christ, "Faithfully Facing Dying," http://www.ucc.org /faithfully_facing_dying (accessed January 12, 2016).

9. Ibid.

10. Ibid.

11. This author was a participant in the discussion at the United Church of Christ General Synod that considered this resolution. The reason that the resolution did not come out in favor of support of assisted dying was because of concern for the vulnerability of handicapped persons and fear of abuse. A "slippery slope" argument directed the deliberation outcome, namely that those most vulnerable and least able to assert autonomy in decision making might have a decision for death made by proxy, and the dangers of such a development were deemed sufficiently serious to prevent the resolution as a clear endorsement of assisted dying from being put to a vote on the floor of the General Synod. There is no evidence of such a slippery slope being in play in those states that allow physician assistance in dying, and numerous safeguards are in place to prevent such abuse, because such a concern is itself reasonable and requires attention, as was given in Oregon's Death with Dignity law.

12. Christian Medical and Dental Associations, "Euthanasia Ethics Statement," at http://cmda.org/resources/publication/euthanasia-ethics-statement (accessed December 31, 2015).

13. Ibid.

14. Christian Medical and Dental Associations, "Physician Assisted Suicide and Euthanasia," http://cmda.org/issues/detail/physician-assisted-suicide-and -euthanasia (accessed December 31, 2015).

15. "Church of England Continues to Oppose Euthanasia: TLC 3.28.05" (March 28, 2005), *Conger: The Religious, Political and Cultural Journalism of George Congar,* https://geoconger.wordpress.com/2005/03/28/church-of-england -continues-to-oppose-euthanasia-tlc-32805/.

16. See the Unitarian Universalist Association, "The Right to Die with Dignity, 1988 Resolution," which honors the requests of patients suffering terminal illness, http://www.uua.org/statements/right-die-dignity (accessed December 29, 2015).

17. Evangelical Lutheran Church of America, "A Message on End of Life Decisions," http://download.elca.org/ELCA%20Resource%20Repository/End_Life _DecisionsSM.pdf (accessed August 3, 2016).

18. "The Lutheran Tradition: Religious Beliefs and Health Care Decisions," ed. Deborah Abbott, revised Paul Nelson (Park Ridge, IL: The Park Ridge Center, 2002): 17, http://www.che.org/members/ethics/docs/1268/Lutheran.pdf (accessed September 19, 2016).

19. Stanley S. Harakas, "The Stand of the Orthodox Church on Controversial Issues," Greek Orthodox Archdioceses of America, http://www.goarch.org/ourfaith /controversialissues (accessed January 4, 2016).

20. Sacred Congregation for the Doctrine of Faith, "Declaration on Euthanasia," May 5, 1980, http://www.vatican.va/roman_curia/congregations/cfaith /documents/rc_con_cfaith_doc_1980050_5_euthanasia_en.html (accessed January 8, 2016).

21. Ibid.

22. *The Catechism of the Roman Catholic Church*, 2284–87, http://www.vatican .va/archive/ccc_css/archive/catechism/p3s2c2a5.htm (accessed August 3, 2016).

23. Ibid.

24. Ibid.

25. See *Catechism of the Roman Catholic Church*, "Suicide," 2280–83, http:// www.vatican.va/archive/ccc_css/archive/catechism/p3s2c2a5.htm (accessed August 3, 2016).

26. Ibid.

27. Pope Pius XII, "Address to an International Congress of Anesthesiologists," November 24, 1957, lifeissues.net, http://www.lifeissues.net/writers/doc/doc _31resuscitation.html (accessed August 3, 2016).

28. Ibid.

29. Double effect is drawn from the Catholic moral tradition, originally from Thomas Aquinas, *Summa Theologica* II-II, Q 64, A7, who asked "Whether It Is Permissible to Kill a Man in Self-Defense?"

30. An expanded version of this discussion can be found in Lloyd Steffen & Dennis Cooley, *The Ethics of Death: Religious and Philosophical Perspectives in Dialogue* (Minneapolis: Fortress Press, 2014), 282.

31. Michael D. A. Freeman, *Lloyd's Introduction to Jurisprudence* 90 (7th ed., 2001), quoted in Alex E. Wallin, "John Finnis's Natural Law Theory and a Critique of the Incommensurable Nature of Basic Goods," 35 *Campbell Law Review* 59 (2012): 59, http://law.campbell.edu/lawreview/articles/35-1-59.pdf (accessed December 30, 2015).

32. Thomas Aquinas, *Summa Theologica*, Ia, IIae 91, http://www.aristotelophile .com/Books/Translations/STIaIIae.91.pdf (accessed September 19, 2016).

33. Michael D. A. Freeman, *Lloyd's Introduction to Jurisprudence* 90 (7th ed., 2001), quoted in Alex E. Wallin, "John Finnis's Natural Law Theory and a Critique of the Incommensurable Nature of Basic Goods," 35 *Campbell Law Review* 59 (2012): 59, http://law.campbell.edu/lawreview/articles/35-1-59.pdf (accessed December 30, 2015).

34. These criteria are advanced in Lloyd Steffen, *Ethics and Experience: Moral Theory from Just War to Abortion* (Lanham, MD: Rowman and Littlefield), 127.

PART II

Ethics and Policy

CHAPTER SEVEN

Ethical Evaluation of Euthanasia in the Islamic Tradition

Tuba Erkoç Baydar and Ilhan Ilkilic

Introduction

Recent rapid advances in the medical world have led to the prolonging of the dying process, and raise issues such as euthanasia, physician-assisted suicide, and assisted death around the world, including in Muslim countries. Death is one of the most salient phenomena that provokes a powerful religious recognition, thus it is not surprising that Islam and Muslims have a meticulous approach to the issues related to death. Taking its cue from this fact, the main topic of this chapter is an investigation of Islam's response to issues related to any intervention into the end of life—with a special focus on the case of euthanasia.

Because legislative regulations pertaining to these problems affect—and in turn are affected by—society as a whole as well as individuals, it seems necessary to examine these issues within their ontological, epistemological, and ethical frameworks. Therefore, this chapter begins by discussing the relevant frameworks from an Islamic perspective. Following a general introduction that investigates the nature and importance of the topic, the first section of this chapter analyzes the ontological understanding and explanation of the human being. After an examination of the Islamic view of human nature and life, the second section deals with the Islamic approach to death. Following the first two sections—which aim to lay a theoretical foundation for the topic—ensuing practical aspects are discussed in the third and fourth sections. The third section evaluates active euthanasia in terms of Islamic morality and investigates the issue of suicide and homicide. The last section discusses termination of treatment within the framework of the evaluation of treatment.

The Islamic Understanding of Humankind

From the perspective of Islamic anthropology, a human being must be defined with reference to qualities such as consciousness, intelligence, and communication skills. There is also a theological dimension to these qualities, entailed in the concept of "relationship": Man's relationship with himself, man's relationship with his environment, man's relationship with other people, and man's relationship with God—the latter determining the nature of all other relationships.[1] In the theological relationship, a human is not only a network of material interactions and a material body; he or she also is a creature that is characterized by spirituality, and his or her value comes from this connection with the divine.[2] Instead of an anthropology that reduces people to their physiology, Islam approaches the human being in terms of both physiological and transcendental qualities. According to Muslim philosopher Muhammad Iqbal (1877–1938), the fact that Man is equipped with both physiological and transcendental qualities does not require a passive submission but an active orientation. Man has a different sense of reality compared to all other species. Among all of God's creatures, Man is the only one that is able to participate consciously in the Creator's creative life.[3] The human being is the only creature in which the secret of existence is hidden. Therefore, we see that Sufis[4] describe Man as a "little universe" (microcosm) or the core of the universe (a miniature model of the world).[5]

It is clearly stated in the Qur'an that human beings have a special place in the universe. Verse 70 of the Surat al-Isra, declares, "Verily we have honored the Children of Adam. We carry them on the land and the sea, and have made provision of good things for them, and have preferred them above many of those whom We created with a marked preferment" (Qur'an 17:70). According to the Qur'an, along with being the best creation of God,[6] the most distinctive feature of Man singling him out from the other creatures is that God has breathed His Spirit into him. Verses 28 and 29 of the Surat al-Hijr say, "And (remember) when thy Lord said unto the angels: 'Lo! I am creating a mortal out of potter's clay of black mud altered. So, when I have made him and have breathed into him of My Spirit, do ye fall down, prostrating yourselves unto him'" (Qur'an 15:28–29). The belief that the angels prostrated themselves before Adam clearly indicates the value of Man in Islamic thought.[7] Additionally, because Man is the caliph of God on earth,[8] whatsoever is in the skies and whatsoever is in the earth has been made serviceable unto him,[9] and he has been assigned to husband and to protect the earth,[10] Man has a very important place in Islamic thought. His importance comes also from the fact that his "nafs"[11] has two aspects. In terms of the intelligible world, man's nafs is affected or enlightened by the supreme principles above him. In terms of the visible world, however, man's nafs affects and governs the bodies below him.[12]

Therefore, it is very important to examine the concepts of "nafs" and "fitrah" (God-given nature) to understand human beings from an Islamic perspective. The human being essentially is composed of the nafs; therefore, answers offered to the question "What is a human being?" also can be seen as answers to the question "What is nafs?"[13] In Islam, the theory of nafs—which has been developed based on the idea that the nafs is spiritual and immaterial—has formed the basis of human contact with the metaphysical world.[14] The word "nafs" lexically means "soul, life, breath, self, human being, and body."[15] It has been used in the meaning of "soul"[16] and "person and inner self"[17] in the Qur'an, and also refers to the spiritual and transcendental aspects of the human beings.

Alongside the concept of "nafs," examining the concept of "fitrah" shows that it also provides important clues for understanding human beings from an Islamic perspective. The concept of "fitrah" in Islamic thought refers to the belief that every human being is created with the same nature.[18] It also represents something that should be considered to find the right way. In the Qur'an, it is declared, for example, "So set thy purpose (O Muhammad) for religion as a man by nature upright—the nature (framed) of, in which He hath created man. There is no altering (the laws of) God's creation. . ."[19] As this verse indicates, the Qur'an advises people to remain stable within the nature in which they were created. In Islamic thought "fitrah"[20] also refers to the purity, superiority, and equality in creation. "Fitrah" does not change from one person to another; therefore, each person has an equal value.[21] According to this doctrine, the human being did not come into existence by chance, or by evolving or descending from other species. In contrast, humans were "specifically" created by God and are creatures whose "humanity" has been ordained by the divine plan.

In sum, in Islam it is not feasible to study human beings from a profane perspective. In addition to physiological qualities, Man also has a transcendental nature and qualities. Because God has breathed into him of His Spirit, Man occupies a special place in the universe. Humans are creatures that have dignity and consciousness. Along with showing Man to be the servant of God, these qualities indicate that great care and attention is required when human life is concerned. Therefore, the human being and issues of euthanasia, termination of treatment, and physician-assisted suicide—all of which are about human life—have led to important discussions in the Islamic world and have been addressed with great hesitation.

Life and Death in Islamic Theology

Euthanasia equates to interfering with the right to life, which is one of the fundamental rights of every human being, and thus is related to perspectives on life, death, test, patience, trust and belief in God, belief in the Hereafter, and the value and inviolability of human life. In particular, being very closely related to the perspective on life and death, euthanasia seems to question whether it is the quality or the inviolability of human life that should be given priority. Supporters of euthanasia who embrace the quality-of-life stance argue that it is meaningless to live a life that fails to comply with Man's honor and dignity. The belief that this world is the only place of life and truth brings with it the desire to get the greatest pleasure from life or to gain maximum advantage for worldly interests. According to Islam, the worldly life—which receives its meaning only with the existence of the Hereafter—should be lived in a manner that is worthy of the dignity of the human being, who is the most honorable of all creatures. In Islamic thought, death is a part of the worldly life and, as Sachedina said, for Muslims the meaning of death cannot be derived from medical facts or scientific investigation alone.[22]

According to the clear statements of the Qur'an, creatures in the universe not only constitute a set of objects but also serve as evidence for the Deity and Lordship of God. The term "World," which in the language of the Qur'an does not have an illustrative but a significative meaning, carrying a moral rather than a geographical content,[23] has been described as a means of play, amusement, commodity, and illusion. In verse 20 of Surat[24] al-Hadîd, which clearly demonstrates the Islamic view of the world,[25] it is very meaningful that worldly life has been described as the likeness of greening of plants after a rain and their yellowing after a disaster, along with being a play and amusement. This statement indicates that this world cannot be the primary goal of a Muslim's life but only a means for attaining that goal. It also indicates that the world is not the permanent dwelling place for Muslims. Both in the Qur'an and in the "hadiths,"[26] the worldly life is depicted as the place of cultivation for the Hereafter, and the deeds performed in the world become meaningful only with the existence of the Hereafter.[27] In this regard, the belief that the world is a place which prepares one for the Hereafter rather than a place out of which one should get maximum pleasure and amusement is very important in Islam.[28]

Related to the belief in the Hereafter, the Islamic emphasis on the concept of test constitutes another point that should be considered when discussing the issue of euthanasia. In this sense, we should pay attention to this statement about the emphasis put on the notion that every human being will be tested: "Do men imagine that they will be left (at ease) because they say, We believe, and will not be tested with affliction?"[29] We can infer from this statement that people should regard the suffering, distress, troubles, and disasters in this world as tests and have patience with regard to them. Additionally, it should also be taken into consideration that the Qur'an—which states that God will not burden people with that which they have not the strength to bear[30]—declares that those who have patience with troubles will have great rewards.

In examining the hadiths, they show that illnesses, calamities, and troubles suffered in this world are regarded as tests, and the rewards for showing patience with them are promised to be given in the Hereafter.[31] In this regard, when the Prophet Muhammad was asked about the plague, he said, "God made the plague a blessing for the believers. None (among the believers) remains patient in a land in which plague has broken out and considers that nothing will befall him except what God has ordained for him, but that God will grant him a reward similar to that of a martyr."[32] This is examined in more detail in the discussion of the issue of treatment. This hadith does not imply that one should do nothing except show patience toward illnesses no matter what happens. On the contrary, as is indicated elsewhere in this chapter, there actually are many hadiths that encourage people to seek treatment.

All the references made above pertaining to the notion that the worldly life will completed with the Hereafter, that those who show patience with troubles in this world will have great rewards in the Hereafter, and that this world is a place of testing indicate one aspect of the Islamic view of the world. Additionally, although the worldly life is described as a temporary place of play, illusion, and testing, it is also essential in Islamic thought to live the worldly life in the best possible way. Indeed, it can be suggested that an understanding of asceticism, which favors a monastic life, is not accepted in Islam. In this sense, it is meaningful that the Prophet

Muhammad warned some of his companions such as Abdullah bin Umar and Uthman bin Maz'um against devoting themselves only to religious activities and emphasized that he himself engaged in both religious and worldly activities.[33]

The Prohibition of Suicide

The prohibition of suicide in Islam arises from the principle of respect for life. Because life comes from God, only God may take life away.[34] Likewise, examining the hadiths shows that those people who commit suicide by throwing themselves from a mountain or by drinking poison are reported to stay in Hell eternally.[35] This indicates that believers are not allowed to kill themselves. As the Prophet stated in the following hadith, even wishing for death is not allowed in Islam: "None of you should wish for death because of a calamity befalling him; but if he has to wish for death, he should say: 'O God! Keep me alive as long as life is better for me, and let me die if death is better for me.' "[36] Considering this admonition, it can be suggested that a person does not have the right to choose either to continue or to end his or her life.

It also is clearly declared in the Qur'an, "cast not yourselves with your hands into perdition,"[37] it is not legitimate in Islam for a person to act in such a way that the integrity of his body is violated. Based on this, just as it is seen not to be allowable to eat less food to the extent that it prevents a person from praying,[38] Muslim scholars also do not recognize a person's right and authority over his or her own body if ensuing actions lead to death.[39] Accordingly, based on the principle that "a person does not have the right and authority over his own body if it leads to any loss of life, even if it is his own life," Abū Ḥanīfa (699–767 CE), the founder of the Hanafi school of Islamic law, nullified the contract signed between the people of Mosul and Umar bin al-Khattab (581–644 CE), the second caliph of the Muslims, because they signed this contract in exchange for their lives. In this respect, we could say that Abū Ḥanīfa is one of the scholars who does not recognize the right to die.[40]

Therefore, considering that committing suicide is strictly forbidden in Islam and that abuse or neglect against the integrity of the human body is not allowed—even if it is done voluntarily—it can be suggested that the right to die is not recognized in Islamic law. Similarly, the abovementioned Islamic notion that God gives life and causes death, that the human soul resides in the body only temporarily, and that only God can take a person's life away, also lead to the conclusion that the right to die is not accepted in Islam.

Ethical Evaluation of Active Euthanasia

The goals of Islam are grouped in five basic principles which seek to promote and preserve people's religion, life, intellect, lineage, and property. These five principles are known as "al-maqasid al-khamsah" (five objectives) or "al-daruriyyat al-khamsah" (five necessities), indicating that they are the most basic and inalienable rights in the sense that without them human life with dignity is impossible.[41] It should be emphasized here that the necessary measures should be taken not only to make these basic principles come into existence but also to help them continue functioning.[42]

Among the principles of "al-maqasid al-khamsah," one principle sometimes may be prioritized over the others.[43] If it is necessary to give priority to one of these principles, this does not necessarily mean that lower-level priorities are less valuable or not valuable at all. In fact, determining such a priority is based on the necessity that the provisions of Islamic law also sometimes must be prioritized. In this regard, we see that the right to life has a primary value in Islam and usually is prioritized over property, lineage, intellect, and even religion. For example, it is declared in the Qur'an that those who are forced to deny their belief in God are allowed to pretend to do so to save their lives.[44] Likewise, those who are in a desperate condition due to lack of food are allowed to eat what under normal circumstances is forbidden.[45] This means that some of the strictly established rules of the religion sometimes can be violated. Similarly, if there is the probability that using water will put a person's life in danger due to extreme cold weather, Islamic law allows the faithful to perform a dry ablution instead of using water.[46] Along with the above-mentioned examples, this example also illustrates how much value Islam attributes to the preservation of human life.

Examining the Qur'anic verses about killing shows that intentional killing or murder is considered as a crime against humanity.[47] In other words, murdering a human being is regarded equivalent murdering all human beings, without making any distinction between them. Regarding this issue, the Qur'an clearly declares, "Whosoever killeth a human being for other than manslaughter or corruption in the earth, it shall be as if he had killed all mankind, and whoso saveth the life of one, it shall be as if he had saved the life of all mankind."[48] In another Qur'anic verse, it is declared, "And slay not the life which God hath forbidden save with right."[49] These two statements clearly indicate that any violation of the right to life is strictly forbidden in Islam. As for punishment, the otherworldly retribution for murdering a believer, according to the Holy Qur'an, is damnation to Hell (the Fire) eternally, forever.[50]

Examination of the hadiths shows that they are in line with the Holy Qur'an with respect to murder. For example, it is emphasized in the hadiths that human life is inviolable and there are both worldly and other-worldly punishments for intentional killing. Further, it is clearly stated that "for God, killing a believer is worse than destroying all the earth,"[51] and the punishment for killing someone intentionally is retaliation.[52] Likewise, the following statement from the Prophet Muhammad also indicates how much value Islam attributes to the right to life: "O people, just as you regard this month, this day, this city as sacred, so regard the life and property of every Muslim as a sacred trust."[53]

Killing, which lexically means to put an end to someone's life for any reason,[54] in Islamic terminology refers to the disembodiment of the human soul.[55] In legal terms, however, it refers to the act of causing the death of a person who has the right to the inviolability of life.[56] According to Islamic law, the crime of killing—one of the most serious crimes committed against other people—is divided into two groups based on whether the act of killing was intentional or accidental, and penal sanctions for this crime are determined accordingly.[57] To determine into which of these two groups an act of killing falls, it is necessary to take into account not only the right that is violated but also the intention of the actor. In fact, in addition to investigating whether the act of killing was completed, the instruments that were used to perform the act and the external circumstances also should be considered. Being defined in general terms as "an act of deliberately killing a person by using lethal instruments such as swords, knives, and arrows,"[58] according to Islamic law intentional killing is different from other types of killing in terms of the intention of the actor and the instruments that are used to perform the act. In other words, it is an agreed-upon idea among Islamic jurists that an act of killing should be considered as intentional if it involves the use of lethal instruments such as swords and knives along with the actor's intent to kill.[59] As for the issue of deliberately killing a person by making him or her drink poison, the majority of Muslim jurists who emphasize the role of intention consider this act as intentional killing. Abū Hanīfa, however, considers this to be quasi-intentional killing, because he emphasizes the use of instruments as much as the role of intention.[60]

According to the majority of Muslim jurists, when deciding if an act of killing should be considered as intentional killing, it is not important whether the victim is a patient who is about to die. In fact, what is important is that the person who is killed was alive and had the security of life as guaranteed by law, and the actor performed the act deliberately and knowingly using a lethal instrument. In other words, the religion, race, gender, or health status of the person is not important.[61] According to Nawawî (1234–1277 CE)—an influential Sunni jurist and hadith scholar—for example, if a patient who is about to die is killed by someone, then the person who performed the act of killing must be punished with retaliation, because it is as if he or she has committed the crime of intentional killing[62]; for Nawawî it is not important whether the person who is killed was a patient who was about to die.

Considering the issues discussed above, it can be suggested that active euthanasia that is performed by giving the patient a lethal dose of medication is similar to the crime of intentional killing; and therefore according to Islamic law it is strictly forbidden.[63] When discussing the case of voluntary active euthanasia, it is important to focus on the question of how the physician's responsibility is affected by the fact that the act of killing was performed upon the request of the patient himself or herself. According to Islamic law, the act of killing does not become permissible through the consent of the person to be murdered. There is, however, disagreement among the Islamic jurists about the effect of the victim's consent on the punishment of the actor.[64]

According to positions held by Turkish scholar Hayrettin Karaman,[65] Saim Yeprem (member of the High Council of the Turkish Directorate of Religious Affairs),[66] Yusuf al-Qaradawî (a present-day Sunni Muslim scholar), Egyptian muftis (Islamic legal experts),[67] and institutions such as the Islamic Medical Association (IMA),[68] and the Islamic Medical Association of North America (IMANA),[69] active euthanasia is strictly forbidden in Islam.

In a meeting of the Fatwa Council of Al-Azhar University, it was been determined that it is not permissible to kill patients to relieve them from pain, no matter what the illness or the stage of the illness. According to this council, it is not permissible for anybody to kill a patient (even with the patient's consent), just as it is not permissible for a patient to kill himself or herself.[70]

Muhammad Sayyid Tantawî (1928–2010)—a former rector of Al-Azhar University—puts forward a more comprehensive explanation for this issue and suggests that human life is a trust from God. Therefore, as God declares in the Qur'an with the statement, "do not cast yourselves into perdition by your own hands" (Qur'an 2:195),[71] human beings should preserve their lives as well as their bodies so as not to cast themselves into perdition.

Lastly, the case of voluntary active euthanasia involves the consent of the person to be murdered; however, this consent does not make the act of killing permissible and it still entails criminal responsibility. When compared to voluntary euthanasia, cases of involuntary and nonvoluntary euthanasia—in which the patient does not provide consent—seem to be even more negative. In fact, it can be suggested that involuntary and non-voluntary euthanasia are regarded as intentional killing by Islamic law, because they are performed without the consent of either the patient or his or her family.

Ethical Evaluation of Withholding and Withdrawing Treatment

In the Islamic world, despite consensus that active euthanasia is forbidden, there is little clarity on the issue of terminating medical treatment.[72] It is debated whether terminating treatment that would have ensured the patient's survival for a longer period, or terminating treatment in such a way as to abandon the patient to death—either by ending treatment or not beginning it—should be considered killing the patient or allowing the patient to die. Before moving on to the various opinions on this subject, it is helpful to first briefly examine how treatment is understood in Islam.

Considering hadith narrations related to treatment shows that the Prophet Muhammad commanded treatment of the sick and stated that everything except death has a cure; in doing so, he encouraged seeking treatment for illnesses. Ibn Taymiyyah (1263–1328 CE)—an Islamic scholar, theologian, and logician—focused primarily on the nature and conditions of treatment, dividing it according to the legal categories of obligatory, encouraged, permissible, discouraged, and forbidden. According to Ibn Taymiyyah, jurists consider seeking treatment through things that are forbidden—such as magic—to be forbidden.[73] Additionally, seeking treatment when it is very likely to be effective and when neglecting it would lead to the illness worsening is obligatory.[74] Ash-Shâfi'î (767–820 CE)— founder of a school of Islamic law—together with some Hanafi[75] and Maliki[76] Sunni scholars considered seeking treatment to be recommended and thus they encouraged it.[77] Although it is thought that Muslim theologian, jurist, and philosopher, al-Ghazâlî (1058–1111 CE), maintained a more cautious approach to discussing treatment in his seminal text, the *Ihya*, in actuality, the title of the section in the book where the subject is addressed shows that al-Ghazâlî does not view the topic in absolute terms; rather, he considers the topic from the perspective of trusting in God. Moreover, examining the text's other topics shows that al-Ghazâlî argues against those who claim that categorically renouncing treatment is more moral.[78] Those Sufis who viewed treatment as inconsistent with trusting in God in general tended to consider treatment impermissible.[79]

Along with the various approaches to treatment mentioned above, there is also a clear objection to causing someone's death by neglecting to do something required by Islamic law. Islamic law places so much importance on the sanctity and inviolability of human life that it considers someone who causes the death of a person by preventing him or her from eating food and drinking water or from receiving treatment as the perpetrator of the killing. Abû Hanîfa—who views the matter on the basis of the causal relationship between an action and its effect—maintains that the death is caused by hunger or thirst, and that although the perpetrator has not committed a murder, he or she has committed another crime.[80] As for an-Nawawî, he considers acts such as intentionally throwing someone who does not know to swim into the water, or throwing someone into water where rescue would be difficult, to be intentional killings—though they might not be outright murder—because someone has died as a result of the acts.[81] The result is that, according to Islamic law, whoever is causing the death of a patient by neglecting a duty must be held responsible for this omission. If the treatment has been terminated with the patient's consent or because of his or her refusal thereof, however, then the action of the patient overrides the action of the person terminating treatment and breaks the tie of cause and effect for the latter. Similarly, when treatment becomes unnecessary or is no longer beneficial, terminating treatment can, under certain circumstances, be considered permissible.

In the modern age, Muslim scholars take different approaches to the topic of terminating or deciding not to initiate treatment.[82] The first approach, which holds that treatment should be continued unconditionally, argues for the necessity of treatment before death even in hopeless cases.[83] Proponents of this approach see no distinction between active and passive euthanasia because the purpose in each case is the same; thus they hold that passive euthanasia, like active euthanasia, should be impermissible.[84] Although the second approach does not claim that treatment before death is obligatory, it still is recommended.[85]

On the topic of treatment being terminated or rejected, Qaradawi views treatment as obligatory for cases in which there is hope of a cure, but also views it as neither obligatory nor encouraged for cases in which experts confirm that treatment will have no effect toward curing the patient and only will prolong the illness. Moreover, Qaradawi holds that these cases should not be thought of as falling within the scope of the euthanasia debate.[86] Sachedina argues that because active euthanasia calls for the "right to die," it is not acceptable from an Islamic perspective. Passive euthanasia is to "allow to die," however, and it is unnecessary for treatment to be applied to terminal patients for their survival.

When it comes to the case of a brain-dead patient being taken off of life support, the conclusion reached in 1986 in Amman by the Islamic Jurisprudence Academy (which is tied to the Organization of Islamic Cooperation) forms the foundation for many countries' decisions on this issue. According to this conclusion, when a person's heartbeat and respiration have stopped completely, his or her doctors have ruled that recovery is impossible, his or her brain function has stopped entirely and for certain, and the brain begins to disintegrate, then the person is ruled to be dead, and all of the legal consequences relating to the individual's death remain.[87] Using this definition, it would be permissible to remove life support from a patient in such situations. At the Meeting to Discuss Contemporary Religious Issues, organized by the Turkish Directorate of Religious Affairs in 2007, the general view was that removing life support from a brain-dead patient is possible.[88]

Conclusion

The time of death is an important moment in which the reactions and positions that people hold about life and the Hereafter are manifested in the most explicit way. For this reason, just as most religions involve a serious contemplation of the concept of death, Islam draws certain conclusions and derives rulings on these matters. The modern period has brought both the development of new technologies and an increase in the problems people face. Death no longer is a moment that people experience in their homes, but rather is one that is suffered through in hospital rooms. This raises many new questions with socioeconomic, ethical, and religious significance.[89]

Issues such as euthanasia, terminating treatment, and assisted suicide all relate directly to human beings and the way in which we understand life. Islam defines Man as a being with traits such as intellect and awareness, having theological significance. Moreover, in Islam, besides having physiological qualities, Man has qualities including consciousness, intellect, and capacity for communication, which gain a special position amongst his qualities by virtue of their having been blown into humans from the spirit of God. Man's special rank and the higher qualities possessed demand that great caution be applied when considering life. For this reason, issues surrounding euthanasia, terminating treatment, and assisted suicide—which revolve around humans and their lives—have led to important debates in the Muslim world and have been taken up with great care and deliberation.

Euthanasia, which amounts to destroying life (a fundamental right), relates to life, death, the meaning of the life of this world, being tested in this life, patience, belief in an afterlife, and the value and sanctity of human life. Belief in the afterlife and seeing this life as a test demanding patience—which are all integral ideas within the Islamic faith—make up the most important determinants of Muslims' valuations in this matter. Thus, within the worldview of Muslims, euthanasia, terminating care, and assisted suicide—all ways of hastening the end of life—require a consideration of these determinants. According to Islamic thought, which takes into account an afterlife along with the life of this world, it is not enough to provide for the well-being and good of Man in this life: one must also protect the well-being and good of Man in the next life.

In Islam, there is a clear understanding of God as the Giver and Taker of life and the soul as a trust given to each human and sheltered in his or her body, such that a human does not even have the right to take his or her own life, because it was God that gave it and it will be God that takes it away. Similarly, because suicide very clearly is forbidden and violence against or neglect of the body as a whole also are not considered permissible, it is obvious that Islam does not allow euthanasia. Despite the consensus that exists in the Muslim world on the impermissibility of active euthanasia, there is no clear consensus on terminating care. It can be said that someone who intentionally terminates care that would have been beneficial and necessary for a patient has caused that patient's death by neglecting a duty required by Islamic law, and thus must be held responsible. If the treatment is terminated on the basis of the patient's own preference or refusal, however, then his or her action breaks the causal relationship between the one terminating care action and death itself. Though it appears that, in cases where treatment is impossible or futile, as long as all conditions have been satisfied, then ending treatment or treatment being refused is permissible. This subject, however, requires more detailed study.

Notes

1. For a detailed analysis of this issue, see Toshihiko Izutsu, *God and Man in The Qur'an: Semantics of the Qur'anic weltanschauung* (Kuala Lumpur: Islamic Book Trust, 2002).

2. Şaban Ali Düzgün, "İnsan Onuru Ve Toplumsal YaŞam İçin Etik," *Kelam Araştırmaları Dergisi* [*Journal of the Islamic Theological Researchers*], 5: 1 (2007): 5.

3. Ibid., 3.

4. A Sufi is a follower of mystical ascetic branch of Islam.

5. Muhammad az-Zuhayli, *Huquq al-Insan fî al-Islâm: Dirase Mukarene* (Damascus: Dâr al-Kalîm at-Tayyeb; 1997), 15.

6. Qur'an, 95/4 (this study used Pickthall's translation of the Holy Qur'an; see: Muhammad Marmaduke William Pickthall, *The Meaning of the Glorious Qur'an* (London: 1930).

7. Abd al-Razzaq al-Qashani, Sharh al-Fusûs al-Hikam (Cairo: Mustafâ al-Bab al-Halebî, 1966), 16.

8. Qur'an, 2/30.

9. Qur'an, 2/29; Qur'an, 31/20; Qur'an, 45/12–13.

10. Qur'an, 33/72.

11. The word *"nafs"* has different meanings, one of them being "soul"; see Mufradat al-Alfaz al-Qur'an, "al-Nafs," Muhammad b. Mufaddal Ragib al-Isfahani (Damascus: Dâr al-Kalem, 2002).

12. Süleyman Uludağ, "an-Nafs," *TDV Encyclopedia of Islam*, 530. http://www.tdvislamansiklopedisi.org/dia/ayrmetin.php?idno=320529&idno2=c320385 (accessed April 13, 2016).

13. Fakhr ad-Din ar-Razî, Mafatih al-Gayb (Cairo: Matbaat al-Amiret ash-Sharafiyya, 1911), V, 642; Süleyman Uludağ, "an-Nafs," 531.

14. Uludağ, "al-Nafs," 531.

15. Al-Isfahani, al-Mufradat, "al-Nafs."

16. Qur'an, 6/93.

17. Qur'an, 3/28.

18. Selçuk Coşkun, "On the Use of 'Fitrah' As a Measure in Determining Whether a Narrated Hadith Belongs to the Prophet Muhammad," *Hadis Çalışmaları Dergisi* [*Journal of Hadith Studies*], 1/VI (2008): 36.

19. Qur'an, 30/30.

20. Yasien Mohamed, "Fitrah and Its Bearing on the Principles of Psychology," *AJISS*, 12/1 (1995): 1–19.

21. Qur'an, 7/189.

22. Abdulaziz Sachedina, *Islamic Biomedical Ethics, Principles and Application* (New York: Oxford University Press, 2009), 145.

23. Mustafa Öztürk, "Kur'an'ın Değer Sisteminde Dünya ve Dünyevi Hayatın Anlamı," *Tasavvuf: İlmî ve Akademik Araştırma Dergisi* [*Sufism Scientific and Academic Research Journal*], 16 (2006): 67.

24. A Surah is a chapter of Qur'an.

25. Know that the life of the world is only play, and idle talk, and pageantry, and boasting among you, and rivalry in respect of wealth and children; as the likeness of vegetation after rain, whereof the growth is pleasing to the husbandman, but afterward it dries up and you see it turning yellow, then it becomes straw. Qur'an al-Hadid, 57/20.

26. A "hadith" is a report describing the words, actions, or habits of the Prophet Muhammad. Jonathan A. C. Brown, *Hadith: Muhammad's Legacy in the Medieval and Modern World* (Foundations of Islam) (Oneworld Publications, 2009), 3.

27. Qur'an, 99/6–8.

28. Rahmi Yaran, Ahirete İmanın Dünya Hayatına Yansımaları, *Din ve Hayat Dergisi* [*Journal of Religion and Life*], 16 (2012): 4–7.

29. Qur'an, 29/2.

30. Qur'an, 2/286.

31. Muhammad Ali al-Bar, *Ahkâm at-Tadawi* (Jeddah: Dar al-Minara, 1995), 37–40.

32. Bukhârî, Abū, *Abd Allāh Muḥammad ibn Ismā'īl ibn Ibrāhīm ibn al-Mughīrah ibn Bardizbah al-Ju'fī, Sahih al-Bukhârî* (Istanbul: al-Maktabah al-Islamiyyah, n.d.), al-Mardâ/3287.

33. Bukhârî, as-Sawm, 56.

34. Jonathan E. Brockopp, "The Good Death in Islamic Theology and Law," in *Islamic Ethics of Life, Abortion, War and Euthanasia*, ed. Jonathan E. Brockopp (Columbia: University of South Carolina Press, 2003), 183; Abd al-Haleem Muhammad Mansur Ali, al-Qatl bi-Dafi' al-Shafaqah fi 'l-Fiqh al-Islami wa-l-Qanun al-Wad'i (al-Maktab al-Jam'i al-Hadith, 2012), 30.

35. Bukhârî, at-Tibb, 56/5778.

36. Bukhârî, al-Mardâ, 19/5671.

37. Qur'an, 2/195.

38. Ali Kaya, Ruh ve Beden Bütünlüğüne Dokunulmazlık Kuramı Bakımından Ölme Hakkı, Marife, 2 (2004): 202.

39. Ibid., 214.

40. Sava Paşa, *İslam Hukuk Nazariyatı Hakkında bir Etüt* (Ankara: Diyanet İşleri, 1955), 89.

41. Ghazâlî, Abu Hâmid Muhammad b. Muhammed, *al-Mustasfâ min 'Ilm al-Usûl* (Beirut: Dar al-Arqam, 1994), V/633–37.

42. The protection of the six basic rights also is considered the common ground of all religions and legal systems—one which provides a juridical basis for religious and legal pluralism. For this reason, these rights are called "objectives of law" ("*maqasid al-shariah*"). According to Islamic theology and jurisprudence, these six principles constitute the unchangeable core of all religions and legal systems in the world. Recep Şentürk, "Adamiyyah and 'Ismah: The Contested Relationship Between Humanity and Human Rights in Classical Islamic Law," *İslam Araştırmaları Dergisi* [*Turkish Journal of Islamic Studies*], 8 (2002): 63.

43. Jasser Auda, Maqasid al-Shariah, *A Beginner's Guide* (United Kingdom: The International Institute of Islamic Thought, 2008), 4.

44. "Whoso disbelieved in God after his belief—save him who is forced thereto and whose heart is still content with the Faith—but whoso findeth ease in disbelief: On them is wrath from God. Theirs will be an awful doom." Qur'an, 16/106.

45. "He hath forbidden you only carrion, and blood, and swine flesh, and that which hath been immolated to (the name of) any other than God. But he who is driven by necessity, neither craving nor transgressing, it is no sin for him. Lo! God is Forgiving, Merciful." Qur'an, 2/173.

46. Shîrâzî, Abû Ishâq Ibrahim, al-Muhadhdhab fî Fiqh ash-Shafi (Bairût: Dâr al-Kutub al-'ilmiyyah, 1990), I, 71.

47. Ali Bardakoğlu, "Katil," *TDV Islam Ansiklopedisi* [*TDV Encyclopedia of Islam*] (Ankara: 2002), XXV/45.

48. Qur'an, 5/32.

49. Qur'an, 17/33.

50. "O ye who believe! God will surely try you somewhat (in the matter) of the game which ye take with your hands and your spears, that God may know him who feareth Him in secret. Whoso transgresseth after this, for him there is a painful doom." Qur'an, 4/94.

51. Nasā'ī, Aḥmad ibn Shu'ayb ibn Alī ibn Sīnān Abū 'Abd ar-Raḥmān al-Nasā'ī, as-Sunan (Beirut: Dâr al- Basha'ir al-Islamiyyah, 1988), 7/83.

52. Ibn Majah, Abū 'Abdillāh Muḥammad ibn Yazīd Ibn Mājah al-Rab'ī al-Qazwīnī, as-Sunan (Delhi: al-Matba' an-Nizami, 1905), ad-Diyat, 8.

53. Bukhârî, al-Hajj, 132.

54. Ibn Manzûr, Lisân al-Arab (Beirut: Dâr al-Ihya at-Turathi al-'Arabi: 1997), 3527.

55. al-Isfahani, Mufradat, "al-qatl," 655.

56. Bardakoğlu, "Katil," 45.

57. Marghînânî, Burhân ad-Dîn, al-Hidâyah: Sharh al-Bidayat al-Mubtadî (Cairo: Dâr al-Salam, 2000), IV/1601.

58. Qâsânî, Badâi' al-Sanai' fî Tartîb al-Sharai (Beirut: Dâr al-Kutub al-Ilmi-yyah, 1997), X, 233.

59. Marghînânî, al-Hidâyah, IV, 16; Nawawî, Abu Zakaria Muhiyî ad-Din Yahya Ibn Sharaf, Rawdat al-Tâlibîn (Beirut: Dâr al-Kutub al- Ilmiyyah, 1992), VII, 7. For a detailed analysis of this issue from the perspective of different schools of thought in Islamic jurisprudence, see Qâsânî, Badâi', X, 237.

60. Nawawî, Rawdat at-Tâlibîn, VII, 12.

61. Bardakoğlu, "Katil," XXVI, 46.

62. Nawawî, Rawdat at-Tâlibîn, VII, 12.

63. Belhaj Arabi, Ma'sumiyat al-Juththa fi 'l-Fiqh al-Islami (Amman: Dar al-Thaqafa, 2009), 116.

64. For a detailed analysis of the views of different Islamic jurists toward this issue, see Qâsânî, Badâi', X, 247; Nawawî, al-Majmu' (Riyad: Dâr al-#afAlam al-Kutub, 2003) XVIII, 395; Ramlî, Muhammad Shams ad-Dîn, b. Shihab ad-Dîn, Nihâyat al-Muhtaj ilâ Sharh al-Minhaj (Beirut: Dâr al-Fikr, 1984) VII, 312; Ibn Rushd, al-Bidayah, II, 332; Qâsânî, Badâi', X, 247; al-Mutii, Muhammad Najib, al-Macmu' sharh al-Muhadhdhab ash-Sharizi (Jeddah: Maktabah al-Irshad, 1977) XX, 319.

65. Hayrettin Karaman, Ötenazi. http://www.hayrettinkaraman.net/yazi/hayat /0403.htm (accessed April 13, 2016).

66. Saim Yeprem, İslam ve Hristiyanlık-Dinlerarası Diyalog için Dini İçerikler, Tasavvurlar ve Duyguların Karşılaştırılması, Dinlerin Gen Teknolojisi, Ötanazi ve Organ Nakline Karşı Tutumları, ed. Konrad Adenauer Foundation (Ankara: 2006), 200.

67. Arabi, Ma'sumiyat al-Juththa, 119.

68. R. M. Yousuf, and A. R. Mohammed Fauzi, "Euthanasia and Physician-Assisted Suicide: A Review from Islamic Point of View," *International Medical Journal Malaysia* 11 (2012): 66.

69. IMANA, "Euthanasia," http://c.ymcdn.com/sites/www.imana.org/resource /resmgr/Files/Publication2.pdf (accessed April 13, 2016).

70. Arabi, Ma'sumiyat al-Juththa, 119.

71. E. Brockopp, "The Good Death in Islamic Theology and Law," *Islamic Ethics of Life, Abortion, War and Euthanasia*, ed. Jonathan E. Brockopp (Columbia: University of South Carolina Press, 2003), 178.

72. Ilhan Ilkilic, "Menschenwürde und ethische Bewertung von Entscheidungen am Lebensende am Beispiel innerislamischer Positionen," *Zeitschrift für Evangelische Ethik*, vol. 60, 88–101 (2016).

73. Muhammad Ali al-Bar, Ahkâm at-Tadawi (Jeddah: Dar al-Minara, 1995), 18.

74. al-Bar, Ahkâm at-Tadawi, 21.

75. A school of Islamic law.

76. A school of Islamic law.

77. al-Bar, Ahkâm at-Tadawi, 25.

78. Ghazâlî, Ihyâ 'Ulûm ad-Dîn (Beirut: Dâr al-Ma'rifah, 1982), IV, 290.

79. al-Bar, Ahkâm at-Tadawi, 37.

80. Qâsânî, Bedâi, X, 239; Nawawī, Rawdat al-Tâlibîn, VII, 8.

81. Nawawî, Rawdat al-Tâlibîn, VII, 13.

82. Mahmud Sadîk Rashvân, *Qatl al-Rahmah wa-Atharuhu fi 'l-Fiqh al-Islamî*, n.d., 791–95.

83. Ilhan Ilkilic, Wann Endet das Menschliche Leben? Das muslimische Todesverständnis und seine medizinethischen Implikationen, in Lebensanfang und Lebensende in den Weltreligionen. Beiträge zu einer interkulturellen Medizinethik, eds. U. H. J. Körtner, Neukirchener Verlag Medien und Recht GmbH, Neukirchen-Vlyun, 165–82, 2006; and Ilhan Ilkilic, "End-of-Life Decisions at the Beginning of Life," in *Health, Culture and the Human Body*, eds. İ. İlkılıç, H. Ertin, R. Brömer, H. Zeeb (BETIM Center Press, Istanbul), 433–44 (2014).

84. Rashvân, Qatl al-Rahmah, 793.

85. For a detailed analysis of this issue see Rashvân, Qatl al-Rahmah, 794.

86. Qaradawi, Qatl al-Rahmah, http://qaradawi.net/fatawaahkam/30/1493 -2012-02-25-11-02-55.html (accessed April 13, 2016).

87. Islamic Jurisprudence Academy (which is tied to the Organization of Islamic Cooperation), 1987, 17.

88. Mehmet Bulut, Güncel Dini Meseleler İstişare Toplantısı (Ankara: Diyanet İşleri Başkanlığı, 2009) 117–53.

89. Ilhan Ilkilic, "Normativity of Heterogeneity in Clinical Ethics," *The American Journal of Bioethics*, vol. 15, 21–23 (2015).

Bibliography

Abdal Haleem, Muhammad Mansur Ali (2012). *al-Qatl bi Dafi' al-Shafakah fi Fiqh al-Islam wa al-Qanun al-Wad'i*, al-Maktaba al-Cami al Hadith.

Al-Bar, Muhammad Ali (1995). *Ahkâm at-Tadawi*. Jeddah: Dar al-Minara.

Auda, Jasser (2008). *Maqasid al-Shariah, A Beginner's Guide*. United Kingdom: The International Institute of Islamic Thought.

Bardakoğlu, Ali (2002). "Katil." *TDV Encyclopedia of Islam*. Ankara. XXV.

Belhaj, Arabi (2009). *Ma 'sumiyat al-Juththa fi 'l-Fiqh al-Islami*. Amman: Dar al-Thaqafa.

Brockopp, Jonathan E. (2003). "The Good Death in Islamic Theology and Law, Islamic Ethics of Life, Abortion." In *War and Euthanasia*, Jonathan E. Brockopp (ed.) Columbia: University of South Carolina Press.

Brown, Jonathan A. C. (2009). *Hadith: Muhammad's Legacy in the Medieval and Modern World* (Foundations of Islam) One World Publications.

Bukharî, Abū 'Abd Allāh Muḥammad ibn Ismā'īl ibn Ibrāhīm ibn al-Mughīrah ibn Bardizbah al-Ju'fī (n.d.). *Sahih al-Bukhârî*. İstanbul: al-Maktabat al-Islamiyye.

Bulut, Mehmet. *Güncel Dini Meseleler İstişare Toplantısı*. Ankara: Türkiye Diyanet İşleri, 2009.

Coşkun, Selçuk, "On the Use of 'Fitrah' As a Measure in Determining Whether a Narrated Hadith Belongs to the Prophet Muhammad," *Hadis Araştırmaları Dergisi* [*Journal of Hadith Studies*], 1/VI (2008).

Düzgün, Şaban, Ali (2007). "İnsan Onuru ve Toplumsal Yaşam İçin Etik," *Kelam Araştırmaları Dergisi* [*Journal of the Islamic Theological Researchers*], 5:1.

Ghazâlî, Abu Hamid Muhammad b. Muhammad (1982). *Ihya al-Ulum al-Dîn*. Beirut: Dâr al-Marifah.

Ghazâlî, Abu Hamid Muhammad b. Muhammad, *al-Mustasfâ min Ilm al-Usûl* (Beirut: Dar-al Arqam, 1994).

Ibn Mājah, Abū (1905). "Abdillāh Muḥammad ibn Yazīd Ibn Mājah al-Rab'ī al-Qazwīnī, as-Sunan" (Delhi: al-Matbaü an-Nizami).

Ibn, Manzûr, Abû Fadl Muhammad ıbn Mukarram b. Ali al-Ansari (1997). *Lisân al-Arab*. Beirut: Dâr al-Ihyâ al-Turath al-Arab.

Ilkilic, Ilhan, "Wann Endet das Menschliche Leben? Das muslimische Todesverständnis und seine medizinethischen Implikationen," in *Lebensanfang und Lebensende in den Weltreligionen*. Beiträge zu einer interkulturellen Medizinethik, eds. U. H. J. Körtner, Neukirchener Verlag Medien, und Recht GmbH (Neukirchen-Vlyun, 2006), 165–82.

Ilkilic, Ilhan, "End-of-Life Decisions at the Beginning of Life," in *Health, Culture and the Human Body*, eds. İ. İlkılıç, H. Ertin, R. Brömer, H. Zeeb (BETIM Center Press, Istanbul, 2014), 433–44.

Ilkilic, Ilhan, "Normativity of Heterogeneity in Clinical Ethics," *The American Journal of Bioethics*, vol. 15, 21–23 (2015).

Ilkilic, Ilhan, "Menschenwürde und ethische Bewertung von Entscheidungen am Lebensende am Beispiel innerislamischer Positionen," *Zeitschrift für Evangelische Ethik*, vol. 60, 88–101 (2016).

IMANA, http://c.ymcdn.com/sites/www.imana.org/resource/resmgr/Files/Publication 2.pdf (accessed April 14, 2016).

Isfahani, Muhammad b. Mufaddal Ragıb, *Mufradat al Alfaz al-Qur'an*, "al-Nafs" (Damascus: Dâr al-Kalem, 2002).

Izutsu, Toshihiko, *God and Man in The Qur'an: Semantics of the Qur'anic weltanschauung* (Kuala Lumpur: Islamic Book Trust, 2002).

Karaman, Hayrettin, Ötenazi, Kürtaj. http://www.hayrettinkaraman.net/yazi/hayat/0403.htm (accessed April 13, 2016).

Kaya, Ali, "Ruh ve Beden Bütünlüğüne Dokunulmazlık Kuramı Bakımından Ölme Hakkı," *Marife Journal* (2004), 2.

Marghînânî, Burhân al-Dîn, *al-Hidâyah: Sharh al-Bidayat al-Mubtadî* (Cairo: Dâr al-Salam, 2000).

Mutii, Muhammad Najeb, *al-Mecmu', ash-Sharh al-Muhadhdhab* (Jeddah: al-Maktabah al-Irshad, 1977).

Nasâ'î, Ahmad ibn Shu'ayb ibn Alî ibn Sînân Abû 'Abd ar-Rahmân al-Nasâ'î, *as-Sunan* (Beirut: Dâr al-Bashair al-Islamiyye, 1988).

Nawawî, Abu Zakaria Muhyî ad-Dîn Yahya Ibn Sharaf, *Rawdhat al-Tâlibîn* (Beirut: Dâr al-Kutub al-Ilmiyyah, 1992).

Nawawî, Abu Zakaria Muhyî ad-Dîn Yahya Ibn Sharaf, *al-Majmu'* (Riyad: Dâr al-#afAlam al-Kutub, 2003).

Öztürk, Mustafa (2006). "Kur'anın Değer Sisteminde Dünya ve Dünyevi Hayatın Anlamı." *Tasavvuf Dergisi* [*Scientific and Academic Research Journal*] 16.

Paşa, Sava (1955). *İslam Hukuk Nazariyatı Hakkında Bir Etüt*. Ankara: Diyanet İşleri Başkanlığı.

Pickthall, Muhammad Marmaduke William (1930). *The Meaning of the Glorious Qur'an*. London.

Qaradawi, Yosuf al-Qaradawî (2016). "Qatl al-Rahma." http://www.qaradawi.net/new/Articles-136 (accessed April 13, 2016).

Qâsânî, Abû Bekr (1997). *Badâi' al-Sanai' fî Tartîb al-Sharai*. Beirut: Dâr al-Kutub al-Ilmiyye.

Qashanî, Abd al-Razzaq (1966). *Sharh al-Fusus Al-Hikam*. Egypt: Mustafa al-Bab al-Halebî.

Ramlî, Imam (1984). *Nihayat al- Muhtaj ila Sharh al-Minhaj*. Beirut: Dâr al-Fikr.

Rashvân, Mahmud Sadîk (n.d.). *Qatl al-Rahmah wa-Atharuhu fî 'l-fiqh al-Islami*.

Râzî, Fakhr ad-Din (1911). *Mafatih al-Gayb*. Cairo: Matbaat al-Amiret aş-Şarafiyyah.

Sachedina, Abdulaziz (2009). *Islamic Biomedical Ethics, Principles and Application*. New York: Oxford University Press.

Şentürk, Recep (2002). "Adamiyyah and Ismah: The Contested Relationship between Humanity and Human Rights." *Classical Islamic Law, İslam Araştırmaları Dergisi* [*Turkish Journal of Islamic Studies*], 8.

Shîrâzî, Abû Ishâk (1990). *al-Muhadhdhab fî Fiqh ash-Shafi*. Beirût: Dâr al-Kutub al-Ilmiyye.

Uludağ, Süleyman (2016). "al-Nafs," *TDV Encyclopedia of Islam*, 530. http://www.tdvislamansiklopedisi.org/dia/ayrmetin.php?idno=320529&idno2=c320385 (accessed April 13, 2016).

Yaran, Rahmi (2012). "Ahiret'e İmanın Dünya Hayatına Yansımaları," *Din ve Hayat* [*Journal of Religion and Life*], 16.

Yasien, Muhamed (1995). "Fitrah and Its Bearing on the Principles of Psychology."
    AJISS, vol. 12. Springer.

Yeprem, Saim (2006). "İslam ve Hristiyanlık-Dinlerarası Diyalog için Dini İçerikler,
    Tasavvurlar ve Duyguların Karşılaştırılması." In Konrad Adenauer (ed.). *Din-
    lerin Gen Teknolojisi, Ötanazi ve Organ Nakline Karşı Tutumları.* Ankara.

Yousuf, Muhammed (2012). "Euthanasia and Physician-Assisted Suicide: A
    Review from Islamic Point of View." *International Medical Ethics*, 11.

Zuhayli, Muhammad (1997). *Huquq al-Insan fi al-Islâm: Dirase Mukarene.* Damas-
    cus: Dâr al- Kalem at-Tayyeb.

CHAPTER EIGHT

An Argument in Favor of the Morality of Voluntary Medically Assisted Death

Robert Young

This chapter develops an argument for the moral justifiability of voluntary euthanasia and physician-assisted suicide (which, as appropriate, the author brackets together and refers to as "voluntary medically assisted death") and defends it against objections that opponents are likely to raise. The argument is concerned only with those competent individuals who want medical help to end their lives either because of suffering intolerably as a result of a terminal medical condition, or because of the loss of independence as a result of an incurable medical condition—such as motor neuron disease— which renders people incapable of ending their own lives. It therefore only in passing comments on the situation concerning requests for medical assistance to die coming from persons who are "tired of life" (or, as some would say, "suffering existentially").[1] Nor does the chapter comment on requests for medical assistance to die from those suffering from serious psychological or psychiatric conditions that dispose them to desire death.[2] Lastly, other than indirectly, the chapter does not comment on the circumstances of those who lack the competence to request medical assistance to die, such as children, those in persistent vegetative states, and those with severe dementia.

Arguing for Voluntary Medically Assisted Death

The most common argument for the moral justifiability of voluntary medically assisted death for those whose incurable or irreversible medical condition involves intolerable suffering or loss of independence is an appeal to two values: The value to individuals of making autonomous choices and the value to individuals who make those choices of promoting their well-being. These values are considered by supporters of voluntary medically assisted death to be individually necessary and jointly sufficient for its moral justification. Neither value on its own is regarded as capable of justifying voluntary medically assisted death; indeed, reliance on either as the sole moral justification would leave each exposed to obvious, albeit different, criticisms.

First, if reliance were placed only on the value to an individual of being able to make autonomous choices then the objection would be that no medical reason could be given for opposing, for example, autonomous requests for medically assisted death made by those people who, for whatever reason, are just tired of life. The second objection would be that although personal autonomy is of value, it isn't the only value of relevance when determining the morality of medically assisted death. Those apt to raise this objection maintain (when they are not complaining that depression and other sometime accompaniments of terminal illness undermine the autonomy of the dying) that the value of personal autonomy always must yield to the inviolable—and hence greater—value of human life. Those opposed to voluntary medically assisted death also would object by stating object that to allow competent individuals to access medical assistance to end their lives would put others in jeopardy of having their lives ended prematurely against their will. Those raising this objection maintain that the value to individuals of being able to make autonomous choices for themselves cannot be permitted to override the value of the lives of vulnerable individuals. At present, the author offers only brief responses to these contentions. Because it is virtually certain that at least the last two of these objections also will be raised against the argument presented here—which yokes individual autonomy and well-being—however, these brief responses are elaborated further below.

It certainly should be acknowledged from the outset that there are disagreements about what counts as medical care. Nonetheless, it is an entirely reasonable response to the first claim to maintain that helping those who are "tired of life" to die—simply because they no longer enjoy living—falls outside the scope of medical care. Because the chapter restricts concerns included here to those wanting help to die who are suffering because of a terminal illness, or are suffering because of an irreversible medical condition that renders them burdensomely dependent on others or on technology, the author says nothing more about this first claim.[3] In the course of spelling out the central argument below, the second claim—namely, that the value of personal autonomy must always yield to the value of human life—is disputed, so for the time being the author says nothing further about that claim. The third claim also is taken up later, when considering whether the empirical evidence concerning the recent legalization in several jurisdictions of voluntary medically assisted death reveals any increase in those jurisdictions of instances of nonvoluntary euthanasia.

Opponents of the moral justifiability of voluntary medically assisted death maintain that (when compared with individual autonomy) it is even more obvious that individual well-being cannot be the sole basis for its justification. The reason is that if it were, then nonvoluntary euthanasia would be as justifiable as voluntary medically assisted death whenever those lacking competence were suffering in ways comparable to those competent to request medical assistance to die.

It is obvious, the argument goes, that the suffering of an incompetent dying person can be every bit as intolerable as that afflicting a competent dying person. So, whether individuals are competent to make autonomous requests for medical assistance with dying is irrelevant to whether their suffering is such that they would be, in the words of proponents of voluntary medically assisted death, "better off dead." (The author states the contention this way because those who deny that a person ever can be "better off dead"[4] and, accordingly, object to medically assisted death in every circumstance, still are entitled to make use of the language of their opponents for purposes of an ad hominem argument against them.) The conclusion drawn is that if individual well-being is proposed as the sole ground for making medically assisted death available to individuals who competently request it, then their competence is, in fact, idle and hence such assistance must be made available regardless of competence. Even so, we should ask whether it is likely that anyone seeking morally to justify voluntary medically assisted death will appeal solely to the well-being of those individuals who might want to avail themselves of such assistance. It is certainly true that some consequentialists (who hold that consequences are all that matters morally) have offered defenses of the moral justifiability of *nonvoluntary* euthanasia solely on the ground of achieving better outcomes for human well-being.[5] Whatever the views of consequentialists might be about justifying nonvoluntary euthanasia, however, this author knows of no consequentialist who has sought to argue for the moral justifiability of voluntary medically assisted death solely on the basis of promoting individual well-being. Hence, it appears unlikely that anyone would seek to justify voluntary medically assisted death solely on the basis of promoting individual well-being.

In view of the reflections provided above, it is clear that supporters of the moral justifiability of voluntary medically assisted death who believe it is to be justified by reference to both personal autonomy *and* individual well-being, must insist not only that the two values be considered in combination but also must maintain that the objections that can be levelled against them when they are offered severally fail to gain any traction when they are employed together. Indeed, that is just what many supporters of the moral justifiability of voluntary medically assisted death have maintained.

Additionally, arguments have been produced to: Defeat the position that human life should be considered inviolable and, accordingly, always should take precedence over the exercise of personal autonomy; show that safeguards can be put in place to ensure that the vulnerable are not exposed to having their lives prematurely ended; and establish that death sometimes can be a better choice for a competent individual than having to endure intolerable suffering or severely burdensome dependence on others or on technology. (The objections mentioned in the preceding paragraphs do not, of course, exhaust the concerns that have been raised by opponents of the moral and legal permissibility of voluntary medically assisted death, but those other concerns have been convincingly responded to by supporters of voluntary medically assisted death.)[6]

This chapter began by noting that the general strategy outlined above is commonly employed to justify the moral permissibility of voluntary medically assisted death. The argument developed below is an elaboration of that strategy. More precisely, it is argued that the values underpinning the general strategy are just those that already have been acknowledged as the foundation for the widely agreed right of competent patients to refuse medical treatment, including life-prolonging treatment; that none of the differences between the right of a competent person to refuse life-prolonging medical treatment and the claim of a competent person to request medical assistance to die constitutes a morally significant difference; and, hence, that voluntary medically assisted death is as morally justifiable as is the refusal by a competent patient of life-prolonging medical treatment.[7]

Informed Voluntary Consent and the Right to Refuse Medical Treatment

This section begins by showing how the right to refuse medical treatment has become established as a human right. It illustrates the process by which this has occurred in two different, but representative, common law jurisdictions, and mentions in passing how it also has been recognized by different means in other jurisdictions. It then argues from its wide establishment as a human right to the moral justifiability of voluntary medically assisted death.

The right of competent people to refuse medical treatment is properly seen as an extension of the legal doctrine of informed voluntary consent (or, as it is more commonly known, informed consent). Even though the doctrine has developed in common law countries chiefly through case law, it subsequently also has gained recognition in other countries by way of conventions concerning human rights. Ultimately, it is founded on the value of personal autonomy. Requiring informed consent for a medical procedure is a way of acknowledging the critical importance of a person's capacity to choose and act autonomously (or, as some would put it, of a person's moral agency).

In a series of landmark court judgments dating back to *Schloendorff v. Society of New York Hospitals*[8] in 1914, courts in various common-law jurisdictions have determined that competent patients who understand a proposed medical procedure, and are able to freely give their consent to its administration, are entitled to make the final determination on what will be done with—and to—their bodies. The scope of this chapter is not broad enough to examine how those court rulings have shaped the more encompassing law concerning informed consent.[9] It is instructive, however, to focus on some key court judgments from two different common-law jurisdictions concerning the idea of refusal of medical treatment. These judgments, along with similar rulings in other common-law jurisdictions, have entrenched the right of competent persons to refuse medical treatment. This right is properly seen as an entailment of the broader requirement for informed consent. As mentioned, recognition of the right also has occurred via conventions on human rights, but detailing the many variations adds little of significance to the story. Suffice to say that in Europe, for example, Article 8 (1) of the European Convention on Human Rights is the acknowledged basis for a qualified (rather than an absolute) right of competent persons to refuse medical treatment. The right is widely recognized throughout Europe, but variations in interpretation regarding when further medical treatment should be considered futile and when it is appropriate to rely on advance directives, have led to differences in practice between the separate jurisdictions, which is why this chapter notes that this is a qualified right.

Here, the illustration of how the right of the competent to refuse medical treatment has come to be established begins by referring to a key U.S. case from 1986—*Bouvia v. Superior Court*.[10] It then turns to Canada, where several key cases have been decided, beginning in 1990 with *Malette v. Shulman*,[11] followed in 1992 by *Nancy B. v. Hotel-Dieu de Quebec et al.*,[12] in 1993 by *Rodriguez v. British Columbia (Attorney General)*,[13] and culminating in 2015 in the rejection by the Supreme Court of Canada of an appeal against the judgment delivered in *Carter v. Canada (Attorney General)* in 2012.[14]

In 1986, hospital staff inserted a nasogastric tube contrary to both the verbal and written instructions of Elizabeth Bouvia—a 28-year-old suffering from cerebral palsy, severe degenerative arthritis, and quadriplegia—who was receiving inadequate nutrition by other means. Crucially, Ms. Bouvia was mentally competent. She wanted the hospital to provide her only with palliative care, so she petitioned for the removal of her feeding tube. The trial court denied her request, stating that her prognosis justified the state's interest in preserving her life. The court said that because Bouvia's intention in refusing treatment was to bring about her death, for it to rule otherwise would be tantamount to aiding and abetting suicide. Bouvia immediately appealed the trial court decision. The California Court of Appeal overturned that decision and in the process affirmed Bouvia's right to refuse life-prolonging medical treatment. In particular, the appellate court held that the state's interest in preserving life could not overcome a competent person's right to refuse treatment. It also held that the trial court was in error in concerning itself with Bouvia's intentions. As far as it was concerned, Bouvia was not intending to bring about her death but merely foreseeing it as a result of her choice. Regardless of what is to be thought of this latter claim (which is considered in more detail below), the significance of the appellate court's judgment resides in its insistence that competent persons have the right to refuse medical treatment, including life-prolonging treatment.

The various Canadian cases mentioned above have extended the position adumbrated in *Bouvia* in several important respects. The first case, *Malette v. Shulman*, established that health care providers must respect refusals of treatment not only when competently expressed at the time of the proposed administration of the treatment, but also when expressed in a competently executed advance directive.

After a head-on collision in Ontario that resulted in the death of her husband, Georgette Malette was rushed by ambulance to hospital and placed in the care of Dr. David Shulman in the Emergency Department. Malette had severe facial lacerations, multiple fractures of facial bones, and blood was streaming from her mouth and nose. She was only semiconscious, was incoherent, and was judged to be in shock. Shulman commenced intravenous administration of glucose and Lactated Ringer's Solution. As he was doing this, a nurse drew his attention to a card she had located in Mrs. Malette's purse that indicated Malette was a Jehovah's Witness. The signed card declared that she was not to be administered blood or blood products under any circumstances. Shulman consulted with an orthopedic specialist and together they decided that it was vital to maintain Malette's blood volume to prevent irreversible shock. It soon emerged that her bleeding could not be controlled and her condition deteriorated rapidly. At the point where her systolic blood pressure dropped below 50 mm Hg and her breathing became seriously distressed, Shulman decided to transfuse her despite the existence of the Medical Alert Card. While Malette was receiving the transfusion, her daughter reached the hospital; she, too, was a Jehovah's Witness. Malette's daughter vigorously objected to the treatment and demanded its cessation. Shulman refused to comply and indicated that he would only cease treating his patient in response to an explicit instruction from the patient herself. He explained that, for all he knew, Malette might no longer subscribe to Jehovah's Witness beliefs, or might have signed the card under duress, or might change her mind once confronted with the prospect of death in the absence of a transfusion. Malette's condition improved after the transfusion and she eventually recovered from her injuries.

Even though Shulman's intervention had almost certainly saved Malette's life she sued for damages on the ground of battery, which, in tort law, is construed as an invasion of a person's bodily integrity without the person's consent, or, in other words, as a violation of the doctrine of informed consent. Under tort law, whether the person is harmed or benefited by such an invasion is irrelevant. The ground for any damages lies in the fact that the person did not consent to the invasion. Although it is true that action taken during an emergency on behalf of a person incapable at that time of giving consent can constitute a legitimate exception to the doctrine of informed consent, Malette argued successfully that the emergency exception did not apply in her case. She successfully contended that her Medical Alert Card made it clear that she would refuse under any circumstance to give her consent to a blood transfusion. Hence, Shulman was found to have committed battery on her person. Shulman appealed, but the appellate court affirmed the trial court ruling.

The right of a competent person to refuse medical treatment was reaffirmed in Canada in *Nancy B. v. Hotel-Dieu de Quebec et al*. The plaintiff was suffering from Guillain-Barre syndrome, which inter alia left her dependent on a ventilator. Her competence was unaffected by the condition. After suffering for several years the effects of her immobility and the need for respiratory support she decided she wished to die and requested removal of the ventilator. Even though her medical attendants did not oppose her request, the matter went to trial because of uncertainty about whether a charge of criminal negligence could be brought against the hospital if the ventilator was disconnected. The court ruled that even though Nancy B.'s refusal of the ventilator would accelerate her death she was entitled to refuse it.

In *Rodriguez v. British Columbia (Attorney General)* the Supreme Court of Canada put beyond any lingering doubt the existence of the right of a competent person to refuse medical treatment, including life-prolonging treatment, when it specifically declared that the right exists even if the withdrawal or discontinuance of treatment will lead to death. *Rodriguez* became famous, however, more for the decision of the Supreme Court (by the narrowest of margins) that Sue Rodriguez could not receive a physician's assistance to help her die. Rodriguez suffered from a form of motor neuron disease, amyotrophic lateral sclerosis (also known as Lou Gehrig's disease). She knew that consequently she eventually would be unable to speak, swallow, or breathe without assistance, and thus wanted assurance that she could decide the manner and timing of her death by being able to call upon a willing physician to help her die without the physician being deemed to have committed a criminal offence. Rodriguez contended that, unlike other dying persons who could achieve their wished-for death simply by refusing life-prolonging medical treatment, she could not, and thus that she was denied her right to equality before the law. Although the Supreme Court of Canada ruled against her, Rodriguez achieved her goal clandestinely a year later with the help of a supportive physician. Significantly, however, in 2012 in *Carter v. Canada (Attorney General)*—a case in which Kay Carter, who was suffering from degenerative spinal stenosis, and Gloria Taylor, who was suffering from amyotrophic lateral sclerosis, each sought to be allowed medical help to die—the Supreme Court of British Columbia held that to the extent that the Canadian Criminal Code's prohibitions on murder and assisted suicide outlaw voluntary medically assisted death they infringe Sections 7 and 15 of the Canadian Charter of Rights and Freedoms. The decision subsequently was appealed by a group opposed to the legalization of voluntary medically assisted death.[15] In 2015, however, the Supreme Court of Canada in a unanimous decision set aside the position it had taken in 1993 and ruled in favor of physician-assisted death in specified circumstances, specifically those that applied in *Carter* but circumstances that also as a matter of fact had applied in *Rodriguez*.[16]

Some Circumstances in Which the Right to Refuse Medical Treatment May Be Exercised

This brief recounting of some key cases in the establishment through case law of the right of a competent person to refuse medical treatment has made clear that the right may be exercised to refuse life-prolonging treatment, and may be exercised either by way of a properly executed advance directive or contemporaneously with the proposed administration of the treatment. In light of these points it is helpful to consider some examples from the range of circumstances encompassed within a competent person's right to refuse medical treatment.

One of these circumstances occurs when a dying patient decides that the suffering being endured has robbed his or her life of its value, and that consequently he or she would be "better off dead." Even though the nature of human well-being and the badness of death both are hotly contested matters,[17] the intuitive meaning of the claim that someone would be better off dead can be grasped without having to completely resolve those matters. Intuitively, what is meant is that, as far as the patient is concerned, the life that remains in prospect lacks positive value *for him or her*. In the sort of circumstance being envisaged, whatever good he or she will experience in the remainder of life pales into insignificance when compared with the negative prognosis (such as the further suffering the patient will have to undergo, or the burdensome dependence on others or on technology that he or she will have to endure). Although death usually is considered the worst-case scenario, when continued life promises ongoing suffering or near-total dependence on others or on technology—and these will not be outweighed by any of the goodness that life makes possible—the usually serious badness of death can be set aside and death be welcomed. This author, along with many other people, believes that this sort of account is on the right track.[18] When life-sustaining treatment is withheld or withdrawn in a circumstance such as that presented above and at the patient's request, it is commonly referred to as an instance of "passive voluntary euthanasia" (although, as is made clear below, the terminology is very misleading).

The same holds true for a second circumstance, namely when treatment that is agreed to be medically futile is withheld or withdrawn at the patient's request. In circumstances such as these, an attending physician can rightly claim that treatment is withheld or withdrawn in compliance with a competent request, and therefore there is no intention on his or her part to end life (but simply an intention to comply with the patient's wish). It is unfortunate that such instances are so often described as amounting to passive voluntary euthanasia because the description is seriously misleading. The reason is that it is the presence of an intention to end life that makes euthanasia different from the withholding or withdrawing of life-prolonging medical treatment.

Thus, even though the withholding or withdrawing of life-prolonging medical treatment in response to a competent patient's request clearly is morally defensible, it serves only to muddy the waters to describe such practices as amounting to "passive voluntary euthanasia." That term only applies to a circumstance in which a physician, in response to a request from a patient for medical assistance to die, withholds or withdraws life-prolonging medical treatment from the patient *with the intention of bringing about his or her death*. This is perhaps an appropriate juncture to make one more point of clarification about terminology: Even though for present purposes it remains convenient to bracket them together, physician-assisted suicide is to be differentiated from all forms of euthanasia by virtue of the fact that the only part the physician plays in bringing about the patient's death is to provide the means to end his or her life.

Consider a third circumstance in which there is again agreement that the continuation of life-prolonging medical treatment would be futile. Suppose that the patient asks to be kept comfortable while he or she dies and thus agrees to be "terminally sedated." For example, the patient might agree to be administered benzodiazapines, or benzodiazapines in combination with morphine, to be sedated for the remainder of his or her life and, as is customary with this practice, for nutrition and hydration to be withheld. It might seem that even in a circumstance such as this a physician still is doing nothing more than acceding to the patient's request.

In at least those instances in which the lack of nutrition and hydration accelerate death to an earlier time than it would have occurred from the underlying disease, the physician should be regarded as intending the patient's death. This is for the obvious reason that, in an instance like this, when the physician withholds nutrition and hydration he or she can have no other purpose than to end a patient's life. In the case where the intention of the physician is to medically assist a patient to die, rather than just to comply with his or her request, this is an instance of voluntary euthanasia (given that what is distinctive of instances of euthanasia is the intention to end life for the good of the patient) rather than an instance of the patient being allowed to die.

Allowing to Die Versus Killing

Many hold that whereas withholding or withdrawing medical treatment, including life-prolonging medical treatment, is morally permissible, voluntary euthanasia is not. This contention harks back to the claim that the value of individual autonomy must yield to the inviolable value of human life; in effect, it is in virtue of our lives supposedly having inviolable value that our being intentionally killed is held to be morally impermissible. At its heart the position relies *either* on there being a morally significant difference between allowing a competent patient to die when he or she so requests and killing a competent patient when he or she so requests *or*, as discussed in the next section, on there being a morally significant difference between foreseeing that an action will lead to a person's death and intentionally bringing about a person's death. These two claims underpin the first two objections to my argument for the moral justifiability of voluntary medically assisted death. The text below responds to them in turn.

The first of these alleged differences rests on the distinction between an omission (of which an allowing to die is considered an instance) and an act (of which a killing is considered an instance). Obtaining agreement on how best to draw the distinction between omissions and acts has not proved easy, but there is a satisfactory way of drawing it so that it can in turn be employed to distinguish an instance of letting die from an instance of killing. The following is a way of drawing the distinction that begs none of the key questions.

A doctor allows a patient to die, but does not kill the patient, if the patient would die from the underlying medical condition were the doctor to withhold medical treatment that would prolong the patient's life or withdraw medical treatment that is keeping the patient alive, provided both that the physician is entitled to withhold or withdraw the treatment and that the patient's underlying medical condition is not a result of something the physician previously has done or has omitted to do.

A brief elaboration on this way of drawing the distinction is the following. Intuitively, for a person to be allowed to die he or she already must be dying from an underlying medical condition. If a physician is appropriately to be thought of as withholding or withdrawing life-prolonging treatment, then he or she must be entitled to do so. This requires that the patient not be dying because of something the physician previously did (for if the doctor were then to withhold or withdraw life-prolonging medical treatment he or she simply would complete the causal process that he or she initiated).

Suppose that this captures the distinction well enough for the present purposes. A more important question remains: Does the distinction as drawn have any moral significance? If it does, then what does it signify for the moral permissibility of voluntary medically assisted death? In general, those who think that only the withholding and withdrawing of life-prolonging treatment are morally permissible maintain that the distinction has moral significance by virtue of reminding us of the inviolability of human life. This argument maintains that it is one thing to die from an underlying medical condition, but is something else entirely to die at another person's hands (regardless of whether those hands are responding to a competent request).

Does this settle matters? No, it does not. As noted above, there are commonly utilized end-of-life practices that involve the withholding or withdrawing of medical treatment (e.g., the withholding or withdrawing of nutrition and hydration from competent patients who are being terminally sedated) which nonetheless amount to the intentional ending of the lives of patients at their request. Moreover, allowing a patient to die can leave the patient worse off than he or she would have been if killed, namely, when allowing a patient to die prolongs his or her suffering without facilitating any compensating goods (like the enabling of opportunities for final farewells). The clear implication is that some instances of allowing patients to die (death being brought about by means of the withholding or withdrawing of life-prolonging treatment) will be morally indistinguishable from instances in which dying patients are helped to die through voluntary euthanasia. That being so, the distinction between letting die and killing cannot alone determine whether voluntary medically assisted death is morally justifiable.

By way of an addendum, it might be thought that, because competent patients are entitled to refuse life-prolonging medical treatment, medical assistance with dying is unnecessary because a competent patient who judges that he or she would be better off dead always can achieve this purpose by refusing nutrition and hydration. Although it is true that competent patients who wish to die can refuse nutrition and hydration, many competent dying patients are likely to find such a strategy unattractive because it means losing control over the timing of their deaths and also might mean having to endure additional unpleasantness. Thus, although the strategy always is available it has to be borne in mind that most competent patients who are set on dying will not wish to adopt such an approach and would prefer to avail themselves of either physician-assisted suicide or voluntary euthanasia.[19]

The Doctrine of Double Effect

There is more to be said about the supposed wrongness of intentionally ending the life of a competent dying person on request. According to the standard interpretation of the traditional "doctrine of double effect," even though it is morally impermissible to intentionally perform certain harmful acts, it is morally permissible to act in ways that it is foreseen will have harmful consequences as long as the following four conditions are satisfied.

1. The harmful consequences are a side effect to the achievement of the act that is directly aimed at.

2. The act directly aimed at is itself morally good, or at least is morally neutral.

3. The good effect is not achieved by way of the harmful effect; that is, the harm is not a means to the good.

4. The harmful effect is not so serious as to outweigh the good effect.

Thus, for example, according to the doctrine it is permissible to administer a drug such as morphine for the relief of suffering (a good effect) even though it is foreseen (i.e., known) that the morphine will shorten life, but it is impermissible to administer morphine with the intention of terminating life (a bad effect). This chapter is not the occasion to give full consideration to the doctrine because, for present purposes, it is necessary only to point out that the doctrine has no application in connection with voluntary medically assisted death. The reason is straightforward: The doctrine is only concerned with actions that involve harmful outcomes but, as was made clear above, for those competent patients who request medical assistance to die because they believe that they will be better off dead, death is a benefit not a harm.[20]

The Right to Refuse Medical Treatment and Voluntary Medically Assisted Death

This chapter previously contended that the finding in various court cases that competent patients are entitled to refuse medical treatment—including life-prolonging medical treatment—has implications for the moral permissibility of voluntary medically assisted death. So far, no morally significant difference has been found between a competent refusal of life-prolonging medical treatment and a voluntary request for medically assisted death. To substantiate this claim, however, at least two counterclaims must be defeated.

One counterclaim is that it does not follow from the fact that a competent patient is entitled to *refuse* life-prolonging medical treatment that a competent *request* for medically assisted death should be honored when made by a terminally ill patient undergoing intolerable suffering or by a person whose burdensome suffering stems from an irreversible medical condition. The second counterclaim is that even if voluntary medically assisted death can be shown to be morally permissible it does not follow that it should be legalized. In other words, for something to be afforded legal protection it is not enough that it be morally permissible. Each of these contentions is important and warrants further consideration; they are considered consecutively here and in the following section.

There is a normative asymmetry between requests for specified medical treatments and refusals of specified medical treatments. The asymmetry is a result of the fact that entitlements arising out of positive rights (i.e., rights to assistance) are weaker than those arising out of negative rights (i.e., rights against interference). Requests are to be located within the former category, refusals within the latter. Notwithstanding that there is this difference, competent patients are entitled to make certain requests for treatment, albeit— by contrast with refusals—there are some obvious limits. First, and most importantly, the medical treatments a competent person is permitted to request are restricted to those that fall within the range of medically indicated treatments (i.e., those that have a reasonable prospect of conferring a medical benefit). Further, because resources are limited, it simply might not be possible to provide certain treatments. Lastly, in jurisdictions where a procedure is illegal, the illegality imposes another limitation on what a competent patient legitimately may request a doctor to do.

The question to be asked is whether the existence of this normative asymmetry between requests and refusals is sufficient to show that requests by competent patients for medical assistance to die should not be fulfilled. Some think that what the asymmetry shows is that it would be morally unjustified for medical personnel to assist their patients to die because to do so would go against the morality of medical care. This author's response is that this is a serious oversimplification. The first point to make in reply is that even if there are limits (such as those mentioned above) to the obligations medical personnel have to fulfill requests from their competent patients, whether a particular request comes within the scope of those obligations remains to be determined. Furthermore, even if doctors are under no obligation to fulfill particular competent requests it still could be *permissible* for them to do so. As it happens, it is possible to be more determinate about this matter because medical personnel have at least one positive obligation to their patients that is of relevance to requests for medically assisted death, and that is to relieve suffering when that is within their capacity. This obligation, of course, can be fulfilled through various measures ranging from palliative care through to terminal sedation. More importantly, no reason has been found for excluding from these measures the administration of voluntary medically assisted death, provided, of course, that it is both medically indicated and legal in the jurisdiction in which it is to be administered. In those jurisdictions in which it is lawful it is acknowledged to be a means of relieving suffering, a hallmark commitment of medical care.

The second point to make in reply is equally significant for the moral justification of voluntary medically assisted death. The previous paragraph stated that doctors have an obligation to relieve suffering when it is within their capacity to do so. Occasionally, to meet that obligation it might be necessary to act in a way that initially, at least, involves doing what is, in itself, bad or harmful to a patient. The justification for doing so is that the harm is a necessary means to the achievement of an outcome that is in the patient's best interests, and thus is for the good of the patient. In other words, an action that if done in isolation would be harmful can be for the best when undertaken in appropriate circumstances. Consider preventive mastectomies wherein healthy breast tissue is surgically removed from those at high risk of breast cancer to lessen the risk of contracting breast cancer at a later date. Suppose, as seems reasonable, that at least some of those undergoing this procedure have requested that their surgeons perform the procedure. A surgeon who agreed about the medical advisability of such a procedure (i.e., considered the procedure to be medically indicated) and fulfilled the request would correctly see the surgical removal of healthy tissue (which, if done in isolation, would constitute a harm) as a means to furthering the good of the patient. In short, the aim of the requested surgery would be to benefit the patient.

Therefore, even though there is a normative asymmetry between competent refusals of medical treatment and competent requests for medical treatment, it is far from obvious that a request made by a competent patient for a medical treatment intended to serve medically indicated best interests is precluded. Moreover, it also is far from obvious that such a request differs in a morally significant way from a refusal of medical treatment by a patient who judges a refusal to be in his or her best interests. Of course, as emphasized here, the requested medical response must be both medically indicated and something that the medical practitioner is entitled to provide.

Accordingly, the spotlight must be on whether it can be in the best interests of competent persons who are terminally ill or burdensomely dependent on others or on technology and consequently want to die to have their requests for medically assisted death satisfied. This chapter has contended that this is the case for those competent individuals who, in light of the prognosis for their medical condition, have assessed their future life prospects and concluded that they would be better off dead. It has further contended that it is morally permissible for doctors to fulfill requests from competent patients for assistance to die in the event that those patients judge that they would be better off dead, the doctors agree that the assistance is medically indicated, and it is legally permissible for the doctors to render that assistance. It is not incompatible with the morality of medical care for them to fulfill such requests. Indeed, as explained above, the administration of medically assisted death sits well with the obligation that medical practitioners must have to relieve suffering when that is within their capacity, and therefore is a legitimate component of medical care.

In sum, the objection that a competent refusal of medical treatment is entirely different from a competent request for medically assisted death overstates the differences between them and should be rejected. A request from a competent patient for medically assisted death when the patient judges that he or she would be better off dead (because of having to endure further unbearable suffering or burdensome dependence on others or on technology) is, in truth, grounded on a similar moral footing to the well-established right of a competent person to refuse medical treatment, including life-prolonging medical treatment.

From the Ethical to the Legal

Many critics of the legalization of voluntary medically assisted death think that its moral defensibility is one thing but its legalization quite another. They maintain that there are powerful reasons for not legalizing the practice and that these reasons show that it would be unsafe to go down the path of legalization.

This section first outlines—and then briefly responds to—these claims. It first turns to the claim that were society to legalize voluntary medically assisted death it would institute a slippery slope that eventually would lead to support for nonvoluntary euthanasia, and thereby put in jeopardy the lives of vulnerable members of society. Whereas it was once the common refrain that the experience in Nazi Germany[21] established a precedent, in recent decades there has been a shift to the claim that the reality of the slope has been confirmed by what has happened, and continues to happen, in the Netherlands and in the United States in Oregon—the two jurisdictions with the longest experience of legalized voluntary medically assisted death.

One (but not the only) way of classifying slippery slope arguments is by reference to whether they are versions of logical, psychological, or arbitrary line forms.[22] The common feature of these different forms is the contention that once the first step is taken on a slippery slope the subsequent steps follow inexorably, whether for logical reasons, for psychological reasons, or to avoid arbitrariness in "drawing a line" between a person's actions.

This section first considers (very briefly) why, at the theoretical level, none of the arguments appears powerful enough to trouble an advocate of the legalization of voluntary medically assisted death. It then comments on the empirical support for opposing its legalization that is allegedly to be found in the experiences of Hitler's Germany, and in the Netherlands and Oregon subsequent to the legalization of voluntary medically assisted death. In particular, it considers the empirical evidence for the claim that the legalization of voluntary medically assisted death in those jurisdictions ushered in the practice of nonvoluntary euthanasia.

Regarding the logical form of slippery slope argumentation, it suffices to say that there is no logical inconsistency in supporting voluntary euthanasia and maintaining that nonvoluntary euthanasia is morally unjustifiable. Those who advocate only voluntary medically assisted death think that a strict limit should be imposed on the practice of euthanasia, a limit that is determined by the competent consent of the patient. This is not to deny that other advocates of voluntary medically assisted death consider that nonvoluntary euthanasia also might be justified in specific instances (e.g., for those in persistent vegetative states who have never indicated their wishes about being helped to die, and for certain severely disabled infants for whom there is only the bleak and hopeless prospect of continued suffering). Rather, it is simply to note that these advocates stand in stark contrast to those who insist both on honoring a competent person's request for medical assistance to die and on fostering his or her best interests. These latter believe that autonomy is the paramount consideration even though they insist that the two values have to function in combination. The difference is not one of logical acumen; it is to be located in the values upheld by the respective supporters.

Regarding the alleged psychological inevitability of moving from voluntary to nonvoluntary euthanasia, it is difficult to see why any such inevitability should be thought to exist. Why, for example, should those who support the legalization of voluntary medically assisted death because they value both the autonomy of the individual and an individual exercising autonomy to determine what would best serve his or her interests, find it psychologically easier to endorse the killing of those who are unable to competently request such assistance? What reason is there to believe that as a result of their support for physician-assisted suicide or voluntary euthanasia, people will be psychologically compelled to administer nonvoluntary euthanasia?

Finally, there is nothing arbitrary about distinguishing voluntary euthanasia from nonvoluntary euthanasia. There is a bright line to be drawn between them. Whether a decision is on one side of the line or the other is wholly determined by whether it is a competent decision, that is, it is both informed and made autonomously. Accordingly, there can be no substance to the charge that only by arbitrarily drawing a line between them can the legalization of voluntary medically assisted death not result in nonvoluntary euthanasia.

The upshot is that none of these versions of the slippery slope argument supplies a convincing theoretical reason against the legalization of voluntary medically assisted death. However, that leaves untouched the empirical evidence from Hitler's Germany, and from the recent experience with legalized voluntary medically assisted death in the Netherlands and Oregon. The period of Nazi rule in Germany is easily dismissed as an example of an inevitable descent down a slippery slope from voluntary euthanasia to nonvoluntary euthanasia. From the 1920s to the 1940s, there never was a policy in favor of, or a legalized practice of, voluntary euthanasia in Germany.[23] Prior to Hitler coming to power there was a practice of killing some disabled persons, but the justification offered never was that their being killed was in *their* best interests; rather, it was said that society would be benefited. Hitler's later revival of the practice, and the widening to include other groups such as Jews and Romanies, was part of a program of *eugenics*, not of euthanasia.

What of the evidence from the legalization of voluntary medically assisted death in the Netherlands and Oregon? In 1991, the Remmelink Report about the medical practice of voluntary medically assisted death in the Netherlands was published. Before that Report it was frequently said that the Dutch experience shows that legally protecting voluntary medically assisted death is impossible without also affording protection to nonvoluntary euthanasia. In the period since the Remmelink Report was issued an additional four national studies of the practice of voluntary euthanasia have been conducted (in 1995, 2001, 2005, and 2010).[24] The findings from these five national surveys have consistently shown that there is no evidence for the existence of a slippery slope, but critics have not been deterred from continuing to advance the criticisms they made before any of the surveys were conducted. A brief summary of the key findings will help to combat the criticisms. Of those terminally ill persons assisted to die (initially under the protection of an agreement between the legal and medical authorities and, since 2002, with legislative support), almost 60 percent clearly have been cases of voluntary medically assisted death as characterized here. Of the remainder, the vast majority of instances have been patients who at the time of their assisted death were no longer competent. For the overwhelming majority of the latter group, the decisions to end life were taken only after consultation between the attending doctors and family members. Further, according to the researchers, most of these instances should be seen as fitting the practice (common in other countries where voluntary medically assisted death continues to be illegal) of giving titrated doses of opioids to relieve pain in the knowledge that this also eventually will end life, or of terminal sedation. These instances therefore should not be thought of as instances of nonvoluntary euthanasia because elsewhere they are not classified in that way and instead are considered to be instances of allowing patients to die. It is true that in a very few cases consultation occurred only with other medical personnel rather than with relatives; however, the researchers point out that families in the Netherlands strictly have no final authority in law to act as surrogate decision makers for incompetent persons, so there is nothing untoward about these cases.

Contrary to the claims of critics, the legalization of voluntary euthanasia has not resulted in an increase in the incidence of nonvoluntary euthanasia in the Netherlands. Given, as noted above, that critics have claimed that legalization of voluntary medically assisted death would put vulnerable dying persons in jeopardy of being killed prematurely and against their will, this is a very significant finding. Moreover, various other considerations negate the suggestion that there has been a slide to the bottom of a morally dangerous slope:

- About a third of all requests for medical assistance to die are rejected as medically inappropriate;
- There have only been a handful of prosecutions of Dutch doctors for failing to follow agreed procedures;
- None of the doctors prosecuted has had a significant penalty imposed by the law courts; and
- The Dutch public has regularly reaffirmed its support for the agreed procedures.

The operation of the law permitting physician-assisted suicide in Oregon[25] has similarly produced no evidence for the existence of a slippery slope. In those places where legal approval for either voluntary euthanasia or physician-assisted suicide has occurred even more recently—including Belgium, Colombia, Luxembourg, and, in the United States, the states of Washington, Montana, Vermont, and California—it is too soon for a clear picture to have emerged. Additionally, such studies as have been published about what happens in other jurisdictions where no legal protection is in place, such as in the various states and territories of Australia, suggest that the pattern for end-of-life care in the Netherlands and Oregon is quite typical. Finally, it sometimes is argued that there might be more danger of the bright line between voluntary medically assisted death and nonvoluntary euthanasia being blurred when euthanasia is practiced in the absence of legal recognition, for then there can be neither transparency nor monitoring.

None of this is to deny that there is a need for safeguards to be put in place to guard against possible abuses of legally protected voluntary medically assisted death. This is particularly important for those who have become incompetent by the time decisions have to be made about whether they should be assisted to die. It is, of course, possible that changes to law could have unintended bad effects. However, if the arguments given above are sound (and the Dutch experience, along with the more limited experience in Oregon, not only is the best available evidence that they are sound, but also is the *only* relevant evidence), then changes to the laws governing medically assisted death in the Netherlands and in Oregon have not produced any such bad effects.

Conclusion

This chapter has pointed out that it is now well established in a large number of jurisdictions—both in those that look to the common law and in those that do not—that a competent patient is entitled to refuse medical treatment, including life-prolonging treatment, and thus effectively has the right to end his or her life. It has shown that it is plausible to infer that the fundamental basis of the right to decide about life-prolonging treatment—respect for a person's autonomy—has direct relevance to voluntary medically assisted death. To extend recognition of the importance of individual autonomy from cases involving the refusal of medical treatment to cases of voluntary medically assisted death requires no dramatic shift in legal policy. No novel legal values or principles need be invoked. Indeed, the fact that suicide and attempted suicide no longer are criminal offences in many jurisdictions indicates that the central importance of individual autonomy for a closely analogous matter already largely has been accepted. That physician-assisted suicide and voluntary euthanasia have not been decriminalized as widely is perhaps best explained along the same lines frequently offered for excluding the victim's consent as a justification for an act of killing—namely, the difficulties thought to exist in establishing the genuineness of the consent. The establishment of suitable procedures for giving consent to voluntary medically assisted death, however, would appear to be no harder than establishing procedures for competently refusing burdensome or otherwise unwanted medical treatment. The latter already has been accomplished in many jurisdictions, so the former should be achievable as well.

Finally, suppose that the sort of moral case proposed herein for legalizing voluntary medically assisted death does come to be judged as being stronger than the case against legalization, and voluntary medically assisted death is made legally permissible in more jurisdictions. Should doctors take part in the practice? Should only doctors administer voluntary medically assisted death? It was shown earlier that respect for both the personal autonomy of patients and their judgment of what is in their best interests can sit comfortably with the morality of medical care. It is these twin values that should guide medical care, not a commitment to preserving life at all costs or without regard to whether patients want their lives prolonged when they judge that life is no longer of value to them. Many doctors in the Netherlands and Oregon, and—judging from available survey evidence—in various other jurisdictions as well, see the practice of voluntary medically assisted death as not just compatible with their professional commitments but as fully in accord with how medical care is best conceived and practiced. That being so, there is no justification for legally prohibiting physicians from providing medically assisted death for patients who are terminally ill, or are overwhelmingly burdened by irreversible medical conditions, and who competently request medically assisted death to relieve their suffering.[26]

Notes

1. Jukka Varelius, "Medical Expertise, Existential Suffering and Ending Life," *Journal of Medical Ethics* 40 (2014): 104–7.

2. For a discussion of the propriety of medically assisted death being made available to those suffering severe depression, which has proved difficult to treat, see Udo Schuklenk and Suzanne van de Vathorst, "Treatment-Resistant Major Depressive Disorder and Assisted Dying," *Journal of Medical Ethics* 41 (2015): 577–83, and various commentaries in the same issue of the *Journal*.

3. Elsewhere, in " 'Existential Suffering' and Voluntary Medically Assisted Dying," *Journal of Medical Ethics* 40 (2014): 108–9, this author has argued that even if medically assisted death is precluded for those who are "tired of life," suicide remains an option.

4. Compare, for example, John Keown in Emily Jackson and John Keown, *Debating Euthanasia* (Oxford and Portland, OR: Hart Publishing, 2012), 90, 98ff, 143f, 163, 172.

5. See, for example, Helga Kuhse and Peter Singer, *Should the Baby Live? The Problem of Handicapped Infants* (Oxford: Oxford University Press, 1985); L. W. Sumner, *Assisted Death: A Study in Ethics and Law* (Oxford: Oxford University Press, 2011), 117–26; and several of the contributors to *The Price of Compassion: Assisted Suicide and Euthanasia*, edited by Michael Stingl (Peterborough, ON: Broadview Press, 2010).

6. See, for example, Robert Young, *Medically Assisted Death* (Cambridge: Cambridge University Press, 2007); and Sumner, op. cit.

7. Arguments drawing on these features have been utilized in Gerald Dworkin, R. G. Frey, and Sissela Bok, *Euthanasia and Physician-Assisted Suicide: For and Against* (Cambridge: Cambridge University Press, 1998), Part 1; Young, op. cit.; and Sumner, op. cit.

8. *Schloendorff v. Society of New York Hospitals,* 211 N.Y. 125 (1914).

9. For extended accounts of the legal and medical developments that have produced the current doctrine see, for example, Ruth Faden and Thomas Beauchamp, in collaboration with Nancy King, *A History and Theory of Informed Consent* (New York: Oxford University Press, 1986); Stephen Wear, *Informed Consent: Patient Autonomy and Physician Beneficence* (Washington, DC: Georgetown University Press, 1998 2nd ed.); and J. W. Berg, P. S. Appelbaum, C. W. Lidz, and L. S. Parker, *Informed Consent: Legal Theory and Clinical Practice* (New York: Oxford University Press, 2001). For a brief account see Robert Young, "Informed Consent and Patient Autonomy" in *A Companion to Bioethics,* ed. Helga Kuhse and Peter Singer (Chichester: Wiley-Blackwell, 2009, 2nd ed.), 530–40.

10. 225 Cal. Rptr. 297 (1986).

11. 72 DLR (4th) 321, 72 OR (2d) 417 (CA) (1990).

12. 86 DLR (4th) 385 (1992).

13. 107 DLR (4th) 342 (1993).

14. B.C.S.C. 886 (2012).

15. For a critique of the judgment by a staunch opponent of the legalization of voluntary medically assisted death see John Keown, "A Right to Voluntary Euthanasia? Confusion in Canada in *Carter." Notre Dame Journal of Ethics and Public Policy* 28 (2014): 1–45.

16. SCC 5 (2015), SCR 331 (2015).

17. Compare, for instance, Ben Bradley, *Well-Being and Death* (Oxford: Clarendon Press, 2009).

18. The author does not deny that critics of voluntary medically assisted death generally object to the claim that a person can be better off dead. Some, like Keown, *Debating Euthanasia,* op. cit, p. 98f, hold that if it is possible for a doctor to judge that someone would be better off dead, then the doctor's duty to benefit the patient requires him or her to do so regardless of the patient's views. If so, then the doctor can have no principled objection to nonvoluntary euthanasia (which, of course, Keown considers an anathema). Others, such as J. David Velleman, "A Right of Self-Termination?" *Ethics* 109 (1999): 606–28, argue that the value that inheres in a person cannot be traded off against the person's interests and so voluntary medically assisted death must be opposed insofar as it is motivated solely by a desire to promote the interests of the person who is to be assisted to die. In short, Velleman thinks that to accede to a competent person's request for medical assistance to die is to disrespect the dignity he or she has as a person (because it destroys the person's rational nature, which is the ground of personhood). There is much more to be said about this view (which is thought by some to find authoritative support in the writings of Immanuel Kant) than is appropriate here, but two points can be stated briefly. First, were Velleman's view compelling it would not just require the moral rejection of suicide and voluntary medically assisted death, but the moral rejection of the right of competent patients to refuse life-prolonging medical treatment. Second, because Kant allowed in his *Lectures on Ethics* that it would be better to choose death than voluntarily to submit to

becoming a galley slave, it is far from clear that Kant would endorse a view like Velleman's. For further discussion of Kant's view on these matters see Michael Cholbi, "Kant on Euthanasia and the Duty to Die: Clearing the Air," *Journal of Medical Ethics* 41 (2015): 607–10. For further discussion of Velleman's view see Frances Myrna Kamm, "Physician-Assisted Suicide, the Doctrine of Double Effect and the Ground of Value," *Ethics* 109 (1999): 586–605; Jeff McMahan, *The Ethics of Killing: Problems at the Margins of Life* (New York: Oxford University Press, 2002), 473–85; Young, *Medically Assisted Death*, op. cit., pp. 74–78; and Sumner, op. cit., pp. 82–84.

19. For discussion of the strategy see, for example, James L. Bernat, Bernard Gert, and R. Peter Mogielnicki, "Patient Refusal of Hydration and Nutrition: An Alternative to Physician Assisted Suicide and Voluntary Euthanasia," *Archives of Internal Medicine* 153 (1993): 2723–28; and Julian Savulescu, "A Simple Solution to the Puzzles of End of Life? Voluntary Palliated Starvation," *Journal of Medical Ethics* 40 (2014): 110–13. Savulescu believes that palliative care can ensure that the otherwise unpleasant side effects of dying from starvation and thirst are avoided.

20. For a helpful discussion of the doctrine of double effect and an extensive bibliography of writings about it see Alison McIntyre, "Doctrine of Double Effect," *The Stanford Encyclopedia of Philosophy,* ed. Edward N. Zalta (Winter 2014 ed.). http://plato.stanford.edu/archives/win2014/entries/double-effect/ (accessed August 14, 2016).

21. For an acclaimed study of those happenings see Michael Burleigh, *Death and Deliverance: 'Euthanasia' in Germany c. 1900–1945* (Cambridge: Cambridge University Press, 1994).

22. Douglas Walton, *Slippery Slope Arguments* (Oxford: Clarendon Press, 1992) remains an excellent resource.

23. See Burleigh, op. cit.

24. For a comprehensive survey see B. D. Onwuteaka-Philipsen, A. Brinkman-Stoppelenburg, C. Penning, G. J. Jong-Krul, J. J. M. van Delden, and A. van der Heide, "Trends in End-of-Life Practices Before and After the Enactment of the Euthanasia Law in The Netherlands from 1990–2010: A Repeated Cross-Sectional Survey," *The Lancet* 380 (2012): 908–15. For discussion of the main issues that have arisen over the several decades in which voluntary medically assisted death has been legally permitted in the Netherlands see J. A. C. Rietjens, P. J. van der Maas, B. D. Onwuteaka-Philipsen, J. J. M. van Delden, and A. van der Heide, "Two Decades of Research on Euthanasia from The Netherlands: What Have We Learnt and What Questions Remain?" *Journal of Bioethical Inquiry* 6 (2009): 271–83.

25. See, for example, L. Ganzini, E. Goy, and S. Dobscha, "Oregonians' Reasons for Requesting Physician Aid in Dying," *Archives of Internal Medicine* 169 (2009): 489–92.

26. Thanks for helpful comments on a draft of this chapter are due to Norvin Richards, and to members of an audience at the University of Melbourne.

CHAPTER NINE

Limiting the Right to Die: Moral Logic, Professional Integrity, Societal Ethos

Courtney S. Campbell

The June 27, 2015, cover of the prominent news journal *The Economist* headlined a cover story titled "The Right to Die."[1] The content and scope of this right was situated in the context of debates over legalization of what the story referred to as "doctor-assisted dying." The story presented a short profile of the case of Brittany Maynard as its illustrative patient.[2] Ms. Maynard, a 29-year-old newly married woman who in the winter of 2014 was diagnosed with terminal brain cancer, had used a prescription provided by a physician in Oregon (following the statutory provisions of the state's "Death with Dignity" law) to hasten her death on November 1, 2014.[3]

An accompanying editorial noted that the Oregon law is often seen as a "model" for legalizing physician assistance in dying, but maintained "we would go further." The editorial advanced a case for expanding the practices legally warranted by "the right to die" to allow for physician administration or provision of lethal medication to (1) persons who are physically incapacitated and cannot self-administer the drugs; (2) persons who are suffering from a chronic, but nonterminal, condition; (3) persons experiencing "mental" pain or suffering; and (4) children facing an imminent death from a terminal condition.[4] It quickly becomes clear that the model jurisdiction for doctor-assisted dying is not Oregon but Belgium. The content and scope of the right to die has been expanded substantially.

Although the extent of this proposal is stunning, in point of fact the argument is, in essence, carrying out a moral logic embedded in prior arguments about the right to die. The claim that a patient has a right to assistance from a physician in hastening his or her death has perennially relied on two major ethical principles, that of respect for personal autonomy, and the duty of professional beneficence to relieve pain and suffering. Under current statutes in Oregon and other U.S. states (California, Vermont, Washington), the right of self-determination is given legal priority, but, as argued by advocates of patient rights, a person's right to die should not be contingent on their physical capacity. Persons with ALS, for example, should not have their rights restricted simply because they are incapable of the motor movement necessary to self-administer the lethal medication. The legal requirement for patient self-administration seems in this respect to be morally arbitrary. Similarly, insofar as a central purpose of medicine is to alleviate patient pain and suffering, it can seem difficult to justify the distinction the laws make in this regard between terminal disease and chronic disease, and between physical pain and mental suffering.

This extension of the moral logic of the right to die to "go further" than physician assistance in hastening the death of terminally ill patients, and to encompass acts of physician administered euthanasia as well as hastened death for nonterminal patients, has indeed been anticipated by some scholars and ethicists for decades. Writing in the era when the scope of the right to die covered rights to refusal of medical treatment, including refusal of medical feeding tubes, bioethicist Daniel Callahan objected to the then-incipient proposals for legalization of physician assistance in patient suicide or euthanasia on the grounds that the moral justification for legalization reflected a "boundless logic."[5] Callahan presciently recognized that once the moral rationale for physician actions to prescribe a lethal dose of medication to terminally ill patients was deemed philosophically and professionally acceptable based in the principles of respect for autonomy and beneficence or compassion, there would be no reason *in principle* to not also permit provision of life-ending medication to patients who suffered in the absence of a terminal illness, nor to patients whose autonomy was more a matter of decision making than physical capacities. The *Economist* editorial board has then developed the embedded moral logic of appeals to the right to die to an anticipated set of philosophical and clinical conclusions, even if the laws in almost all jurisdictions have not yet arrived there.

The purpose of this chapter is to provide a critical account of prominent arguments about the content, meaning, and scope of the right to die. As illustrated by the forgoing, it presents the concept of the right to die to make a moral claim that encompasses not only a patient's *right to refusal* of medical treatments at the end of one's life, but also a *terminally ill* patient's right to a *hastened death* through physician-prescribed medication or through physician-administered euthanasia based in the principle of respect for autonomy, as well as a *chronically ill* patient's right to a hastened death through physician-prescribed medication or through physician-administered euthanasia based in the principle of beneficence or the professional duty to relieve pain and suffering.

This entails a critical analysis of arguments about personal autonomy and self-determination, certainly, but also those arguments directed toward the responsibilities of physicians (and occasionally, pharmacists or nurses) that reflect considerations of professional integrity. Insofar as moral positions on patient autonomy and physician integrity have implications for questions of legalization, it also is necessary to address the impact of an expansive scope of the right to die for citizens, intermediate communities such as hospice organizations or religious communities, and the general societal ethos. This argumentation presumes a distinctive cultural context for modern dying, with which the chapter begins.

A Context of Dying

It is very difficult in the field of biomedical ethics to find an argument or position that doesn't at some point or another find a moral foundation in the principle of respect for personal autonomy or self-determination. From ethical issues about reproductive choices and the beginnings of life to medical research or testing in the prime of life, to decisions about life's endings, the rights of patients to informed and voluntary decision making in medical care are paramount. The profile of patient rights to self-determination is seldom higher than in discourse over the right to die.

As alluded to above, a core philosophical argument for expanding the right to die to include forms of hastened death has been constituted by an appeal to the right of self-determination, the principle of respect for patient autonomy, and informed patient choice. In this core argument, a mentally competent patient is considered to have *moral* authority about both *who* decides and *what* is to be decided with respect to end-of-life care. The various state statutes that currently permit physician assistance in the hastened death of a terminally ill patient reiterate this emphasis on patient self-determination by requiring rational decision-making capacity, knowledge of the anticipated outcomes of the procedure as well as alternatives, and the voluntary choice, expressed consistently over some duration of time, of a terminally ill patient. Significantly, physician reports of patient rationales in Oregon for choosing physician-assisted dying as the method of ending life have consistently indicated patient concerns about losing autonomy as the primary end-of-life consideration; the proportion of patients whom physicians report stating such concern has remained steady at ~91 percent for nearly two decades.[6]

Nonetheless, the concept of the right to die seems at first glance to be a very puzzling moral and legal claim. After all, "rights" are justifiable claims against others for their nonintervention (a "negative" right) or their assistance (a "positive" right). We appeal to our rights as grounds for preventing others from depriving us of an important interest. Thus there is an important philosophical correlation between rights and duties; an appeal to a "right" represents a claim that some others have a "duty." A valid moral right means that others have moral duties to refrain from intervening with our decisions or our actions or a duty to assist us in achieving our ends. Ultimately, however, no person or medical technology will prevent us from experiencing dying and death. Hence, the moral and legal puzzle: How can we have a "right" to something that will happen no matter what anyone else does? The evolving meanings and scope of the right to die can be rendered clearer by attentiveness to historical and cultural context.

The "right to die" entered into the discourse of medical law, biomedical ethics, and public usage in the mid-1970s as part of the moral upheaval that occurred within medical care at the end of life in the wake of the case of Karen Ann Quinlan, a college student who suffered cardiac failure from a drug and alcohol overdose, followed by the onset of a permanent vegetative state. Ms. Quinlan became a tragic symbol of the ways that new medical technologies could prolong biological life for years—even decades—without providing any significant medical benefit to the patient. It also became evident as the Quinlan case unfolded that life extension in the absence of patient improvement and benefit also engendered moral and spiritual distress in family members and in professional caregivers.

The Quinlan case is widely regarded as the first "right to die" case in the United States, and became precedent setting in several respects.[7] Significantly, the claim by patients to refuse or terminate life-prolonging treatment, such as respiratory support, was legally recognized and ethically justified on grounds of patient autonomy and privacy and encompassed patient freedom from invasive medical procedures. The case recognized the rights of family members, such as Ms. Quinlan's parents, to authorize treatment termination when a patient lacks decision-making capability.

Further, physicians and other professional care providers who participated in decisions about "pulling the plug" were not considered to have violated professional ethics or legal standards of due care.

The Quinlan case did not resolve all issues, however, and it required 15 years of ongoing litigation and ethical discourse about patient rights, proxy rights, and physician responsibilities in the use of medical technology in end-of-life care before a threshold "right to die" case came before the U.S. Supreme Court. The Court considered the rights of the parents of Nancy Cruzan—a Missouri woman who, like Karen Ann Quinlan, had been in a persistent vegetative state for several years following an auto accident—to refuse a different life-extending medical treatment, nutrition, and hydration provided by intubation, on behalf of their daughter. The Supreme Court extended the scope of the arguments made in the *Quinlan* case, ruling in *Cruzan* that tube feedings were a "medical" treatment that could be legitimately refused by a patient, or by an authorized proxy, with "clear and convincing" evidence that the patient would have wanted the treatment stopped or refused. (The Court's evidentiary standard meant that the Cruzans were not able to have the feeding tubes removed from the body of their daughter until additional information about her wishes came forward at the state level.)[8]

Although this brief historical narrative could be substantially and substantively extended, the preceding provides sufficient background through which discourse about "the right to die" acquires intelligibility. Such language points to two primary considerations: the *circumstances* of dying and *decision-making authority* regarding choices to continue or refuse life-sustaining medical technology. The appeal to "the right to die" signals that, in the perception of patients, proxies, and advocates of patient rights, it is now *more difficult* to die in a manner consonant with the patient's values. *That* is the fundamental deprivation that right-to-die discourse seeks to rectify.

In one of the earliest philosophical reflections on the right to die, written shortly after the public furor about the Quinlan case, Hans Jonas likewise affirms the "strange" and "exceedingly odd" construct of this right. Jonas turns to the emergence of life-prolonging medical technologies as the context for the emergence of the right to die. He situates the "novel problem" addressed through this right as, "medical technology . . . can still put off the terminal event of death beyond the point where the patient himself may value the life thus prolonged, or even is still capable of any valuing at all."[9] Jonas sought to establish a philosophical basis for the right to die as a specification of the right to refuse treatment, even as he acknowledged that more "worrisome cases are those of the more or less captive, such as the hospitalized patient with terminal illness, whose helplessness necessarily casts others in the role of accessories to realizing his option for death."[10]

In his recent book, *Being Mortal*, physician Atul Gawande uses a variety of patient narratives to highlight some reasons why various lines have become blurry in contemporary medicine, with the consequence that for many patients it has in fact become more difficult to die relative to prior eras of medicine.[11] Ironically, some of these reasons are attributable to the success of medicine rather than medical failures. For example, the causes of death in the 21st century are significantly different than found a century previously. The majority of persons in generations prior to World War II experienced death from infectious disease, such as polio, influenza, or tuberculosis. Various antibiotics, including penicillin, have altered the general patterns in the population significantly such that nearly 90 percent of persons currently living will die from a chronic ailment, such as heart disease, cancer, lung and pulmonary diseases, diabetes, and Alzheimer's disease.

The implications of this shift for personal and cultural experience of the dying process are profound. The "chronicity of disease" and death refers to a ubiquitous social pattern in which many people are diagnosed of their terminal condition several years before they actually die. They experience a period of gradual decline in health, with accompanying comorbidities, which can limit their physical well-being and social interactions, and thus diminish quality of life. This is a significant consideration with respect to the debate about physician-assisted dying and euthanasia. According to the Oregon data, ~89 percent of patients who request physician assistance to hasten their death under the state statute indicate a concern that due to their terminal condition, they are "less able to engage in activities making life enjoyable."[12]

A contributing factor to the lengthening duration of the chronicity of disease is the research development and successful clinical application of innovative biomedical technologies. As illustrated by the Quinlan and Cruzan cases, biomedical technology can prolong biological life for what could be seen as an indefinite period. Advances in technologies such as pacemakers, chemotherapy, and transplantation can provide proportionate benefits for several years, but at some point the ultimate wrenching question of when to stop treatment must be addressed. The professional "default" in the absence of clear direction from the patient is "do something,"[13] and although there almost always is something else medicine can do, continued technological interventions mean it might no longer be clear, even for physicians, just when a person is actually irreversibly dying: "In the past few decades, medical science has rendered obsolete centuries of experience, tradition, and language about our mortality and created a new difficulty for mankind: how to die."[14]

Prompted in part by the logistics of access to life-sustaining technologies, in part by the economics of health care delivery, the dying process has become increasingly institutionalized. Although in the past two decades an increasing number of deaths in this country have occurred in a patient's home and under hospice care, it still is the case that a majority of deaths occur in institutionalized settings, such as hospitals, nursing homes, or assisted-care facilities. This displacement of dying to institutions means that terminally ill persons can experience dying as a profoundly alienating experience. They receive care from strangers in a setting where the presence of technology is pervasive and nearly everything—from food to time—is unfamiliar and disjointed from their life narrative, including the patient's control over his or her choices.

Perhaps most significantly, end-of-life care can entail a constant series of choices about medical treatments for which there has been inadequate preparation and little communication between patient, family, and physician. Ideals of shared decision making often fail to address the realities of difficult choices in circumstances of uncertainty. In Gawande's interpretation, physicians evade the hard conversations and are excessively optimistic about the patient's prognosis, and duration and quality of life, even in the presence of a terminal condition.[15] This new difficulty has meant for many patients that dying is constructed as beyond their control, and not simply because of an irreversible biological process. The chronicity of modern dying is complemented by control by institutions, by technologies, and by professionals—meaning that death is medicalized and "medically managed." Against this background, patients and their advocates continue to invoke a "right to die" to retain some control and influence over the circumstances of dying and about decision-making authority. Through this appeal, death is brought into the realm of choice.

Applications of the "Right to Die"

The "right to die" is both a rhetorical appeal about the circumstances of modern dying as well as a normative claim regarding who should have authority to make decisions about end-of-life care and treatments. This construction of the right to die does not settle either the scope of the situations in which such a right is relevant, nor in what context it should be exercised, nor does it resolve the normative moral and legal question of *what* should be decided. The right to die has been appealed to in arguments about patient rights to *refuse* medical treatment, whether these involve a respirator, a feeding tube, or antibiotics (or other medical treatments). This was the basic point of contention in the historical origins and evolution of the right to die as illustrated in the Quinlan and Cruzan cases, and more recently still in the case of Terri Schiavo in Florida.[16] The right of patients (or authorized proxies) to refuse or stop medical treatment is now firmly established in law, in patient advance directives, and in medical ethics.

The more controversial context morally and legally regarding a patient's right to die has evolved from arguments regarding treatment cessation to arguments about patient requests for physician assistance in dying. The right to die subsequently has been cited in arguments about the patient's right to *control* their dying or to *medical assistance* in death, as well as the right of a patient to *die with dignity*, or to "end their life in a humane and dignified manner," which is how the right is articulated with respect to the various death-with-dignity statutes in U.S. states. For the remainder of this chapter, the author leaves aside the question about patients' rights to refuse treatment and concentrates on the right to die as a claim for physician-prescribed medication to hasten death, as in the case of Brittany Maynard, as well as the "further step" advocated by *The Economist* of physician administration of lethal agents.

The distinction between a right to refuse or terminate treatment and a right to request assistance in ending one's life corresponds closely with the conceptual distinction in moral philosophy between negative and positive rights. A negative right is a claim by a moral agent of noninterference against others, who have a corresponding duty to not interfere, intervene, or restrict the decisions or actions of the moral agent. The assertion of a negative right—including what Justice Brandeis called the most comprehensive and valued of any right, "the right to be left alone"[17]—provides a zone of moral and legal space within which a person can enact his or her values in accordance with personal self-determination.

Negative rights in general tend to be very stringent, that is, there are relatively few moral claims that can justifiably override them. Additionally, a negative right generally is applicable against all other persons or institutions (the government, medicine, religious communities) that might be in proximity to the moral agent. These other persons or institutions comply with the right, and fulfill their own corresponding moral duty, by not intervening or interfering with the agent's exercise of the right. It generally takes minimal physical effort to comply with another person's negative right; essentially, one complies by "staying out of the way" of the actions of the moral agent. Negative rights thereby imply a corresponding duty on the part of other persons or institutions to respect the person's choices and not interfere with the enactment of autonomy, at least insofar as the action does not impose a risk of harm to others.[18]

The core civil liberties recognized in the legal system, such as the rights to life, to liberty, to freedom of religion, to speech, to a free press, and to peaceful assembly, are classical illustrations of negative rights. In exercising any of these rights, the moral agent makes a claim against others to refrain from interfering in the exercise of these rights. There are likewise several clear examples of the concept of negative rights in biomedical ethics. The most broad and all-encompassing is the right to respect for personal autonomy, including respect for the moral agent's decision-making authority. A second negative right with profound implications is the right to privacy, which provides protections in the contexts of reproductive decision making, control over disclosures of medical information, and research, including research in genetic testing.

The right to refuse medical treatment is among the most prevalent and significant of negative rights in biomedical ethics and health care decision making. It stems from a broader negative right to bodily integrity; in a medical setting, treatments or procedures such as respirators, dialysis machines, pacemakers, feeding tubes, and antibiotics are understood as "invasive" procedures that, without the authorization of the moral agent, violate his or her freedom to bodily integrity. Professionals have a moral duty to remove or to not initiate these invasive procedures upon the informed and voluntary request of the patient or of an appointed proxy who is acting to advance the patient's values.

The contrasting but complementary set of rights—which involve a moral agent's claim of *assistance* from another in bringing about a desired end—are designated as positive rights in moral philosophy. A justified positive right generally is not claimed against all others, but rather against a specified other person with whom the moral agent is in some kind of special relationship. The other person specified has a corresponding positive duty to provide the requested assistance. Thus, compliance with a positive right requires not simply forbearance from action, as with a negative right, but the performance of some action. Positive rights thus tend to have a more limited scope of applicability because they are binding only for persons within a specified relationship—such as the physician-patient relationship—rather than with strangers, as is the case with negative rights.

There are some positive rights that have broader social applicability in American society, such as the right to education, although the means by which this is exercised are variable, for example, public school, private school, or home school. Other positive rights in the social realm are much more controversial, among which is the right *to* health care. This right often is held to require a stronger argument in justification because it is not clear who the right is claimed against, or what party is responsible for the performance of the duty. It might be the state in general or a specific professional organization entrusted by the state to oversee implementation.[19]

There are positive rights *within* health care that are well accepted and justified because of the special relationship between patient and physician. Among the core positive rights is the right to informed consent, which at minimum means that to assist or facilitate a patient's deliberation about a proposed treatment the physician has a duty to disclose information to the patient (or proxy) about a procedure, alternatives to the procedure, and risks of the procedure. A second illustration of a core positive right is the patient's right to confidentiality. This requires the physician (as well as health care institutions) to take steps to ensure that the patient's medical information is protected from nonmedical parties, such as insurers or employers.

The most contested positive right in medical ethics is the right to die as understood and specified as a claim for assistance or intervention from a physician to hasten dying. This right entails a correlative duty on the part of the medical profession, or of a particular medical professional, to provide such assistance. Such a claim raises important questions about not only the meaning of patient self-determination but also about the moral responsibilities of medicine. Further, it invites scrutiny of the underlying ethos of a society that has legitimated medicine with the status of a profession attributable to its distinctive dedication to, knowledge of, and techniques for healing, curing, and caring. However interpreted and construed, the right to die is necessarily about more than the individual patient; its exercise, according to Callahan, also is a "social act" insofar as facilitating the desired end requires participation of others.[20] We now turn to an examination of arguments critical of the scope and applicability of the right to die in each of these realms of moral discourse—patient self-determination, physician integrity, and social ethos. These arguments affirm absolute or qualified opposition to legalizing physician assistance in dying through the prescription and administration of a lethal medication to hasten a patient's death.

The Critique of Autonomy and Self-Determination

This chapter first examines three arguments against legalized physician-assisted death or physician-administered euthanasia that focus their critique on the core rights-based premise of patient self-determination. A first argument contends it is contrary to the meaning of autonomy and self-determination to use personal freedom to end life. A second position challenges the autonomous decision-making capabilities of patients facing terminal illness and concludes that patients experience impaired judgment to such an extent that their decision-making autonomy and authority is compromised. The third position, alluded to previously, claims that the right of autonomy and self-determination is limited in scope to noninterference and negative rights, and such principles cannot substantiate a positive right to physician assistance in death.

The Critique of the Autonomous Self

Leon Kass, former chair of the President's Council on Bioethics, raises a very sharp critique of the right to die as a philosophical and political conception, claiming that "the notion is groundless and perhaps even logically incoherent."[21] Kass contends the language of rights, as applied to human dying and death, distorts our self-understanding or relationships, and our view about death. He recommends that we banish language about the right to die from our moral and political vocabulary.[22] Kass's position is indebted to arguments historically developed in objections to suicide by theologians such as Thomas Aquinas, and variations of the argument are developed by philosophers such as John Locke and Immanuel Kant. The central claim is that freedom or liberty is so integral to who we are, to our shared human nature, that self-determination cannot be given up by the self in circumstances such as intentionally hastening one's death without diminishing the dignity of the human person. It is a self-contradiction to make a choice that irrevocably ends any further choices.

Autonomy often is held to be an unrestricted and absolute principle in regard to matters pertaining to one's self. As articulated by John Stuart Mill in his classic essay, "On Liberty," "over himself, over his body and mind, the individual is sovereign."[23] The substance of Mill's harm principle is that moralistic, legalistic, or paternalistic restrictions on the choices and actions of an autonomous person are legitimate only if such decisions and acts place others at some risk of being harmed. Kass likewise understands claims of rights to have a "non-negotiable and absolutized" character. Rights are "in principle, absolute and unconditional" or "absolute and unqualified" claims.[24]

Even more troubling on Kass's view than the absolute nature of claims to rights, however, is that the "new" rights—among which is the right to die—reflect a cultural valuation of a different kind of selfhood, a self which affirms its radical independence from others, from community and relationships, from history, and from nature. The right to die, among other rights, represents the emergence of a Nietzschean self, "a self-made self" that asserts "the rights of the untrammeled will."[25] Thus, Kass's criticism of the right to die is not simply a matter of moral principle, or of the moral and professional practices that might follow from the principle, but more fundamentally a disagreement about selfhood and the nature of human nature.

Although Kass is culturally observant in recognizing that "the present American climate requires one to talk of rights if one wishes to have one's way is such moral matters,"[26] he overstates the moral primacy or absoluteness of "rights" language. Even Mill's strong advocacy of respecting a person's liberty, choices, and actions nevertheless does not constitute a moral carte blanche. In particular, Mill argued that the possession of liberty does not empower a person to alienate their right of freedom through indentured servitude or slavery: The principle of freedom cannot require that he should be free not to be free. It is not freedom, to be allowed to alienate his freedom."[27] Our political culture also recognizes that the basic rights of the person can, in compelling circumstances, be overridden by other moral and political claims either of individuals or the community. There are then inherent limits to self-determination.

The question at this point is whether this limit within the logic of autonomy itself can be extended from the case of slavery to that of ending life. That is, assuming a person makes an informed and voluntary choice to end their life, would such an action violate the very nature for which freedom is bestowed and valued? Mill himself does not extend his argument on abdicating liberty to a decision to use one's liberty to end life, but the German philosopher Kant makes this argument explicit. Kant also invokes a conception of self to support his claim, thus anticipating the second major line of critique Kass directs against the right to die.

Kant's reasoning is based on intrinsic duties to self and he contends that using one's freedom to take one's life (suicide) necessarily degrades a person and their dignity to the level of "creature." Insofar as one of his formulations of the Categorical Imperative is to "treat humanity, whether in your own person or in the person of any other, never merely as a means to an end," an act of suicide is morally wrong insofar as it involves treating oneself *merely* as a means to an end. The action does not comport with the objective and rational moral law that is one's duty to obey.

The use of freedom to end life not only violates what Kant calls the "perfect duty" to one's self, but it does so in a manner that entirely precludes the performance of any other duties to one's self or to others. Insofar as the goodwill is the necessary and sufficient condition for the performance of duty, self-killing reflects a degraded will that annuls the foundations of all other duties. Thus, although for Mill it is the conditions of freedom that preclude the alienability of freedom, for Kant it is the conditions of duty and moral law that preclude ending the continuation of duty through ending one's life. "To destroy the subject of morality in one's own person is to root out the existence of morality from the world, so far as this is in one's power; and yet morality is an end in itself."[28]

The idea that it seems contrary to the notion of self-determination to act in such a way as to foreclose further self-determination comprise what Kass takes to be the implicit incoherence of the right to die. Self-preservation is a requirement of the rational moral law and good reasons can be presented for restricting such a choice for physician-assisted dying as not in full concord with the conditions of freedom, or the conditions of morality, and as inauthentic to personal dignity. The philosophical argument that we are not free to abandon our freedom has parallels in religious argumentation that the moral agency of human beings is limited by human accountability before God and responsible stewardship over God's gifts, including life and freedom. Indeed, in its position statement on physician-assisted suicide, the U.S. Conference of Catholic Bishops echoes Kant in claiming, "A choice to take one's life is a supreme contradiction of freedom, a choice to eliminate all choices."[29] This isn't to say that a person may not act in such a manner contrary to their liberty, but rather that they cannot do so without abandoning rational grounds. This line of reasoning forms the background to the claim taken up in the subsequent section that imputes impaired judgment to requests for physician assistance in a hastened death.

Before proceeding to the issue of impaired judgment, two responses to the arguments rooted in incoherence and the nature of the self are briefly presented. It seems problematic to argue against the moral absolutism of rights claims with an absolutistic count of human nature. In particular, it is to invariably interpret a person's request to hasten his or her own death as irrational or nonrational when they are with near-certainty within the last six months of their mortality. In this set of circumstances, death will occur with a high degree of probability no matter what is done. A terminally ill person's decision to request assistance in their death arguably could reflect not an intent to alienate their freedom or obliterate morality as much as an understandable response to a biological condition of mortality, of having our agency slowly dissipated by the natural processes of dying from underlying disease. It thereby seems problematic to argue that the person who has received a terminal diagnosis is confronting a circumstance analogous to that of a person tortured by internal demons or external circumstance to end their life prematurely. Instead, such a decision could manifest high levels of moral reflection, critical thinking, and conscious awareness of one's relationships.[30]

Further, the objection of incoherence might not apply to all circumstances of physician assistance in death. A conceptual distinction between a physician prescription for lethal medication and physician-administered euthanasia is that, in the former situation, the terminally ill person retains some semblance of meaningful control over the final action rather than being entirely subject to the will and power of another person. Indeed, data from Oregon and Washington indicate that the medication is used in approximately two of every three cases in which it is prescribed.[31] A request does not necessarily mean an irreversible abdication of freedom, for the patient can choose not to consume the medication. Thus, the cogency of the argument made by Kass and others seems to have more resonance in the circumstance of physician-administered euthanasia.

The Critique of Impaired Judgment

The moral argument for legalized physician-assisted dying or physician-administered euthanasia has continually presupposed the autonomous moral agency of patients facing a terminal illness. Enacted laws bestow the presumption on the decision-making capacity of the patient; a psychiatric evaluation of the patient is a secondary alternative initiated only in circumstances in which a physician has some medical reason for doubting the possession of capacity. It is little surprise then that one critique of the autonomy argument appeals to a different set of empirical "facts" about the decision-making status of a terminally ill person. Critics contend that such a person is suffering from depression or other deficits in cognition, such as comprehension, to an extent that their judgment about a literal life-and-death decision is necessarily impaired. As articulated by physician Ezekiel J. Emanuel, "depression, hopelessness, and psychological distress are the primary factors motivating the great majority" of patients interested in a hastened death with a physician's assistance.[32]

Research studies have long recognized that, as part of the dying process, terminally ill persons necessarily experience sadness, resignation, and loss of hope. A terminally ill patient's expression of a *desire* to die, however, according to Chochinov and Schwartz could be interpreted as "clear evidence of a major depression, which may affect the competence of the patient to make such decisions."[33] Indeed, in making a very sharp critique of the Oregon Death with Dignity statute, Hendin and Foley concur with Emanuel that, "most of those [persons] who respond to terminal illness with a desire to hasten death are suffering from depression."[34] A patient's request for physician assistance in dying signifies, on this interpretation, "the depression speaking" (analogous to "the pain speaking" in other contexts) and implies the person's capacity for choosing between alternative courses of actions has been substantially compromised. It therefore follows that the legal presumption in favor of a terminally ill patient's decision-making capacity is misplaced, and consequently, all persons seeking to avail themselves of physician assistance in dying should undergo psychiatric consultation.

As with the preceding argument, an important conceptual claim serves as background for this argument, namely that there is little conceptual and psychological difference between an act of suicide by nonterminal persons and hastening death under legalized physician-assisted death statutes. In circumstances in which a nonterminal person has experienced a significant life disruption or reversal such that they desire to end their life, the presumption is that the choice of suicide is nonautonomous and nonrational and that interventions of a medical and social nature are warranted to prevent a premature death. The argument on impaired judgment thereby appropriates the conventional model of the meaning of suicide to categorize what occurs when a terminally ill patient requests or takes a medication prescribed by a physician with the intent to hasten death. This understanding lies back of the insistence of opponents that ingesting a prescribed medication to hasten death should rely on the nomenclature of physician-assisted "suicide" rather than "doctor-assisted dying."[35]

It seems to follow on this position that the primary moral imperative at issue is not respecting autonomy, but rather protecting vulnerable persons from the imposition of an inauthentic autonomy and a premature, hastened death. That is, the ethical paradigm shifts from respecting self-determination to that of beneficence. Further, some research studies have called into question the efficacy of physicians' skills in assessing depression. One such study—conducted prior to the implementation of the Death with Dignity Act in Oregon—revealed that 28 percent of 2,761 Oregon physicians believed that they could not reliably diagnose depression.[36] Hence, the statutory requirement that physicians make a referral for a psychological evaluation of a patient who requests physician assistance in death on the grounds of presumed impaired judgment seems to provide less protection for vulnerable patients from incompetent or nonautonomous choices than otherwise might have seemed the case.[37]

The claim that decision-making capacity in a person who is terminally ill could be compromised cannot be discounted; indeed, this possibility is recognized within the legal statutes themselves. Even the fallback provision in the death-with-dignity statutes for psychiatric referral to assess decision-making capability in circumstances of diagnostic uncertainty by the physician might not provide sufficient safeguards: A different research study found that, in the absence of a long-term relationship with a patient, only 6 percent of psychiatrists in Oregon believed they could make a determination of competency following one patient visit.[38] Nonetheless, even if there are some circumstances in which some terminally ill patients have compromised decision-making capacities, there are certainly insufficient numbers to warrant an imperious universal judgment that just by making an inquiry or request for a hastened death, a patient has displayed depression or a morally significant manifestation of impaired judgment.

The argument from impaired judgment is circumstantially applicable only and cannot support an absolute or exceptionless interpretation that, were there a right to die established, terminally ill patients who request some form of physician assistance in dying nonetheless lack the autonomy and decision-making capacity to exercise such a right. Many philosophical arguments[39] have presented a compelling case that in certain circumstances, especially those confronting terminally ill persons, a choice for suicide or assistance in hastening one's death can be rational and satisfy all the requirements for a reflective and autonomous informed consent, including decision-making competence, sufficient information disclosure, comprehension or understanding, and voluntariness. Alternatively, the experience of depression as part of the process of coming to terms with one's mortality is not a sufficient reason for determining that the terminally ill person has compromised decision-making capacity. Indeed, insofar as patients have been empowered with all sorts of decision-making authority, and a negative right to die with respect to refusing life-prolonging medical treatments, it's difficult to see just why a person would suddenly lose that capability when requesting that their death instead be hastened through a medication prescribed by a physician.

The most compelling evidence against the impaired judgment objection comes from the testimonials of patients who have opened to the world a window on their dying. The award-winning independent documentary *How to Die in Oregon*[40] profiles several patients who clearly meet criteria for autonomous decision making. Additionally, most recently, the poignant narrative related by Ms. Brittany Maynard regarding her decision to opt for physician assistance in dying following diagnosis of terminal brain cancer should put to rest the objection that, *in principle*, a person who makes a request for death has experienced compromised decision-making capacity.[41] Maynard's story and advocacy was deemed a compelling contribution to the enactment in 2016 of the California End of Life Option Act, which permits physician prescription of lethal medication for terminally ill patients.

The argument from impaired judgment thus has only limited applicability and cannot be a foundation for rejection of a positive right to die or an absolute proscription of assisted dying facilitated by physicians. One expectation of opponents, which supports concerns of a missed diagnosis of impaired judgment, nonetheless has been borne out by experience. Hendin and Foley anticipated that because "the Oregon law does not require [psychiatric consultation], one fears that over time an increasingly smaller percentage of patients will be referred for independent psychiatric evaluation."[42] This expectation or "fear" has in fact materialized. Although it was the case that in 1998, the first year of legalization in Oregon, more than one in four patients (27 percent) who made a request for physician-assisted death were referred for a psychological consultation or psychiatric evaluation, the most recent data (2014) indicate a referral rate of less than 3 percent of patients.[43] It is unclear, however, that this effect is attributable to the cause cited by Hendin and Foley. This decline is certainly more a function of increased patient screening by the Compassion & Choice advocacy group, as well as to a more informed public and profession, leading to patient self-selection and increased physician experience.

The impaired judgment objection to the right to die and to physician-assisted death is reliant on contingency and empirical evidence that is unjustifiably generalized to the entire population of terminally ill patients. As with circumstances of treatment refusal, policy should presume competency and decision-making capability in terminally ill persons unless and until there is strong evidence to the contrary for any given patient.

The Argument from the Moral Logic of Rights

The significant body of medical jurisprudence and bioethics literature has, since the mid-1970s and the case of Karen Ann Quinlan, portrayed the right to refuse medical treatment as a right of noninterference asserted by patients against paternalistic moral authority exerted by other persons or institutions, such as the medical community, religious institutions, or the state. Philosophical and political advocates of physician-assisted death and physician-administered euthanasia claim that the discussion about treatment refusals established ethical and legal precedents relevant to the positive right to die. The various death-with-dignity statutes are interpreted as "building on" or "expanding" on the rights to noninterference about treatment refusal or termination that patients already possess.[44]

In general, it is more difficult for a society rooted in liberal political philosophy, with its historical emphasis on freedom from oppression and tyranny, to generate a robust array of positive rights comparable to the numerous negative rights invoked in political, social, and philosophical discourse. In part, this is attributable to the thesis of "correlativity," that is, for each right that is affirmed, there is a correlative duty on the part of others, or some others.[45] In the specific circumstances of a right to physician-assisted death or euthanasia, the patient is claiming both a negative right or right of noninterference with regard to respecting his or her choice, and a right to *assistance*, or *aid*, in facilitating the choice. A claim for assistance lies within the moral logic of positive rights, but the existence of a positive right cannot be derived from a negative right. This is not to say that there can't be a positive right to such assistance, but rather that any such right requires an argument independent of those invoked to support rights of noninterference. The rights to treatment cessation cannot be the philosophical grounding for the more expansive right to die required in the context of physician-assisted death or euthanasia.

In arguing for the moral legitimacy of physician assistance in a patient's hastened death, Margaret Battin contends, "If we acknowledge the right [to die], we must be prepared to acknowledge a corresponding duty, and if we hold that suicide is a fundamental right, we must be prepared to ensure that the duty is met."[46] Individual patients as well as society can present good reasons for having the members of the medical profession assume such a responsibility. It is not clear, however, that a patient can claim a positive right to assistance in death from any given physician, including a physician with whom the patient has been in a medical relationship of long duration. It is noteworthy that all of the states that have approved regulatory statutes for physician-assisted death also have made practice exemptions for physicians who are opposed to providing such assistance. There is, in these states, no legal duty of a physician to participate in a patient's request.

Even if the right to medical assistance in dying cannot be claimed against any particular physician, it might be claimed against the medical profession as a whole. The assumption of a general duty to assist is embedded in the ethos of the medical profession—its core commitment is not exhausted by refraining from harm, but encompasses providing medical care that benefits and promotes the welfare of the patient. The question is then whether the professional duty of beneficence can support a specific positive duty to assist in hastening the death of a patient. This chapter next considers two arguments that answer this issue differently.

Battin derives from the physician commitment to beneficence—to "provide help to those in need"—what Battin designates as a "graduated obligation" on the part of physicians to assist a patient in his or her suicide according to the patient's "medical impairment" or "medical need." On Battin's account, the strength of the physician's obligation increases gradually in proportion to greater serious illness or disability afflicting the patient;

the most compelling obligation is "imposed" when patients are "fully disabled or in severe, untreatable, terminal pain."[47] Physicians may refuse to provide requested assistance only when they have "moral scruples" against participation.

This argument seems to fall short of providing a robust, positive patient right and a correlative duty for physicians to provide assistance in the dying of a patient. It is not evident at all that terminally ill patients have a "medical need" for death that can *only* be achieved through physician prescription of a medication intended to hasten death. There are, after all, several "last resort" methods in which death can be brought about for a terminally ill patient, including the so-called gold standard of palliative and hospice care, refusal of medical treatment, voluntary stopping of eating and drinking, and palliative sedation.[48] Indeed, the existence of such alternatives leads scholars like Emanuel to determine that the expansive right to die is unnecessary: "Patients who are being kept alive by technology and want to end their lives already have a recognized constitutional right to stop any and all medical interventions, from respirators to antibiotics. They do not need physician-assisted suicide or euthanasia."[49]

Further, by framing the patient's request for death as a response to a "medical" impairment or need, Battin medicalizes the process of dying and contributes to the medical "management" of death. We need to ask here in what sense is death a "medical" problem? Excessive use of life-prolonging technology in circumstances of medical futility is a medical problem, or inadequate use of pain medications is a medical problem. These can be remedied by appropriate use or cessation of the technology and appropriate medication dosage. It is not clear without further argument that a patient's request for a hastened death is similar to these situations such that it grounds both a patient right and imposes a professional duty on the physician. Battin's use of the language of "scruples" to refer to the purported basis for a physician's act of declining to assist a patient functions to diminish the force of objections to physician participation rooted in a principled ethic intrinsic to medicine.

Daniel Callahan reasons from essentially the same premise as Battin, with one important difference. Rather than invoking the *professional* commitment to beneficence, Callahan maintains there is an embedded *societal* duty to relieve the suffering of our fellow human beings.[50] Society then entrusts the enactment of the societal duty to the knowledge and skill of the medical profession when pain and suffering are symptoms of underlying illness and disease. This shifts the moral ground for physician assistance in dying from respect for patient autonomy to the ethic of beneficence. The question then arises as to whether a terminally ill patient has a positive right, grounded in the physician's socially bestowed duty, to relief of pain and suffering through a prescribed medication or a lethal injection that hastens death. As Callahan frames the issue, "Ought the general duty of the physician to relieve suffering encompass the right to kill a patient if, in the judgment of the patient, that is desired and seems necessary?"[51]

Callahan distinguishes between two kinds of suffering, a first form which consists of what he calls the "psychological penumbra of illness," which can include fears, uncertainty, dread, and anguish of the patient in confronting their medical condition. A second form of suffering can be considered existential suffering; it "touches on the meaning of suffering for the meaning of life itself.[52] The scope of the physician's duty to alleviate pain and suffering certainly encompasses responding to the first form of patient suffering; the physician's commitment is to rely on "counseling, pain relief, and cooperative efforts with family and friends, [and] do everything possible to reduce the sense of dread and anxiety, of disintegration of self, in the face of a threatened death."[53] Medicine does not, however, have the expertise, wisdom, or societal authorization to address existential suffering. The physician's responsibility to relieve pain and suffering is comprised of relieving "only the problem of illness, not the problems of life itself," including what may seem to be a pointless death.[54] In short, Callahan's account rejects Battin's claim that patients could have a "medical" need for, or medical assistance in, relief of their metaphysical or existential suffering instigated by a terminal illness through request for a hastened death. Expanding the scope of the physician's action without a justifying rationale for a duty will, for Callahan, "open the way for a corruption of their vocation."[55]

It is important to note that the state "death with dignity" statutes that legalize physician assistance in dying all ground the patient's claim to assistance in the patient's rights of self-determination and informed consent. They do not make any reference to the extent of patient pain or the intensity of patient suffering, which both distinguishes them from laws in European nations and, in the view of advocates, provides an important procedural safeguard against abuse inasmuch as patient pain and suffering are most often very subjective. Nevertheless, whether moral analysis starts from the scope of the patient's rights to self-determination or the scope of the physician's responsibility to alleviate pain and suffering, it is difficult to generate moral reasoning that bestows an unqualified positive moral right for patients to a physician's assistance in a hastened death or that can support a physician duty to assist in the specific way requested by the patient. Even Battin argues the physician's obligation is "fully compelling" only in rare circumstances—full disability or complete, severe, terminal pain—that are beyond the scope of current state statutes, but not beyond the aspirations of *The Economist* relying on the Belgian model. The physician's duty to relieve pain and suffering as it pertains to treatment of the terminal illness can be met through recourse to several alternative measures that a physician can use, and is otherwise limited by the breadth of the physician's knowledge and expertise.

Several objections to a patient's positive right to die—meaning a right to physician prescriptions or lethal injections—which are rooted in critiques of autonomy and self-determination, do not seem to present a compelling case for an exceptionless prohibition. Terminally ill patients can exercise autonomy comparable to patients in the prime of health or to patients who are faced with a decision about refusing treatment. The choices of a terminally ill patient facing death do not necessarily require the abdication of freedom or the obliteration of moral choice. Although patient autonomy is a necessary condition of a moral choice, however, it is not clear that it is, of itself, a sufficient condition. Indeed, as intimated by the preceding discussion, the assistance the patient requires of a physician entails that we also consider arguments pertaining to medicine's moral integrity.

Physician Assistance and Medicine's Ethical Integrity

It is not societally, philosophically, or professionally compelling to uncouple the issue of the right of a patient to a hastened death from the physician's or medicine's vocational responsibility or duty to participate in such a death. As Jonas recognized in his influential article, "to defend the right to die . . . the real vocation of medicine must be reaffirmed."[56] If these are treated as separable questions, as is the case in most professional and bioethical literature, then medicine becomes a morally neutral profession, and the vocation of physician no more than a technician. Patient autonomy is a necessary but not sufficient condition of moral analysis because (a) the precedent-setting negative rights of patient choices to terminate or refuse treatment leave open the question whether there is a positive right to die and a positive duty to provide assistance to hasten death, and (b) medicine as a profession is constituted by a set of values and commitments that comprise its "profession," that is, its ethical integrity and accountability. These values and commitments are independent of, and cannot be reduced to, patient self-determination.

There is at least implicit recognition even by advocates of a positive right to die that physicians are moral agents, not merely technicians of the body, and professional integrity should be considered in discussion. If the issue at stake was *only* about respecting patient autonomy, there would be no reason in principle for right-to-die proponents to not also advocate for physician-administered voluntary euthanasia. Many philosophical arguments, and some legal jurisprudence, have in fact considered physician-assisted death and physician-administered voluntary euthanasia to be morally equivalent.[57] Nonetheless, it is necessary to raise the question that if patient self-determination was the sole ethical consideration, then why did the states of Oregon, Washington, Vermont, and California draw boundaries around their end-of-life statutes and permit physicians to prescribe medications to hasten a terminally ill patient's life, but retain legal prohibitions on physician administration of a lethal injection? The latter is, after all, permitted with regulatory oversight in the Netherlands, Belgium, and Switzerland. This author's contention is that, at least in part, the policy and moral line was drawn to accommodate physician moral agency and the professional ethics of medicine.

Here we develop this issue initially through a crystallizing publication by a distinguished team of physicians and medical educators in response to an anonymous story published in *The Journal of the American Medical Association*, titled "It's Over Debbie."[58] The story related an episode in which a gynecology resident provided a lethal injection of morphine to an emaciated female patient who was dying from ovarian cancer, a clear illustration of voluntary euthanasia, and perhaps even nonvoluntary euthanasia. In their response, the authors—Willard Gaylin, Leon Kass, Edmund Pellegrino, and Mark Siegler—observed:

> This issue [medical killing] touches medicine at its very center; if this moral center collapses, if physicians become killers or are merely licensed to kill, the profession—and, therewith, each physician—will never again be worthy of trust and respect as healer and comforter and protector of life in all its frailty.

The authors further claimed that "the deepest meaning of the medical vocation" had been violated by the resident, and consequently, "the very soul of medicine is on trial."[59]

This crystallizing commentary drew acclaim, and also criticism, in part due to the distinctive way that it framed questions about the ethical integrity of medicine. The authors drew upon, and unified, utilitarian, deontological, and virtue-based concepts of ethics to mount a provocative moral critique of the *JAMA* scenario as well as an argument against future incidents of killing in the name of and with the power of medicine. If the medical community could not unite around *this* moral center, the commentary implies, then such a community ceases to exist; if medicine cannot affirm the principle to refrain from killing patients as central to its vocation, then its status as a moral practice and profession is irreparably diminished. The ethical integrity of medicine would be diluted to the point that the physician would not meet the ideals of "healer and comforter" and instead would be a "morally neutered technician" who fixes an annoying problem but lacks an overarching sense of the human good served by his or her practice. It is very clear, at least in this account, how the ethical integrity of medicine might be threatened by physician-administered euthanasia. At the moral core of medicine is a principle to not use the power with which society bestows physicians to engage in direct killing of vulnerable persons.

The question is whether there is comparable risk to the integrity of medicine from practices of physician-assisted death. If there is no moral difference between physician prescriptions of lethal medication to hasten death and physician-administered euthanasia, as some proponents of legalization claim, and as advocated by *The Economist,* then it would seem that legalizing physician prescriptions to hasten death would threaten medicine's moral integrity just as much (or just as minimally) as euthanasia would.

By contrast, it is quite possible to identify a central moral difference between the two practices, one with clear implications for medicine's integrity, namely, the physician's "assistance" in writing a prescription is very different than the physician's "administration" of euthanasia. In the context of physician-assisted death, physicians are necessarily called upon for their diagnostic and technical skills: They diagnose a terminal condition and the patient's decision-making capacity, provide information for informed choices, and write a prescription. Physician "assistance" also might be construed to include "emotional and moral support, [and] the continuous presence or at least availability of the physician" for the patient.[60] The patient retains self-determination, however, and decides whether to ingest the medication. This places the physician at a psychological and moral distance from the actual death. Physician participation in assisting a hastened death then seems to resolve what seemed to be irreconcilably conflicting claims in the scenario of physician-administered active euthanasia: The physician is able to refrain from killing, avoid becoming the direct cause of death, and still respect patient self-determination. The compromise posed to the ethical integrity of medicine seems to vanish.

Of course, it is hoped that there is more—much more—to the ethics of medicine than respecting patient autonomy and not killing patients. If we return again to the *JAMA* commentary, and consider the values that the prohibition of killing in medicine is portrayed as protecting, we gain insight into why the integrity issue surfaces even in the context of physician-assisted death. The authors were concerned not just to assert abstract principles, but to claim that medicine is morally constituted by trusting relationships and by a commitment of healing, and that it is this "soul" that needs affirmation. Members of the profession are responsible for obtaining knowledge, developing technical skills, and applying both knowledge and skill in the compassionate care of patients. There is a moral core and an ethos to the practice and the profession of medicine for which its members are accountable, just as much as their accountability for technical expertise. There are certain nonnegotiables, such as commitments to heal, principles to not harm and to benefit, and responsibilities of non-abandonment of the vulnerable, without which medicine can no longer be medicine but becomes another form of social practice. It is important to examine these appeals to the integrity of the physician-patient relationship, to healing, and to solidarity with vulnerable persons, and assess their implications for an expansive patient right to die.

The Relationship Argument

The relationship between physician and patient is at the core of medicine and medical ethics, and yet few people would dispute that the relationship is undergoing significant transformation. Physician-writer Abraham Verghese observes that the reliance on technology, both diagnostic and informational, as a mediator between the physician and patient has led to the construction of the "iPatient," in which quantifiable data *about* the patient has supplanted professional interaction *with* the patient.[61] Others have observed an increasing market-model and commodification overlay on medical practice, such that patients are now "consumers" and physicians are "providers." In contrast to even recent historical relationship models of physicians and patients as covenant or contractual partners, the economic model threatens to dilute the trust necessary for a healing relationship and the ethics of medicine to the minimal financial security of caveat emptor.[62] Even Battin, for all her cogent philosophical advocacy of a patient's right to physician-assisted suicide, contends that the prevalence of a commercial or business model of medicine could necessitate a more limited form of assistance by physicians—that is, technical assistance—to minimize risks of abuse.

There has been strikingly little data on the physician-patient relationship presented in states that have legalized physician prescriptions to hasten death; however, what is available suggests the broader account of physician assistance beyond technical competence. The accumulated data from 16 years in Oregon indicates that the median duration for those relationships in which a patient has requested a lethal prescription from the physician is 13 weeks, which is a comparatively short period. This is especially notable given that a patient must be diagnosed by an attending and a consulting physician with a condition that gives the patient 6 months (~26 weeks) or less to live to be eligible to request the medication to end life. Additionally, the ongoing presence of the physician commended by Battin is infrequent; the prescribing physician is present when the patient ingests the medication or dies from the medication in only about one of six cases.[63]

In their articulation of models of the physician-patient relationship, Emanuel and Emanuel situate the technician role of the physician within what they designate as the "informative model." This model stipulates a "clear distinction between facts and values"; the physician has responsibility for presenting the facts of a disease condition and treatment options, and the realm of values is supervised and directed by the patient. "As technical experts, physicians have important obligations to provide truthful information, to maintain competence in their area of expertise, and to consult others when their knowledge or skills are lacking." In the informative or technical model, however, physician or professional integrity can be largely irrelevant, for "[t]here is no role for the physician's values, the physician's understanding of the patient's values, or his or her judgment of the worth of the patient's values."[64]

Although the authors concede that the informative model "has become dominant in bioethics and legal standards," they express strong criticism, asserting that "it embodies a defective conception of patient autonomy, and it reduces the physician's role to that of a technologist."[65] It is clearly difficult to determine how prevalent an information model is in the context of physician-assisted hastened death, but physicians meet their minimal legal responsibilities by technical methods: making a diagnosis, providing information, and writing the prescription. Philosophic or political arguments on the right to die tend to draw on assumptions about the relationship between physician and patient that are extrinsic to the ethos of medicine. In short, patient values dictate medical practice, although the basic concept of medicine as a *moral* profession is diminished.

It must be noted that in those circumstances where the physician-patient relationship is *publically* narrated or documented, the relationship between physician and patient exemplifies trust. Dr. Timothy Quill's commitment to his patient "Diane," as related in his influential narrative that initiated the practice of public legitimation and professional accountability of physician-assisted suicide, represents a profound trusting relationship cultivated over the course of years, not weeks.[66] Additionally, the central relationship between patient Cody Curtis and Dr. Katherine Morris displayed through the documentary, *How to Die in Oregon*, presents a physician who embodies the essential moral qualities of the healer, including compassion, presence, and nonabandonment. This author's experience with physicians in Oregon who have both participated in patient requests for physician assistance in death and with physicians who have refused, on principle or in circumstance, to participate has revealed physicians who are deeply committed to relationships with their patients. Such persons clearly have technical competence and expertise, but they see themselves much more as companions and advocates than as technicians.

Although the moral and professional issue raised by the relationship argument requires further conceptual and empirical inquiry, it could be that such inquiry will reveal the concern about an ethically compromised relationship and detached and technical physician role to be more theoretical than actual. Nonetheless, this author contends that the burden of proof is on participating physicians to explain and justify how their care for patients who request a lethal prescription fits seamlessly within their general philosophy of care and the profession's commitment to healing. Further, we should be suspect of analyses of the right to die that reduce medical ethics in the way that Battin does to "physician scruples."

The Argument from Healing

The question of whether the right to die imposes a correlative duty of positive assistance on the part of physicians cannot be answered solely through appeals to patient autonomy. The role of physicians requires assessment of the meaning of medicine as a moral calling and profession. Within this setting of professional integrity, the physician's vocation cannot be constructed entirely by the provision of cure. The diseases, or disease conditions, that afflict terminally ill patients and ultimately bring about their deaths, cannot be cured. It would represent a morally diminished sense of vocation if medicine had nothing to offer patients when cure is not possible. Medicine thus must have complementary objectives and perhaps even a superordinate end or purpose.[67] For many physicians as well as scholars in the philosophy of medicine, that overarching telos of medicine is summarized by the concept of "healing," of "making whole" what has been fragmented or destroyed. Medicine is frequently identified as a "healing profession," and its practitioners cultivate not only the science of medicine but also the "arts" of healing.[68] The construction of the physician as a "healer" manifests an understanding of medical integrity with important relevance for physician responsibilities in end-of-life care.

Healing has been described as "the proper activity of the profession of medicine,"[69] or, as articulated by physician-ethicist Edmund Pellegrino, "Medicine is a healing relationship."[70] Although healing certainly overlaps with curing, they are distinguishable in important ways. As physician Eric Cassell states, "One of the most basic errors of the modern era of medicine [is] to believe that patients cured of their diseases . . . are also healed; are whole again."[71] The concepts are thus not coextensive. It is possible to contend that curing does not guarantee healing, and also that healing can occur even if, as with the circumstances of terminally ill patients, there cannot be a cure for the disease.

When medicine cannot save life, when it cannot cure the disease, the professional "default" is to more technology that prolongs biological life. When medical options seem limited to life prolongation at some burden to the patient physically, the claim of a right to die through physician-assisted death can seem a preferable alternative. The option of physician-hastened death, reliant on a technology in its own way, however, ignores the prospect that medicine can always heal even when cure is impossible and can remain faithful to its core mission even if there is no prospect for cure. Pellegrino contends that the physician's core commitment is an ethical commitment, and consists in "the promise of help that shapes the nature of every healing act and defines the requirements for successful healing—even when cure is not possible."[72] The physician invariably must seek to heal and to care in the absence of cure.

The nature of healing within medicine is a subject beyond the scope of this chapter; the question here is whether physicians oriented to a professional identity as healers rather than technicians compromises professional integrity and the internal ethos of the profession through assistance in hastening patient's deaths through prescribed medications or administration of lethal injections. Certainly some scholars have made such a case. Richard McCormick, a pioneering founder of the bioethics field, argued that the question of physician-assisted death only can arise when there is a convergence of certain cultural and professional trends that culminate in what McCormick designates as the "absolutization of autonomy" and the "independence" of medicine from a moral tradition.[73] That is, a right to physician-assisted death is a coherent moral perspective in contexts where patient self-determination is deemed to be a sufficient ethical paradigm and where medicine's imperatives and integrity are governed by economics rather than ethics.

Within this convergence, political, professional, and patient advocacy for physician-assisted death represents what McCormick refers to as "a flight from compassion." Compassion, or the capacity to enter into the experience of illness of the patient and live through the suffering with them, is the "more" to healing that is not exhausted by curative medicine; compassion is a constituent virtue of the healer. Physician participation in assisting terminally ill patients to die manifests, for McCormick, a profession that has neglected compassion and the arts that comprise healing. Instead, contemporary medicine verges on becoming indistinguishable from a business and its very direct utilitarian morality of maximization.

Pellegrino's argument, although normatively built primarily around the proscription of medical killing delineated in the *JAMA* commentary, is connected to an interpretation of medicine's healing commitments: "A critical examination of the moral basis of medical practice must proscribe euthanasia because it contravenes the primary healing purposes of the medical activity."[74] Not only do patients have other alternatives, such as palliative care and hospice care, but physicians, as healers, also have other alternatives, including being present to terminally ill patients through their ordeal, providing sufficient pain control, and assuming an embodied responsibility to meet the patient's needs for relationship, touch, and nonabandonment.

Medicine is not a morally neutral profession and its commitment to caring and healing—even when curing is not possible—is a constitutive feature of its morality and integrity. It is not clear, however, that developing the ethical commitments embedded in healing can carry the entire argument that negates the positive right to die on grounds that physician-hastened death violates the ethical integrity of medicine. It is no coincidence, after all, that the virtue of compassion has been incorporated into the name of the most prominent patient rights advocacy organization for physician-assisted death, that of *Compassion* and Choices in Dying. The organizational nomenclature conveys that participation in a patient's choice to hasten his or her death is an expression of compassion, rather than a "flight" from compassion as claimed by McCormick. Furthermore, even physicians such as Cassell—who have argued for the integral place of healing in medicine, and for the distinction between healing and curing—have asserted that, in carefully regulated circumstances, physicians can legitimately assist terminally ill patients to die.

This does not mean that a physician *must* participate in a patient request for a prescription, but only that the appeal to the healing intrinsic to medicine does not provide a sufficient rationale for *refusing*. The appeal to healing as a ground for objection is much stronger (as argued above) when the question is physician-administered euthanasia and the physician cannot evade responsibility for the death of the patient. Nonetheless, the healing ethos of medicine entails that a burden of proof be imposed on those who advocate for legalization of the right to die in all its forms; these advocates must make a compelling argument as to how a correlative physician duty to assist does not erode personal and professional integrity.

The Argument from Solidarity

Implicit in the preceding arguments regarding relationship and healing is a moral commitment of medicine and of physicians to be present for persons who are sick and to not abandon patients who are terminally ill. The argument from solidarity arises as an independent claim about medicine's integrity on the basis of two interrelated points about human nature. The first claim is that, in contrast to the individualistic construction of the self that is presupposed in advocacy for physician-assisted death, human beings are fundamentally relational and community-oriented beings. We experience our lives in a web of relationships, with family, friends, colleagues, associates, congregations, and larger communities. Such relationships provide a matrix for learning and for experiencing a shared dependency and vulnerability; our vulnerability to the vicissitudes of aging, disease, disability, and dying bursts illusions of independence and evokes interdependency with others. A moral community emerges through presence to the humanity of each other in these relationships of interdependency.

The second point is that by assuming responsibility for medical caregiving to the ill, medicine has undertaken and expresses an identity-conferring commitment to make common cause with populations that are among society's most vulnerable and marginalized. Clearly, terminally ill persons are a very vulnerable population. They are experiencing deprivations of the most fundamental sort: loss of control, loss of a future, loss of decision-making authority, loss of bodily integrity, loss of privacy, perhaps loss of home or the familiar, and ultimately culminating in loss of life. In this context of pervasive loss, medicine has a moral responsibility to be a meaningful and healing presence, ensuring terminally ill persons that their sickness unto death does not mean isolation or ostracization, and that they have not been abandoned. Though their disease condition might not be amenable to cure, patients can experience healing as members of a community to the very end of their lives.

The solidarity appeal also is rooted in the shared value of compassion. The etymological meaning of compassion means "suffering with" the person that is suffering from their affliction. The expression of the virtue thus requires a relational context: it implies continual presence of a caring community or professional. In his critique of physician-assisted dying,

Pellegrino makes a direct connection between the capacity for compassion and the witness of solidarity to the ill: "True compassion is an emotion accompanied by a desire to help, but to help in a way that communicates our solidarity with the sufferer without losing our ethical bearings in the process." Indeed, "co-suffering" as the embodiment of compassionate presence "confirms our solidarity with the sufferer."[75]

For many observers, including this author, the possibility of compassionate caring for, and healing of, terminally ill persons in a setting in which medical cure is not possible is envisioned and embodied in hospice care. The hospice philosophy of care—which includes commitments to patient self-determination, the highest quality of life while dying, "bearing witness" to and alleviating the patient's physical pain and emotional and spiritual suffering, and companionship and nonabandonment of the patient—exemplifies a profound commitment of solidarity with the terminally ill. Significantly, the movement for legalization of physician-assisted death has forced hospice associations to reconsider some of their basic assumptions and philosophies of care.[76]

Taking each on its own, the arguments from relationship, healing, and solidarity cannot sustain an unequivocal or exceptionless prohibition of physician assistance in hastening a patient's death through a lethal prescription or euthanasia. When these arguments are viewed as complementary rather than solitary, however, and as issuing from a moral core of medicine, they provide a compelling moral direction, namely, that there should be no positive moral duty or obligation on any physician to acquiesce in a patient's request for assistance in death. Importantly, the "Death with Dignity Acts" that have received voter or legislative approval contain a provision that there is no legal duty on any particular physician, health care professional, or health care institution, to participate in a patient request. *That* provision presumes there is more morally at stake in debates regarding the right to die than patient self-determination, or to put it somewhat differently, the goals and purposes of medicine cannot be reduced to respect for autonomy.

As noted, there is little to no data available regarding physicians who refuse to acquiesce in a patient's request for medical assistance in their hastened death. In particular, it would be important to understand the rationales for physician refusals. Although this often is attributed to religious reasons, anecdotal evidence suggests other factors can be relevant, including (a) unfamiliarity with or lack of relationship with a patient, (b) disagreements about the medical status (diagnosis or prognosis) of a patient, (c) professionalism, and (d) personal values. It would be especially significant to understand whether a physician who refuses to participate is saying, in effect, "This action is wrong," or "This action is wrong *for me* personally," or "This action is wrong *for physicians*, myself, and others."

Societal Ethos and Moral Symbolism

The focus of the solidarity argument on our communal nature and on the status of vulnerable persons provides a bridge between the professional ethic and concerns about recognition of a positive right to die for the societal ethos. The prospective social impact of legalized physician-assisted death for vulnerable persons is of particular importance in a health care context that emphasizes utilitarian commitments to cost-effectiveness and rationing of health care services. Two cases from Oregon are illustrative of the reality of this objection.

Randy Stroup was a 53-year-old man diagnosed with prostate cancer, with a prognosis of somewhere between two to four months of remaining life. Stroup had undergone one chemotherapy treatment that was unsuccessful in halting the spread of the disease, and his physician and Stroup agreed to try a different chemotherapy method. The oversight board for the state insurance plan refused to authorize reimbursement for this second round of chemotherapy, however, holding that it did not satisfy the plans "5 year, 5 percent" rule—that is, that in undergoing the chemotherapy, Stroup would be expected to have a 5 percent chance of being alive after a five-year period. Instead, Stroup's condition met state requirements for comfort and palliative care, and Stroup was informed this included "physician aid in dying" as provided in the Oregon Death with Dignity statute. Stroup was offended and indignant and took the rejection to mean that the state had "placed a price tag on [his] life" and that the state "would pay to kill me, but won't pay to help me."[77] Stroup then brought his situation to public attention and the state plan reversed its decision, authorizing payment for his treatment. Stroup died within a month of beginning his second round of chemotherapy.

The story of Barbara Wagner unfolded similarly. Wagner, a lifelong smoker, had been treated for lung cancer, and after first- and second-line treatments had failed, her oncologist recommended a third-line drug, Tarceva, for which study results had indicated life extension of four to six months in 8 percent of patients. The state health plan refused to authorize this treatment because of the "5 year, 5 percent" rule, but it would provide coverage for comfort and palliative care, including access to a prescription to end life under the Death with Dignity law.[78] In the wake of a media firestorm over public disclosure of the story, the manufacturer of Tarceva provided the drug to Wagner without cost. Like Stroup, Wagner also died shortly after beginning treatment.

What can we make of these two stories? There is little question that the specifics of the cases are aberrations within the general patterns of physician-assisted death. However, the social and health care context in which such circumstances are even possible should not be overlooked. The American health care system spends excessively on medical treatment of questionable or negligible benefit to the patient during the last year of life, and especially during the final six months of life. Policy, insurance, and professional reforms that will make the delivery of all health care more consistent with principles of responsible stewardship and cost-effectiveness are necessary, lest patients experience a more direct and draconian form of health care rationing. Physicians likewise can be placed in an untenable conflict of interest between professional imperatives and economic mandates. This context for decision making is very different than in European countries where access to universal health care removes conflicts of policy and professional interest with respect to physician-hastened death.[79]

The moral difficulty is not generated solely by initiatives for efficiency and cost-effectiveness in health care but rather by the coupling of cost-effectiveness with methods of hastening the death of terminally ill persons. The moral issue is best framed as a question not of instrumental rationality—the most efficient and effective means to desired ends—but rather of *symbolic* rationality. The symbolism conveyed to Stroup and Wagner was that society and the health care system were uncaring about their disease, and callous and insensitive toward their suffering. The societal myth is that no expense will be spared to save a human life; the value of each human life transcends, we claim, economic valuation.[80] The initial notices of funding refusals received by both Stroup and Wagner were thus interpreted by them, and by a sympathetic public, as a form of betrayal of the symbol of priceless value of a human life, and an exemplification of society's abandonment of terminally ill persons.

This is not to say that the denial of coverage by the state health plan for the different methods of chemotherapy requested in these circumstances was morally mistaken. Indeed, given the fairly late-stage cancers both patients experienced, the morally preferable alternative would have been for them to be enrolled in a hospice program where they would have received comfort and palliative care, rather than curative measures. This is clearly not the current conventional social wisdom about end-of-life care, which instead emphasizes "fighting" to the end to "beat" cancer. That is—given society's declared "war" on cancer—appropriated into various militaristic metaphors in medicine, opting for comfort, palliation, and hospice care can be a symbolic admission of "defeat" on the part of both physicians and patients.

Although both the societal ethos about the inestimable value of human life and the social myth that no expense will be spared to save a life should be critically challenged, it remains important that terminally ill persons are not vulnerable to subtle pressure from the society or from their families to hasten their death for the purposes of saving on medical expenses or balancing a health care budget. It would be both terribly ironic and morally tragic if disputes about the ethics of physician-assisted death—which have been articulated through the discourse of the *right* to die—become intertwined with disputes about rationing end-of-life care, which have commonly been articulated through the discourse of a *duty* to die.[81] The maintenance of this proverbial firewall between costs of treatment and hastened death, between the right to die and the duty to die, will continue to be an important social justice consideration regarding legalization of physician-assisted death.

As significant as it is to recognize the implications of how affirmations of a right to die could, in a health care culture of cost-effectiveness and efficiency, evolve into a duty to die, there is yet a more encompassing moral critique of a societal commitment to efficiency and the risks this commitment poses to vulnerable persons. In this critique, which has been articulated consistently in the past two decades in the tradition of Roman Catholic moral theology,[82] physician-assisted death is interpreted as a symptom of societal moral decline. This decline in the societal ethos has crossed a threshold such that actions that are morally wrong have become legitimated by the state through the language of rights.

In his encyclical *Evangelium Vitae* (*The Gospel of Life*), Pope John Paul II drew attention to what he portrayed as the "emergence of a culture which denies solidarity and in many cases takes the form of a veritable 'culture of death.' "[83] This societal ethos is supported and sustained by "powerful cultural, economic and political currents" that promote excessive concerns with efficiency. The papal pronouncements are directed in large measure against world views of secularism, moral relativism, individualism, and materialism; at the same time, this critique is directed at practical manifestations of these worldviews, particularly social acceptance of legalized rights to abortion, capital punishment, discrimination against persons with disabilities, and practices that exploit the vulnerabilities of a person who is at the end of life, that is, persons whose care requires resources that are inefficient from a purely technical maximization of efficiency perspective. The integrity of the medical profession is eroded as part of the societal moral decline:

> Even certain sectors of the medical profession, which by its calling is directed to the defense and care of human life, are increasingly willing to carry out these acts against the person. In this way the very nature of the

medical profession is distorted and contradicted, and the dignity of those who practice it is degraded.[84]

John Paul II makes a clear connection between the underlying world-views, an ethics of efficiency, and the risks to socially marginalized persons. A "symptom" of the culture of death prevalent in all prosperous societies, he claims, is

> an attitude of excessive preoccupation with efficiency and which sees the growing number of elderly and disabled people as intolerable and too bur-densome. These people are very often isolated by their families and by society, which are organized almost exclusively on the basis of criteria of productive efficiency, according to which a hopelessly impaired life no lon-ger has any value.[85]

The Pope thus identifies euthanasia (and "so-called assisted suicide") as an illustrative practice of the culture of death: reflecting what is portrayed as a "misguided pity" regarding patient suffering, John Paul II observed that "euthanasia is sometimes justified by the utilitarian motive of avoid-ing costs which bring no return and which weigh heavily on society."[86] Civil laws that authorize or regulate physician-assisted death or euthanasia cannot be a "true, morally binding civil law"; the Pope follows Thomistic teaching in claiming such laws are "unjust laws." They should be con-scientiously opposed rather than obeyed and physicians and health care personnel should receive an unqualified exemption from participation in the laws. It is this refusal to assist in injustice, and not the right to die, that John Paul II considers "a basic human right."[87]

Certainly, the practices that the Pope critiques, be it legalized abortion, capital punishment, or euthanasia, have a long history of both practice and philosophy advocacy that predate current preoccupations with efficiency. Moreover, the "utilitarian" rationales cited in *Evangelium Vitae*, though pres-ent in justificatory arguments, are really a background legitimation to the primary rights-based arguments. The papal focus, however, is more on the culture and the background worldviews that legitimate the culture. The important claim is that the ethics of physician-assisted death, however much it concerns personal self-determination and individual autonomy, cannot be reduced morally to a private self-regarding action. The question itself is situated within a particular cultural context and influenced by prevalent worldviews, ideologies, and mythologies. Further, the question has moral ramifications for various intermediate communities in the society, including the healing professions, hospice programs, and religious communities.

Conclusion

This chapter examines various arguments regarding the cogency of a right to die. There are sound arguments in philosophical ethics, in public policy, and in law for understanding the right to die as a right to noninterference through which a person with a terminal illness can request the cessation or refusal of life-sustaining medical interventions. These positions have been understood to establish precedents for expanding the scope of the right to die as a right to medical assistance in a hastened death, requiring legalization of such practices as physician prescriptions for a lethal medication self-administered by a patient, or physician administration of the lethal medication through an injection.

This conceptual expansion of the right to die—and the correlated legitimation of various practices in medicine—has been challenged on several grounds. This chapter has claimed that, within the moral logic of rights, a positive right to assistance from a physician cannot be derived from a negative right to noninterference. Additionally, it is misleading to characterize a right to assistance as entirely a question of a private action enacted through patient self-determination. All rights claims presume some moral community and relationships, and the most significant community with respect to physician-assistance in death is the medical profession. Medicine is not a morally neutral profession nor are its practitioners technicians: medical practice is shaped by defining commitments of integrity, healing, and solidarity with vulnerable persons. Insofar as individual rights historically are articulated as claims of the person for freedom from tyranny and political oppression, the social and political context of the right to die bears careful scrutiny. In particular, moral assessment requires differentiating the discourse and the exercise of rights in health care from cost-effectiveness movements. Indeed, in the context of a market-based system, the right to die can be experienced by some patients as a duty to die. Ultimately, arguments advocating legalized physician-assisted death or physician-administered euthanasia for terminally ill patients (or for chronically ill patients experiencing protracted pain and suffering) bear a burden of proof that they can meet justificatory standards of authorization, cause, proportionality, intention, discrimination, and last resort.

Notes

1. "The Right to Die," *Economist*, June 27, 2015, 9. http://www.economist.com /news/leaders/21656182-doctors-should-be-allowed-help-suffering-and-terminally -ill-die-when-they-choose (accessed September 23, 2016).

2. "Final Certainty," *Economist*, June 27, 2015, 16. http://www.economist.com /news/briefing/21656122-campaigns-let-doctors-help-suffering-and-terminally-ill -die-are-gathering-momentum (accessed September 23, 2016).

3. The Brittany Maynard Fund, http://www.thebrittanyfund.org/ (accessed September 23, 2016).

4. "The Right to Die," *The Economist*.

5. Daniel Callahan, *The Troubled Dream of Life: Living with Mortality* (New York: Simon & Schuster, 1993), 107.

6. State of Oregon, Oregon Health Authority, "Death with Dignity Act: Current Report (2014)." https://public.health.oregon.gov/ProviderPartnerResources /EvaluationResearch/DeathwithDignityAct/Documents/year17.pdf (accessed September 23, 2016).

7. Peter G. Filene, *In the Arms of Others: A Cultural History of the Right-to-Die in America* (Chicago: Ivan R. Dee, 1998).

8. Filene, *In the Arms of Others*, 161–83.

9. Hans Jonas, "The Right to Die," *Hastings Center Report* 8 (1978): 31.

10. Jonas, "The Right to Die," 33, 36.

11. Atul Gawande, *Being Mortal: Medicine and What Matters in the End* (New York: Metropolitan Books, 2014) 149–90.

12. State of Oregon, "Death with Dignity Act: Current Report (2014)."

13. Gawande, *Being Mortal*, 174.

14. Ibid., 158.

15. Ibid., 167–68.

16. Vincent Barry, *Bioethics in a Cultural Context* (Boston: Wadsworth, Cengage Learning, 2012), 1–2.

17. J. Brandeis, Dissenting Opinion, *Olmstead v. United States*, 277 U.S. 438 (1928).

18. John Stuart Mill, "On Liberty," in *The English Philosophers: From Bacon to Mill*, ed. Edwin A. Burtt (New York: The Modern Library), 955–56.

19. James F. Childress, *Practical Reasoning in Bioethics* (Bloomington: Indiana University Press, 1997), 237–62.

20. Daniel Callahan "Reason, Self-Determination, and Physician-Assisted Suicide," in *The Case Against Assisted Suicide: For the Right to End-of-Life Care*, ed. Kathleen Foley, Herbert Hendin (Baltimore: Johns Hopkins University Press, 2002), 60.

21. Leon R. Kass, *Life, Liberty, and the Defense of Dignity: The Challenge for Bioethics* (San Francisco: Encounter Books, 2002), 202.

22. Kass, *Life, Liberty, and the Defense of Dignity*, 228–29.

23. Mill, "On Liberty," 956.

24. Kass, *Life, Liberty, and the Defense of Dignity*, 204, 212.

25. Ibid., 217, 226.

26. Ibid., 211.

27. Mill, "On Liberty," 1031.

28. Immanuel Kant, *The Doctrine of Virtue*, trans. Mary J. Gregor (Philadelphia: University of Pennsylvania Press, 1964), 85.

29. United States Conference of Catholic Bishops, "To Live Each Day with Dignity: A Statement on Physician Assisted Suicide," 2011. http://www.usccb .org/issues-and-action/human-life-and-dignity/assisted-suicide/to-live-each-day/ (accessed March 2012).

30. David Hume, "Of Suicide," in *Ethical Issues in Death and Dying,* 2nd ed., ed. Tom L. Beauchamp and Robert M. Veatch (Upper Saddle River, NJ: Prentice Hall, 1996), 122–26.

31. State of Oregon, "Death with Dignity Act: Current Report (2014)"; Washington State Department of Health, "Death with Dignity Report, 2014." http://www .doh.wa.gov/portals/1/Documents/Pubs/422-109-DeathWithDignityAct2014.pdf (accessed March 15, 2015).

32. Ezekiel J. Emanuel, "Whose Right to Die?" *The Atlantic,* March 1997, 73–79. http://www.theatlantic.com/magazine/archive/1997/03/whose-right-to-die /304641/ (accessed September 23, 2016).

33. Harvey M. Chochinov, and Leonard Schwartz, "Depression and the Will to Live in the Psychological Landscape of Terminally Ill Patients," in *The Case Against Assisted Suicide: For the Right to End-of-Life Care*, ed. Kathleen Foley, and Herbert Hendin (Baltimore: Johns Hopkins University Press, 2002), 267.

34. Kathleen Foley, and Herbert Hendin, "The Oregon Experiment," in *The Case Against Assisted Suicide: For the Right to End-of-Life Care*, ed. Kathleen Foley, and Herbert Hendin (Baltimore: Johns Hopkins University Press, 2002), 150.

35. It is of interest that the State of Oregon used the terminology of physician-assisted suicide in the initial years (1998–2005) of its public reporting on its Death with Dignity Act. That is, the State did not interpret "suicide" as necessarily linked to "impaired judgment."

36. Melinda A. Lee, Heidi D. Nelson, M.D., M.P.H., Virginia P. Tilden, R.N., D.N.Sc., Linda Ganzini, M.D., Terri A. Schmidt, M.D., and Susan W. Tolle, M.D. "Legalizing Assisted Suicide—Views of Physician in Oregon," *New England Journal of Medicine* 334 (1996): 310–15.

37. Felicia Cohn, and JoAnne Lynn, "Vulnerable People. Practical Rejoinders to Claims in Favor of Assisted Suicide," in *The Case Against Assisted Suicide: For the Right to End-of-Life Care*, ed. Kathleen Foley, and Herbert Hendin (Baltimore: Johns Hopkins University Press, 2002), 238–60.

38. Linda Ganzini, Darien S. Fenn, Melinda A. Lee, Ronald T. Heintz, and Joseph D. Bloom, "Attitudes of Oregon Psychiatrists Toward Physician-Assisted Suicide," *American Journal of Psychiatry* 153 (1996): 1469–75.

39. Richard Brandt, "The Morality and Rationality of Suicide," in *A Handbook for the Study of Suicide*, ed. Seymour Perlin (Oxford: Oxford University Press, 1975), 61–76; Margaret P. Battin, *Ethical Issues in Suicide* (New York: Simon and Schuster, 1995), 131–53.

40. *How to Die in Oregon.* 2010. Documentary film by Peter D. Richardson. Clearcut Productions. www.howtodieinoregon.com (accessed September 29, 2016).

41. The Brittany Maynard Fund, http://www.thebrittanyfund.org/ (accessed September 23, 2016).

42. Foley, Hendin, "The Oregon Experiment," 153.

43. State of Oregon, "Death with Dignity Act: Current Report (2014)."

44. Robert P. Jones, *Liberalism's Troubled Search for Equality: Religion and Cultural Bias in the Oregon Physician-Assisted Suicide Debates* (Notre Dame, IN: University of Notre Dame Press, 2007).

45. Joel Feinberg, *Social Philosophy* (Englewood Cliffs, NJ: Prentice-Hall, 1973), 59.

46. Margaret P. Battin, *Ethical Issues in Suicide* (New York: Simon and Schuster, 1995), 195.

47. Ibid., 219.

48. Timothy E. Quill, "Physician-Assisted Death in the United States: Are the Existing 'Last Resorts' Enough?" *Hastings Center Report* 38 (2008): 17–22.

49. Emanuel, "Whose Right to Die?"

50. Daniel Callahan, *The Troubled Dream of Life: Living with Mortality* (New York: Simon & Schuster, 1993), 94–95.

51. Ibid., 95.

52. Ibid., 100.

53. Ibid., 101.

54. Ibid., 102.

55. Ibid., 102.

56. Jonas, "The Right to Die," 36.

57. Ronald A. Dworkin, Thomas Nagel, Robert Nozick, John Rawls, Thomas M. Scanlon, and Judith Jarvis Thomson, "The Philosophers' Brief," in *Physician Assisted Suicide: Expanding the Debate*, ed. Margaret P. Battin, Rosamond Rhodes, and Anita Silvers (New York: Routledge, 1998), 431–41.

58. Anonymous, "It's Over Debbie," *Journal of the American Medical Association* 259 (1988): 272.

59. Willard Gaylin, Leon R. Kass, Edmund D. Pellegrino, and Mark Siegler, "Doctors Must Not Kill," in *Arguing Euthanasia: The Controversy over Mercy Killing, Assisted Suicide and the "Right to Die,"* ed. Jonathan D. Moreno (New York: Simon and Schuster, 1995), 33–36.

60. Battin, *Ethical Issues in Suicide*, 220.

61. Abraham Verghese, "Culture Shock: Patient as Icon, Icon as Patient," *New England Journal of Medicine* 359 (2008): 2748–51.

62. William F. May, *The Physician's Covenant: Images of the Healer in Medical Ethics*, 2nd ed. (Louisville, KY: Westminster John Knox Press, 2000), 89–111.

63. State of Oregon, "Death with Dignity Act: Current Report (2014)."

64. Ezekiel J. Emanuel, and Linda Emanuel, "Four Models of the Physician-Patient Relationship," *Journal of the American Medical Association.* 267 (1992): 2221–26.

65. Emanuel and Emanuel, "Four Models of the Physician-Patient Relationship," 2226.

66. Timothy E. Quill, "Death and Dignity: A Case of Individualized Decision Making," *New England Journal of Medicine* 324 (1991): 691–94.

67. Mark J. Hanson, and Daniel Callahan, *The Goals of Medicine: The Forgotten Issues in Health Care Reform* (Washington, DC: Georgetown University Press, 1999).

68. David Schenck, and Larry R. Churchill, *Healers: Extraordinary Clinicians at Work* (New York: Oxford University Press, 2012).

69. Richard C. Vance, "Healing," in *Encyclopedia of Bioethics*, 3rd ed., ed. Stephen G. Post (New York: Macmillan Reference, 2004), 1051.

70. Edmund D. Pellegrino, "Doctors Must Not Kill," in *Euthanasia: The Good of the Patient, The Good of Society*, ed. Robert I Misbin (Frederick, MD: University Publishing Group, 1991), 30.

71. Eric J. Cassell, *The Nature of Suffering and the Goals of Medicine* (New York: Oxford University Press, 1991), 69.

72. Edmund D. Pellegrino, "Being Ill and Being Healed: Some Reflections on the Grounding of Medical Morality," in *The Humanity of the Ill: Phenomenological Perspectives,* ed. Victor Kestenbaum (Knoxville: University of Tennessee Press, 1982), 160.

73. Richard A. McCormick, "Physician Assisted Suicide: Flight from Compassion," *The Christian Century* 108 (1992): 1132–34.

74. Pellegrino, "Doctors Must Not Kill," 35.

75. Edmund D. Pellegrino, "Compassion Is Not Enough," in *The Case Against Assisted Suicide: For the Right to End-of-Life Care*, ed. Kathleen Foley, and Herbert Hendin (Baltimore: Johns Hopkins University Press, 2002), 49, 51.

76. Courtney S. Campbell, "Moral Meanings of Physician-Assisted Death for Hospice Ethics," in *Hospice Ethics: Policy and Practice in Palliative Care*, ed. Timothy W. Kirk, Bruce Jennings (New York: Oxford University Press, 2014), 223–49.

77. *How to Die in Oregon.*

78. Barry, *Bioethics in a Cultural Context*, 389–90.

79. Margaret P. Battin, "A Dozen Caveats Concerning the Discussion of Euthanasia in the Netherland," in *Arguing Euthanasia: The Controversy over Mercy Killing, Assisted Suicide and the "Right to Die,"* ed. Jonathan D. Moreno (New York: Simon and Schuster, 1995), 88–109.

80. James F. Childress, *Priorities in Biomedical Ethics* (Philadelphia: The Westminster Press, 1981), 83.

81. John Hardwig, "Is There a Duty to Die?" *Hastings Center Report* 27 (1997): 34–42.

82. Joseph Cardinal Bernardin, *Consistent Ethic of Life* (Kansas City: Sheed & Ward, 1988).

83. John Paul II, *Evangelium Vitae* (*The Gospel of Life*), 1995, par. 12. http://w2.vatican.va/content/john-paul-ii/en/encyclicals/documents/hf_jp-ii_enc_25031995_evangelium-vitae.html (accessed August 16, 2016).

84. Ibid., par. 4.

85. Ibid., par. 64.

86. Ibid., par. 15.

87. Ibid., par. 72–74.

CHAPTER TEN

Respect for Personal Autonomy in the Justification of Death-Hastening Choices

Paul T. Menzel

Patient decisions to hasten death run the gamut from widely accepted to very controversial: refusing extraordinary lifesaving medical treatment, withdrawing continuing life-support, withholding lifesaving treatment by advance directive (AD), voluntarily stopping eating and drinking, withholding food and water by mouth by AD, and physician-assisted dying. This chapter explores how firm the moral support provided by respect for personal autonomy is for a person's prerogative to make each of these choices.

The most widely accepted of these choices is competent voluntary refusal of lifesaving medical treatment. A primary justification for a person's prerogative to make such a decision is personal autonomy. The scope of the care that may be refused includes acute treatments as well as continual life support, and permissible refusal includes not only initial withholding but midstream withdrawal. Is that scope wide enough to include critical care in nonterminal as well as terminal illness situations? Food and water by mouth, not just medical treatment? Which of these by AD?

This analysis constitutes an extended comparison of justifying prerogatives to make these various choices on the basis of respect for autonomy. Simplistic arguments from autonomy provide inadequate justification for even some of the less controversial, widely legal choices in this spectrum. Understanding the more nuanced use of respect for autonomy that protects these choices has an important implication for physician-assisted dying: its justification by autonomy is stronger than what is provided for by some of the more widely accepted choices.

Introduction

Whether a person has the "moral liberty" to make a choice is an important dimension of moral judgment. The morally right choice also is important, but is a different kind of judgment. Views on what is right can vary greatly, although who should have the prerogative—the moral right, the moral liberty—to make the choice is easier to determine. Health care providers and patients likely want to know which of a patient's potential choices are "morally protected"—that is, what actions do they have a moral right to choose. This is still a moral judgment of actions, but the judgment is about the actions of others in respecting or not respecting a patient's choice.

A society's discussion of death-hastening choices often is focused on patients' moral liberty to choose, and not as much on what is right or wrong for them to choose. Legalization decisions certainly have this focus, as do institutions' policies about what they will permit within their ranks. To be sure, people sometimes argue against the liberty to make a certain choice by claiming that the choice would be morally wrong—a patient's taking lethal drugs, for example. Generally that type of argument is too simple. Unless we are thoroughgoing "moralists," sometimes people ought to be at liberty to do things that are wrong.

To be sure, people may be barred from making certain choices because those choices are wrong in a particular way—that they harm others, for example. Choices that hasten a person's own death, however, typically have their overwhelmingly primary effect on the person who makes them. It is, after all, that person's life that is at stake. For this reason, much of the focus here is on patients' moral rights and liberties. The death-hastening choice context is tailor-made for personal autonomy to play a major role.

How powerful a role? Over what kinds of decisions? Over what time span and in what conditions? Pursuing these questions requires clarifying the principle of respect for personal autonomy and why it has moral weight.

Respect for Personal Autonomy

One use of "autonomy" is descriptive, referring to a capacity for deci-sion making that someone does or does not have. Another is normative, referring to a value that people should encourage and respect or a principle that has weight in moral judgment. The two are related; as a value or prin-ciple, autonomy will have no weight—will not apply—without the mental capacity referred to by autonomy in its descriptive sense. This chapter does not, however, attempt to delineate in any detail what this capacity is. The focus is on the normative sense. It also typically speaks of "respect for autonomy," not just "autonomy," and often adds "personal autonomy" to make clear that the decisions that this value or principle paradigmatically protects are primarily self-regarding.

Definitions of normative autonomy vary greatly.[1] A widely used textbook refers to autonomy as the principle that bids us to "respect the capacity of individuals to choose their own vision of the good life and act accord-ingly" and to engage "the patient's own powers of deliberation, choice, and agency."[2] This chapter narrows the concept somewhat and regards autonomy in the medical context as patient *self-determination* that reflects the wider notion of *respect for persons*. Normative autonomy does not bid us to abide by all patient choices, only the choices of patients about *their own lives* (*self*-determination) when they are acting in their capacity *as persons* (reflective, deliberating agents).

Why should such autonomy have moral weight? An objection imme-diately arises: A person's preferences and desires might be volatile, fragile, and superficial—a function of serendipitous and questionable factors in individuals and their environments. A "consumerist" sense of preferences arguably reflects a thin form of individualism, providing only a veneer of normative force.[3] A better understanding focuses on respect for persons. Two of the first things such respect militates against are deception and coercion. If deception is routinely legitimate and does not require special justification, then how can individuals relate to each other as reflective, decision-making persons rather than as beings to be manipulated? And if coercion is routinely justified, what is the point of being a person, with capacity for reflection, value formation, and choice? Thus, patients gener-ally must be told the truth of their medical situation, and coercion must be carefully limited.

Autonomy as self-determination gains much of its force by association with our most basic conceptions of ownership. "It's my life, not yours" is obviously true when said by a patient to a provider of lifesaving care. Consciousness itself demands this use of possessive pronouns—at least self-consciousness does. "My life" is life with my body, with my mind. Thus, I have normatively privileged use of my life and mind, and when I use them to labor, work, and create, the products are rightfully mine (or partly mine). Thus, the right of people not to be enslaved is a fundamental right. Others inevitably do and might influence my mind and body, but they cannot simply control it without my consent. The title of the 1981 film about patient choice, *Whose Life Is It Anyway?*[4] captures this fundamental reason for patient self-determination. Here it is referred to as "self-ownership."

It does not close the door to all paternalism—others making decisions about matters in your life for your benefit. Sometimes—rarely—others might know better than you what will be for your own self-defined benefit. The cases in which others are most justified in paternalistically pulling decisions about your life away from you occur when you yourself will predictably say later that others were correct. Such exceptions do not really compromise the strong moral pull of autonomy as self-determination but reflect respect for autonomy in a temporally extended form.

Patient autonomy gains considerable normative power from the central observation of self-ownership, but it also gains justification from several moral theories. John Stuart Mill defended personal liberty and self-determination in *On Liberty*,[5] a classic application of utilitarian theory, and Immanuel Kant articulated respect for persons, never treating them merely as a means, as a basic form of the Categorical Imperative.[6] Applying the other universalization form (always act so you can will the maxim of your action to become a universal law of nature) quickly generates obligations not to deceive, and typically not to coerce. Onora O'Neill refers to the autonomy thus protected as "principled autonomy" to distinguish it from an individualism focused on consumer preferences.[7] Liberty simply to follow one's preferences, whatever they might be, has shallow moral roots, but the liberty and self-determination characterized by the rejection of deception and careful limitation of coercion has both utilitarian and Kantian justifications. Properly understood, respect for autonomy is not a mere consumerist culture.

Refusing Lifesaving Medical Treatment[8]

The right to refuse lifesaving treatment is a moral right, not merely a legal right; the obligations others have to respect it are moral, not only (or even necessarily) legal. The scope of the care that patients may refuse includes both acute lifesaving care and continual life-support. It encompasses withdrawing care midstream and holds regardless of whether the patient's illness is "terminal." Along with the right of informed consent and refusal generally, it is one of the central principles of modern medical ethics. In this chapter's discussion of the moral protection that normative autonomy provides death-hastening decisions, the right to refuse lifesaving treatment is the initial, most clearly protected right—the "anchoring" right.

Its moral explanation might seem obvious but is not always simple. In legal terms, administering medical treatment to competent persons without their informed consent is *battery*, the unauthorized harmful *or offensive* invasion of the body or contact with it. One might wonder why, in cases where we have every reason to think medical treatment is not harmful (and in fact is greatly helpful), it is still offensive to administer it without patient consent. The most plausible explanation is that to touch or invade the body of a person capable of consent, without his or her consent, is morally offensive for two very stubborn reasons.[9] One is bodily integrity: Treatment typically is an invasion of the body, and if anything should be within persons' province of control, their own bodies should be. A second is patient autonomy—combining its descriptive and normative senses: Patients can be asked, they are (usually) capable of responding if asked, therefore they should be asked. A stubborn, basic moral judgment is involved here: *Beings with the capacity to consent should be asked, and their choice be respected.* If we do not ask, we do not treat them as the persons with agency that they are.

There are other reasons for the right to refuse treatment beyond these, though not as central and more contingent. Treatments often can be more effective if the patient is involved as a decision maker. Treatments often involve risks, even the risk of death; those should be evaluated by the person who is taking the risk. Moreover, given the risks involved and the inevitability that treatment will sometimes harm, patients' trust in physicians and caregivers erodes if the responsibility for making decisions is not shared. These considerations add to the ethical case for the right to refuse treatment, but its core is self-ownership, self-determination, and respect for persons—that is, normative autonomy.

That said, questions still arise about how far the right to refuse lifesaving treatment should extend. It has its strongest justification in situations of terminal illness and continual pain—who better to discern the value of the remaining life with suffering than the person experiencing it? How much of this point changes when the person who would refuse lifesaving care is not terminally ill?

Perhaps very little. If anything, in nonterminal illness suffering can be longer and all the worse. Moreover, although an illness might not be officially "terminal" in the sense of death being likely within six months, life still could be on a steady downhill progression in which the patient is losing the things he or she most associates with being "alive" (in progressive dementia, for example). Yet, what if the refusal occurs in a situation that is not terminal at all—an anorexic 25-year-old refuses tube feeding, for example? May we add a tasteless liquid to her drink to revive her appetite?

In such nonterminal situations two further factors are relevant: the degree of bodily invasion and the potential for "retrospective consent." Surgery and tube feeding are different than a tasteless pill or food additive. Retrospective consent also can affect our judgment. If providers have very good reason to think that a patient will end up saying, after recovery, that it was right to give him or her lifesaving treatment though he or she had refused it at the time, treating without current consent could be justified.[10] Such justification is not straight, hard paternalism in which the patient's choice is overridden, but rather an appeal to the patient's own eventual consent. Physicians override refusal out of respect for a patient's autonomy temporally extended.

Even if likely retrospective consent and little or no bodily invasion occasionally justify treating a patient despite refusal, the default rule remains the right to refuse. The burden of proof falls not on the patient to show that consent is required, but on any party who wants to treat in the face of refusal to show that limitations are justified because bodily invasion is minor or the likelihood of retrospective consent is very high.

Moreover, perhaps the most frequently cited good reason for treating patients in the face of refusal is that they lack sufficient decision-making capacity. Here treatment is certainly not really a compromise of or exception to the patient's right to refuse and respect for persons that lies behind it, but a logical aspect of the right itself.

A patient's moral right to refuse lifesaving treatment has inherent limitations: when there is insufficient decision-making capacity, high probability of retrospective consent, or little bodily invasion in delivering treatment. These limiting circumstances do not reflect any weakness in the central justification that autonomy with its constitutive elements of self-ownership, self-determination, and respect for persons provides.

Voluntarily Stopping Eating and Drinking (VSED)

Does autonomy support a moral right to refuse food and water by mouth as strongly as it supports a right to refuse lifesaving treatment? If it does, patients' range of choice is greatly expanded. People can effectively hasten death by refusing lifesaving treatment only if they have a condition that requires treatment. No such contingencies of medical circumstance limit the death hastening capacity of VSED.

Legally, in the United States at least, people effectively have a right to refuse to eat and drink.[11] In one of its articulations, the moral and legal right to VSED derives from the right to refuse life-sustaining medical treatment (LSMT). To be sure, stopping eating and drinking is not per se the refusal of treatment, and providing food and water by mouth, even with extensive assistance for those who are unable to feed themselves, is not by itself an intrusion. Yet a moment's reflection on what happens if we do not respect a person's decision to stop eating and drinking reveals how tightly connected such a decision is to the right to refuse treatment. The only way to keep alive the person who steadfastly refuses to eat and drink is to insert some sort of feeding tube, using whatever force is necessary. In practice, VSED thus becomes an instance of the right to refuse lifesaving treatment, and autonomy's support will presumably transfer to VSED. The prospect of physically restraining competent patients to insert feeding tubes against their will is so demeaning and repugnant that we quickly acknowledge a right to VSED.[12]

A right to VSED also has a simpler explanation as a manifestation of bodily integrity. U.S. Supreme Court Chief Justice Rehnquist might have seen it this way: "It seems odd that your bodily integrity. . . [would be] violated by sticking a needle in your arm but not by sticking a spoon in your mouth."[13] Without the consent of the patient, neither is a warranted intrusion. Insofar as protection against bodily invasion is part of what is meant by normative autonomy, autonomy could protect VSED just as it protects refusing treatment.

As powerful as these arguments are, they hardly dispose of the matter. An opposing view is implied by the statement on nutrition and hydration by the U.S. Bishops' Pro-Life Committee (1992). The statement begins with the long-standing Roman Catholic position that *intentionally* ending life is impermissible. Acting to intentionally end life includes not only active killing but some omissions. Often the purpose of an omission such as not being treated is "to relieve the patient of a particular procedure that was of limited usefulness . . . or unreasonably burdensome." If so, then even if nutrition and hydration are omitted, the omission is not a decision to intentionally end life and should not be equated with suicide. At other times, however,

> the harsh reality is that . . . withdrawal of nutrition and hydration . . . directly intend[s] to bring about a patient's death. . . . Whether orally administered or medically assisted . . . [food and fluids] are sometimes withdrawn not

because a patient is dying, but precisely because a patient is not dying (or not dying quickly) and someone believes it would be better if he or she did. . . . We must be sure that it is not our intent to cause the patient's death—either for its own sake or as a means to achieving some other goal.[14]

The bishops often couch their view in terms of what can be "withheld" or "withdrawn," language that fits medically assisted food and water better than refusal of food and water by mouth. The view is nonetheless clear: in the typical case, by intentionally and with certainty causing one's own death, VSED is impermissible suicide. When family and caregivers cooperate with such action and facilitate it with good palliative care, they assist a suicide. Neither the act itself nor the assistance is morally permissible.

Outside a framework such as Roman Catholic moral theology in which intentional killing is inherently wrong, the matter could look very different. Why should hastening death *intentionally*, and with certainty *ensuring* it, and being *the primary cause* of it, make the act morally wrong if what it brings about, death sooner rather than later, is a good thing as compared to living with great suffering or a chronic condition like severe dementia? These characteristics of VSED's relationship to death—intention, certainty, causation—might make VSED "suicide," *but do they make it wrong*? On the basis of autonomous persons' choice to see death coming sooner rather than later as a good thing, the intentionality, certainty, and causation hardly make VSED worse. If anything, they make it better. As long as stopping eating and drinking is voluntary and not foisted on patients by others, why is it not within their moral prerogative as much as refusing LSMT? How is their self-determination or respect for them as persons any less at stake?

The strongest argument against VSED as a moral and legal right, though, does pivot directly off its character as suicide. In U.S. law, suicide is not a crime in the sense that a person who accomplishes or unsuccessfully attempts it is not punished. But it is not a person's legal right, either— others may stop it and in most jurisdictions others are not allowed to assist it.[15] This greatly complicates the situation. To be a comfortable path to death, VSED should be accompanied by palliative care, but if it is correctly deemed "suicide" because it intentionally and with certainty causes one's death, comfortable and humane VSED usually involves assisted suicide.[16] This poses little moral difficulty if there is nothing wrong with assisting suicide, but it complicates the legal and moral situation greatly if there is.

In practice, such doubts about the right to VSED based on its typical involvement with assistance are likely overcome by our negative reaction to the alternatives. We react with "revulsion at the prospect of physically overcoming and restraining people" to feed them against their will.[17] We think it hypocrisy to let people embark on hastening death by VSED but then pull them back when they become incapable of resistance. We think it heartless not to provide them with palliative care if they are carrying out the act regardless. We thus likely see medically supporting VSED as permissible *even if VSED is suicide and assisting suicide is not generally permissible.* Such permission is crucial if VSED is actually going to be used as a significant comfortable option for assuring a hastened death in the many jurisdictions where physician-assisted death by direct lethal injection means is illegal.

Adequate justification for a right to VSED is not provided by simply reiterating the autonomy-based reasons for the right to refuse LSMT. Additional complications must be addressed, but the means for persuasively addressing them are available in various moral frameworks: If suicide is not inherently wrong, if VSED is not suicide, or if—although it is—assisting it is still permissible. Respect for personal autonomy remains a strong reason for VSED as a person's moral right, though the route to a convincing conclusion on this score has to employ considerations beyond autonomy.

Refusing Lifesaving Medical Treatment by Advance Directive

For patients who lack competent decision-making capacity, the right to refuse LSMT does not apply. If, however, they previously had such capacity, previous autonomous choice still could have weight in later decisions. A patient might have written a substantive advance directive conveying what treatments in what circumstances should be refused. Or a patient might have named a proxy decision maker to make decisions for him or her as a matter of *substituted judgment* (estimating what the patient would have chosen in the circumstances if he or she now still was able to decide).

Whether through substantive AD or appointed proxy and substituted judgment, the justification for the prerogative to refuse lifesaving treatment for a no longer competent patient would seem to be the same normative autonomy—self-determination and respect for persons as decision-making agents—that justifies the right to refuse LSMT when the person was competent in the first place. If this influence of the patient's previous choices and values is by clear, informed, and sufficiently specific directive, then his or her current incapacity tends to be ignored and the previous directive regarded as his or her decision even in the current situation. The life that will be affected, after all, is still *the patient's life*; the full moral weight of self-determination therefore still is in play. This is referred to here as the *precedent autonomy* view of ADs.

To constitute precedent autonomy, the moral force of any substantive AD must track the same basic considerations that give force to a competent patient's choice. How informed is the person is about the medical condition to which he or she understands the treatment would apply, about his or her prognosis with and without the treatment, about its risks? How adequate is his or her mental capacity to absorb such information and make decisions based on it? How voluntary and free from pressure and coercion are his or her choices?

These same elements affect the normative force of choices expressed in a directive. When by AD a person refuses a type of treatment, to what conditions with what range of prognoses does he or she understand this refusal to apply? Was he or she knowledgeable about those when writing the directive? Was it made voluntarily and without coercive pressure? The clearer, more knowledgeable, and more unquestionably voluntary a directive is, the greater its moral force for later caregivers and decision makers.

The notions of validity and applicability summarize these considerations. A directive has normative force in a given situation if it is *valid*—made voluntarily and with sufficient understanding of the things to which it speaks. But it must also, now when the patient is incompetent, be *applicable*—the conditions to which the person intended it to apply must now in fact be present. A good directive thus must be clear and substantive enough to later be applicable. If the directive conveys little understanding of and direction about the conditions for which a treatment later might be refused, how can it be an appropriate substitute for the informed choice the person would make if he or she were still competent? Many directives, undoubtedly, do not have enough clear content to make them truly applicable. A practical way of blunting this common deficiency is to supplement the substantive AD with another directive appointing a proxy.

These difficulties in meeting a reasonably high standard of validity and applicability are ongoing everyday challenges to the authority of ADs in a precedent autonomy framework. People might tend not to be very demanding of directives on these scores because they stubbornly hold two moral beliefs: *people do not lose their rights when they become incompetent* (those rights just have to be exercised for them by others), and *the life a person lives in incompetence is still his life.* Thus a right to refuse LSMT by AD could be seen as nearly as strongly justified by self-determination and respect for persons as is the competent person's right.

The matter, though, is not so simple. A fundamental difficulty, the "then-self" versus "now-self" problem, intrudes. The directive's competent writer (the "then-self") could request, for example, that no treatment that would prolong life in a significantly diminished or painful condition be provided because he or she does not want to live if the patient has to "live like that." Yet precisely the situation that motivates writing an AD and brings it into operation—incompetence—also can affect a person's values, attitudes, and desires. The now incompetent individual (the "now-self") might not regard "life like that" as being unbearable. In the form of self in which the patient is now living, he or she is not autonomous, does not care about autonomy, is not aware of the directive, and might no longer value many of the things about life that were the basis for writing the directive. So why should the directive be followed?

Some critics—notably Rebecca Dresser and John Robertson[18]—conclude that the directive is irrelevant. The now incompetent patient should be treated solely on the basis of current best interest, not his or her previous wishes, even if the directive clearly and accurately expressed those wishes. "Precedent autonomy" is a misnomer: the moral force of autonomy is lost when autonomy is no longer present. To respond that this fails to respect the patient's autonomy manifested in the directive is hardly persuasive, for what Dresser and Robertson are disputing is the very relevance *to the current patient* of that autonomy.

A compelling response to the Dresser/Robertson rejection of any weight for ADs based on autonomy is Nancy Rhoden's. Their position, she notes, amounts to *treating previously competent patients no differently than patients who were never competent*: both are to be treated only on the basis of best interest. But should we ever treat a person who has had a long life as a competent, full, and vital person as if he or she never had been competent and deserves no respect for having been an autonomous person? We must not.

> Someone who makes a prior directive sees herself as the unified subject of a human life. She sees her concern for her body, her goals, or her family as transcending her incapacity. . . . One . . . component of treating persons with respect [is] that we view them as they view themselves. If we are to do this, we must not ignore their prior choices and values.[19]

If this is correct, ADs must have some authority.[20] Dresser and Robertson are right in noting that the patients incapacitated at the time when their directives are to be acted upon do not understand autonomy, exemplify it, or care about it, but that does not mean previous wishes may be ignored. If it is not autonomy per se that is being dealt with here, it is something very close: the narrative identity people see in their lives. Norman Cantor states the view this way: "A person, by nurturing and developing a body, character, and relationships has earned a prerogative to shape a life narrative—including the medical fate of a succeeding incompetent persona."[21]

Ronald Dworkin attempts to capture this claim within the framework of best interest, not precedent autonomy, through the notion of "critical interests."[22] A person's "experiential" interests can change significantly with chronic incompetence, but a person's overall best interest still is connected with previous choices. Competent, autonomous persons have beliefs, desires, and values that form something more than experiential interests—"critical" interests based on "second-order" desires that emerge when people reflect on events and on the first-order desires that they just have. Critical interests are based on evaluations that are more than mere preferences—convictions, for example, about "what helps to make . . . [one's] life good on the whole."[23] For some, that involves how one's life should end.

Unlike experiential interests, critical interests can exist even after one no longer experiences them. If someone cares about what happens to his or her property, family, or reputation after he or she dies, for example, then the person has critical interests in these things even after he or she has died, when the person will have no experience of whether his or her interest is thwarted or satisfied. This is also true for any conviction a person might have that his or her life as a whole would be better if it did not extend into years with an eventually fatal chronic disease such as severe dementia. Refusing to implement someone's directive would harm the person just as unfairly tarnishing his or her reputation would.

The notion of critical interests could formally put the defense of ADs back into a best-interest-of-the-patient framework, but autonomy as self-determination about one's whole life—something only a person has the capacity to exercise, and an essential part of what must be respected to respect them as a person—is still the underlying justification. Whether the matter is put into Rhoden's directly autonomy-focused terms, uses Cantor's language of owning a life narrative, or employs Dworkin's notion of critical interests, self-determination and respect for persons still provide the normative force in these arguments for ADs.

Yet because of the then-self/now-self problem, autonomy's normative power can diminish when a directive is used to temporally extend one's right. Autonomy does not generate the same weight without limitations when a decision to refuse LSMT is made by AD, even when a directive is thoroughly valid and now clearly applicable. The reason is that contrary experiential interests can intrude when the person is incompetent. The critical interest a person has in dying sooner rather than later, expressed in an AD and still present when now the person is incompetent, does not always outweigh a contrary experiential interest in survival.[24]

Imagine, for example, James, age 90. For years he has been gradually declining physically and mentally, and he recently had a series of strokes.

In his recovery he has now plateaued, regaining enough control to walk short distances with a walker and slowly feed himself, though he usually ambulates by wheelchair and must be spoon-fed to eat. With his stroke-induced dementia he can carry on no conversation, and he no longer can occupy himself with TV or an activity such as a Word Find. James seems to recognize his most frequent caregivers, although maybe not as particular persons; it's doubtful whether he recognizes his wife and son as his wife and son. Nonetheless, he is consistently good-natured and smiles when someone looks at him directly and speaks kindly. He makes soft appreciative sounds in many circumstances.

James' AD specifies that once he cannot recognize his closest friends and loved ones, converse with them as specific individuals, or occupy himself with even simple activities, he should receive no lifesaving treatment of any sort, including antibiotics. Now he has contracted pneumonia, readily curable with an antibiotic, and otherwise almost certainly fatal. His directive applied to the situation clearly specifies not providing the antibiotic. James therefore has a critical interest in the pneumonia not being treated. Yet he is not suffering or in pain, and he experiences some real though modest enjoyment of life; he still has some experiential interest in surviving.

This is not an easy case, but it would be much easier (in favor of not treating his pneumonia) if the *full* weight of autonomy carried into incompetence through his directive. Rhoden's, Cantor's, and Dworkin's arguments show that his directive's earlier choices to determine the course of his life must be accorded significant weight, but now he still has an experiential interest in continuing to live. And if his directive is not followed, he undoubtedly will not know that fact and will experience no consternation, a factor very different than if he were competent and was given the antibiotic against his wishes. Even with less than the full original weight from autonomy, if James were to slide a bit further into dementia to where he could not anticipate tomorrow or appreciate having lived from yesterday, a decision to follow his directive would be easier. The subjective value to him of survival would then be low enough that his strong critical interest in not being treated would more easily outweigh it.[25]

Directives and the patient autonomy that lies behind them still very much count when a person loses competence, but sometimes a stronger case can be made for going against prior wishes than ever could be made for going against current wishes when a person is competent and refuses lifesaving treatment. That amounts to saying that ADs, though accepted in many Western cultures as a natural extension of self-determination, do not transmit decisions with the same full force of autonomy that contemporaneously competent decisions have. Advance directives are compelling but problematic vehicles for self-determination. They command our attention and support, but their discerning application is far from simple.

Stopping Eating and Drinking by Advance Directive

Voluntary stopping eating and drinking by advance directive (SED by AD) is more complex yet. The normative weight of autonomy carried forward diminishes more than with a directive for refusing treatment. Not a great deal more, however; a directive for SED still can have moral force if the circumstances are right. This has significant practical importance. Many people want not to live years into severe dementia as much as or more than they want not to suffer for a few weeks or months at the end of life. They might choose to take preemptive action while they are still decisive (VSED or suicide), but then they often sacrifice valuable years of life. The only other way they can assure that they will not live into years of severe dementia is to have an implementable directive to withhold food and water by mouth.

All the characteristics required to justify following a directive to refuse treatment apply to a directive for SED. It must convey clearly the condition(s) in which feeding is to be stopped.[26] The person writing the directive must be reasonably knowledgeable about what SED involves, about the likely course of decline it causes, and about the medical situations to which the individual says it should apply. The directive also must be made voluntarily. The last two characteristics are required for the directive to be *valid*, the first for it to be *applicable*.

Assuming the directive is valid and applicable, implementation will still be vulnerable to the basic then-self/now-self problem that can confront any AD. A morally cogent strategy must be in place to handle it, whether implementing a directive for SED or of any other sort.[27] Even if the then-self/now-self problem about survival is cogently addressed, however, SED encounters further issues. The patient might express a desire to eat when the directive is being implemented, and food and water is basic *personal care* that caregivers often see as a more unconditional obligation to provide than medical treatment.

Using the example presented above, suppose that James' directive, described previously in regard to refusing a lifesaving antibiotic, also directs that his eating and drinking be stopped when he reaches a certain stage of decline. Also suppose, however, that when that time comes and we do not feed him, he reacts. Not brought to his eating table, he grimaces, looks puzzled, holds out his hand, and utters pleading sounds. His behavior is not a change of mind about his directive; he is cognitively incapable of that.[28] And the then-self/now-self problem is blunted by the fact that his experiential interest in surviving is low; he does not anticipate being alive tomorrow, and tomorrow he will not remember having survived from today. Yet here he is in front of us, wanting to eat. Even without much experiential interest in survival, he has an immediate experiential interest in being fed.

In one scenario, James did not address this complication in his directive. We then cannot reasonably infer that he would want us just to follow the directive and not be fed; that might or might not be his desire. Perhaps we should make a "not yet" decision: don't stop food and drink *yet*, but be attentive to his directive, knowing that as his dementia continues to deepen he will reach a point where he will not have as much, if any, desire for food.[29]

Suppose, conversely, the other scenario—James did address this kind of situation in his AD, requesting that we administer distress-relieving drugs or appetite suppressants and proceed with withholding food and water. We can address the then-self versus now-self problem by considering the same critical interests and narrative identity that emerge from normative autonomy and constitute the moral authority of any AD. Having clarified in his directive what to do in the circumstance where he still desires to eat, what difference should it make that it is withholding food and water by mouth, not refusal of lifesaving treatment, that he has requested? From the perspective of self-determination and respect for persons, it is hard to see a difference. Writing his directive, he wanted one as much as the other. Any weight from autonomy that is diminished already has been diminished by the choices being delivered by AD at all.

Should, however, a person have the prerogative to forbid later caregivers from providing basic *personal care*, not just medical care? Providing food and water by mouth and manually assisting with it is not medical care. The same considerations of bodily intrusion that make imposition of medical care so objectionable might not characterize the personal care here (the person fed is not resisting). Withholding food and water by mouth in a fairly typical such case might not fall within the proper scope of an AD. At least one major court has said it does not.[30]

In regard to Rhoden's objection that we should never treat a person who was previously competent the same as a never-competent person, though, and in relation to the other considerations of self-determination and respect for persons that justify moral rights both to VSED and to refusing lifesaving treatment, it is hard to see why personal care should be any less within someone's control. The life the care preserves is just as much *this person's life* as is the life at stake in refusing treatment, and personal care is care *of this person* as much as medical care is. A person's AD generally could address all sorts of considerations related to mental deficiency and mental health, not just medical ones.[31]

Caregivers might claim that they are more unconditionally obligated to provide a basic element of life such as food and water than to provide medical care that requires patient consent. Indeed, caregivers could believe that their obligations to provide basic personal care are more absolute, but what is the moral justification for this? If caregivers should not provide even the most basic medical care against a person's will, and if they have eventually come to accept that ADs preserve much of the moral weight of autonomy that justifies a person's right to refuse such care, then *are* they any more obligated to provide assistance with eating and drinking that a patient has refused by AD? Arguably, they are not.

Thus, although directives for SED raise additional moral complications not inherent in directives to refuse lifesaving treatment, they still have considerable moral weight based on the same elements of autonomy that underlie a right to VSED. If a competent person's moral right to VSED is nearly as firm as his or her right to refuse LSMT, and if the person's right to refuse lifesaving treatment largely can be preserved for future incompetence by an AD, why should his or her right to VSED not similarly be preserved when the person becomes incompetent, especially if the person has left specific instructions about what to do if he or she expresses a desire to eat when the directive becomes applicable? Perhaps the personal care/medical care distinction makes a moral difference, but, if so, then the difference needs to be justified and not merely asserted.

Physician-Assisted Dying (PAD)

How much of the strength of these arguments from self-ownership, self-determination, and respect for persons extends to physician-assisted dying? Some slippage in the moral weight of autonomy, although not a great deal, is observed when moving from refusing LSMT to VSED, to refusing LSMT by AD, and to SED by AD. Does any more slippage, or even as much, occur in moving from the primary reference case of a competent patient refusing LSMT to a competent patient actively causing his or her death with a physician-prescribed drug?

Physician-assisted dying (sometimes termed "aid-in-dying") falls within the broader conceptual category "physician-assisted suicide" (PAS). Conceptually, PAS is not limited to patients who are terminally ill (unlikely to live more than six months, in typical definition). Because the patient with terminal illness is sufficiently close to death, "physician-assisted *dying*" is a more transparent label when a terminal illness condition is attached. Because the lethal drug is taken by the patient, and not administered by the physician, it is physician-*assisted* dying and not euthanasia.[32]

The morally relevant differences between PAD and refusing LSMT potentially are many. Some are "external" differences—such as allegedly greater potential for abuse in permitting PAD than in permitting refusal of lifesaving treatment, alleged drop in trust of physicians if they depart from their traditional role as healing, and never killing. These differences are relevant in any comprehensive moral assessment of whether people have a moral right to employ PAD, but they are set aside here because they do not directly affect the moral weight normative autonomy brings to the assessment. At best, they only constitute countervailing considerations that in the real world of practice could outweigh autonomy in deciding whether PAD should be permitted.

Three other differences in the very nature of PAD might more directly affect the normative force of autonomy: the difference between active killing and letting death come, differences in coercion, and differences in co-responsibility. Do any of these affect how strongly autonomy protects PAD compared to refusing LSMT?

Active Killing

In PAD, the patient with the physician's assistance actively kills himself or herself by doing something; in refusing LSMT he or she allows death to come by not having something done. Not only in PAD, however, but in refusing lifesaving treatment, a person might very much intend death to come, and refusing treatment can be a cause of death just as taking a lethal drug is. Intention and causation therefore are not real differences. The real difference in PAD is the certainty and speed with which death comes.

Whether the killing/letting die distinction is morally relevant has generated a huge amount of literature,[33] but the general relevance of the distinction is not the concern here. This section's focus is whether the distinction makes any difference in the normative weight that autonomy brings to the decision for PAD as compared to a decision to refuse treatment. If with PAD, undesired life (including pain, suffering, dependency, and subjective indignity, for example) would end more quickly and with greater certainty, and this is what the person whose life it is strongly desires and believes to be best, the normative force of autonomy would appear to be just as strong if not stronger than with refusing lifesaving treatment. This might be balanced out by a factor that leans the other way: bodily intrusion occurs when a person is treated against his or her will, something not present when one is denied the opportunity for PAD. The outcome? Probably a draw.

Coercion

By not allowing a person to use PAD, nothing is forced on the person; in failing to respect a person's refusal of treatment something is forced upon a person—treatment. On the surface, this argument seems cogent, but only on the surface. Not respecting a person's refusal of treatment is forcing *something* on this person, but not allowing PAD also is forcing upon the person a segment of life that he or she doesn't want to live. Life generally is not termed a "thing," but it is certainly as much an intrusion into a person's life to be required to live additional time in a condition one very much thinks does not allow life to be worth having as it is to tell the person that he or she cannot refuse lifesaving care. From the perspective of ownership of one's life, self-determination, and respect for decision-making persons, the two are not different.

Co-Responsibility

In PAD the patient brings another person, the prescribing physician, into a co-responsible role. By contrast, though refusing lifesaving treatment might subsequently involve physicians in complementary roles such as palliative care, they do not thereby become co-responsible for the refusal. The moral protection that autonomy and self-determination provide is first and foremost for actions for which the person himself or herself is solely responsible. In the patient's self-determination he or she might want to bring others into co-responsible roles, but that is a secondary circle of autonomy.

This argument is no more convincing than the previous two. There is indeed a difference in the range of people responsible in PAD as compared to refusing LSMT. But why should it be assumed that courses of action that call others into co-responsibility are any less important for self-determination, or any less at issue in respect for persons?

In the last analysis, none of these three differences provide good reason to think autonomy provides less moral protection for PAD than it does for refusing lifesaving treatment.

Finally, no analysis of the role of normative autonomy in justifying a moral right to PAD would be complete without considering the well-known

Kantian objection to suicide that focuses on respect for the intrinsic worth of persons: If the persons for which respect is owed are intrinsically valuable for their own sake, *the very person* may not be sacrificed to accomplish what is *good for* the person.[34] Therefore, PAD, all other forms of suicide, and euthanasia are forbidden by respect for persons, no matter how much the persons themselves might desire these measures. Even outside of any attachment to Kant's moral philosophy, the claim is attractive. Respect for autonomous persons expresses the conviction that all persons have an intrinsic worth residing in their capacity for reflective choice and self-determination, thus the person is more important than anything that is good for him or her.

The argument warrants lengthy discussion. The analysis here is necessarily brief and uses the critique provided by Jeff McMahan. McMahan interprets the argument as treating "the person as an instrument of his rational nature. . . . If a person's life ceases to be worth living, he is required simply to suffer through it if the alternative . . . involves the sacrifice of his rational nature."[35] This view of respect for persons might be an accurate interpretation of Kant's argument, but it is difficult to see it as conveying the contemporary sense of normative autonomy that involves more-direct respect for people's reasonable choices, especially those about their own lives. Still using Kantian categories, McMahan points out the difficulty in seeing the choice of PAD as a person treating himself or herself merely as a means to his or her own desires when those desires themselves are formed by the person with a capacity for reflective choice. McMahan concludes,

> We can concede that persons have a value that is independent of their good, yet hold that respect for that value is nevertheless manifested in an active concern for their good, at least when that coincides with respect for their autonomous will. There is simply no sense in which a person's worth is upheld or affirmed by her mere persistence [making her persist] through suffering.[36]

Even if the Kantian argument against PAD was persuasive on a contemporary understanding of normative autonomy, it would face another difficulty in the context of the discussion here about the relative strength of the moral protection autonomy provides PAD. The argument also could apply to cases of refusing lifesaving treatment in which the patient clearly intends thereby to die as soon as he or she can. The key elements of causation and intention are present, and the choice to refuse is made understanding full well that forgoing treatment will lead to death.

Autonomy—self-ownership, self-determination, respect for persons— provides nearly as much moral protection for physician-assisted dying as for refusing lifesaving medical treatment. Plausible objections to such parity can be made, but very little in these objections survives analysis.

Conclusion

The moral right of competent patients to refuse lifesaving medical treatment is the most justified, "anchoring" right of patients among death-hastening decisions. Much of its justification stems from respect for personal autonomy. Extending this right to voluntarily stopping eating and drinking requires addressing challenging questions about suicide and assisting suicide that refusing lifesaving treatment seldom confronts. Those challenges can be met, although the resulting protection provided VSED by autonomy is less direct, and other moral considerations sometimes must be employed.

Extending the anchoring right to using advance directives to refuse lifesaving treatment for times of incompetence faces the additional problem of conflicts between then-self and now-self. A further extension, to stopping eating and drinking by advance directive, raises even more difficult then-self/now-self conflicts, as well as the objection that personal care is not within the legitimate scope of directives. The ethical challenges to both extensions by AD can be met by careful distinction and often subtle argument, but meeting them reveals certain limits to the justification that autonomy can provide ADs. In some cases a directive cannot be said to be applicable because it is not clear enough for the current circumstance; in other cases proxies and caregivers should say "not yet" and hold off implementation because of the altered interests of the incompetent patient.

At first glance, physician-assisted dying appears to run into greater slippage in the justification provided by autonomy than the extension of refusing lifesaving treatment by advance directive. Analysis, however, shows that the moral protection provided PAD by respect for personal autonomy is virtually as strong as what is provided for a competent patient's refusal of lifesaving treatment. Moral protection for PAD, and probably for VSED, too, is no more, and perhaps even less, problematic than refusing lifesaving treatment by advance directive.

Notes

1. Onora O'Neill, *Autonomy and Trust in Bioethics* (Cambridge: Cambridge University Press, 2002), 21–23.

2. Bonnie Steinbock, Alex J. London, and John D. Arras, eds., *Ethical Issues in Modern Medicine*, 8th ed. (New York: McGraw Hill, 2009), 36, 45.

3. O'Neill, *Autonomy and Trust*, 47–48.

4. *Whose Life Is It Anyway?* (film), John Badham, director (Beverly Hills, CA: Metro-Goldwyn-Mayer, 1981).

5. John Stuart Mill, "On Liberty" (1863), in *Utilitarianism, On Liberty and Other Essays*, ed. Mary Warnock (London: Fontana, 1962).

6. Immanuel Kant, "Groundwork of the Metaphysics of Morals" (1785), trans. Mary J. Gregor, in Kant, *Practical Philosophy* (Cambridge: Cambridge University Press, 1996), 4: 387–463.

7. O'Neill, *Autonomy and Trust*, 86–95.

8. Significant parts of the substance of this and the next three sections are drawn from Paul T. Menzel, "Refusing Lifesaving Medical Treatment and Food and Water by Mouth," in *Ethics at the End of Life: New Issues and Arguments*, ed. John K. Davis (London: Taylor & Francis Group, Routledge, 2017). The current chapter systematically focuses on the role of autonomy; the essay referred to does not.

9. Norman Cantor, "On Hastening Death Without Violating Legal and Moral Prohibitions," *Loyola University Chicago Law Journal* 37 (2006): 101–25, at 106.

10. The prediction of retrospective consent was a primary justification doctors used in 1973–74 in treating burn victim Dax Cowart against his strong objections. For a description of this well-known case, see Keith Burton, "Dax's Case As It Happened," in *Dax's Case: Essays in Medical Ethics and Human Meaning*, ed. Lonnie D. Kliever (Dallas: Southern Methodist University Press, 1989) and in *Ethical Issues in Modern Medicine*, ed. Steinbock, London, and Arras, 343–47. *See also* Dax Cowart and Robert Burt, "Confronting Death: Who Chooses, Who Controls?" *Hastings Center Report* 28 (1998): 1: 14–24; and *Ethical Issues in Modern Medicine*, ed. Steinbock, London, and Arras, 348–53.

11. Thaddeus M. Pope and Lisa E. Anderson, "Voluntarily Stopping Eating and Drinking: A Legal Treatment Option at the End of Life," *Widener Law Review* 17 (2011): 2: 363–427. Cantor, "On Hastening Death," 109–12.

12. Cantor, "On Hastening Death," 112.

13. In oral argument in *Vacco v. Quill*, 521 U.S. 793 (1997) (No. 95-1858) at 13:39 to 13:46, available at http://www.oyez.org/cases/1990-1999/1996/1996_95_1858 /argument (accessed August 16, 2016). As oral argument, Rehnquist's view here is only dictum, not case law precedent. See Pope and Johnson, "Voluntarily Stopping Eating and Drinking," 414.

14. U.S. Bishops' Pro-Life Committee, "Nutrition and Hydration: Moral and Pastoral Reflections" (Washington, DC: U.S. Catholic Conference, Inc., 1992), in *Ethical Issues in Modern Medicine*, ed. Steinbock, London, and Arras, 391–97, at 393.

15. Assisted suicide (assisted by physicians) is legal in only five U.S. states (Oregon, Washington, Vermont, Montana, and California) and Switzerland, Belgium, and the Netherlands, permitted there typically only in restricted circumstances of terminal illness or unbearable suffering. The exception is Switzerland, where neither terminal illness nor a minimum level of suffering is required. The only Swiss restriction is that the person assisting must be acting unselfishly. See Penney Lewis, "Assisted Dying: What Does the Law in Different Countries

Say?" BBC World report, at http://www.bbc.com/news/world-34445715?SThisFB (accessed August 16, 2016).

16. At least it would be *supported*, if not assisted, suicide.

17. Cantor, "On Hastening Death," 112.

18. Rebecca Dresser and John S. Robertson, "Quality of Life and Non-Treatment Decisions for Incompetent Patients," *Law, Medicine and Health Care* 17 (1989): 3: 234–44.

19. Nancy Rhoden, "The Limits of Legal Objectivity," *North Carolina Law Review* 68 (1990): 845–65, at 860.

20. In speaking of the "authority" of ADs this author does not intend to accord them anything like final control. The term only means that they should be respected as having normative force and therefore a substantial role in decision making.

21. Norman Cantor, "Is It Immoral for Me to Dictate an Accelerated Death for My Future Demented Self?" http://blogs.harvard.edu/billofhealthj/2015/12/02/is-it-immoral-for-me-to-dictate-an-accelerated-death-for-my-future-demented-self/, 5 (posted Dec 2, 2015).

22. Ronald Dworkin, *Life's Dominion: An Argument about Abortion, Euthanasia and Individual Freedom* (New York: Alfred A. Knopf, 1993), 201–32.

23. Dworkin, *Life's Dominion*, 201.

24. Paul T. Menzel and Bonnie Steinbock, "Advance Directives, Dementia, and Physician-Assisted Death," *Journal of Law, Medicine and Ethics* 41 (2013): 2: 484–500, at 495.

25. Two coauthors and I have called this the "balancing" or "sliding scale" model of handling the tension between then-self and now-self: weigh up together the person's respective experiential and critical interests. See Menzel and Steinbock, "Advance Directives . . . and Physician-Assisted Death," 495–96, and Paul T. Menzel and M. Colette Chandler-Cramer, "Advance Directives, Dementia, and Withholding Food and Water by Mouth," *Hastings Center Report* 44 (2014): 3: 23–37, at 28–29.

26. If the directive is for SED in dementia, that could be a defined stage on the Functional Assessment Staging Test (FAST) scale for dementia. See Barry Reisberg, "Functional Assessment Staging Test (FAST)," *Psychopharmacology Bulletin* 24 (1988): 653–59, and Menzel and Chandler-Cramer, "Advance Directives . . . and Withholding Food and Water by Mouth," 33.

27. For example, per the "balancing" or "sliding scale" approach referred to in note 25, the patient could have both a modest experiential interest in surviving and a strong critical interest in not living longer, and those competing interests would be weighed.

28. See Paul T. Menzel, "Changing One's Mind in Dementia: A Problem for Advance Directives," in *Ethics at the End of Life: New Issues and Arguments*, ed. John K. Davis (London: Taylor & Francis Group, Routledge, 2017).

29. Menzel and Chandler-Cramer, "Advance Directives . . . and Withholding Food and Water by Mouth," 34.

30. Court of Appeal for British Columbia, *Bentley v. Maplewood Seniors Care Society*, 2015 BCSC 91, appealing British Columbia Supreme Court decision *Bentley v. Maplewood Seniors Care Society*, 2014 BCSC 165. See also Thaddeus M. Pope, "Prospective Autonomy and Ulysses Contracts for VSED," one of two sections of T. M. Pope and B. J. Richards, "Decision-Making: At the End of Life and the Provision of Pretreatment Advice," *Journal of Bioethical Inquiry*, DOI 10.1007/s11673-015-9652-6.

31. Lisa Brodoff, "Planning for Alzheimer's Disease with Mental Health Advance Directives," *The Elder Law Journal* 17 (2010): 239–308.

32. The following analysis uses the particular form of PAD legalized in three U.S. states (Oregon, Washington, and California): Eligibility requires voluntariness, a prognosis of terminal illness, and availability of good palliative care. There is no requirement concerning suffering. See Lewis, "Assisted Dying."

33. For one extensive collection, see Bonnie Steinbock and Alastair Norcross, eds., *Killing and Letting Die*, 2nd ed. (New York: Fordham University Press, 1994).

34. A well-known articulation and qualified defense of the Kantian argument is by David J. Velleman, "A Right of Self-Termination?" *Ethics* 109 (1999): 606–28. Jeff McMahan critically discusses the argument in *The Ethics of Killing: Problems at the Margins of Life* (New York: Oxford University Press, 2002), section on "Respect for the Worth of Persons," 473–85.

35. McMahan, *The Ethics of Killing*, 479.

36. Ibid., 485.

CHAPTER ELEVEN

Intention, Permissibility, and the Consistency of Traditional End-of-Life Care

Joseph Boyle

The Challenge to the Received Practice of End-of-Life Care

Today, the received standards of practice in end-of-life care are widely disputed in many jurisdictions. Those who question what this chapter calls the "received practice" seek to qualify its key prohibitory element—the prohibition against intentional killing—in favor of a standard of practice that incorporates physician-assisted death, that is, assisting in the patient's suicide, providing euthanasia upon the patient's request, or both. That revision is called for, they say, so as to respond adequately to the demands of competent patients to reduce their intolerable suffering and to respect their autonomy.

The rationale for this revision of the received practice is essentially comprised of views about the extent of beneficence, and the relative value of autonomy, maintaining life, reducing suffering, and protecting the vulnerable. In addition to the debates these normative matters have initiated, the prohibition against intentional killing and its role in the received practice provide a distinct topic for reflection and debate.

Within modern jurisprudence, medical practice, and commonsense morality, there exist two significant precedents for qualifying this blanket prohibition against intentional killing. First, suicide is not a crime, nor is it any sort of wrong cognizable by the state. This provides, it is said, at least some sort of right to commit suicide. Second, the right of a competent person to refuse any medical treatment for any reason (or none) provides, it is said, at least a restricted right to die that is in tension with the prohibition. That tension pervades the structure of end-of-life care. For those expecting death in weeks or months and who are suffering greatly, the relief of that suffering provides an alternative to interventions for the sake of extending life, even when the interventions promise nontrivial extension of life. In some cases, the palliative regime requires that life-extending treatments be set aside. In others, some life-extending care is compatible with the palliative option, and nevertheless is rejected. Facing these options, many patients, family members, and caregivers opt for measures for the relief of suffering, but recognize that that might mean that the patient will die sooner. Decisions having this sort of life-shortening effect are common and are widely acknowledged as being in principle morally correct. As a result of these decisions, however, life is predictably and deliberately shortened—and shortening life, like killing, brings life to an end sooner than the alternative choice. In addition to foregoing life-extending treatments in favor of palliative care, patients sometimes have been offered— and sometimes have accepted—medical interventions aimed at easing suffering even when they understood that such interventions predictably cause or risk earlier death. Here, the decision is similar to killing insofar as it causes earlier death or makes it more likely. Such actions are even harder to square with the prohibition against intentional killing than is declining further treatment. Yet the legitimacy of such decisions is widely accepted within commonsense morality and medical ethics.[1]

Those who wish to maintain the received practice do not regard the cited precedents as decisive; and they deny that the tensions noted are true contradictions. That is primarily because they take for granted the limitation of the prohibition against killing to *intentional killing*. Both terms in the expression—"killing" and "intentional"—have been invoked to avoid the counterexamples and the tensions in the received practice of end-of-life care. Thus, for example, one might suppose that refusing treatment is not *killing*, and thus is not even presumptively in tension with the prohibition, and that using life-shortening analgesics or sedatives is not *intentional* killing. Invoking such distinctions thus becomes the focus of the objection that the received practice is not coherent either with established commonsense morality or with itself. If invoking these distinctions is unjustifiable casuistry, then the practice is reasonably revised toward qualifying the prohibition that generates the difficulties. If justifiable, the case against the traditional practice is shown to be an element of an alternative normative conception, and not a rationale to replace an incoherent ethical practice.

This indicates that the multifaceted objection precisely to the coherence of the received practice constitutes an important public argument for assisted death: The noncriminal status of suicide and the right to refuse medical treatment are widely accepted within the law and commonsense morality, and accepted by the received practice. The prohibition against intentional killing is in tension with these moral standards and with key elements in palliative care. These tensions can be eliminated easily without introducing new and controversial ethical notions, simply by qualifying that prohibition.

The goal of this chapter is to show that this argument—that the received practice is inconsistent with key elements of commonsense morality and is internally incoherent—fails.

Killing Is Prohibited, Not Letting Die: An Inadequate Response

One of the strategies for responding to part of this challenge is to limit the killing prohibited specifically to actions causing death. According to this approach, what counts morally is that in "assisted death" *actions* are involved, whereas in foregoing treatment the patient is *allowed* to die.

This distinction between killing and letting die in itself perhaps is supposed to be morally significant by virtue of the limitation of the agent's causal control over the death—the underlying disease or injury kills the patient, not anything the patient or caregiver does. Limiting killing in this way is meant to show that decisions to forgo life-extending treatment are not killing. Thus, a person's exercise of the right to refuse further treatment or decision to embrace palliative care is not killing, but rather is letting die.

The limitation of the agent's causal control in allowing something to happen, however, does not break the link with the agent that suffices for moral responsibility, namely, the link between the agent's decision and what happens as a result. Allowing something to happen—for example, a patient's death—is distinct from causing it to happen, when the process leading to that outcome is unfolding and an agent could do something to prevent that result from happening but does not.[2] A caregiver can let something happen inadvertently or negligently, but it is deliberate decisions not to prevent a patient's dying that are involved in end-of-life debates. In these decisions agents recognize that a process that likely will lead to death is under way and believe that they could do something to prevent the death from occurring when expected. An agent would not undertake the preventive intervention if he or she thought that doing that would not affect the outcome, or that intervention's effect was trivial, for example that it is unlikely to prevent death within the time frame in which it was expected to occur without intervention. In other words, a caregiver allows someone to die only when that agent has a sufficient understanding of the process leading to it reasonably to expect its happening in some time frame, and when he or she also has a sufficient understanding of the possible effectiveness of preventive interventions.

Consequently, it is true that when a person deliberately allows something to happen, then the causal connections between refraining from action and the outcome allowed are more complex than when someone judges that he or she can guarantee an outcome, or make it very likely, by doing something. Causal connections, however, and in particular counterfactual judgments justified by them—namely, that had someone intervened preventively, the event that would have occurred likely would not occur— exist and are taken into account. Dependence upon this more complex causal judgment does not imply that a decision based on it is unconnected with the happening of something one chose not to prevent. Although an agent does not cause the outcome by initiating the causal chain believed will bring it about, a person exercises agency in respect to it on the basis of deliberation taking into account the causal connections an agent believes exist between an action he or she has the power to take and the outcome.

Therefore, decisions to withhold life-extending treatments, regardless of whether they are morally justified, include responsibility for the patient's dying earlier than he or she otherwise would die. If that responsibility is not to be culpability for a wrong, rather than merit for beneficence, other factors besides the fact that one chose not to prevent the outcome must be invoked.

Philippa Foot thought that such factors exist. She suggested that the moral significance of the doing/allowing distinction is founded on its connection with the distinction between positive and negative rights and duties—a distinction deeply embedded in commonsense morality.[3] Because negative duties—to refrain from harming—generally are more stringent than positive duties—to provide assistance—people generally are required to allow what they should prevent when the alternative is to cause harm. Thus, it is not that causing a result and allowing a result *just as different ways agency is realized* are to be morally distinguished. Rather, in a class of moral conflicts—namely, when acting to assist also harms— the distinction has moral significance. In those cases, allowing harm is justified. This appears to provide a basis for resolving some of the tension within the received practice, namely, that between withholding lifesaving treatment and killing: one could not kill without inflicting the harm of death to assist the person in his or her suffering.

According to the classification of duties as negative and positive, the moral objection to killing is that it causes the harm of death, which violates a negative duty even when undertaken to provide a form of assistance such as relieving suffering. The permissibility of letting someone die justified by the classification is clearest when it is a refusal to kill to relieve suffering. It also applies in other cases, however, where the presence of several positive duties requires reasonably situating within a person's entire set of responsibilities the duty to maintain life, such as when a caregiver lets a patient die because the duty to relieve suffering is more insistent than the duty to maintain life. In other cases where duties are not in competition, letting a harm occur would seem to be as impermissible as inflicting that harm.[4]

However, complications emerge. A caregiver can let a patient die precisely for the sake of ending the patient's life. The clearest cases are where the letting die occurs outside the context of conflicting duties, where an agent lets someone die out of malice or indifference. Such a decision, however, can occur in a context where there is a conflicted duty to assist that person. In such a case, the decision to withhold treatment has little to do with declining to provide help due the patient, and everything to do with ending that person's life. The fact that there is only a positive duty to assist the person in staying alive is incidental to the decision; for a person allows death to occur because he or she seeks precisely that outcome. This indicates that use of the killing/letting die distinction to apply the distinction between positive and negative duties requires a further condition to succeed, and that condition is the agent's intention. Without that condition, a decision to let a patient die that might be justified by the fact that preventing death is a positive duty is undertaken for a reason that makes the act of "letting die" indistinguishable from the act of killing. Whether an agent lets a person die as a way to end his or her life, or takes action to kill that person, the same moral considerations should apply. Consequently, when an agent allows harm intentionally as a way to achieve certain ends, that should be as stringently prohibited as inflicting that harm.

Foot allowed, but downplayed, the relevance of intention in cases in which an agent allows a person to die in order to get him or her dead, "It does seem relevant that in allowing him to die we are aiming at his death, but presumably we are inclined to see this as a violation of negative rather than positive duty."[5] Both clauses seem true, but we can wonder about their connection: Aiming at death seems to be precisely the factor that renders this letting die to be a violation of a negative duty and not a positive duty.

Therefore, the prohibition against killing obviously applies to cases where treatment is withheld precisely for the sake of shortening a life, as when someone refuses to assist a critically injured person that he or she planned to murder. More controversially, it applies to common bioethical cases; for example, cases when hydration and nutrition are withheld as part of terminal sedation, to "get it over with" faster, also seem excluded by the prohibition.[6] The fact that something was allowed to take place, even if covered by a conflicting positive duty to prevent it, does not by itself put the allowing into a different moral category than the causing of that event. An agent's decision to allow must include the intention to avoid the evils that preventing would involve—such as conflicts with negative duties or failing in other responsibilities.

In short, this section argues that the effort to clarify the terms of the prohibition against killing by limiting morally significant killing to causing death does not itself provide a basis for the coherence of the received practice. Linking the killing/letting die distinction to the classification of duties as negative and positive introduces moral relevance that the distinction lacks, but that link is insufficient for the needed coherence without appeal to intention.

The Intention-Based Response: The Rule of Double Effect

The argument presented in the previous section gives focus to the conception of intentional killing relevant for the received practice—the kind of action excluded in the prohibition. Intentional killing cannot be restricted to intentionally taking action for the sake of ending a person's life, and instead includes any decision someone makes to secure that state of affairs, whether as a final end or as a condition for pursuing further goals. The intentional pursuit of a person's death—by doing something or by refraining from some preventative action—thus is what the absolute prohibition excludes. This reference to intention therefore is necessary for any account of the needed coherence.

Foot produced a counterexample to show, in effect, that the role of intention in the received practice cannot apply to all cases. The counterexample, however, does not succeed. A drug that will save five patients can be made only by producing a gas that emits toxic fumes and can be vented only to a nearby room that is occupied by a patient. The patient's death is not intended, yet this action obviously would be wrong—as wrong as intentionally killing the patient to get a cadaver for body parts. The harm is *inflicted* on the person by the doctor's action, so it violates a negative duty.[7] Therefore, Foot held, the negative duty not to inflict harm is morally dispositive, not the fact that the harm is not intended. The present author agrees both that the death is not intended and that the action that killed the patient is wrong, but does not agree that the negative duty was morally dispositive. Such a duty would generally and stringently prohibit inflicting bad results on people, and that is on its face an excessive, even impossible demand. People knowingly cause many events whenever they act. The events caused by many, if not most, actions have some bad results—bad enough to provide a reason for prohibiting those actions. Given the ubiquity of such results, however, a universal and stringent prohibition of actions causing them is unreasonable. Thus, the intuitive credibility of Foot's judgment that it is wrong unintentionally to inflict death on a nearby patient to save others cannot plausibly be based on a general and very stringent prohibition against causing or "inflicting" evils such as death. This suggests that, as in Foot's example, when unintentionally inflicting such a result is wrong, more is involved than simply that a bad result is inflicted. Some human relationships impose duties to not harm other parties even as an unintended side effect of important actions. Some duties of parents, and of caregivers more generally, appear to be this type. Refusing to inflict harm on a patient as a side effect of helping others also seems to be one of these duties.

The necessity of intention for establishing the coherence of the received practice is highlighted by the role it plays in securing that coherence. Intention is used to distinguish a type of action that is without exception prohibited from other decisions that shorten life. These latter are sometimes (even often) permissible. The former includes and the latter do not include the intention of "earlier death." In other words, inferences from the impermissibility of the former to that of the latter are ruled out, as are inferences from the permissibility of the latter to that of the former.

This is a very specific and distinctive role for intention that is different from and irreducible to the several widely accepted ways that intentions are agreed to be morally relevant; for example, in the determination of responsibility, the assessment of character, and the specification of the meaning of some actions.[8] Nevertheless, intention's role in the received practice exemplifies a more general view concerning the connection between impermissibility and intention. This is the doctrine or principle of "double effect," or at least one version of it, which this text calls the "rule of double effect" (RDE). Philippa Foot perspicuously formulated the rule and explained its key elements: "it is sometimes permissible to bring about by oblique intention what one may not directly intend."[9] Foot explained the sense of "directly intend" and "oblique intention" in her formulation: What you directly intend are your means and ends; what you indirectly intend are the foreseen consequences of your action. Unintended side effects are thus distinguished from one's long-term or intermediate goals and from the actions one takes to realize them.

The expression "double effect" was introduced by Thomas Aquinas, who noted that an action can have two effects, one of which is intended and the other not intended, but *"praeter intentionem"* or outside the agent's intention. This author believes that Aquinas meant that the same action can be intentional under some descriptions and not intentional under others. Aquinas used this distinction in an argument that an indefeasible prohibition of an act described in terms of its intended effect does not also prohibit an action described in terms of an unintended effect of the same type as the first action. The case he discussed was a private person's killing in self-defense. If that action were intentional killing, then it simply would be excluded by the prohibition against intentional killing by private persons. If the defensive action was not intentional killing, however, and the assailant's death was "outside the intention," then the action could be permissible if other conditions are met.[10] More generally: intending a bad result is taken to be sufficient for an action's being simply impermissible; bringing about a bad result as an unintended result of one's intentional act is not simply impermissible; if it is impermissible, other considerations are needed. Following Aquinas's lead, traditional formulations of the RDE point to other considerations of two types: The action having the bad side effect must be permissible independent of considerations about the bad side effect, and that action must be important enough to justify bringing about the bad side effect—the action must be proportional to the bad result.[11]

The rule of double effect plainly requires a conception of a "bad result." Following Foot's formulation, this chapter deems a result to be bad if and only if it contributes to an action's being impermissible. It might seem arbitrary to define bad results deontically as this chapter follows Foot in doing. Indeed, a more teleological conception—that bad results are harms—is at least as intuitively plausible an explication of the commonsense meaning of "bad result."

Foot's conception, however, is preferred here because of its clear focus on the connection between intending a bad effect and impermissibility. The teleological conception does not distinguish this matter from that concerning the determinants of the impermissibility of the bad effect. The factors contributing to an action's impermissibility are presupposed by, but distinct from, the implications of that impermissibility for determining the impermissibility of other actions, in particular those having bad effects of the type involved in the impermissible action.[12]

The prohibited actions from which the RDE blocks inferences comprise a distinctive type of prohibited action. This chapter does not consider other kinds of prohibition. The prohibitions in which intention plays the role specified are those satisfying two conditions: (1) They prohibit an action because of its description as an action of a certain kind, independently of factors articulated in further descriptions of the action; and (2) the description under which the action is prohibited picks out the features in virtue of which the action is indefeasibly impermissible. For an action wrong in virtue of features included in its description as a "such and such" type of action presents a ground for an inference about the wrongness of an action with features of that kind.

The second condition is needed because the conception of a bad result can function as it does in the RDE only if bad effects of some type are taken not only as contributing to the impermissibility of an intentional action but also as *guaranteeing* it when they are intended. For, if intending the bad result of an impermissible action were not sufficient for its impermissibility, blocking inferences from that impermissibility could not turn generally on the presence or absence of the intention of the bad result. Intending the bad result might remain a factor of moral relevance, but one that could be offset by others; perhaps it is of little importance in grounding the impermissibility of the intentional action. Such possibilities would undermine any effort to block inferences from the impermissibility of the intentional action based on the intention of the bad effect. That might or might not be relevant to its impermissibility, and the features contributing to impermissibility might well be present in actions in which the bad effect is not intended.

This condition implies the first condition: that the impermissibility involved is that of an indefeasible prohibition. The intentional action is taken to be impermissible because it is an action of a certain kind—namely, intentionally bringing about a bad result of the sort specified in the first condition. Because being of that type of action is taken to be sufficient for the impermissibility of any instantiation of the kind, further moral considerations expressed in additional true descriptions of the particular instantiation cannot change its moral valence, because they leave in place the description of the action as prohibited. If that description could be displaced by further considerations, the intention of the bad result would not be sufficient for impermissibility.[13]

Some contemporary philosophers regard the absolutist framework of the RDE as providing a decisive reason for rejecting it. Those finding something plausible in it and accepting this common view about absolutism seek to develop formulations of double effect that do not require such a framework.[14] This objection and the alternatives to the RDE to which it has led are not the subject of this inquiry, which seeks to articulate and defend a conception of the connection between intention and impermissibility that has a chance of providing a basis for the coherence of the moral components of the received practice. This chapter does not address them because their very terms show that they are not meant to do that work. Giving some weight to the compelling sense that intending evil and harming persons intentionally is especially morally problematic, for example, seems justifiable. That weight, however, does not and is not meant to justify anything general enough to block inferences from the impermissibility of actions involving intentional harms.[15]

The clarifications in this section are not meant to justify the rule of double effect. Rather, they are meant highlight the distinctive role the RDE ascribes to the connection between intention and impermissibility, and to explore some of the key suppositions about the type of prohibitions the RDE is meant to deal with. These explorations of the RDE are in the service of providing a general ethical doctrine that exhibits the moral structure of the received practice. Because the RDE exhibits the moral structure of the received practice, it provides a way into assessing the coherence of that practice. Other double effect doctrines that do not exhibit this moral structure cannot do that.

It is precisely the distinctive role of intention articulated in the RDE that critics of the received practice, including many of the most eminent contemporary moral philosophers, reject: this is work that intention simply cannot do. Some of the main reasons for this verdict are discussed in the next section.

Criticisms of the RDE and Responses

Knowing Intentions

Perhaps the most common objection to the RDE is that intentional actions must be clearly distinguishable from their unintended results, but that it is difficult or impossible to distinguish them. There actually are two objections here. The first is that rationalizing abuse of the idea of intention cannot be controlled. In a nod that acknowledges the precise moral role that intentions play in existing thought and practice, those wishing to evade moral and legal responsibility for a questionable action commonly describe what they do so as to suggest that the wrongful elements are mere side effects, as does the hypothetical euthanizing doctor who says that his only goal is eliminating suffering, and that the patient's death is only an unintended side effect. Elizabeth Anscombe exposed the emptiness of this rationalizing dodge.

> For after all we can *form* intentions; now if intention is an interior move-
> ment, it would appear that we can choose to have a certain intention and
> not another, just by saying, e.g., within ourselves: "What I *mean* to be doing
> is earning my living, and *not* poisoning the household" or "What I *mean* to
> be doing is helping those good men into power; I withdraw my intention
> from the act of poisoning the household, which I prefer to think goes on
> without my intention being in it." The idea that one can determine one's
> intentions by making such a little speech to oneself is obvious bosh.[16]

This author would add only that making a speech, even a quiet one to oneself, is a human action, that is, it is itself an intentional act—and we might wonder about that intention. Thus, as Anscombe said, "It is nonsense to pretend that you do not intend what is the means you take to your chosen end."[17] The pretense is made possible by a rationalizing dis-tortion of the idea of intention—one that reflection, such as Anscombe's, can unmask for what it is.

The second objection emerges sharply once this pretense is exposed: How can the action descriptions under which an action is intentional be distinguished analytically from those under which it is voluntary but not intentional? If that cannot be done, then the distinction between what is intended and what is caused as a side effect vanishes as a serious notion of moral analysis; their "closeness" provides an insurmountable practical difficulty for the RDE.[18]

Anscombe provided a general strategy for addressing this question. The strategy is forensic and, without some important nuances, is as follows. If asked why someone did something under a certain description, and the agent honestly refuses the question, then the agent did not intend the action under that description. If the question is accepted and answered, then the action is intentional under that description. Thus, the further intention of a goal indicated by a person's not refusing the question why he or she acted in some way establishes that the action thus described is intentional. Although Anscombe did not highlight it, the query can be pushed further by questioning how the intentional action thus revealed is connected to the further goal expressed in answering the initial question.

Anscombe illustrated some of the complexities, but also the power of the strategy in her famous example of pumping poisoned water—a set of actions that move poisoned water from a well to a home occupied by a malicious gang.[19] Questions about some descriptions of the actions of a person pumping the water reasonably will be rejected by the agent if that agent did not know he or she was doing that—for example, if the person was unaware that his or her pumping was casting a shadow. Some questions about descriptions of the action will be rejected, not because the agent was unaware that he or she was doing that, but because that description was of no interest, not part of why the agent acted—when casting a shadow was noticed, but was of no interest to the agent. Some questions are rejected even if the action described as poisoning people is queried. The question "Why are you poisoning these people?" addressed to the worker who pumped the water he or she knew to be poisoned allows the following and possibly true response: "I know that what I did would poison these people, but I am hired to pump water to the house and paid to do that. I could care less about them; I was just doing my job." One can push back at this response, especially by seeking clarity on whether the actions undertaken were altered in any way so as to facilitate the poisoning. The response could be true, however, and unlikely to absolve the worker for responsibility for the action, regardless of whether poisoning was intentional.

It is not clear whether Anscombe's strategy can give definitive answers for all cases of "closeness." Nevertheless, this strategy plausibly deals with most of the cases raised by end-of-life care. For example, if a doctor does not refuse the question of why he provided a drug dose sufficient for killing a suffering patient and answers the question by saying that he did it to end the patient's suffering, it is fair to pursue further how doing just what he did—giving precisely that dose of drugs—served the purpose he acknowledges. If the connection is left mysterious, it is right to press on to exclude the possibility that, although his action was aimed at relieving suffering as an end, it also included killing the patient *as a means*, and so was intended. To take a withholding treatment example: If hydration and nutrition are withheld as part of a regime of terminal sedation, then the doctor can be asked why he or she chose to refrain from these actions. If the answer is "to get it over with," then a description of the decision not to act under which it is intentionally shortening life—morally speaking, intentionally killing—applies to the decision. If the answer is that the patient cannot absorb hydration and nutrition in his or her condition, or that any assimilation will make no difference to the patient's life or welfare, then the intention is to avoid harm or waste.

As these examples suggest, the forensic account provides a way to clarify the issues arising from the fact that intention makes reference to an aspect of agency not available to narrowly empirical third-party verification. This limited inaccessibility of intentions does not, however, imply that they are unexpressed internal wishes and preferences. If intentions were such purely mental realities, then the epistemological and deontic objections to the RDE would be unanswerable. Without a connection to what a person actually chooses to do or refrains from doing and to the reasons for which the person makes the choice, the so-called mental component of action is related in a completely contingent way to what that person does. As Anscombe's strategy indicates, the question is not what the agent wished, wanted, or hoped for, but why the agent performed an action under a description. If the question is refused, then it is fair to push on: "What were you doing then, if not the action you say was not intentional?" The intentions that the rule of double effect addresses are what distinguish the means to the agent's ends from among the events known that the exercise of agency inevitably causes. They are not "further intentions" of long-term and ultimate purposes, but the very intention of the agent's intentional action.[20] The "intentionalness" of an intentional act makes reference to an immediate goal revealed by the answering the questions about why a person acts as he or she does, not to the constellation of interests in the background of action.

Consequently, although doctors might well have conflicted or unclear intentions and feelings about an end-of-life decision, the medical steps they take or decline are surely intentional actions whose intentions are clarified when the doctors are asked why they did what they did and how doing that serves that purpose. These matters can become quite clear even when more ultimate intentions are obscure and when there is considerable "absence of a clear purpose."[21]

A further consequence is that doctors who would like to assist patients in dying, but who are effectively deterred by legal sanction from doing so, are not intentionally killing when they strictly follow protocols for palliative interventions, even when hoping that they will end life as soon as possible. In cases where death is caused as a side effect, there generally is a clear manifestation of the intention in the medical steps taken in the circumstances, their connection to the stated medical goal, or in the exact drugs in the precise dosages prescribed. Similarly, being happy that a suffering patient will die as a result of discontinuing treatment does not by itself constitute that decision as intending that the patient die sooner; the former might be a feeling or a wish that is not the reason for the decision.[22]

Intending Bad Results and Impermissibility

The more radical criticism of the RDE is that the connection between intention and permissibility at the center of the rule simply does not exist. Intentions are not found among the factors that render actions impermissible.[23]

In several discussions of double effect, Elizabeth Anscombe indicated why actions that are simply prohibited must be those truly described as intentionally causing a result, and not simply voluntarily causing the result. She argued, saying the following:

> The distinction between the intended, and the merely foreseen, effects of a voluntary action is indeed absolutely essential to Christian ethics. For Christianity forbids a number of things as being bad in themselves. But if I am answerable for the foreseen consequences of an action or refusal, as much as for the action itself, then these prohibitions will break down. If some innocent will die unless I do a wicked thing, then on this view I am his murderer in refusing: so all that is left to me is weighing up evils. Here the theologian steps in with the principle of double effect and says: "No, you are no murderer, if the man's death was neither your aim nor your chosen means, and if you had to act in the way that led to it or else do something absolutely forbidden."[24]

Anscombe's larger concern here, and in a handful of similar statements,[25] was with the breakdown of absolutist moral theory into incoherence or toward consequentialism when the role of intention is excluded. This concern tends to overshadow a more elementary point embedded in these arguments.

Anscombe supposes (1) that murder is absolutely prohibited, and, for the sake of the argument, (2) that the prohibition does not discriminate between intentional actions of killing and causing death as a side effect. Clearly, on these suppositions the prohibition against killing breaks down if a choice that causes death as a side effect is a refusal to intentionally kill; and it would also break down if the action one refused to do were a distinct kind of absolutely prohibited action that also had the side effect of killing.

Anscombe made this point in a collection of Catholic writings about modern warfare.[26] Her point about limiting absolute prohibitions to intentional actions concerns the logic of prohibitions generally, however, and thus applies to any ethical or legal system that includes indefeasible or exceptionless prohibitions of actions of a specified kind. Because this is a claim about the nature of absolute prohibitions, it applies to religiously based prohibitions, to those based on rational or "natural law" ethics, and to publicly promulgated legal prohibitions. If there are grounds for positive, legal prohibitions sufficient to justify ruling out some actions just because they are of a specific kind, they too must be limited. But why, one might ask, are they limited by the presence of the *intention* of the evil result?

This author believes that there is a general reason why the distinction between intentional actions and the unintended side effects of different intentional actions provides a reasonable limitation of absolute prohibitions. Very generally, and without the qualifications in a full account, the reason is that intentional acts are avoidable—a person can choose not to do them. Bad side effects, however, generally are not avoidable in this way.[27] Sometimes, regardless of what a person does in accord with moral principle, a bad side effect occurs, as Anscombe's hypothetical shows. Because prohibiting what one cannot avoid regardless of whatever is chosen involves being obliged to do the impossible, absolute prohibitions against bringing about bad side effects are not rational. Intentional actions are reasonably prohibited, however, even though complying with them is sometimes very difficult. These are general points about human agency and its limitations, and about the connection of these limitations to what might reasonably be impermissible; they are not particular moral evaluations or elements of controversial normative theories.

This argument supports the RDE's supposition that the means to one's goals are taken to be intended, and that the distinction between means and unintended side effects is morally significant. Both of these assumptions have been criticized. The limitations of human power implying that absolute prohibitions be limited to intentional actions—because they are in an agent's power simply to avoid, whereas bad side effects are in many cases unavoidable—help fix the relevant sense of intention. Some conceptions of intention, such as that invoked by Francis Kamm in her famous "triple effect" doctrine,[28] imply that means need not be intended. Means, however, are the immediate result of agency and more immediately in the agent's power to activate or not activate than is anything else.

This argument shows why the difference between means and unintended side effects can bear the moral weight the RDE assigns to it, a view that many people find implausible.[29] It is true that means are not as ethically fundamental as goals—for example, basic goals seem to define our moral selves, in a way the means we often reluctantly adopt do not. We are not committed to goals as more than aspirational ideals, however, unless we choose to do something about realizing them, and what we choose to do is the means. That is not the case for unintended side effects.

The argument put forth in this section seeks to show how the role of intention specified in the RDE is justified. Its relevance to the coherence of the received practice can now be summed up. Palliative measures—even those that risk shortening life—are obviously permissible, and presumptively the duty of care providers; certainly, intentionally causing patients to suffer simply would be wrong. Choosing to address that suffering at the risk of shortening life accepts this risk as a side effect of doing something of considerable moral importance, which is sometimes obligatory for some people, although not in all cases unqualifiedly obligatory. Moreover, the reality of these responsibilities does not justify killing patients to relieve their suffering. When the choice is precisely whether to kill, an agent has the power to not do that. The constraint on the power to avoid either contributing to suffering or shortening life as side effects of all the options available does not stand when the choice is to kill. That is not a side effect. Considerations about the intentions of doctors' and patients' intentional actions are not arbitrary constraints on overcoming suffering.

The Noncriminal Status of Suicide and the Right to Refuse Treatment

The argument of the preceding section aimed to show that the prohibition against intentional killing is in fact consistent with the permissions of the received practice, because the role of intention used in the RDE is not groundless or without application in the norms shaping the received practice. The prohibition, however, also appears inconsistent with other entrenched parts of commonsense morality; in particular, with the fact that suicide is not criminal and that refusing life-extending treatment is the right of a competent person—a right not contingent on the patient's not intending death in that refusal. Assessing the sources of these apparent inconsistencies requires normative judgments independent of the role of intention in the received practice; for example, judgments about the nature of the autonomy involved in the right to refuse treatment, and the grounds for the noncriminal status of suicide. Still, unless the received practice can deal with these apparent inconsistencies, the RDE might secure its strictly internal consistency but not attain consistency with moral judgments that are very widely shared.

In committing suicide, the person ending his or her life acts intentionally, and because that is not a crime the law provides a counterexample to the universal prohibition against intentional killing. The noncriminal status of suicide does not imply its moral permissibility, but rather that suicide is not reasonably prohibited by criminal sanction. That judgment about the criminal law is surely compatible with the conviction that suicide is morally impermissible—a person who holds that suicide is wrong but that it should not be against the law is not stating an inconsistency.

The historical grounds for decriminalizing suicide seem not to have included public endorsement of suicide, but rather recognition of the limits of criminal law in dealing reasonably with it.[30] To the extent that this is the positive legal ground for excluding suicide from liability for criminal sanctions, the liberty is compatible with substantial social disapproval of suicide and explains why third parties have been forbidden to participate.

Generally, third parties have *no right* to help and may, and often are encouraged to, interfere. Thus, the liberty to commit has been very restricted.

Still, many people believe that suicide is permissible in some circumstances, so the morality of suicide is likely an area where common morality is indeterminate. Even if suicide were morally permissible in some cases, however, that does not involve one person's killing another, which obviously raises public moral issues not raised when a person commits suicide without the help of others. Moreover, the prohibition against intentionally killing others, not the more general moral prohibition of killing including self-killing, is the prohibition dominating the received practice.

As with the law on suicide, it could be argued that the right of competent persons to refuse medical treatment implies that commonsense morality endorses a person's decision precisely to end his or her life. But that is not so; the right of a competent person to refuse medical treatment is a reasonable allocation of the authority over medical decisions generally—not only decisions at the end of life—to the person who must live with the treatment and its results, and who, if competent, is best able to assess the meaning for his or her life. The core provision in this right is the requirement that other private persons not touch a person without the person's permission; this requirement articulates a realm of autonomy by empowering a person to refuse unwanted interference in his or her bodily self.[31] The autonomy this right protects is, on this account, limited. It sets a condition on what others may do to a person's bodily self; it does not imply that others must act to facilitate a person's desires, and so it does not establish a presumption that a person has the right to direct others, such as doctors, to pursue a treatment option that is excluded by the prohibition against killing.[32]

It is true that someone might use this empowerment to commit suicide—to choose precisely to shorten his or her life—but that is not the point of the empowerment, and in the eyes of those who believe suicide to be immoral it is an abuse of the entitlement. In this respect, the right is similar to other all-purpose social empowerments, such as property or privacy, which are susceptible to abuse. The supposition that the intentions of those who create and sustain such empowerments must include the abuse they recognize to be likely is not reasonable. Some of those abusing any empowerment might rejoice at the opportunity it provides for their actions, but that abuse is plainly parasitical on an empowerment justified otherwise, or otherwise rationalized in the case of thoroughly evil empowerments.

Consequently, the right to refuse medical treatment is not inconsistent with a prohibition against intentionally killing others. The claim that the right to refuse treatment that will shorten life gives evidence for the social acceptability of suicidal choices is not warranted by the autonomy that this right uncontroversially protects. At most this right allows that a person may appeal to this right as a way to end his or her life. It does not endorse that decision or warrant others to do anything to further it beyond respecting the right that protects it.

Those who honor the refusal might act out of respect for the established empowerment without intending to shorten the life of the person refusing treatment; this can be true even if they know that the person refusing treatment does intend to shorten his or her life. If they act in a spirit of full cooperation with a patient they believe to be choosing to end life by exercising this right, however, then they surely are willing that the patient succeed in ending his or her life, but if they do nothing at all to make that will effective then they are not acting for that goal and therefore not intending it. When it is simply a matter of honoring a refusal of life-extending treatments, the possibilities for such action—required and justified by the right and by it alone—appear limited.

Shaping the Normative Debate About Assisted Death

The argument presented here is meant to place in focus the nature of the ethical burden faced by defenders of the received practice. That burden does not include defending an incoherent practice. Still, the justification of the prohibition against intentional killing is not achieved by the RDE; that is a distinct and prior matter. The initial judgment that an action is indefeasibly prohibited can be made only if it is judged to be a bad sort of action, so bad that all actions of that type should be avoided to the greatest extent possible. That normative judgment is not made by the RDE but it is needed for the RDE to have work to do. Once established, this judgment practically requires limiting the prohibition to intentional actions of bringing about the effect in question, and only at that point does the RDE apply.

Because the RDE cannot have application without absolute prohibitions, the received practice is committed to the existence of such prohibitions. That is not a popular idea, but it is not crazy either, especially because the prohibitions of law and organized professional groups are the prohibitions involved. The purposes of these prohibitions include coordinating the actions of members of a community. That purpose is frustrated if all the community's prohibitions are to be applied at the discretion of the individuals guided by them. Thus, it is no surprise that that the debate about assisted death is conducted as a debate concerning the *qualification* of an absolute prohibition against intentional killing done by private persons, including by doctors, in favor of another absolute prohibition of more limited scope—the prohibition of intentional killing by private persons other than doctors, who may kill or assist in the suicide of those suffering and wanting to end their lives, when specified conditions about competent consent and level of suffering are met.

This debate is hindered, not advanced, by the supposition that the received practice is deeply incoherent, or that the RDE is what grounds the prohibition against intentional killing, or that any reasonable prohibition against killing simply could not be of the sort to which the RDE might apply.

Notes

1. Wayne Sumner, *Assisted Death: A Study in Ethics and Law* (Oxford, New York: Oxford University Press), 27–71. The formulation of the challenge to the coherence of what the present author calls the "received practice" of end-of-life care is indebted to Sumner's discussion; but the formulation is not a report of his view. Use of the expression "assisted death" follows his terminology.

2. Philippa Foot, "The Problem of Abortion and the Doctrine of the Double Effect," in *Virtues and Vices* (Berkley and Los Angeles, University of California Press, 1978), 26.

3. Foot, "The Problem of Abortion," 27.

4. Ibid., 26–27.

5. Ibid., 28.

6. Joseph Boyle, "The Relevance of Double Effect to Decisions About Sedation at the End of Life," in *Sedation at the End of Life: An Interdisciplinary Approach,* ed. Paulina Taboada (Dordrecht: Springer 2015), 96–97.

7. Foot, "The Problem of Abortion," 27–28.

8. T. M. Scanlon, *Moral Dimensions: Permissibility, Meaning, Blame* (Cambridge, MA, London: Harvard University Press, 2008), 27–88.

9. Foot, "The Problem of Abortion," 20.

10. Thomas Aquinas, *Summa Theologica* (New York, Boston: 1947) 1471–72 (Pt. II-II, q. 64, Art.7); Joseph Boyle, "*Praeter intentionem*" in *Aquinas, The Thomist* 42, 1987, 657–61, provides commentary.

11. Joseph Boyle, "Toward Understanding the Principle of Double Effect," *Ethics* 90 (1980), 529–31; Joseph Boyle, "Who Is Entitled to Double Effect?" *The Journal of Medicine and Philosophy* 16 (1991), 475–78.

12. Judith Jarvis Thomson, "Physician Assisted Suicide: Two Moral Arguments," *Ethics* 109 (1999), 511–12; Sumner, *Assisted Death*, 58–60. Thomson and Sumner mount an argument against the relevance of the RDE by using the teleological conception of bad result and arguing that death is not a harm in the end-of-life cases. These arguments are believed to have their force not as a critique of the RDE but of the soundness of the prohibition it deals with.

13. Joseph Boyle, "Intention, Permissibility, and the Structure of Agency," *American Catholic Philosophical Quarterly* 89 (2015), 461–66.

14. Warren Quinn, "Actions, Intentions and Consequences," *Philosophy and Public Affairs* 18 (1989), 334–36; Boyle, "Intention, Permissibility," 469.

15. Thomas Nagel, *The View from Nowhere* (New York, Oxford: Oxford University Press, 1986), 175–82; Boyle, "Intention, Permissibility," 472–74.

16. G. E. M. Anscombe, *Intention,* 2nd ed. (Cambridge, MA, London: Harvard University Press, 2000), 42 (paragraph 25).

17. Anscombe, "War and Murder," in *Collected Philosophical Papers,* Vol. 3: Ethics, Religion and Politics (Minneapolis: University of Minnesota Press, 1981), 59.

18. Foot, "The Problem of Abortion," 22, introduced the term "closeness" to refer to the difficulty in distinguishing means and unintended side effects. Foot seems to have seen it as a difficulty for the RDE but not a disabling problem for all applications. Foot's concern has been extended to all applications. Jonathan Bennett, "Foreseen Side Effects Versus Intended Consequences," in *The Doctrine of Double Effect: Philosophers Debate a Controversial Moral Principle,* ed. P. A. Woodward (Notre Dame, IN: 2001), 85–118, has developed this objection relentlessly.

19. Anscombe, *Intention,* 37–47 (paragraphs 23–26).

20. Anscombe, *Intention,* 1 (paragraph 1) distinguishes an action as intentional from the intention with which the action is done and from future intentions.

21. Timothy Quill, Rebecca Dresser, and Dan Brock, "The Rule of Double Effect—A Critique of Its Use in End-of-Life Decision Making," *New England Journal of Medicine* 337 (1997), 1770.

22. Thomson, "Physician Assisted Suicide," 515 seems to suppose otherwise, especially in her variation on Chief Justice Rehnquist's observation concerning Eisenhower's intentions in respect to the deaths of American soldiers at Normandy. Her hypothetical is that he did intend them, but that this made no difference whatsoever to the plan. She concluded that intention is irrelevant to impermissibility.

23. Thomson, "Physician Assisted Suicide," 514–16; and Scanlon, *Moral Dimensions,* 8–36, provide the most compelling statements of the objection.

24. Anscombe, "War and Murder," 58.

25. Elizabeth Anscombe, "Modern Moral Philosophy, in *Collected Philosophical Papers* Vol. 3, 33–36; "Medalist's Address: Action, Intention, and 'Double Effect,' " in Woodward, *The Doctrine of Double Effect,* 60–65.

26. Anscombe, "War and Murder," 51.

27. Boyle, "Intention, Permissibility," 476–78.

28. Frances Kamm, "The Doctrine of Triple Effect and Why a Rational Agent Need Not Intend the Means to His End," *Proceedings of the Aristotelian Society Supplement* 74 (2000), 21–39.

29. Quill et al., in "The Rule of Double Effect" argue from legal precedents that the distinction is unsound; Sumner, *Assisted Death,* 68–70, addresses Nagel's position on intending evil, not the RDE as formulated here.

30. John Finnis, "A British 'Convention Right' to Assistance in Suicide?" *The Law Quarterly Review,* Notes, 131 (2015), 1–8.

31. Germain Grisez, and Joseph Boyle, *Life and Death with Liberty and Justice: A Contribution to the Euthanasia Debate* (Notre Dame, IN: University of Notre Dame Press, 1979), 86–96.

32. Quill et al., in "The Rule of Double Effect," treat autonomy as a more fundamental determinant of permissibility than intention.

CHAPTER TWELVE

Assisted Dying and Palliation

Ben A. Rich

This chapter addresses two distinct but related questions: (1) Are there important ethical and/or legal distinctions between assisted dying (AD) and palliative measures that have neither the purpose nor the effect of hastening death, and if so how should those distinctions influence the availability and acceptability of these two options? (2) Where assisted dying has been made available as a matter of law and medical practice, what if any impact has this had upon the provision of palliative care?

For purposes of this chapter, AD includes both lethal prescriptions administered by the individual and voluntary active euthanasia by a physician. In seeking to answer these questions the chapter necessarily touches upon the subject matter of other chapters in this volume, particularly Chapter 1 on the legal history of AD in the United States, Chapter 10 on autonomy and the right to die, and Chapter 11 on the doctrine/principle of double effect.

The first question, particularly with regard to the comparative ethics of the two practices, is a normative one. Reasonable minds almost inevitably differ, which is precisely what an extensive review of the scholarly and professional literature indicates. A critical consideration is how law and public policy should accommodate the difference. The second question essentially is an empirical question. The challenge is to distinguish reliable information from mere anecdote and determine what conclusions can be drawn from it. Consideration of these questions begins by positioning them within the range of what are characterized as "palliative options of last resort." Of course, whether AD should be considered a palliative option under any circumstances goes to the very core of the ethical debate.

The Ethical Challenge: Delineating the Acceptable Range of Palliative Options of Last Resort

In a frequently cited article, palliative options of last resort (POLR) are identified as voluntarily stopping eating and drinking (VSED); aggressive palliative measures (e.g., high-dose analgesics such as morphine), palliative sedation (PS), AD (assisted dying, lethal prescription), and voluntary active euthanasia (VAE).[1] Because the focus of this chapter is on the two questions set forth in the Introduction, the majority of the discussion and analysis is devoted to comparison and contrast between AD and aggressive palliative measures used in the most challenging end-of-life clinical scenarios. Because VAE is legal in only a few countries and has not played a significant role in the extended public policy debates about end-of-life care due to its perceived potential for abuse, it is not discussed further hereinafter. Nevertheless, its general unavailability in most countries raises legitimate issues about justice, and fairness for patients who have decisional capacity and wish to utilize AD but are physically incapable of self-administering lethal medication. Before moving to a more detailed consideration of PS and AD, the chapter briefly reviews the other components of the POLR panoply.

With regard to VSED, this chapter suggests that strictly speaking it is not a palliative measure at all, but rather a means by which a patient for whom the dying process has become unbearably protracted can bring about his or her death in a nonviolent manner.[2] In this sense, VSED is similar to AD in that it is a means for the patient to exert some measure of control over the time and manner of an inevitable and imminent death from an underlying terminal condition. The only connection between VSED and palliation would be if the patient began to experience distress, either from the underlying terminal condition or from the absence of nutrition and hydration. In such instances, palliative measures may be clinically indicated to maintain the patient's comfort. It is well recognized, however, that in the advanced stages of a terminal illness many patients experience relatively little hunger or thirst. There is an emerging consensus that palliating a patient's symptoms under these conditions does not constitute assisting in a patient's suicide.[3]

The aggressive use of pain medications in the care of the dying has at times been characterized in ways that suggest it could be a form of euthanasia, that is, "hanging the morphine drip" and "slow euthanasia."

Indeed, one article that generated a considerable degree of consternation and critical commentary among hospice and palliative care professionals, the authors of which used the second term as its title, also included palliative sedation (also called "terminal sedation") in that category.[4] The rather sinister implication of the article was that rather than the acceptable clinical practice of titrating analgesia to therapeutic effect to alleviate distress, the intent of the physician was to hasten the patient's death by delivering a dosage of morphine sufficient to suppress respiration. Much of the ethical and legal discourse on POLR concerns issues of both causation and intent to which this chapter now turns.

The Role of Causation and Intent in the Ethics of End-of-Life Care

Appearances to the contrary notwithstanding, ascribing X, but not Y, as the cause of Z is not an entirely objective (value-free) process, hence the well-recognized distinction between factual causation and legal causation.[5] In the context of the death of a patient, for example, however disconcerting it might be to those not versed in legal theory, the inquiry is not what *is* the cause, but rather what *should be deemed to be* the cause as a matter of law, ethics, and public policy. To illustrate this point, this chapter briefly considers the legal concept of "proximate cause" and its reliance on the so-called but for test. As a matter of law, X will be considered the cause of Y if Y would not have happened when and as it did *but for* X. It is also important to note that causation is not restricted to affirmative acts insofar as the law is concerned, that is, a failure to act (omission) when there is a legally recognized duty to do so can also be deemed a cause of that which could have been prevented but for the omission.

To appreciate the normative dimensions of proximate cause determinations in the law, consider two instances in which a physician disconnects the ventilator from a patient whose continued life is dependent upon it. In the first scenario, the physician disconnects the ventilator in response to the patient's decision and request for discontinuation. In the second one, the physician directly disregards the patient's request to continue life support. Further assume that, in both cases, the patient dies as anticipated very soon after the disconnection takes place. In the first instance, the law—following the traditional approach—would find the proximate cause of the patient's death to be the underlying medical condition which necessitated mechanical ventilation. In the second instance, however, the law would likely hold the physician responsible for homicide on the grounds that it was the discontinuation of mechanical ventilation, not the underlying medical condition, which caused the patient's death. Nevertheless, one can reasonably conclude that *but for* the discontinuation of mechanical ventilation, neither patient would have died when and as he or she did. The disparate approach of the law to these two scenarios is based upon ethical and public-policy considerations which prioritize patient autonomy and informed consent/refusal.

In December of 2009 the causation issue played a major role in the AD case of *Baxter v. Montana*. The trial court ruled that the Montana homicide laws violated the state constitution insofar as they might be applied to a physician who provided a lethal prescription at the request of a terminally ill patient. Preferring to not invoke constitutional law if another approach were available, the Montana Supreme Court surveyed the relevant state statutes and concluded, "We find no indication in Montana law that physician aid in dying provided to terminally ill, mentally competent adult patients is against public policy."[6]

The critical portion of the court's decision for purposes of this chapter examines the causal connection between the writing of a lethal prescription and its ultimate role in bringing about a patient's death. In the course of this examination the court compares and contrasts the decision and action of a physician to discontinue a life-sustaining intervention at the request of a patient or a patient's proxy. One reason the court focuses on discontinuing life-sustaining treatment is that the Montana Rights of the Terminally Ill Act specifically immunizes physicians from any civil, criminal, or professional liability for acceding to the request of a terminally ill patient or his or her proxy to withdraw life-sustaining measures. In the court's judgment, such a statutory provision "authorizes physicians to commit a direct *act* [italics in original court opinion] of withdrawing medical care, which hastens death."[7] The court then contrasts this with writing a lethal prescription at the request of a terminally ill patient, which it characterizes as consisting "solely of making the instrument of the 'act' available to the terminally ill patient. The patient then chooses whether to commit the act that will bring about his own death."[8]

The majority opinion in *Baxter* directly challenged the prevailing view, including that expressed by the U.S. Supreme Court, on both causation and intent. At the heart of that prevailing view was what has been recently characterized as a moral (and by implication legal) fiction that when life support is withdrawn from a patient the cause of death is the underlying medical condition necessitating life support, whereas when a patient takes a lethal medication the cause of death is that medication.[9] From this perspective arises the purported moral distinction between merely allowing a patient to die and actively killing a patient. It is the legitimacy of this distinction which the Montana court challenges by arguing that, from the perspective of proximate cause, a physician who writes a lethal prescription that a patient might take at some indeterminate future date is at best tenuously linked to the patient's ultimate demise should he or she choose to take the medication, whereas a physician who withdraws a life-sustaining intervention without which the patient will be expected to die within a matter of minutes or hours is much more directly and immediately linked in a causal way to the patient's death.

This view by the Montana court in *Baxter* is consistent with the analysis of Beauchamp and Childress in their highly regarded treatise *Principles of Biomedical Ethics*, wherein they argue that the "killing" versus "letting die" distinction suffers from multiple flaws, among them that it masks rather than highlights the critical factors involved in assessing permissible conduct, one of which is the patient's consent and the pursuit of shared therapeutic objectives.[10]

More recently, the Supreme Court of Canada also addressed the issue of AD in the case of *Carter v. Canada*. The core holding of the tribunal was that Section 241 (b) of the criminal code was unconstitutional to the extent that it prohibits AD for a competent adult who consents to the termination of life and who has "a grievous and irremediable medical condition (including an illness, disease, or disability) that causes enduring suffering that is intolerable to the individual in the circumstances of his or her condition."[11] The section in question provides that anyone who aids or abets a person in suicide commits an indictable offense and no person may consent to death being inflicted upon them. The high court drew upon a voluminous trial court record which took into consideration evidence from Canada and jurisdictions in which the practice is permitted regarding critical issues such as medical ethics, current end-of-life practices, the risks associated with AD, and the feasibility of safeguards. Significantly, one finding by the trial court that appeared to be influential in the Supreme Court's review of the issues, but that most certainly would be strongly contested by opponents of AD, is that the "preponderance of the evidence from ethicists is that there is no ethical distinction between physician-assisted death and other end-of-life practices whose outcome is highly likely to be death."[12]

Also resonating with the Canadian high court was the trial judge's findings that the absolute prohibition on assisting another person to end their life could only be upheld if it were the least-drastic means of achieving an admittedly legitimate legislative objective, which is to provide safeguards for vulnerable persons who might seek to end their lives under circumstances of mental illness or incapacity, duress, oppression, or the undue and improper influences of third persons. After considering all of the evidence presented by opposing parties to the case, the trial judge concluded, and the high court found fully substantiated and persuasive, that "the risks inherent in permitting physician-assisted death can be identified and very substantially minimized through a carefully designed system imposing stringent limits that are scrupulously monitored and enforced."[13] Similarly, the court found persuasive the trial judge's conclusion that there was no concrete and credible evidence that the practice of AD would be likely to lead down some hypothetical slippery slope toward state-sanctioned homicide. These consequentialist considerations concerning AD are explored in a subsequent section of this chapter.

The Supreme Court of Canada specifically addressed something that too often has been overlooked or insufficiently noted in the protracted debate over AD, which is that concerns about a possible lack of decisional capacity and vulnerability arise in all end-of-life medical decision making, and most certainly encompasses decisions by health care proxies or surrogates to discontinue life-sustaining interventions from a patient who lacks decisional capacity. It follows from this that there is no basis upon which to believe that patients who are undergoing life-sustaining interventions that request their discontinuation or who refuse nutrition and hydration are any less vulnerable or susceptible to biased decision making than those who seek AD. Despite these risks, current law, ethics, and clinical practice (in Canada, the United States, and many other Western nations) permit patients or surrogates to discontinue life-sustaining measures knowing or expecting that doing so will cause or hasten the moment of death.

The Supreme Court suspended the application of its decision for 12 months, presumably to allow for the development of policies, procedures, and practice parameters to accommodate AD by physicians who are willing to offer it to qualified patients. One very significant distinction between what the decision will permit in Canada and the practice of AD in certain jurisdictions in the United States is that in Canada there will be no requirement that the requesting patient be diagnosed with a terminal condition. Rather, all that is required to secure access to AD is that the patient has the capacity to consent, and the patient has been diagnosed with a serious and incurable medical condition that causes enduring suffering that is intolerable to the patient in his or her circumstances. This would appear to encompass severe chronic medical conditions such as congestive heart failure, but more controversially also perhaps mental illnesses that cause suffering but do not deprive the patient of decisional capacity. Although an in-depth analysis of the comparative risks and benefits of extending access of AD to nonterminally ill persons with major chronic psychiatric conditions or perhaps even what has come to be called "weariness of life" is beyond the scope of this chapter, it is important to note that arguments supporting of such extensions consistently appear in the medical literature.[14]

Moving to the question of intent, there is, of course, a wide range of medications that can be clinically indicated in the last days or even weeks of life to control pain, suffering, anxiety, and other forms of distress. Some of these could have the side effect of reducing respiratory drive or the level of consciousness. The presumption (always rebuttable in troubling cases) is that the goal and specific intent of the prescribing professional is ensuring the patient's comfort, not causing or hastening death. When the U.S. Supreme Court addressed the issue of a purported constitutional right to AD in 1997, some of the most often-cited language is the following passage from a concurring opinion by Justice Sandra Day O'Connor: "a patient who is suffering from a terminal illness and who is experiencing great pain has no legal barriers to obtaining medication, from qualified physicians, to alleviate that suffering, even to the point of causing unconsciousness or hastening death."[15] This language was interpreted by many commentators as encompassing both aggressive symptom management and PS. The permissive approach of the law to these measures was deemed to map onto their ethical acceptability.

The intent of the clinician when providing one or more of the POLR panoply is deemed critical from an ethical standpoint. The intention to relieve pain and suffering was traditionally deemed to be acceptable, whereas the intent to hasten the patient's death was not, even in circumstances in which that, too, is the patient's wish because in his or her estimation the meager benefits of continued existence are far outweighed by the burdens of illness and disability. Discussions of intent in the context of the care of the dying often invoke the doctrine or principle of double effect (DE). (A detailed discussion of DE is provided in Chapter 12.) For purposes of this chapter, note that despite references to DE by many courts, including the U.S. Supreme Court, one major incongruity between traditional legal doctrine and the theological/moral view of DE is routinely overlooked or otherwise discounted. One of the four key elements of DE maintains that a person can foresee the negative consequence of an action without intending it. At least in the criminal law, quite to the contrary, the governing legal principle is that every competent person should be presumed to intend the natural and probable consequences of his or her actions, and therefore legitimately may be held accountable for them.[16]

The DE view of intent is further compromised by its arguably simplistic, black-or-white approach. This is precisely the point made by Timothy Quill in his often-cited piece on the inherent "ambiguity of clinical intentions" wherein he reflects upon the complex, fluctuating, and often even contradictory intentions in play when a physician is caring for a seriously ill person in the terminal phase of illness.[17] Moreover, the DE analysis in these clinical situations posits death as the negative consequence. When the only alternative to death is unbearable refractory suffering, however, many would not view death as a negative consequence.[18]

The Complexities and Challenges of Palliative Sedation

Palliative sedation, originally referred to as "terminal sedation," often has been proffered as the morally acceptable alternative to AD for terminally ill patients with severe, refractory distress. Before delving into the particulars of the practice and its purported moral superiority to AD, it is appropriate to address this semantic issue of how to properly refer to it. From its inception, sedation to unconsciousness as a means of relieving refractory terminal distress was characterized as "terminal sedation." The problem with this terminology is that raises more questions than it answers—questions of clinical, ethical, and legal significance. To describe the intervention in this manner begs the question of the meaning of terminal in the context of sedation. Some people incorrectly believed that it meant that sedating a patient to unconsciousness actually caused the patient's death, and hence those who administered PS might be presumed to intend the patient's death. In the usual and customary circumstances in which it is provided, there is no evidence to support this belief.[19] The ambiguity is further exacerbated by the related but distinct question of whether sedation to unconsciousness will be accompanied by the withholding of artificial nutrition and hydration. If that is the case, then the timing of PS becomes a critical factor. If total sedation were to be induced not merely days, but weeks prior to the patient's anticipated demise from the underlying terminal condition, then in fact the cause of death might be neither the sedating medications nor the terminal illness, but rather dehydration or other complications arising from the withholding of artificial nutrition and hydration. For this reason, most clinical practice guidelines support the practice only when the patient's death is considered imminent (hours to at most a few days).[20]

It also is important to note that often sedation is to a state of less than total unconsciousness. After all, the therapeutic goal is to relieve the patient's refractory distress, not produce complete unconsciousness. The approach is to titrate the sedating medications "to effect," the presumably desired effect being relief of the patient's distress. For all of these reasons, the current consensus view among palliative care professionals is that PS is a more accurate term for the practice. Nevertheless, some critics continue to insist that this is an unwarranted euphemism that mischaracterizes what is really going on in many cases.[21]

One basis for the argument that PS is consistent with prevailing standards of medical ethics and AD is not goes to the question of intent. Whereas, the argument goes, a physician who prescribes a lethal medication in response to a qualified patient's request must necessarily intend to bring about the patient's death, a physician who provides palliative sedation to a dying patient experiencing refractory distress merely intends to relieve that distress by reducing or completely removing the patient's capacity to experience it. Nevertheless, mindful of the highly nuanced and multifaceted nature of intention in the clinical setting previously noted, another view provides that the intent of a physician who responds to a terminally ill patient's request for AD may be to respect that individual's wish for an added measure of control over the time and circumstances of his or her death. If, as has been the case with approximately one-third of patients in Oregon who obtained a lethal prescription, the patient ultimately chooses not to take the lethal medication, then neither the intent nor the purpose of the prescribing physician has been frustrated because the clinical objective was respect for patient autonomy and choice not death by means of the lethal medication.

The Nature of Suffering and Practice Parameters for Palliative Sedation

Opponents of AD maintain that PS is well accepted, readily available, and ethically preferable. As previously noted, however, the prevailing view is that PS should be offered only when the patient is within hours or at most a few days from death. Consequently, in jurisdictions where AD is not a legal option, this constraint can pose a barrier to optimal patient care in some circumstances. For many patients in the terminal phase of illness, predicting the time of death is not an exact science. Studies indicating a tendency of physicians to overestimate survival have significant implications for patient access to PS.[22] Patients with distress that is refractory to less-aggressive measures but who are believed to be weeks or perhaps even months from death may be denied PS out of concern that if artificial nutrition and hydration are withheld then the patient's death will not be from the underlying terminal illness. The fact that the withholding of nutrition and hydration is at the request of the patient or the patient's proxy rather than imposed by the physician as a condition precedent to PS does not appear to have influenced clinical practice guidelines for PS.

Another major limitation on access to PS is the purported distinction between types of suffering associated with terminal illness. The American Medical Association, for example, has issued guidelines for PS that distinguish between clinical and nonclinical or "existential/spiritual" suffering.[23] This distinction appears to have been derived from an earlier position paper on AD issued by the American College of Physicians–American Society of Internal Medicine (ACP-ASIM) in 2001.[24] The thrust of the position paper is a reaffirmation of the organization's unqualified opposition to AD. Perhaps in an effort to reassure members of the medical profession and the public that dying patients will not be consigned to unbearable suffering for want of a lethal prescription, the discussion of PS is included in the statement. In elaborating on the ethical acceptability of PS under appropriate clinical circumstances, however, the statement introduces the purported distinction between clinical and nonclinical suffering at the end of life, captured in the following language:

> When patients continue to suffer from physical symptoms or psychiatric syndromes despite the best efforts at palliation, physicians should vigorously pursue the alleviation of these symptoms, even at the risk of unintentionally hastening death. But when the patient's suffering is interpersonal, existential, or spiritual, the tasks of the physician are to remain present to "suffer with" the patient in compassion, and to enlist the support of clergy, social workers, family and friends in healing the aspects of suffering that are beyond the legitimate scope of medical care.[25]

This language and the categorical distinction it introduces between types of refractory terminal suffering is fraught with both clinical and ethical implications. Because it subsequently has been embraced by the AMA without further analysis or justification, however, it warrants some extended analysis here because of these implications.

Both literally and figuratively, physician and bioethicist Eric Cassell can be said to have written the book on suffering. Growing out of his seminal article in the *New England Journal of Medicine*, Cassell's considerable body of work on suffering is built upon a foundational examination of the nature of persons.[26] He maintains that without an adequate understanding of the nature of persons in general and each person as a unique individual, we cannot begin to understand and adequately respond to another person's experience of suffering. The dichotomization of suffering in the above-referenced policies, with the implication that distinct categories of suffering can be clinically diagnosed and must be treated differently even in their refractory phases, runs directly counter to Cassell's conceptual analysis of the phenomenon. His language below is particularly pertinent to this point.

> It is evident in thinking about suffering that it is not possible to divide the problem into physical, psychological, and social aspects without losing your grasp of it. In fact, reflecting on suffering should make it possible to see that there is nothing about the body that is not also psychological and social, nothing about social that is not physical and psychological, and nothing about the psychological that is not physical and social. We are of a piece. What happens to one part of us happens to the whole and what happens to the whole happens to every part.[27]

The AMA policy, and clinical practice guidelines that also purport to impose this distinction between categories of suffering, seek to legitimate the denial of PS to certain dying patients who have been "diagnosed" with the "wrong" kind of suffering. Cassell views this approach as harkening back to the flawed notion of mind-body dualism and a fundamentally flawed concept of person and of the nature of human suffering. In a critique of the AMA policy (in collaboration with the author of this chapter) Cassell notes with a certain irony, "Now, if the AMA policy becomes the standard of care, dying patients whose distress is genuinely intractable and has been labeled 'existential' in nature will have no viable medical option of last resort except in those jurisdictions in which a lethal prescription is allowed."[28]

This idea, now pervasive in the palliative medicine community (if the professional literature is reflective of the practice), that an accurate assessment of the precise nature and severity of the patient's suffering can be made and should determine whether and when PS is offered, highlights one of the more significant practical distinctions between PS and AD.[29] To access a lethal prescription in jurisdictions in which AD is legal, the patient only is required to have a confirmed prognosis of six months or less, possess decisional capacity, and to have made both oral and written requests for the medication within a specified period of time. Assessment of the nature, severity, duration, or intractability of the patient's suffering is neither required nor routinely undertaken by clinicians willing to write such prescriptions in these circumstances. It is sufficient that as a part of the informed-consent process the physician advise the patient of all available alternatives, including hospice and palliative care, social, psychological and pastoral counseling, and VSED.[30]

Despite the tacit embrace of PS by the palliative care community of professionals as ethically acceptable and universally legal means of responding to suffering in the terminally ill, there nevertheless appears to be an enduring perception among clinicians that sedation to unconsciousness accompanied by a decision to withhold artificial nutrition and hydration poses a significant risk of hastening death or indeed constitutes a kind of death. This concern is also reflected in the contemporary philosophical literature, in which death often is described as the complete and permanent absence of consciousness.[31] In this context, also note an important philosophical distinction between human personal life and human biological life.[32] Within the bioethical discourse over brain death and vegetative patients, proponents of higher brain or neocortical death argue that permanent unconsciousness constitutes the death of the person.[33] Thus to render a patient—even one who is near death from a terminal illness—permanently unconscious with the intent to maintain total sedation until death occurs is to be in some sense causally implicated in their demise.

The disinclination to be causally connected to the death of the patient at least partially explains the ubiquitous clinical practice guideline provision that PS should be offered only when the patient, based upon the exercise of sound clinical judgment, is within hours, or at most a few days from death due to the underlying terminal condition. It has enabled advocates for PS (conservatively applied) to maintain that it does not hasten death. For some patients who experience otherwise severe and refractory distress weeks or more before death is anticipated, these guidelines and clinician concerns could create insurmountable barriers to a peaceful death.

The Impact of Assisted Dying on Hospice and Palliative Care

This chapter next turns to the second question to be addressed: What has been the impact on hospice and palliative care in jurisdictions where AD is legally available? It is important to distinguish reliable evidence and valid data/statistics from anecdotal cases subject to perception bias and conflicting views of underlying situational factors. As the saying goes, "the plural of anecdote is not data."

When the Oregon Death with Dignity Act (ODWDA) was initially before the electorate in 1994, the major opposition came from the Roman Catholic Church, certain disability rights groups, and politically conservative right-to-life organizations. Interestingly, the thrust of their challenge to legalizing and regulating AD primarily was consequentialist and not deontological in nature. Rather than attempting to persuade voters that AD was categorically wrong on moral grounds, which was most certainly the formal position of the Catholic Church and the American Medical Association, the major talking points presented a parade of horrible consequences that they insisted would invariably follow from allowing terminally ill patients to secure a lethal prescription from a physician. The list included the following:

- Only or primarily patients who are poor, uninsured, or without access to palliative care services will seek this option in desperation.

- Many of the people who pursue this option will be depressed and their request will simply be a cry for help.

- Insurance companies will invoke this option to deprive seriously ill patients of effective but expensive therapies.

- Patients will lose trust and confidence in their physicians.

- Progress in the promotion of hospice and palliative care will be undermined.

- Legalization of AD for decisionally capable terminally ill patients will lead inexorably to its expansion to patients who are not terminally ill and those who lack decisional capacity (the slippery slope).

Now more than 15 years of data is available on the operation of the Oregon Death with Dignity Act, provided by the Oregon Department of Health Services. Overwhelmingly, patients who secured and utilized a lethal prescription had health insurance, were enrolled in hospice and were exercising their rights under the law to determine the time and manner of their imminent death.[34] Recent studies have found no evidence of the adverse sequelae predicted by the opponents of the law. For example, there has been no effort to expand the scope of AD to decisionally incapacitated or nonterminally ill patients.[35] In states where AD has been legalized, physicians working in end-of-life care have observed that with the enactment of such laws there actually has been an increased, rather than decreased, level of attention to the quality and availability of palliative care.[36] The availability of AD has not resulted in a diminution of patient trust that their physician will pursue their best medical interests.[37] This finding is consistent with the results of a survey of patients conducted almost a decade earlier, which found that the overwhelming majority of patients expressed no reservations about continuing to trust physicians should they be among those who provide AD to patients who seek it.[38]

An important ethical consideration is the emotional impact of AD on the death of patients who utilize this option where available and upon their families. Studies on the quality of dying for such patients, and the impact upon families not only fail to reveal any adverse mental health impact, but also found that patients who utilize AD and their families were more prepared for and accepting of death.[39] These studies also tend to confirm the patient demographics represented in the ODWDA data previously noted. Compared to other terminally ill patients who do not pursue this option, those who do are younger, predominantly white, more highly educated, enrolled in hospice, and strongly motivated by the impending loss of control.[40]

Opponents of AD have consistently challenged the portrayal of patients who utilize AD as determined, independent individuals making an autonomous and authentic choice to assert control over the dying process. Rather, they continue to insist, many of these patients are depressed, overwhelmed by both physical and emotional distress, and fearful that good hospice and palliative care will be insufficient for their needs. Evidence from the medical literature suggests otherwise. One study noted that physicians, hospice professionals, and family members of patients in Oregon who pursue aid-in-dying generally do not believe that depression influences choices for a hastened death. This observational hypothesis was tested by following a number of patients through the dying process. Interestingly, those who received a lethal prescription actually were found by validated measures to have a lower desire to die and lower helplessness scores. Most significantly, although 25 percent of patients who requested a lethal prescription had clinical depression, 75 percent of those who actually received prescriptions for a lethal medication did not.[41]

Throughout the history of AD in Oregon, the three reasons most often given by patients for considering or utilizing this option have been (1) loss of autonomy, (2) loss of dignity, and (3) loss of capacity to engage in activities which make life enjoyable.[42] Because the data also indicate that most of these patients were enrolled in hospice, it is important to note the stance of the Oregon hospice community AD. The website of the Oregon Hospice Association (OHA) takes the position that terminally ill patients need not choose between hospice and AD. It goes on to state: "A hospice should never deny a person its services because he or she has asked a doctor for a prescription, even when the hospice intends to exercise its right not to be involved. The Oregon Hospice Association supports patient choice."[43] The OHA statement indicates that every hospice patient who expresses an interest in or desire for AD is routinely provided a psychosocial assessment and monitored for mental health issues. Thus, individuals with mental health issues are screened out and will not qualify for a lethal prescription. The fact that most patients who utilize the AD option in Oregon are enrolled in hospice also might be explained in part by the influence of the *ODWDA Guidebook for Health Care Professions*, which urges physicians to encourage patients who express an interest in AD to consider enrolling in hospice if they have not already done so.[44]

Data from the state of Washington provide additional evidence that most patients who seek a lethal prescription do not do so out of desperation or clinical depression. The Seattle Cancer Care Alliance (SCCA), the site of care for the Fred Hutchinson–University of Washington Cancer Consortium, implemented a Death with Dignity Program in early 2009. That program was monitored and data collected through 2011. The most common reasons patients sought to participate in the program were identical to those noted above for Oregon. Each potential participant was assigned a patient advocate whose credentials were a licensed clinical social worker employed by the SCCA. As a matter of practice, all patients of the SCCA receive a first-line psychological evaluation by a social worker regardless of whether they express interest in participating in the Death with Dignity Program. In the report presenting the data, the authors note that no participants in the Death with Dignity Program during this period of nearly three years were deemed to require a mental health evaluation for depression or decisional incapacity. This is in contrast to 4.8 percent of patients generally in Washington who sought AD and 6.7 percent in Oregon.[45] Families of patients who utilized AD under the program described the death as peaceful and expressed gratitude even when the prescription was never filled or utilized, because of the sense of control it had provided to the patient. Some physicians at SCCA who initially declined to participate in the program subsequently decided to do so based upon their favorable perception of its administration and the level of patient/family satisfaction reported.

Hospice, Palliative Care, and Assisted Dying: Are They Compatible?

The traditional hospice mantra has been "we neither hasten nor prolong life." The mantra could be plausibly reworded as "we neither hasten nor prolong the process of dying." The clear implication is that doing either would be in some sense ethically problematic. This is one of the sticking points—if not *the* major one—between those who promote AD as an acceptable end-of-life option and those who oppose it. Until recently, state and national hospice organizations actively opposed initiatives such as the ODWDA. Experience with that and similar laws, however, has changed the views of some in the hospice and palliative care communities. The American Academy of Hospice and Palliative Medicine has adopted a neutral position on AD, reflecting the wide range of views of its membership on this issue. Following this lead, as well as that of the American Public Health Association—which has an official position supporting AD—other medical organizations have shifted their positions from opposed to neutral, including most recently the California Medical Association in 2015.

A compelling case in point is that of Ann Jackson, who for 20 years (concluding in 2008) was executive director and CEO of the OHA. In testimony before the Public Health Committee of the Connecticut General Assembly in March of 2013, when the Compassionate Aid in Dying bill was before the assembly, Jackson recounted how in her professional capacity as head of a state hospice association and as a matter of personal conviction she opposed the ODWDA on both occasions when it was on the ballot (1994 and 1996).[46] Subsequently, she experienced an epiphany, and now readily acknowledges that it was cavalier to even consider the possibility that hospice and palliative care professionals could meet all of the needs of every dying patient such that the ODWDA was unnecessary. She alludes to many conversations with hospice professionals in the years following the implementation of the ODWDA. Regardless of their individual position on AD, they consistently reported that following its implementation, conversations about death and dying improved significantly.

Similar sentiments have been expressed by the director of palliative care services at the University of Vermont Medical Center, who notes that not only has the Vermont AD law raised awareness about improving end-of-life care, it "brought with it a whole parallel movement to try to more broadly look at the needs of people facing serious illnesses at the end of their lives."[47] Moving beyond the experience in the United States, studies from countries in Western Europe where AD is available provide similar perspectives. A recent study reviewing data from the Netherlands, Belgium, and Luxembourg concluded that legal regulation of AD appears to have actually promoted the expansion of palliative care services generally.[48]

The purported incompatibility of AD and access to high-quality palliative care are therefore contestable propositions. Reasonable minds knowledgeable and proficient in palliative care take different positions. A paper describing the situation in Belgium asserts that "most values of palliative care workers and advocates of euthanasia are shared. If Belgium's experience applies elsewhere, then advocates of the legislation of euthanasia have every reason to promote palliative care, and activists for palliative care need not oppose the legalization of euthanasia."[49] Similarly, a chapter in a recent text on the Netherlands' experience with AD concludes, "Excellent palliative care and physician-assisted death may go together, both in practice and in principle."[50]

The devil, as the saying goes, is in the details. Careful studies of the interplay of hospice professionals and hospice patients who seek to utilize AD in Oregon and Washington reveal a broad continuum of practices. Understanding the existence and particulars of this continuum is important if we are to accurately assess the significance of the fact that most patients in these jurisdictions were enrolled in hospice. In Oregon, for example, one often-cited study described four models of hospice participation in AD: (1) full (within legal parameters), (2) moderate, (3) limited, and (4) nonparticipation (or uncooperation).[51] A subsequent analysis of hospice policies in Washington identified a somewhat similar range of hospice positions on patients seeking to utilize AD.[52] The existence of these marked variations in approach to AD in the Pacific Northwest indicates that there is not, in fact, a monolithic hospice stance in unqualified opposition to any involvement of hospice professionals in AD. With regard to the question being considered in this section of the chapter, there is no indication that the quality of care provided by hospices characterized as participating in a patient's choice of AD in some meaningful way is different from or in some objective sense inferior to those that preclude any involvement. Moreover, none of the hospice programs considered would go so far as to discharge a patient who was determined to access and utilize AD.

The gradual proliferation of AD in Europe and North America in recent years presents, as one commentator has observed, a "defining question" on the role and mission of hospice when respect for patient choice involves AD.[53] One chapter in a recent text on hospice ethics includes a detailed framework of questions for deliberation over the moral implications of AD for hospice.[54] Clearly many hospice and palliative care professionals are engaged in a serious reconsideration of the place, if any, that AD should have in the care of dying patients. For some, the availability of AD should be viewed not as a threat but as a challenge to demonstrate to terminally ill patients that in most circumstances a peaceful and dignified death can be achieved without resort to a lethal prescription.

Conclusion

A consideration of the topics and issues addressed in this chapter, and indeed this volume as a whole, indicates the diversity and fluidity of perspectives on interventions intended to or which have the risk of causing or hastening death. What appears to be quite clear is that, at least in liberal Western democracies, there is a clear trend toward expanding the options for patients facing terminal conditions. This trend is reflected in many developments over recent decades, including voter initiatives such as those in Oregon and Washington legalizing AD, judicial decisions recognizing the liberty/autonomy interests of terminally ill patients in orchestrating the end of life, health-professional organizations' adoption of official positions of neutrality or in support of AD, and public opinion surveys reflecting a clear majority of persons who believe this option should be available to them. At some level, each of these indicates a slowly emerging social consensus that previously rigid ethical and legal distinctions between AD and palliative care are no longer accepted, at least when considered outside of adherence to strict religious doctrine.

In part these changing attitudes about AD are likely influenced by the absence of any compelling evidence that the quality or availability of palliative care is in any way undermined by the availability of AD. Safeguards incorporated into the laws, policies, and guidelines for AD in the jurisdictions that permit it have been generally effective to prevent the victimization of vulnerable populations and ensure that only those patients who genuinely desire and meet the prerequisites for utilizing AD actually have access to it.

Notes

1. Timothy E. Quill, Bernard Lo, and Dan W. Brock, "Palliative Options of Last Resort: A Comparison of Voluntary Stopping Eating and Drinking, Terminal Sedation, Physician-Assisted Suicide, and Voluntary Active Euthanasia," *JAMA* (1997) 278: 2099–104.

2. Natasa Ivanovic, Daniel Buche, and Andre Fringer, "Voluntary Stopping of Eating and Drinking at the End of Life—a Systematic 'Search and Review' Giving Insight into an Option of Hastened Death in Capacitated Adults at the End of Life," *BMC Palliative Care* (2014) 13: 1–8.

3. National Hospice and Palliative Care Organization, Commentary and Position Statement on Artificial Nutrition and Hydration, September 12, 2010. http://www.nhpco.org/sites/default/files/public/ANH_Statement_Commentary.pdf (accessed August 10, 2015).

4. James A. Billings and Susan D. Block, "Slow Euthanasia," *Journal of Palliative Care* (1996) 12: 21–30.

5. Jane Stapleton, "Legal Cause: Cause-in-Fact and the Scope of Liability for Consequences," *Vanderbilt Law Review* (2001) 54: 941–1004.

6. *Baxter v. Montana,* 224 P. 3d 1211 (2009).

7. Ibid. at 1222.

8. Ibid. at 1222.

9. Franklin G. Miller, Robert D. Truog, and Dan W. Brock, "Moral Fictions and Medical Ethics," *Bioethics* (2010) 24: 453–60.

10. Tom L. Beauchamp and James F. Childress, *Principles of Biomedical Ethics* (New York: Oxford University Press, 2009), 175–76.

11. *Carter v. Canada (Attorney General),* 2015 SCC 5, p. 7.

12. Ibid. at paragraph 23.

13. Ibid. at paragraph 105.

14. Udo Schuklenk and Suzanne van de Vathorst, "Treatment-Resistant Major Depressive Disorder and Assisted Dying," *Journal of Medical Ethics* (2015) 41: 577–83.

15. *Washington v. Glucksberg,* 521 U.S. 702, 736–37 (1997).

16. Ben A. Rich, "Causation and Intent: Persistent Conundrums in End-of-Life Care," *Cambridge Quarterly of Healthcare Ethics* (2007) 16: 63–73.

17. T. E. Quill, "The Ambiguity of Clinical Intentions," *New England Journal of Medicine* (1993) 329: 1039–40.

18. Robert A. Pearlman, Kevin C. Cain, Donald L. Patrick, Malka Appelbaum-Maizel, Helene E. Starks, Nancy S. Jecker, and Richard F. Ulhmann, "Insights Pertaining to Patient Assessments of States Worse than Death," *Journal of Clinical Ethics* (1993) 4: 33–41.

19. M. Malroni, C. Pittureri, E. Scarpi, L. Piccinini, F. Martini, et al., "Palliative Sedation Therapy Does Not Hasten Death: Results for a Prospective Multicenter Study," *Annals of Oncology* (2009) 20: 1163–69.

20. Nathan I. Cherny and Lukas Radbruch, "European Association for Palliative Care (EAPC) Recommended Framework for the Use of Sedation in Palliative Care," *Palliative Medicine* (2007) 23: 581–93.

21. Margaret P. Battin, "Pulling the Sheet Over Our Eyes," *Hastings Center Report* (2008) 38: 27–30.

22. Paul Glare, Kirian Virik, Mark Jones, Malcolm Hudson, Stefan Eichmuller, et al., "A Systematic Review of Physicians' Survival Predictions in Terminally Ill Cancer Patients," *BMJ* (2003) 327: 195.

23. American Medical Association Council on Ethical and Judicial Affairs, "Sedation to Unconsciousness in End of Life Care," *CEJA Reports* 5-A-08.

24. Lois Snyder and Daniel P. Sulmasy for the Ethics and Human Rights Committee, American College of Physicians—American Society of Internal Medicine, "Physician Assisted Suicide—Position Paper," *Annals of Internal Medicine* (2001) 135: 208–16.

25. See note 24 at 212.

26. Eric J. Cassell, "The Nature of Suffering and the Goals of Medicine," *New England Journal of Medicine* (1982) 306: 639–45.

27. Eric J. Cassell, "The Nature of Suffering: Physical, Psychological, Social, and Spiritual Aspects," in *The Hidden Dimension of Illness: Human Suffering,* ed. Patricia L. Stark and John P. McGovern (New York: National League of Nursing Press, 1992).

28. Eric J. Cassell and Ben A. Rich, "Intractable End of Life Suffering and the Ethics of Palliative Sedation," *Pain Medicine* (2010) 11: 435–38.

29. Nathan I. Cherny and Lukas Radbruch, "European Association for Palliative Care (EAPC) Recommended Framework for the Use of Sedation in Palliative Care," *Palliative Medicine* (2009) 23: 581–93.

30. Task Force to Improve the Care of Terminally Ill Oregonians, *The Oregon Death with Dignity Act Guidebook for Health Care Professionals* (2008). https://www.ohsu.edu/xd/education/continuing-education/center-for-ethics/ethics-outreach/upload/Oregon-Death-with-Dignity-Act-Guidebook.pdf (accessed October 27, 2015).

31. John Martin Fischer, "Death," in *Encyclopedia of Ethics* (2nd ed.), Lawrence C. Becker and Charlotte B. Becker eds. (New York: Routledge, 2001), 377–78.

32. Ben A. Rich, "Postmodern Personhood: A Matter of Consciousness," *Bioethics* (1997) 3–4: 206–16.

33. Robert M. Veatch, "The Impending Collapse of the Whole-Brain Definition of Death," *Hastings Center Report* (1993) 23: 18–24.

34. Oregon Public Health Division, Oregon's Death with Dignity Act—2014. https://public.health.oregon.gov/ProviderPartnerResources/EvaluationResearch /DeathwithDignityAct/Documents/year17.pdf (accessed November 23, 2015).

35. Margaret P. Battin, Agnes van der Heide, Linda Ganzini, Gerritt van der Wal, and Bregje D. Onwuteaka-Philipsen, "Legal Physician-Assisted Dying in Oregon and the Netherlands: Evidence Concerning the Impact on Patients in 'Vulnerable' Groups," *Journal of Medical Ethics* (2007) 33: 591–97.

36. Melinda A. Lee and Susan W. Tolle, "Oregon's Assisted Suicide Vote: The Silver Lining," *Annals of Internal Medicine* (1996) 124: 267–69.

37. Mark Hall, F. Trachtenberg, and E.J. Dugan, "The Impact on Patient Trust of Legalizing Physician Aid in Dying," *Journal of Medical Ethics* (2005) 31: 693–97.

38. Mark A. Graber, Barcey I. Levy, Robert F. Weir, and Robert A. Oppliger, "Patients' Views About Physician Participation in Assisted Suicide and Euthanasia," *Journal of General Internal Medicine* (1996) 11: 71–76.

39. Linda Ganzini, Elizabeth R. Goy, Steven K. Dobscha, and Holly Prigerson, "Mental Health Outcomes of Family Members of Oregonians Who Request Physician Aid in Dying," *Journal of Pain & Symptom Management* (2009) 38: 807–16.

40. Linda Ganzini, Elizabeth R. Goy, and Steven K. Dobscha, "Oregonians' Reasons for Requesting Physician Aid in Dying," *Archives of Internal Medicine* (2009) 169: 489–92.

41. Linda Ganzini, Elizabeth R. Goy, and Steven K. Dobscha, "Prevalence of Depression and Anxiety in Patients Requesting Physicians' Aid in Dying: Cross Sectional Survey," *BMJ* (2008) 337: a1682.

42. See Note 30 at 2.

43. Oregon Hospice Association, "Hospice and Oregon's Death With Dignity Act." http://oregonhospice.org/hospice-and-dwd/ (accessed November 29, 2015).

44. Task Force to Improve Care of Terminally-Ill Oregonians, *The Oregon Death with Dignity Act: A Guidebook for Health Care Professionals* (2nd ed. 2008). https://www.ohsu.edu/xd/education/continuing-education/center-for-ethics/ethics -outreach/upload/Oregon-Death-with-Dignity-Act-Guidebook.pdf (accessed November 29, 2015).

45. Elizabeth Trice Loggers, Helene Starks, Moreen Shannon-Dudley, Anthony L. Back, Frederick R. Appelbaum, and F. Marc Stewart, "Implementing a Death with Dignity Program at a Comprehensive Cancer Center," *New England Journal of Medicine* (2013) 368: 1417–24.

46. Ann Jackson, Testimony Before Public Health Committee of Connecticut General Assembly, "Support for CT Bill 5236: Compassionate Aid in Dying 2014." March 17, 2013. https://www.cga.ct.gov/2014/PHdata/tmy/2014HB-05326-R000317-Ann, %20Jackson,%20End%20of%20Life%20Care%20Consulting-TMY.PDF (accessed December 2, 2015).

47. Lisa Schencker, "Assisted-Suicide Debate Focuses Attention on Palliative, Hospice Care," *Modern Healthcare*. May 16, 2015. http://www.modernhealthcare .com/article/20150516/MAGAZINE/305169982 (accessed December 3, 2015).

48. Kenneth Chambaere and Jan L. Bernheim, "Does Legal Physician-Assisted Dying Impede Development of Palliative Care? The Belgian and Benelux Experience," *Journal of Medical Ethics* (2015) 41: 657–60.

49. Jan L. Bernheim, Reginald Deschepper, William Distelmans, Arsene Mullie, and Luc Deliens, "Development of Palliative Care and Legalization of Euthanasia: Antagonism or Synergy?" *BMJ* (2008) 336: 864–67.

50. Dick Willems, "Palliative Care and Physician-Assisted Death," in *Physician-Assisted Death in Perspective*, eds. Stuart J. Younger and Gerrit K. Kimsma (New York: Cambridge University Press, 2012), 211.

51. Courtney S. Campbell and Jessica C. Cox, "Hospice and Physician-Assisted Death: Collaboration, Compliances, and Complicity," *Hastings Center Report* (2010) 40: 26–35.

52. Courtney S. Campbell and Margaret A. Black, "Dignity, Death, and Dilemmas: A Study of Washington Hospices and Physician-Assisted Death," *Journal of Pain and Symptom Management* (2014) 47: 137–53.

53. Bruce Jennings, "Unreconcilable Differences?" *Hastings Center Report* (2011) 41: 4–5.

54. Courtney S. Campbell, "Moral Meanings of Physician-Assisted Death for Hospice Ethics" in *Hospice Ethics: Policy and Practice in Palliative Care,* eds. Timothy W. Kirk and Bruce Jennings (New York: Oxford University Press 2014), 245–47.

CHAPTER THIRTEEN

Capacity and Assisted Dying

Colin Gavaghan

Much divides supporters and opponents of voluntary euthanasia (VE) and assisted suicide (AS). One thing that tends to unite them, however, is a concern that anyone choosing those options must be making an autonomous choice. For supporters, only those will qualify as truly VE.[1] For many opponents, doubts about that form a large measure of their opposition.

What precisely is required for a decision to be autonomous is much debated. At a minimum, however, it requires an agent who is capable of making decisions. This attribute is variously described as decision-making capacity or competence. Although perhaps not in itself sufficient to establish that a choice is autonomous, decision-making capacity is a necessary qualification for anyone seeking to avail himself or herself of VE or voluntary AS. It is also a necessary element for anyone whose support for VE or AS is predicated on respect for autonomy.

Any jurisdiction considering allowing VE or AS then must turn its attention to questions of capacity: What it means, how it is to be evaluated, what safeguards can be put in place to ensure it is present and in the right degree. To some extent, these are not new challenges. The sorts of end-of-life (EoL) decisions that currently are permitted in all Western democracies—such as the right to decline life-prolonging treatment—pose hard questions about capacity assessment. Whether VE/AS poses new or different varieties of challenges, or just brings those challenges into sharper focus, is considered elsewhere in this chapter.

Even in those jurisdictions where neither VE nor AS are allowed, the capacity of the person attempting suicide can be relevant for various legal purposes. In England, prosecution guidelines issued by the Director of Public Prosecutions have made it clear that "[a] prosecution is more likely to be required if . . . the victim did not have the capacity (as defined by the Mental Capacity Act 2005) to reach an informed decision to commit suicide."[2] Although it does not follow that the presence of capacity will result in a decision not to prosecute, capacity evidently is an important factor in the decision as to whether prosecution is in the public interest.

If prosecution and conviction occur, then the autonomous nature of the deceased's wishes could play a part in mitigating any sentence handed down. In New Zealand, Sean Davison's conviction for assisting his mother to die could have resulted in a maximum sentence of 14 years' imprisonment. Davison received only five months of home detention, in part because of the judge's recognition that his mother "was still strong-willed" and put Davison "under some pressure."[3]

The question of the autonomy and decision-making capacity of the suicidal party, then, could be relevant for a range of purposes. Leaving aside the argument that a request to die can *never* be fully autonomous—at the very least, the burden of proving this lies with those making such a charge—there are a number of hard questions that arise in relation to capacity and VE/AS. This chapter discusses

- The presumption of capacity;
- Mental disorder (with particular reference to depression);
- Stability of values; and
- Influence and duties to die.

These are all particular challenges about assessing capacity that have arisen in the context of VE/AS. Whether they are unique or particular to that context is certainly questionable, but there is no doubt that they arise there with particular poignancy. Before turning to those challenges, however, this chapter first explains the standard account of capacity, as well as some more contentious elements that sometimes are suggested.

Standard Requirements for Capacity

The legal test for decision-making capacity varies slightly between jurisdictions but generally relates to a set number of criteria. Applebaum and Grisso set these out in an influential series of papers and relate them to the individual's abilities

- to communicate a choice,
- to understand relevant information, and
- to manipulate information rationally.[4]

Variations derived from this approach are found in the capacity tests of various jurisdictions.[5]

Courts occasionally have sought to supplement these requirements with additional criteria, such as that the person must *believe* the information being conveyed.[6] This requirement has proved controversial, though in practice it seems not to have been used to support a finding of incapacity.[7] Supplemented or otherwise, the standard approach to capacity is concerned with the decision-making *process*, rather than with the *content* of that decision. At least in theory, the test of capacity should be substantively neutral.[8] This is consistent with the fundamentally liberal tenet that the state and its agents should be neutral as between various rival conceptions of "the good life." Jonathan Herring has suggested a rationale for this approach.

> With an increasing lack of trust in medical expertise and a breakdown in agreed moral values, it has become highly controversial to declare what is or is not in a patient's interests. To replace such paternalism with an assessment of what the patient wants avoids controversial judgements. Hence, we have the "triumph of autonomy."[9]

A number of commentators doubt how clearly this division between procedural and substantive factors can be maintained. At the very least, as Natalie Banner has pointed out, "[o]ften it is precisely the decision outcome, such as a treatment refusal, that alerts clinicians to the fact that there may be a mental impairment influencing the decision-making process."[10]

The distinction between an "unwise" decision alerting health care providers to the possibility of incapacity, and that decision itself supporting a finding of incapacity, is a subtle but important one. This chapter considers this in more detail elsewhere in addressing the potential compatibility of mental illness and capacity.

Capacity often is said to be decision specific. That is, individuals typically are deemed capable of making particular decisions, rather than being deemed capable or incapable across the board. (Of course, there are exceptions, such as unconscious patients, who will evidently lack capacity for any decisions.) A higher standard of capacity generally is regarded as necessary for complex decisions. A patient with dementia, for example, might be capable of deciding what they want for supper, but is not capable of making a decision about potentially lifesaving surgery. More controversially, it often is said that the degree of capacity should vary with the *gravity* of the decision. Thus, a life-or-death decision could be assumed to require the highest level of capacity.[11]

In addition to these standard features, a number of additional criteria for capacity have been suggested, including having had personal experience of particular treatments[12] or to place the capacity oneself in the shoes of another.[13] It would seem that, for the most part, courts have been reluctant to accept these additional requirements.

In addition to the patient's own mental capacities, it is also important when determining whether a decision is autonomous to inquire into surrounding circumstances. Thus, a decision typically will not be deemed valid unless the patient is *sufficiently* informed about the treatment options and likely outcomes, and unless his or her decision is *sufficiently* free from controlling influences of others. As is discussed later, neither of these are absolute requirements; no patient can possess all the information that might possibly be relevant to their decision, and no decision is ever entirely free from all outside influences. The concern for law is only that the decision is free and informed enough.

Some Challenges Regarding Capacity in Relation to Voluntary Euthanasia / Physician-Assisted Suicide

Presumption of Capacity

In most medical contexts, adult patients are presumed to possess decision-making capacity. The Mental Capacity Act 2005 (England and Wales), for example, provides that "[a] person must be assumed to have capacity unless it is established that he lacks capacity."[14] This applies, at least in theory, to patients who decline medical treatment even in the face of medical advice.

In contrast, many of the laws that have permitted assisted suicide or euthanasia have placed the burden of confirming capacity firmly on the other side. That is to say, assistance only is permissible when the applicant's capacity has been positively confirmed. Oregon's Death with Dignity Act, for example, requires that the patient's capacity must be positively confirmed both by an attending (127.815 § 3.01) and a consulting (127.820 § 3.02) physician.

A legal presumption serves as a sort of epistemic placeholder: "a putative fact which, while in the circumstances perhaps no more than probable or plausible, is nevertheless to be accepted as true provisionally—allowed to stand until concrete evidential counterindications come to view."[15] It is the default position adopted in the absence of evidence to the contrary.

Whether the presumption of capacity should be extended to voluntary euthanasia and physician-assisted suicide (PAS) depends in large part on the rationale underlying that presumption in those other circumstances. If the reasons for a general presumption to that effect apply also to VE/PAS, then it seems to follow that the same presumption should apply there.

There are various reasons why a presumption can be adopted in law. A presumption, for example, could reflect what the best evidence shows usually to be the case. This might explain, for example, the common presumption that a woman's husband is the father of her children. Similarly, it could be that the general presumption of capacity reflects a reality wherein most adults do in fact possess decision-making capacity. If that is the case, then the issue of whether the same presumption should apply in the VE/AS context is an empirical one. If the best evidence suggests that most applicants for VE/AS are competent, then it seems that the same presumption should be applied. If in contrast the best available evidence suggests the contrary, then the opposite presumption could well apply; the burden of proof should lie with those claiming capacity.

Part of the reasoning for a positive requirement—and hence, a reversed presumption—seems to derive from empirical assumptions that, although the majority of patients will be competent, many or most—or at least more—of those applying for VE/PAS will have compromised capacity. Yet the evidence in this regard is unclear. On the one hand, there is reason to believe that a large number—perhaps a great majority—of those who attempt suicide either lack capacity or are affected to some extent by mental disorder.[16] (As discussed below, the presence of mental disorder does not in itself establish that the person lacks capacity, but it at least can serve as a warning in that regard.)

Conversely, it might be prudent to be somewhat cautious in assuming that the same holds true for those seeking to avail themselves of VE or AS through "official" channels. A 2007 study by Margaret Battin and colleagues found that applicants for assisted dying under Oregon's Death with Dignity Act included more people with mental illness than did the general population, but they still accounted for only 30 percent of the total.[17] As the authors note, however, there are reasons to be somewhat careful in interpreting this finding, and it might be that an empirically informed presumption requires more data than are currently available.

Alternatively,[18] a presumption could come into being because it is considered that the danger of being wrong in a particular way outweighs the danger of being wrong in a different way. The presumption of innocence in criminal trials, for example, is not predicated on a belief that most people accused are in fact innocent, but rather reflects a normative belief that it is worse to convict an innocent person than to acquit a guilty one.

The suggestion that any doubt should be resolved in favor of preserving life is one that has evident appeal in such circumstances, and it is one to which courts have at times had recourse.[19] Whether being provided with assistance is always the worst outcome for applicants, however, is somewhat questionable. As noted in several recent cases,[20] denying an applicant the option of assistance in dying should that become necessary could serve as a perverse incentive for them to take their own lives while they have the capacity to do so—and hence, die sooner than they would have wanted.

Even if a presumption predicated on avoiding the worst outcome might justify a presumption against capacity in VE/AS situations, it is less clear why the same would not apply in the context of treatment refusals. It is unclear, for example, why a patient seeking to decline a lifesaving medical intervention is risking any less than one seeking positive assistance in dying. In fact, for a variety of reasons, the latter scenario might be less dangerous. Those jurisdictions that have allowed VE or AS all have required additional qualifying criteria than a competent request; some, for example, require a terminal diagnosis, and others require evidence of unendurable suffering. Others require a mandatory "cooling off" period. All of those additional checks—that is, over and above what is required in treatment-refusal cases—seem to suggest that the chances of a terrible mistake are if anything less in the VE/AS situation than in the treatment-refusal situation.

The explanation for the differing treatment might lie on the other side of the scale. The patient refusing treatment and the patient requesting VE/AS might both be seeking death, but the means by which they could be prevented are rather different. Perhaps the general presumption of capacity reflects the harm, the indignity, and the violation of rights that could result if doctors routinely were allowed to impose unwanted treatment on actually competent patients. In this analysis, the "worst-case scenario" might not be death at all, but rather the significant bodily intrusions and indignities that would accompany force-feeding or other enforced prolongations of life.

Although not wholly implausible, it is unclear that this distinction serves to support a different presumption regarding capacity. It seems more likely that, in the majority of cases, the similarities between the various classes of end-of-life decisions outweigh the differences, and that the greatest danger lies in a potentially salvageable life being lost on the basis of an incompetent decision. If so, then an argument emerges for a consistent approach to the presumption of capacity. No argument is given here about the form that presumption should take; perhaps all people seeking to end their lives should be presumed to lack capacity, or maybe only those who wish to make life-ending choices contrary to medical advice. The presumption of capacity possibly should apply in all such cases. In any event, the case for treating them differently stands in need of further argument.

Mental Disorder and Capacity

The relationship between capacity and mental disorder is not straight-forward. Historically, the presence of mental illness often was deemed to preclude the possibility of capacity. As Applebaum and Grisso have explained, "Nineteenth-century medicine, for example, expressed the belief that mental illness invariably destroyed decision-making capacities, rendering patients unable to make valid decisions of any kind."[21] As they go on to explain, however, "With the growth of informed consent law after the middle of the twentieth century, the assumption that people with mental illness were uniformly deficient in decision-making abilities and should be considered legally incompetent began to be called into question."

By the late-20th century, common-law courts had explicitly recognized that it was possible for people affected by mental disorders to retain aspects of decision-making capacity. In a highly influential English case, it was held that the patient's schizophrenia did not preclude him from having the capacity to decide about whether to have his gangrenous leg amputated.[22] Although mental illness might undermine some aspects of capacity, or capacity to decide about certain things (for example, a patient with anorexia might not be competent to decide about feeding), it should not be taken to imply global incapacity.

As discussed elsewhere in this chapter,[23] the presence of mental illness can serve either as a qualifying or disqualifying condition for VE/AS. Its role in both capacities has been contentious. In the Netherlands, controversy has surrounded whether psychological suffering should satisfy the criterion of intolerable suffering—a question that divides supporters of VE in all jurisdictions.[24] In other jurisdictions, attention has focused on whether people affected by mental disorders should automatically be excluded from eligibility. In Canada, the Special Joint Committee on Physician-Assisted in Dying, although recognizing "that there will be unique challenges in applying the eligibility criteria for MAID where the patient has a mental illness," did not recommend that such patients should be denied assistance on that basis.

Cases involving mental illness may prove challenging to address for health care practitioners, but the Committee has faith in the expertise of Canadian health care professionals to develop and apply appropriate guidelines for such cases. The difficulty surrounding these situations is not a justification to discriminate against affected individuals by denying them access to MAID.[25]

Jeanette Hewitt has suggested a checklist of questions that might allow us to identify those with mental illness whose suicidal wishes are nonetheless rational.

1) That the person is not acting impulsively because of acute psychological distress or acute psychotic phenomena; 2) That suicidal thoughts are not causally linked to command hallucinations or persecutory delusional beliefs; 3) That the person is able to realistically appraise current circumstances and probable futures; 4) That the person is able to appreciate the possibility for alternative action and the costs and consequences of his or her decision; 5) That the cause of suicidality is not directly linked to an obviously treatable or remediable condition; 6) That the person perceives his or her suffering to be unendurable; and 7) That the person has a realistic perception of death.[26]

Although there could be no reason to assume that mental disorder precludes capacity in all cases, it is easy to see how the existence at least of a disorder that manifests in cognitive deficits might at least raise doubts about a cognitive concept of capacity. A greater challenge, perhaps, arises in relation to affective disorders.

Depression and Mood Disorders

Although the presence of mental disorder in general provides a challenge in the context of EoL issues, it is probably depression that figures most commonly in debates around VE and PAS. The image of vulnerable people availing themselves of assisted dying while in the throes of an acute depressive episode is a powerful one, and it is scarcely surprising if the prospect turns some people away.

Gloria Taylor, one of the appellants in *Carter*, felt the need to emphasize, "I know that I am dying, but I am far from depressed."[27] In similar terms, Lecretia Seales stressed that, "I am not depressed. I have accepted my terminal illness and manage it in hugely good spirits considering that it's robbing me of a full life."[28]

The insistence that they were not depressed might be seen to fit with a narrative that views a depressed wish to die as suspect. On the face of it, this is hardly surprising. For many, the image of a depressed person availing themselves of VE/AS calls to mind similar concerns as expressed on one anti-euthanasia website.

> Depressive illness distorts a person's thinking so that they can't think clearly or rationally. It would appear difficult for the depressive person to be both competent and in a position to make a rational decision about choosing assisted suicide.
>
> The suicidal person suffering from depression typically undergoes severe emotional and physical strain. This physical and emotional exhaustion impairs basic cognition, creates unwarranted self-blame, and generally lowers overall self-esteem, all of which easily lead to distorted judgements.
>
> This suggests that intervention to keep an individual alive is actually the course most likely to honor that individual's true wishes or to respect the person's "autonomy."[29]

Valerie Gray Hardcastle and Rosalyn Walker Stewart group together cases "in which the person attempting suicide is depressed, deranged, or otherwise in the grip of some psychological disorder." "Here," they say, "the medical profession is almost unanimous in its disapproval: suicides committed under emotional duress are not to be tolerated, for emotional duress is treatable."[30]

Is it reasonable to group depressed people alongside those who are "deranged"? Is it reasonable to conclude that all such people are "treatable"? (The authors of that article argue that "[m]any psychotics are in continual agony and have no reasonable hope for a cure.") If so, should that fact alone render them ineligible for VE/AS?

In fact, as is explored in this section, the relationship between depression and capacity/autonomy is a good deal more complicated than is sometimes recognized. Specifically, the predominantly cognitive approach to capacity adopted in most common-law countries has something of an uneasy relationship with affective conditions such as depression. Whether this should lead to modifying that approach, or making allowance for depressed suicides, is an issue that merits closer consideration. Before turning to that, it is worthwhile to consider another question: what exactly do we mean by "depressed"? Authors such as Allan Horwitz and Jerome Wakefield have argued that

> the recent explosion of putative depressive disorder, in fact, does not stem primarily from a real rise in this condition. Instead, it is largely a product of conflating the two conceptually distinct categories of normal sadness and depressive disorder and thus classifying many instances of normal sadness as mental disorders.[31]

The question of what qualifies as "depressive illness" is potentially very important if a diagnosis is to serve either as a qualifying or disqualifying condition. As is argued elsewhere in this chapter,[32] the way in which mood disorders are defined also could raise a concern about definitional circularity, which could have the effect of seriously limiting any "right to die."

With regard to the relationship between depression and capacity, the picture too is unclear. Depression certainly *can* impact all of the standard elements of capacity. One team of leading researchers in this area explained, "There appears to be little disagreement that major depression can have an impact on cognitive functions related to decision making. Impairments may exist in concentration . . . , information processing, and reasoning, among others."[33]

Although cognitive symptoms can accompany depression, this is not invariably the case. Research in this area is limited,[34] but the research suggests that although depression can have an impact, depressed people vary widely in terms of their decision-making capacities, with many performing at least as well as the non–mentally ill control group.[35]

The potential compatibility of depression with the standard account of capacity has led some writers to question the adequacy of that account, and in particular, its almost exclusive reliance on cognitive capacities. One concern is that, although a depressed patient could have a nonpathological grasp of options and likely outcomes, how he or she *feels* about those options and outcomes could be heavily skewed by the disorder. Is it possible that a cognitively lucid person could nonetheless be acting in the throes of "pathological pessimism,"[36] "undervaluing positive outcomes while focusing on negative outcomes of treatment and thus skewing the weights given to treatment outcomes in favour of treatment risks"?[37]

The assumption that people with depression have deficiency in terms of gauging the likelihood of outcomes has been called into considerable doubt. Recent research tends to suggest that, if anything, those with depression have a *more* realistic grasp of probability.[38] For Sharot and colleagues, what often are seen as "negativity biases" among depressed people in fact could be better characterized as "realism relative to an objective standard or by an absence of a positivity bias relative to healthy individuals."[39]

From the perspective of a cognitive standard of capacity, then, we should be wary of any assumption that depression is incompatible with capacity. Of greater concern is perhaps the possibility that the depressed person could be, in the words of Dan Brock, "value impaired."[40] The concern here is that, although a depressed person might be no less able to estimate the likelihood of a particular outcome, the effect of the depression is to undermine his or her capacity to care about it.

Supplementing the notion of capacity with a concern for value impairment has some appeal, but it is a step to take cautiously. For one thing, it raises the prospect that the question "How much should I care?" is one having an objectively right answer. The danger here is that this could significantly erode the substantive neutrality that underpins the standard "procedural" approach to capacity. The patient in the *Kings College* case certainly possessed an idiosyncratic and unusual notion of what made her life valuable. To deny her the option of making decisions based on that value system is to elevate one set of normative value judgments over another, in a manner that would involve a very radical revision of the standard account of capacity.

A more promising approach to such unsettling cases might be to enquire as to the extent that the values and choices expressed while depressed are consistent with those that have characterized the majority of the patient's nondepressed life. A dramatic inconsistency might imply that the current values and choices are a product of the depressive illness rather than an authentic expression of the patient's autonomy. Even here, however, there is cause for some caution.

Stability of Values

Even within a substantively neutral approach to capacity, it is common for capacity to be thought to require a minimal level of stability or consistency of values or preferences. Although stability of values rarely features in formal legal requirements for capacity, it is something that has received considerable attention in academic commentaries. As Buchanan and Brock have argued, "a competent decision maker . . . requires *a set of values or conception of what is good* that is at least minimally consistent, stable, and affirmed as his or her own."[41]

A requirement of minimal consistency can refer to several different things. Inconsistency between stated value and actual choice—or between stated ends and chosen means—might be an indication of a major flaw in the reasoning process. As Banner has noted, "inconsistencies in what a person believes or values and what he ostensibly decides to do may indeed look bizarre and potentially hint at a lack of capacity."[42] A patient who says that his or her greatest fear is pain but continually refuses pain medication could be displaying a disordered decision-making process.

Alternatively, the concern might relate to stability of values. A patient whose preferences fluctuate from day to day, or even hour to hour, can be thought to be exhibiting some defect in capacity. It is probably uncontroversial to accept that some degree of consistency or stability should be demanded as requirements for capacity. The difficulty lies in determining to what degree those factors must be present. As Banner has pointed out:

> We hold numerous competing and incompatible beliefs, values and desires, and it is indeed part of the process of making a decision that we become aware of and modify these, change our minds and often make decisions that represent a compromise between such conflicts. . . . Furthermore, we may legitimately change our minds and adopt radically different views from those previously held. This is especially true in the context of medical decision-making, where often life-changing decisions are made, in the context of circumstances that have not been foreseen or previously considered.[43]

It is certainly true that most of us value a number of different things, and that these different values and interests sometimes can come into conflict. Trite examples abound, but in the end-of-life context the respective desires to live a long life and to avoid extreme suffering or indignity could be expected to coexist in most people. It is entirely possible that for many of us the question of which of those interests or values matters most is not something that we are capable of answering in the abstract. The ranking of values can vary between situations. It is even possible that I have no insight into that priority ranking until those values are tested in the crucible of real-life decision making.

All this is to say that we perhaps should be wary of demanding too high a level of stability or consistency when patients make EoL choices. That someone's request for VE seems out of character could be a reason to scrutinize that request more closely, but it need not be evidence of compromised capacity. As Beauchamp and Childress observe (in discussing the work of Agnieza Jaworska),

> a patient might request a highly invasive treatment at the end of life against his previous judgment about his best interests because he has come to a conclusion that surprises him: he cares more about living a few extra days than he had thought he would. Despite his long-standing and firm view that he would reject such invasive treatments, he now accepts them.[44]

This, they suggest, "is not uncommon in medical contexts."

It presumably would be unthinkable to deny lifesaving treatment to a patient on the grounds that choosing treatment is out of keeping with the patient's previous character or statements. Normally, it would be said that such a patient had changed his or her mind; that, when push came to shove, the patient had come to realize that he or she valued life—or feared death—more than previously realized. Typically, people would be slow to draw an inference of lost capacity.

My suggestion is to be cautious about inferring lost capacity in the opposite situation—when a previously stoical patient decides that he or she has endured enough. Rather than a betrayal of his or her previous values, this simply could reflect the reality that reserves of energy and determination are not infinite.

Out-of-character choices and changed priorities could provide reasons to scrutinize someone's capacity more closely, but such choices and priorities do not in themselves provide a reason to conclude that capacity is compromised. People change their minds, and people faced with grave or arduous situations might change their minds quite dramatically. The decisions that are made in a range of hypothetical situations can differ a great deal from the decisions made when faced with real-life situations. Provided the changed values are themselves relatively stable and consistent, they might be better seen not as a symptom of incapacity, but of a very human response or adaptation to a radically new situation.

Influence and Coercion

It is trite to observe that no decisions are made in a vacuum. All are subject to some degree of influence. As Herring has observed,

> We are all inevitably influenced by our family and broader society. How we view ourselves and what we value in life are conceptions of the values that are influenced, caused, or constituted by our social relationships and social conditions. Social-relational factors are essential in the development of our capacity for autonomous decision making. We are probably overconfident, if anything, of being actually capable of shaking off the shackles of their relational and social context to form values genuinely "of their own. . . ."[45]

As Herring goes on to acknowledge, however,

> a relational autonomy approach must recognize that relationships can undermine as well as enhance autonomy. Social relationships or social conditions can undermine our capacity for autonomous decision-making by influencing the content and impairing the authenticity of our affective attitudes. A relationship of domestic abuse, for example, can rob a person of self-worth, self-respect, and self-esteem and thereby the ability to assign weight to their preferences and desires, which is essential to practical reasoning. Where this sense of self-worth is impaired, a person is vulnerable to deferring excessively to the preferences and desires of others.[46]

But when does that influence undermine autonomy? In their highly influential analysis, Beauchamp and Childress sought to distinguish different forms of influence.

> Control of another person is necessarily an influence, but not all influences are controlling. . . . Many influences are resistible, and some are welcomed rather than resisted. The broad category of influence includes acts of love, threats, education, lies, manipulative suggestions, and emotional appeals, all of which can vary dramatically in their impact on persons.[47]

For Beauchamp and Childress, overt appeals to reason and argument—what they call persuasion—are least likely to threaten autonomy. Indeed, such persuasive attempts even could be thought an integral part of informed consent: "Reasoned argument in defense of an option is itself a form of providing information and is often vital to ensuring understanding."[48]

The more problematic categories of influence, in terms of respecting autonomy, are described respectively as coercion and manipulation. Coercion occurs when "one person intentionally uses a credible and severe threat of harm or force to control another."[49] It is presumably uncontroversial to deem this incompatible with autonomy, thus it is not considered further.

Manipulation, conversely, might—on Beauchamp and Childress' analysis—sometimes be compatible with autonomy. It consists of "swaying people to do what the manipulator wants by means other than coercion or persuasions," for example through "a deliberate act of managing information that non-persuasively alters a person's understanding of a situation and thereby motivates him or her to do what the agent of influence intends."[50]

On some approaches, appeals to emotion are problematic for autonomy, because when successful they circumvent the agent's rational faculties. Others might view that as an artificially rationalistic model of decision making. After all, it could be argued that few of us make important decisions in a manner wholly detached from emotions.

For the courts, the sorts of factors that are likely to render an influence coercive include the state of mind of the patient at the time (e.g., being in great pain, confused, or under the effect of trauma or medication) and their relationship with the persuader. Close familial relationships sometimes are considered particularly suspect.[51]

All of this sounds quite reasonable. Yet, as Emily Jackson has pointed out, "Doctors and relatives will often try to persuade patients of the merits of undergoing a procedure which they believe will benefit the patient."[52]

Not uncommonly, such attempts can look considerably more like emotional manipulation than rational persuasion. Very often, they also involve exactly the sorts of close relationships that are identified as being potentially threatening to autonomy.[53] If an attempt to persuade an elderly relative to go on living is compatible with an autonomous decision, it is hard to see why an attempt to persuade them to die would automatically vitiate autonomy and capacity.

It could be argued, then, that a substantively neutral notion of capacity would take account of the *manner* that influence is brought to bear on the patient, including any particular vulnerabilities and particular relationships between persuader and patient. Those considerations, however, should apply regardless of the *content* of the views that the persuader is seeking to impart. There is no obvious reason to suppose that pressure in one direction poses more of a threat to autonomy than pressure in the other.

Conversely, it should be remembered that autonomy is not the only ethical principle in play. Perhaps concerns about harms and benefits could provide a legitimate reason for greater scrutiny of "persuasion to die" rather than "persuasion to live." Those choices also can be seen as asymmetrical in the obvious sense that, in many cases,[54] the latter type of decision can always be revisited later, whereas the former is very final.

The distinction, then, might be a reasonable one. Once again, however, it is one that seems to require some degree of departure from the putative substantive neutrality of the law's approach to capacity and consent. The different treatment of "persuasion to die" and "persuasion to live" would rest on the likely outcomes of those interventions, rather than their effect on the decision-making process.

Duty and "Being a Burden"

Although, in theory, all attempts to persuade are somewhat challenging from the perspective of autonomy and capacity, there is a specific example of influence that in the VE/AS context causes considerable and understandable concern. This the oft-articulated concern that elderly and ill people, particularly, will be made to feel that they have a "duty to die." The idea has somewhat fallen out of fashion but, from time to time, there have been serious arguments advanced in bioethical literature about a possible ethical duty to die. One (in)famous account comes from John Hardwig, who argued for such a duty on a relational basis: "Tragically, sometimes the best thing you can do for your loved ones is to remove yourself from their lives. And the only way you can do that may be to remove yourself from existence."[55]

Margaret Battin has proposed a more global variant of this duty, predicated on a Rawlsian concern for a fair distribution of scarce resources.[56] My concern here, though, is not to consider whether the idea of a duty to die is plausible or compelling, but rather with the more modest question of whether believing oneself subject to such a duty presents a challenge to autonomy or capacity. This concern was recently and powerfully articulated by members of the English Supreme Court.

> [T]here would be a direct concern about weak and vulnerable people in the same unhappy position as Applicants, who do not have the requisite desire (namely "a voluntary, clear, settled and informed decision to commit suicide"), but who either feel that they have some sort of duty to die, or are made to feel (whether intentionally or not) that they have such a duty by family members or others, because their lives are valueless and represent an unjustifiable burden on others.[57]

In a similar vein, John Finnis has recently written of "the patient's subjection to the pressure of the thought that my being killed is what my relatives expect of me and is in any case the decent thing to do, even though I utterly fear it and perhaps perceive it as the uttermost and ultimate indignity."[58]

This situation, Finnis suggests, would not be a manifestation of autonomy at all, but rather, "an odious, devastating subjection to the needs and will of others."[59]

The notion of a "duty to die" occupies a strange place in law, and in culture. Legally, although it is recognized by some senior judiciary as being a reason to resist a move toward legalized VE/AS, it is not always regarded as a factor that vitiates capacity. In the *Kings College* case, among various reasons for wishing her life to be over, the patient listed a concern about being a burden.[60] The possibility that her capacity was thereby undermined was not even considered by the court.

In terms of cultural and social attitudes, the landscape has been a shifting one. Margaret Battin has noted a number of societies and notable thinkers that, at different times, seem to have recognized some sort of "duty to die" as being incumbent upon the elderly, the ill, or some other cohort of the population.[61] For those of us of 21st-century Western sensibilities, however, the idea seems unfeasibly harsh and inhumane, redolent perhaps of the brutal totalitarianism of the middle years of the previous century.

Duties to die can take a variety of forms. They might be expressed overtly or implicitly. They can arise from the individual's deepest moral convictions or be impressed upon them by others, perhaps at times of vulnerability. A concern in the *T* case, for example, was that the patient's mother might have (what exactly the mother said was never determined) exhorted her daughter to decline the blood transfusion at a point when she already was weak and confused.[62]

Persuading someone to act on the basis of a putative duty could, in certain circumstances, certainly pose problems for the person's autonomy and capacity. It is not clear that this is any more true, however, than any other attempt to persuade. A relative who successfully persuades a sick or confused patient to choose one treatment rather than another—or perhaps to reject conventional medicine in favor of faith healing or homeopathy— might also raise concerns about the extent to which that patient's capacity was undermined thereby. The problem seems to arise from the extent to which they are able to overcome the reasoning capacities of that patient, rather than from the specifics of what they are persuading them to choose.

Some of the concern about duties to die, however, is not confined to the scenario where ideas of duty are foisted onto a patient by some other party. Some of the suspicion about such duties to die seems to set a very high— perhaps impossibly high—bar for the independence of such choices. In discussing duties, Hazel Biggs has argued that

> [w]here choosing suicide amounts to one person wanting to sacrifice herself for the good of others because she feels socially pressured, serious misgivings arise about whether that person is making an autonomous decision. Whether the pressure is real or imagined, covert or overt, doubts persist about the quality and efficacy of choices made in those circumstances.

This might seem reasonable; social pressure could in fact threaten capacity—though more needs to be said about when influence becomes pressure. Biggs, however, then goes on to claim that "[t]hey may appear to be autonomous but are clearly defective if influenced by the needs of others."[63]

Is it really the case that taking account of the needs of others is incompatible with autonomy? Is my decision-making capacity undermined because I care not only about my own needs, but also about those of the people closest to me? Perhaps even, as one judge put it in a famous English case, "a belief that finite resources are better devoted to enhancing life than simply averting death"?[64]

The notion that only self-interested or self-regarding choices are truly autonomous seems implausible. It seems to rely on the sort of extreme version of individual autonomy that recently has been the subject of much criticism from feminist and relational ethicists[65] and proponents of principled autonomy. Onora O'Neill has argued in favor of a broadly Kantian notion of autonomy, according to which "[a]utonomy is manifested in a life in which duties are met, in which there is respect for others and their rights, rather than in a life liberated from all bonds."[66]

Cultural attitudes toward those who sacrifice their lives out of duty seem decidedly ambivalent. Captain Lawrence Oates, who famously sacrificed his own life in an (ultimately unsuccessful) attempt to save his fellow Antarctic explorers, is still regarded by many as a hero. It is uncommon to think of his sacrifice as being coerced or nonautonomous simply because it might have arisen from a sense of duty.

The judiciary seem to share this ambivalence. In a recent New Zealand case about assisted suicide, the judge took care to distinguish cases of "altruistic" suicide, such as when a soldier throws himself onto a hand grenade to save his comrades. Such cases of altruistic sacrifice are not, the judge held, properly to be considered cases of suicide at all.[67]

Yet, somehow the image of a weak or aged person making such a sacrifice seems harder to reconcile with our ideas of heroism and altruism, and easier to accommodate within a paradigm of vulnerability. Certainly, some elderly or sick people are vulnerable in certain ways, but it is not obviously true that they are more vulnerable to coercive notions of duty than, for example, young and healthy soldiers who were indoctrinated with ideas of camaraderie and patriotism.

It seems, then, that acting from a sense of duty surely can be consistent with autonomous choosing. Indeed, on some analyses, it is the purest manifestation of autonomy. Additionally, being concerned in part with the interests of other people—whether one's closest family, or with society at large—need not be an indication of compromised capacity, any more than prioritizing one's own interests. Neither should we be quick to deny the option of altruistic sacrifice to those whose age or physical infirmity takes them outside conventional ideas of heroism; such patronizing stereotypes threaten dignity as well as autonomy.

Rather, the concern should be cases where those "duties to die" appear a result of undue influence from others, rather than from the patient's own value system. Just as with any medical decision, that influence should be assessed with a view to a range of factors, including the relationship between the parties and, in particular, any significant power imbalance; the circumstances in which the influence was brought to bear (was the patient confused or in a weakened state?); and the extent to which the patient has had an opportunity properly to reflect on his or her decision, in full possession of information about alternatives.

Finally, it is suggested that parties be slow to second-guess the patient's perception of the impact of their death on others. The authors of one article on this topic warned that

> [i]deally, the person would have considered the potential adverse effects of
> their suicide upon family and friends and evidence of such concern would
> help to complete the picture of competence. Evidence of distorted or patho-
> logical perceptions of the effect on family and friends (e.g., "they want me
> dead") will be of obvious relevance.[68]

But who is to judge whether the perceptions are distorted? The medical
team can form its own impression about the truth of these beliefs—but
such impressions are likely to be formed on the basis of limited contact
and information. Though the patient's own views *might* be distorted or
borne of paranoia, it also is possible that the patient in fact has a more
accurate perception of the wishes and motives of his or her relatives. Certainly, medical professionals should be cautious about assuming that those
views are distorted simply because they do not tally with their own perceptions or expectations.

Pressure *By* the Patient

Much of the attention around threats to autonomy in relation to VE/AS
have related to the capacity of the patient. Hazel Biggs, however, raised
the possibility that those being asked to provide assistance also could find
themselves placed under considerable pressure.

> People who are asked to assist in the suicide or euthanasia of a patient or
> loved one, might feel compelled to comply out of loyalty or compassion,
> regardless of their own misgivings. Just as a patient might find her auton-
> omy constrained by concerns about the impact of her actions upon others,
> so those who care for her, either professionally or emotionally, may find
> their autonomy compromised by being asked to participate in, or condone,
> conduct that will result in loss of life.[69]

This might well be true, but does it provide a persuasive reason to reject
VE/AS? As more-or-less autonomous agents, people often are faced with
pressures and duties—real or imagined—to undertake unwelcome tasks.
Many of those who undertake caring roles for seriously ill or disabled relatives do so out of a sense of duty—often at considerable cost to their own
careers, aspirations, and their other relationships. As with the altruistic
self-sacrificers considered earlier, in such situations the sense of obligation
does not generally weaken our admiration for such people. The extent
to which we regard their autonomy as being compromised might rely on
factors such as the persistence and force of the appeals for assistance and

the availability of alternatives. This, however, is likely to be true of a great many duties; there is nothing evidently unique about VE/AS.

Conclusion

For those whose support for VE/AS is predicated to some extent on a support for personal autonomy, a range of hard questions exists in determining that an applicant has the requisite capacity to make an autonomous choice. For some, these difficult questions reveal certain deficiencies in how they approach the issue of capacity; perhaps it is too individualistic, or too focused on, for example, cognitive rather than affective criteria. For others, it simply is too hard to admit to the possibility at all.

I suggest that, as hard as those questions might be, they are in general no more difficult than those encountered in the context of other end-of-life decisions. If a person's mechanisms for dealing with compromised or threatened autonomy are adequate in cases such as those considered in this chapter, then it is unclear why these mechanisms would not be adequate for purposes of AS/VE. Conversely, if such mechanisms are inadequate for purposes of VE/AS, then it is urgent that we revise the way we presently approach treatment refusals.

A tentative suggestion is that there is probably a degree of merit in both of those positions. Certain putative threats to capacity in the VE context—such as the "duty to die"—are probably overstated; but certain aspects of the present approach to treatment refusals—such as the emphasis on cognitive rather than affective criteria—could require closer analysis (subject to the stated caveat that the mere presence of a diagnosis of mood disorder need not always mean incapacity). Regardless, there is no obvious reason why we should not strive for consistency across all EoL choices. Although there could be other reasons to regard VE as more ethically problematic than treatment withdrawal or refusal, they seem unlikely to relate to the issue of decision-making capacity.

Notes

1. This is not to deny support for nonvoluntary euthanasia for suffering by incompetent people. For example, the idea has been seriously considered that "psychiatric patients lacking autonomy could be candidates for physician-assisted death" Jukka Varelius, "Mental Illness, Lack of Autonomy, and Physician-Assisted Death," in *New Directions in the Ethics of Assisted Suicide and Euthanasia*, ed. M. Cholbi and J. Varelius, 59–77.

See also Valerie Gray Hardcastle and Rosalyn Walker, "Supporting Irrational Suicide." *Bioethics* (2002) 16(5): 425–38, 433. "We believe that there are clear cases in which supporting so-called irrational suicides and providing for calm and peaceful deaths are morally and medically preferable to the alternatives." By definition, however, support for "voluntary" euthanasia is predicated the voluntariness of the request, and hence, the requester's capacity to make a voluntary decision.

2. Director of Public Prosecutions, "Policy for Prosecutors in Respect of Cases of Encouraging or Assisting Suicide" (October 2014).

3. *R. v. Davison* (HC, Dunedin CRI 2010-012-4876, 24 November 2011) at [33].

4. Paul S. Applebaum and Thomas Grisso. "The MacArthur Treatment Competence Study. I Mental Illness and Competence to Consent to Treatment." *Law and Human Behavior* (1995) 19(2):105–26.

5. In England and Wales, the Mental Capacity Act 2005, for instance, sets out broadly the same test, though in a negative form:

Section 3(1)
For the purposes of section 2, a person is unable to make a decision for himself if he is unable—

(a) to understand the information relevant to the decision,
(b) to retain that information,
(c) to use or weigh that information as part of the process of making the decision, or
(d) to communicate his decision (whether by talking, using sign language or any other means).

6. *Re C. (Adult: Refusal of Treatment)* [1994] 1 All ER 819; *Chief Executive of the Department of Corrections v. All Means All* [2014] NZHC 1433.

7. The willingness at least to *consider* counterfactuals has sometimes been enough to satisfy the requirement that the information be "believed." In *Kings College Hospital NHS Foundation Trust v. C. and Another* [2015] EWCOP 80, a patient who had attempted suicide sought to decline the period of dialysis that her doctors believed would probably restore her to full health. The judge noted at paragraph 87 that "on occasions [the patient] has expressed herself in terms of categorically rejecting her prognosis in a way which gives the impression that she does not believe or accept that prognosis." However, he went on to observe that "on other occasions it is clear that her rejection of her prognosis is the result of her having considered it and given it no weight as against other factors more important to her."

8. Section 1(4) of the Mental Capacity Act 2005, for example, provides that "[a] person is not to be treated as unable to make a decision merely because he makes an unwise decision."

9. Jonathan Herring, *Vulnerable Adults and the Law* (Oxford: Oxford University Press, 2016), 53.

10. Natalie Banner, "Can Procedural and Substantive Elements of Decision-Making be Reconciled in Assessments of Mental Capacity?" *International Journal of Law in Context* (2013) 9(1): 71–86, 73. *See also* Kenneth Veitch, *The Jurisdiction of Medical Law* (Aldershot: Ashgate, 2007).

11. "The more serious the decision, the greater the capacity required." *In re T.* (Adult: refusal of treatment) [1993] Fam. 95, 113, per Lord Donaldson.

12. In one English case, a doctor was unwilling to accept a paralyzed patient's refusal of treatment on the basis that "[h]e thought that it would take up to two years to gain the experience necessary to have an informed opinion. Patients in the position of Ms. B, in his view, could only appreciate fully through experience." *Ms. B. v. An NHS Hospital Trust* [2002] EWHC 429 (Fam), [62].

13. One expert witness in *Kings College Hospital NHS Foundation Trust v. C. and Another* concluded that the patient lacked capacity in part because she had "no ability to place herself in her daughters' shoes when considering the effect of her refusing treatment."

14. Section 1(2). See also, for example, Protection of Personal and Property Rights Act 1988, s 5 (New Zealand); Guardianship and Administration Act 2000, Schedule 1, Principle 1 (Queensland, Australia); Guardianship and Administration Act 1990, s 4(3) (Western Australia).

15. Nicholas Rescher, *Presumption and the Practices of Tentative Cognition* (New York: Cambridge University Press, 2006), 4.

16. "The orthodox psychiatric view is that suicide always, or nearly always results from psychological disturbance, and thus it is always necessary to intervene in suicide attempts whenever possible." Hewitt, "Why Are People with Mental Illness Excluded from the Rational Suicide Debate?" 361.

17. Margaret P. Battin, Agnes van der Hilde, Linda Ganzini, Gerrit van der Waal, Bregje D. Onwuteaka-Philipsen, "Legal Physician-Assisted Dying in Oregon and the Netherlands: Evidence Concerning the Impact on Patients in 'Vulnerable' Groups," *Journal of Medical Ethics* (2007) 33: 591–97, 596.

18. These two options are not exhaustive of the possible reasons for a legal presumption. A presumption also can arise out of expediency. Many jurisdictions have a "common calamity" rule, which creates a presumption that, if two parties had died in the same incident and it is impossible to determine which died first, the younger will be presumed to have survived the elder. There is no particular reason to presume that this will have been true, and it is hard to see why it would in general be worse to adopt the opposite presumption. For purposes of inheritance, however, the law must sometimes reach some conclusion on the matter, and that is the rule that has been adopted. These sorts of presumptions exist to provide certainty in the law, but there is no particular reason to suppose that they reflect the true situation. This text assumes that the presumption of, or against, capacity is not of this nature.

19. In the context of a dispute about advance directives, Munby J. held that the burden of proof rests on those who "seek to establish the existence and continuing validity and applicability of an advance directive. So if there is doubt that doubt falls to be resolved in favour of the preservation of life." *H. E. v. A Hospital NHS Trust* [2003] EWHC 1017 (Fam), [23].

20. *Carter v. Canada* 2015 SCC 5; *Seales v. Attorney-General* [2015] NZHC 1239.

21. Applebaum and Grisso, "The MacArthur Treatment Competence Study. I," 107.

22. *Re C. (Adult: Refusal of Treatment)* [1994] 1 All ER 819.

23. Colin Gavaghan, "In Word, or Sigh, or Tear: Depression and End of Life Choices," in *Inspiring a Medico-Legal Revolution,* ed. G. Laurie and P. Ferguson (Ashgate, 2015): 231–55.

24. As Jeanette Hewitt explains, both libertarian and utilitarian rationales for VE run into difficulties when the candidate is mentally ill:

> Discussions of rational suicide have typically focused on pain associated with physical suffering; rarely has psychological suffering been seen as a reasonable inclusion either because it is seen as being insubstantial and ephemeral or because it is attributed to an underlying mental illness which is remediable.

"Why Are People with Mental Illness Excluded from the National Suicide Debate?" *International Journal of Law and Psychiatry* 36 (2013) 358–65, 360. For further discussion, see Udo Schuklenk, and Suzanne van de Vathorst "Treatment-Resistant Major Depressive Disorder and Assisted Dying," *Journal of Medical Ethics* (2015) 41(8): 589–91.

25. "Medical Assistance in Dying: A Patient-Centred Approach." Report of the Special Joint Committee on Physician-Assisted Dying (2016).

26. Hewitt, "Why Are People with Mental Illness Excluded from the Rational Suicide Debate?" 364.

27. *Carter v. Canada* (Attorney General), 2015 SCC 5, at [12].

28. *Seales v. Attorney-General* [2015] NZHC 1239, at [29].

29. http://www.life.org.nz/euthanasia/abouteuthanasia/abouteuthanasia2/ (accessed)

30. Gray Hardcastle and Walker Stewart, "Supporting Irrational Suicide," 425–38, 426.

31. Allan V. Horowitz and Jerome C. Wakefield, *The Loss of Sadness: How Psychiatry Transformed Normal Sorrow into Depressive Disorder* (Oxford: Oxford University Press, 2007), 6. *See also* G. Parker, "Classifying Depression: Should Paradigms Lost Be Regained?" *American Journal of Psychiatry* (2000) 157(8): 1195–203.

32. Colin Gavaghan, "In Word, or Sigh, or Tear."

33. P. S. Appelbaum, T. Grisso, E. Frank, S. O'Donnell, D. J. Kupfer, "Competence of Depressed Patients for Consent to Research," *American Journal of Psychiatry* (1999) 156(9): 1380–84, 1380.

34. Thomas Hindmarch, Matthew Hotopf, and Gareth S. Owen. 2013. "Depression and Decision-Making Capacity for Treatment or Research: A Systematic Review," *BMC Medical Ethics* 14:54.

35. Applebaum and Grisso, "The MacArthur Treatment Competence Study. I" Owen, Richardson, et al., "Mental Capacity to Make Decisions on Treatment in People Admitted to Psychiatric Hospitals."

36. Aaron T. Beck, A. John Rush, Brian F. Shaw, and Gary Emery, *Cognitive Therapy of Depression* (New York: The Guilford Press, 1987).

37. A. Rudnick, "Depression and Competence to Refuse Psychiatric Treatment," *Journal of Medical Ethics* (2002) 28: 151–55, 152.

38. James A. Shepperd, Patrick Carroll, Jodi Grace, and Meredith Terry, "Exploring the Causes of Comparative Optimism," *Psychologica Belgica* (2002) 42(1–2): 65–98; Tali Sharot, *The Optimism Bias: Why We're Wired to Look on the Bright Side* (New York: Random House, 2012).

39. C. W. Korn, T. Sharot, H. Walter, H. R. Heekeren, R. J. Dolan, "Depression Is Related To An Absence of Optimistically Biased Belief Updating About Future Life Events," *Psychological Medicine* (2014) 44(3): 579–92, 584.

40. Dan W. Brock, "Patient Competence and Surrogate Decision-Making," in R. Rhodes, L. P. Francis, and A. Silvers (eds.), *The Blackwell Guide to Medical Ethics* (Oxford: Blackwell Publishing, 2007), 130.

41. Buchanan and Brock, *Deciding for Others*, 25.

42. Banner, "Can Procedural and Substantive Elements of Decision-Making Be Reconciled in Assessments of Mental Capacity?" 71–86, 77.

43. Ibid.

44. Tom L. Beauchamp and James F. Childress. *Principles of Biomedical Ethics* (7th ed. Oxford University Press, 2013), 103–4.

45. Herring, *Vulnerable Adults and the Law*, 57–58.

46. Ibid.

47. Beauchamp and Childress, *Principles of Biomedical Ethics*, 94.

48. Ibid., 95.

49. Ibid., 94.

50. Ibid., 95.

51. *In re T. (Adult: Refusal of Treatment)* [1993] Fam. 95.

52. Emily Jackson, *Medical Law: Text, Cases, and Materials* (2nd ed.) (Oxford University Press, 2010), 281.

53. Consider, for example, prominent anti-euthanasia campaigner Ilora Finlay's account of persuading her mother to accept treatment. "Mum wanted to die, but convincing her to live gave us both a gift beyond measure." *Daily Mail* (March 20, 2010).

54. Not all decisions to accept treatment will be reversible. For the devout Jehovah's Witness persuaded to accept a blood transfusion, or the pregnant Roman Catholic woman who agrees to an abortion, they might have to live with a substantial burden of guilt.

55. John Hardwig, "Dying at the Right Time: Reflections on (Un)Assisted Suicide," in *Ethics in Practice*, ed. Hugh LaFollette (3rd ed. Blackwell, 2007), 95.

56. Margaret Pabst Battin, "Global Life Expectancies and International Justice: A Reemergence of the Duty to Die?" in *Ending Life: Ethics and the Way We Die* (New York: Oxford University Press, 2005), 280–99.

57. *R. (Nicklinson) v. Ministry of Justice* [2014] UKSC 38, per Lord Neuberger at [86]. A similar argument is advanced by Lord Sumption at [228].

58. John Finnis, "Euthanasia and the Law," in *Human Rights and Common Good: Collected Essays Volume III* (Oxford University Press, 2011), 251–70, 262.

59. Ibid.

60. *Kings College Hospital NHS Foundation Trust v. C.*, at [59].

61. Margaret Battin, "Age Rationing and the Just Distribution of Health Care: Is There a Duty to Die?" *Ethics* (1987) 97(2): 317–40.

62. *In re T. (Adult: Refusal of Treatment)* [1993] Fam. 95.

63. Hazel Biggs, *Euthanasia: Death with Dignity and the Law* (Oxford: Hart Publishing, 2001), 97.

64. *Airedale NHS Trust v. Bland* [1993] AC 789, 813.

65. See, for example, Michelle Taylor-Sands, *Saviour Siblings: A Relational Approach to the Welfare of the Child in Selective Reproduction* (Routledge, 2013); Jonathan Herring *Relational Autonomy and Family Law* (Springer International Publishing, 2014).

66. Onora O'Neill, *Autonomy and Trust in Bioethics* (New York: Cambridge University Press, 2002), 83.

67. *Seales*, [137] and [143].

68. Cameron Stewart, Carmelle Peisah and Brian Draper, "A Test for Mental Capacity to Request Assisted Suicide," *Journal of Medical Ethics* (2001) 37: 34–39.

69. Biggs, *Euthanasia: Death with Dignity and the Law*, 110.

Bibliography

Appelbaum, P. S., T. Grisso, E. Frank, S. O'Donnell, and D. J. Kupfer (1999). "Competence of Depressed Patients for Consent to Research." *American Journal of Psychiatry* 156(9): 1380–84.

Applebaum, Paul S., and Thomas Grisso (1995). "The MacArthur Treatment Competence Study. I Mental Illness and Competence to Consent to Treatment." *Law and Human Behavior* 19(2):105–26.

Banner, Natalie F. (2013). "Can Procedural and Substantive Elements of Decision-Making Be Reconciled in Assessments of Mental Capacity?" *International Journal of Law in Context* 9(1): 71–86.

Battin, Margaret P. (1987). "Age Rationing and the Just Distribution of Health Care: Is There a Duty to Die?" *Ethics* 97(2): 317–40.

Battin, Margaret P. (2005). "Global Life Expectancies and International Justice: A Reemergence of the Duty to Die?" In *Ending Life: Ethics and the Way We Die*. New York: Oxford University Press, 280–99.

Battin, Margaret P., Agnes van der Hilde, Linda Ganzini, Gerrit van der Waal, Bregje D. Onwuteaka-Philipsen (2007). "Legal Physician-Assisted Dying in Oregon and the Netherlands: Evidence Concerning the Impact on Patients in 'Vulnerable' Groups." *Journal of Medical Ethics* 33: 591–97.

Beauchamp, Tom L., and James F. Childress (2013). *Principles of Biomedical Ethics*, *7th ed.* New York: Oxford University Press.

Beck, Aaron T., A. John Rush, Brian F. Shaw, and Gary Emery (1987). *Cognitive Therapy of Depression*. New York: The Guilford Press.

Biggs, Hazel (2001). *Euthanasia: Death with Dignity and the Law*. Oxford: Hart Publishing.

Brock, Dan W. (2007). "Patient Competence and Surrogate Decision-Making". In *The Blackwell Guide to Medical Ethics*, edited by Rhodes, R., L. P. Francis, and A. Silvers. Oxford: Blackwell Publishing.

Buchanan, Alan E., and Dan W. Brock (1989). *Deciding for Others: The Ethics of Surrogate Decision Making*. Cambridge: Cambridge University Press.

Bullock, Emma C. (2015). "Assisted Dying and the Proper Role of Patient Autonomy." In *New Directions in the Ethics of Assisted Suicide and Euthanasia*, edited by Michael Cholbi and Jukka Varelius. Springer, 11–25.

Director of Public Prosecutions (October 2014). "Policy for Prosecutors in Respect of Cases of Encouraging or Assisting Suicide."

Dworkin, Gerald (1998). "Public Policy." In Dworkin, Frey, and Bok. *Euthanasia and Physician-Assisted Suicide: For and Against*. Cambridge: Cambridge University Press.

Faden, Ruth, Tom Beauchamp, and Nancy King (1986). *A History and Theory of Informed Consent*. Oxford, Oxford University Press.

Finnis, John (2011). "Euthanasia and the Law." In *Human Rights and Common Good: Collected Essays Volume III*. Oxford University Press.

Gavaghan, Colin (2015). "In Word, or Sigh, or Tear: Depression and End of Life Choices." In *Inspiring a Medico-Legal Revolution*, edited by Graeme Laurie and Pamela Ferguson. Ashgate. 231–55.

George R. J. D., I. G. Finlay, and D. Jeffrey (2005). "Legalised Euthanasia Will Violate the Rights of Vulnerable Patients." *BMJ* 331(7518): 684–85.

Gray Hardcastle, Valerie, and Rosalyn Walker (2002). "Supporting Irrational Suicide." *Bioethics* 16(5): 425–38.

Hardwig, John (2007). "Dying at the Right Time: Reflections on (Un)Assisted Suicide." In *Ethics in Practice, Third Edition*, edited by Hugh LaFollette. Blackwell, 91–102.

Herring, Jonathan (2016). *Vulnerable Adults and the Law*. Oxford: Oxford University Press.

Hewitt, Jeanette (2013). "Why Are People with Mental Illness Excluded from the Rational Suicide Debate?" *International Journal of Law and Psychiatry* 36: 358–65.

Hindmarch, Thomas, Matthew Hotopf, and Gareth S. Owen (2013). "Depression and Decision-Making Capacity for Treatment or Research: A Systematic Review." *BMC Medical Ethics* 14:54.

Horwitz, Allan V., and Jerome C. Wakefield (2007). *The Loss of Sadness: How Psychiatry Transformed Normal Sorrow Into Depressive Disorder*. Oxford: Oxford University Press.

Jackson, Emily (2010). *Medical Law: Text, Cases, and Materials, 2nd Edition*. Oxford: Oxford University Press.

Korn, C. W., T. Sharot, H. Walter, H. R. Heekeren, R. J. Dolan (2014). "Depression Is Related to an Absence of Optimistically Biased Belief Updating About Future Life Events." *Psychological Medicine* 44(3): 579–92.

O'Neill, Onora. *Autonomy and Trust in Bioethics* (2002). New York: Cambridge University Press.

Owen, G. S., G. Richardson, A. S. David, G. Szmukler, P. Hayward, and M. Hotopf (2008). "Mental Capacity to Make Decisions on Treatment in People Admitted to Psychiatric Hospitals: Cross Sectional Study." *British Medical Journal* 337.

Parker, G. "Classifying Depression: Should Paradigms Lost Be Regained?" (2000). *American Journal of Psychiatry* 157(8): 1195–203.

Rescher, Nicholas (2006). *Presumption and the Practices of Tentative Cognition*. New York: Cambridge University Press.

Rudnick, A. (2002). "Depression and Competence to Refuse Psychiatric Treatment." *Journal of Medical Ethics* 28: 151–55.

Schuklenk, Udo, and Suzanne van de Vathorst (2015). "Treatment-Resistant Major Depressive Disorder and Assisted Dying." *Journal of Medical Ethics* 41(8): 589–91.

Stewart, Cameron, Carmelle Peisah, and Brian Draper (2011). "A Test for Mental Capacity to Request Assisted Suicide." *Journal of Medical Ethics* 37: 34–39.

Varelius, Jukka (2015). "Mental Illness, Lack of Autonomy, and Physician-Assisted Death." In *New Directions in the Ethics of Assisted Suicide and Euthanasia*, edited by Michael Cholbi and Jukka Varelius. Springer, 59–77.

Veitch, Kenneth (2007). *The Jurisdiction of Medical Law*. Aldershot: Ashgate.

Wheat, Kay (2000). "The Law's Treatment of the Suicidal." *Medical Law Review* 8(2): 1, 182.

CHAPTER FOURTEEN

Advance Directives for Euthanasia

Eric Vogelstein

The use of advance directives is widely regarded as an important way of respecting the autonomy of medical patients after they become incompetent to make their own decisions.[1] Via an advance directive, a patient can indicate what medical treatment he or she wants, or doesn't want, in various circumstances that might occur in the future. If a patient prefers not to be kept alive in a vegetative state or coma, for example, he or she can indicate as much; or if the patient would rather pass away than be permanently dependent on a ventilator, he or she can direct potential treatment decisions to avoid that scenario.[2] Advance directives are commonly thought to be extremely helpful for *surrogate decision makers* (either the patient's next of kin or someone the patient has specifically designated)—those who are charged with deciding what care incompetent patients receive. Surrogates often are unsure of what their loved one would want and are faced with the challenging task of figuring that out based on what they know of the patient's personality and values. Often, there simply isn't enough information to go on, and the decision is nothing more than an educated guess. If patients provide prior instructions, however, then surrogates have the information they need to make the choice that coheres with the patient's wishes, and thus it is far more likely that the patient's autonomy will be respected—at least, that is the case according to the conventional wisdom.

This chapter addresses whether there are pressing ethical problems that arise when advance directives are combined with the practice of *euthanasia*. As used here, the term "euthanasia" refers to an act whereby a clinician directly ends the life of a patient for the patient's own good or at the patient's request, where the proximate cause of death is the clinician's act itself as opposed to a prior, underlying illness or injury (e.g., euthanasia occurs when a clinician injects a patient with a lethal dose of medication; it does not occur when a clinician disconnects life-support).[3]

Many people argue that euthanasia ought to be legal because the practice stands to respect the autonomy and promote the well-being of seriously ill medical patients. If euthanasia indeed should be legal, the question naturally arises whether to permit advance directives for euthanasia (ADEs). Prima facie, the same arguments that would justify euthanasia for competent patients seem to justify ADEs—given that we ought to permit euthanasia per se, it seems that such an act should be treated simply as another form of treatment, and thus as a legitimate candidate for the type of care to which advance directives would apply. Consider, for example, a case in which a patient has a terminal illness with a clear trajectory, and that the end-stages of that illness will involve severe pain that cannot be adequately relieved without sedation to unconsciousness or near-unconsciousness, and an inability to meaningfully or adequately communicate one's wishes. In that case, the patient might prefer euthanasia once those conditions come to pass, but would be unable to make the euthanasia request at such a time—thus, an advance directive for euthanasia, it seems, would be appropriate. That said, if such a patient were undergoing continuous life-sustaining treatment, he or she could simply state in advance that he or she wishes such treatment to be withdrawn—in that case, one might claim, euthanasia would be unnecessary. However, not all patients in the type of case at issue will require life-sustaining treatment, in which case an ADE might be the only option that is consistent with the patient's desire not to live in such a condition. Further, many patients prefer to die quickly and painlessly rather than endure the slow, painful, and uncertain death that could come with the withdrawal of life-support. Indeed, a quick death would seem to be in the patient's best interests, considering the alternative.

Despite the legitimate reasons why patients might want an ADE, however, it is worth considering the possibility that—even if advance directives are ethically appropriate tools in general, including for the withdrawal of life-sustaining treatment—there is something problematic about their use for euthanasia. That is the issue addressed in this chapter—the issue of whether there are any *special* problems with the use of ADEs. It will be suggested that there is a plausible argument according to which ADEs indeed come with their own unique moral drawbacks. That argument is based on the premise that there are significant problems with the use of advance directives in general, in terms of how effective they are as tools for respecting patients' autonomy. It will be suggested that the upshot of those problems might be exacerbated in the case of ADEs, such that even if advance directives are ethically appropriate tools in general (i.e., even if their benefits ordinarily outweigh their costs), they are not appropriate for euthanasia (i.e., their benefits do not outweigh the *exacerbated* costs that come with ADEs) at least in a key class of cases. That, the chapter suggests, is the best prospect for an argument against the use of ADEs. Because that argument's premises will not be uncontroversial, however, this author stops short of a full-fledged endorsement of the argument, and concludes simply that it is *plausible* to hold that there are particular and significant moral problems with ADEs—problems that *might* warrant restricting or even banning the use of ADEs, even if both euthanasia and advance directives should otherwise be permitted.

Problems with Advance Directives

Despite their relatively widespread endorsement, advance directives are not without their problems. Some have argued that advance directives are not the effective tool for respecting patient autonomy that their proponents believe them to be—in particular, that the patient's prior instructions for care, or lack of care, often do not actually describe what the patient would want in the circumstances at issue (despite the patient's belief that they do).[4] This section describes what the author considers to be the most pressing of such problems. The following section explains how those problems pose a potentially serious ethical problem for the use of ADEs—a problem that does not necessarily apply to other sorts of advance directives, including directives for the withdrawal of life support.[5]

Knowing What We'd Want: The Problem of Affective Forecasting

One major problem with advance directives relates to *affective forecasting*—predicting how we will feel and what we will want in the future—especially as it pertains to situations with which we are not familiar or circumstances we have not experienced directly. This is particularly relevant to the use of advance directives—after all, in an advance directive we must predict how we will feel, what we will want, and how we will react to and cope with circumstances in which we do not currently find ourselves, and make a decision about treatment based on that prediction.

If that prediction is itself suspect, then so is the authority of the advance directive—it would, in that case, fail as an accurate representation of what we would *actually* want were we to be in such circumstances.

Yogi Berra is purported to have said, "It's tough to make predictions, especially about the future." Surely that is correct. But one might think that an exception to this general rule would be predictions about *ourselves*: what we would want, and how we would feel, given various possible future contingencies. After all, we have intimate *knowledge* about ourselves—specifically, about our *dispositional* features; that is, how we are inclined to react in different circumstances, based on characteristics including our values and desires, emotional tendencies, character traits, and psychological strengths and weaknesses. For that reason, we are, it seems, *predictable*. To some extent that is no doubt true. As it turns out, however, humans are very often quite bad at affective forecasting, especially when it comes to the types of predictions made in advance directives.

To see where we go wrong in affective forecasting and how such errors impugn the effectiveness of advance directives, it will be helpful to understand two basic ways in which we make the relevant sort of predictions. One way in which we make such predictions is that we *imagine* ourselves in the relevant circumstances and then infer, based on how we feel in response to the imagined scenario, that we would feel similarly in *actual* such circumstances. In the case of advance directives, we would imagine ourselves having the relevant medical condition(s), and in so doing imaginatively simulate how we would feel and what we would want if we were in such circumstances. The reaction to the simulation then would be used as strong evidence of how we actually would react if we had the medical conditions at issue, and on that basis we would make decisions for treatment or lack thereof. For example, when deciding whether we would wish to continue living if permanently confined to a bed, attached to a ventilator, and unable to communicate, we imagine how we would feel, what life would be like, and whether we would be able to satisfy our desires and honor our values, if in such a state. If the reaction to that imaginative simulation were sufficiently positive (e.g., "it wouldn't be a good quality of life, but it seems better than death"), then we would opt for continued treatment. If the reaction were sufficiently negative (e.g. "I wouldn't want to live like that"), then we might opt for removal of the life-sustaining ventilator.

Imaginative prediction, however, is a tenuous strategy for affective forecasting. One reason is that the way we feel when considering a hypothetical scenario is easily influenced by our mood and background emotional state, which in turn can be influenced by random factors. In one famous study, for instance, subjects reported higher overall life satisfaction on sunny days than on rainy days—thus, subjects believed that the way they felt *when* thinking about their lives was *caused* by thinking about their lives, when in fact it was caused (in large measure) by the weather.[6] Along similar lines, it has been shown that fear can be mistaken for, or cause feelings of, sexual attraction—one's feeling of attraction, in such cases, is *not* caused by features of the person to whom one feels attracted, but by (for example) the fear-inducing swaying of the suspension bridge one is on.[7] The point is this: We often are awash in various contingent affective dispositions that can taint the way we respond to all circumstances, imagined and real. Thus, affective responses to imagined circumstances are very often *not* stable indicators of our dispositions to react in specific ways to particular scenarios, but rather are the result of random fluctuations in our psychological makeup, caused by fleeting factors outside our control and unbeknownst to us.

Additionally, we are prone to a *particular* sort of bias in imaginative prediction when it comes to determining to what degree positive states of affairs will make us happy and negative states of affairs will make us unhappy—a bias that is directly relevant to the sort of decisions made in advance directives. The bias is based on a well-known psychological phenomenon called "focalism." Focalism implies that when confronted with a hypothetical case, the novel and salient characteristics of the scenario play a dominant role in determining emotional reaction, and people tend to ignore or downplay other more ordinary or mundane aspects of the case that nevertheless could have a greater role to play regarding how a person actually would feel in such a situation.[8] If, for example, someone asked you to consider how happy you would be with your life, overall, if you lost your left hand, you naturally focus on the loss of your hand, rather than all the other things that make for a happy life, such as fulfilling work, personal and professional accomplishment, and loving relationships with family and friends. Thus, the simulated emotions that accompany imagining losing your left hand will be disproportionately negative, because the "in focus" feature of the scenario is itself negative—one's response to *that* aspect of the case will dominate, in comparison with one's responses (or lack of responses) to other aspects that are not in focus but that might nevertheless significantly mitigate or compensate for the loss of one's hand. Thus, one will tend to overestimate the badness of such an event. And because advance directives call on us to make predictions in unfortunate circumstances, we will tend to think that such situations would be worse for us than they actually would be. This may lead, for example, to a directive forbidding life-sustaining treatment in a situation in which we would want to continue living, were we to actually find ourselves in such a state.

The other main method of affective forecasting is theoretical rather than imaginative: it involves invoking our *beliefs* about how we are likely to feel and what we are likely to want in various sorts of situations. That is, we have *theories* about our own affective dispositions, and we rely on those theories to predict our affective responses. Consider, for instance, a person who is very physically active and strongly values both living an active life as well as being highly self-sufficient. This person believes that he or she could not be happy without significant mobility and independence, based on what he or she knows of his or her own current values and desires. On that basis, this person concludes that being permanently bedridden or paralyzed would be worse than death, and thus indicates in an advance directive that he or she is to receive no life-saving treatment if being in such a state is to be the result.

As it turns out, however, theorizing about our affective dispositions is also highly prone to error—our theories, in other words, are very often wrong. A mundane yet telling example is that we are bad at predicting how much variety we desire in food choices over time. In one study, subjects were asked to choose a snack for each of three consecutive Mondays.[9] People tended to choose a mix of items, for example, two of their favorite and one of their second-favorite item; they were disappointed, however, on the days that they did not get their favorite snack. In this case, the subjects theorized that they preferred a certain kind and degree of variety over time, when in fact they did *not* prefer such variety—they were wrong about what they would want in the future situations they were charged with deciding about *because* they believed a false theory about themselves. This is just one example; but it is representative of a broader phenomenon.[10] The upshot is this: If, as the research suggests, we're prone to having false theories regarding simple and familiar aspects of ourselves, such as which snacks we prefer, then so much the worse for complex and unfamiliar cases—just the sorts of cases about which we are asked to choose in advance directives. Although we might *think* we know ourselves well enough to predict what we'd want in various possible future medical situations, it is highly questionable whether that is indeed the case.

Furthermore, research shows that we are prone to a particular false theory about ourselves that directly calls into question the sorts of choices made in advance directives—we fail to appreciate the power of our *psychological immune system*, that is, the degree to which we are able to mentally adapt to negative circumstances.[11] In other words, we believe that in response to events that negatively impact our well-being we will suffer emotional and psychological harm to a degree *far greater* than the degree to which we will *actually* suffer those effects—in reality, the emotional and psychological harm of such events is far more muted, and in many cases disappears almost entirely over time. The failure to recognize the strength of our psychological immune system is known as "immune neglect." Like focalism, immune neglect can cause us to overestimate how bad things will be, and thus contribute to decisions in advance directives that fail to cohere with what we actually would want and how we actually would feel in such circumstances.

As a case in point, patients with serious illnesses generally rate their quality of life as being significantly *higher* than others rate the patients' quality of life—even others who have an intimate knowledge of the relevant illnesses and the patients, such as close family members and health care professionals.[12] In one telling study, the following question was presented to healthy people, oncologists, and current cancer patients: *Would you accept a grueling course of chemotherapy for three extra months of life?* Six percent of oncologists answered "yes," 10 percent of healthy people answered "yes," and 42 percent of current cancer patients answered "yes."[13] The likely explanation of this stark discrepancy between how current cancer patients view their own quality of life and how others view it is that the non-patients suffer from a combination of immune neglect and focalism—phenomena that are minimized once you actually *experience* the condition in question. Thus, advance directives suffer from what one author calls the *Green Eggs and Ham* phenomenon: Unless a person has directly experienced a certain condition, he or she cannot accurately predict what his or her feelings and desires would be if the person actually found himself or herself in that condition.[14] The reference here is to the famous Dr. Seuss story, in which the protagonist inaccurately predicts that he will dislike green eggs and ham—once he tries them, he discovers that they are delicious. The protagonist might have imaginatively simulated eating green eggs and ham and felt disgusted; he might have relied on the theory that foods that are both green and not vegetables will taste bad. But regardless of how he arrived at his affective forecast, he could not know what green eggs and ham would taste like without actually trying them. Likewise, without having experienced the medical condition about which we are deciding, we are in a poor position to know what we would indeed want vis-à-vis treatment were we to have such a condition, especially given the natural biases of focalism and immune neglect. This seriously impugns the accuracy of many advance directives, and thus the degree to which honoring such directives stands to respect their authors' autonomy.

Balancing Specificity and Generality: The Problem of Translation

An additional problem with the accuracy of advance directives is based on the difficulty of *translating* written directions in an advance directive into concrete instructions for treatment, or lack of treatment, in complex context-driven cases in the real world. Often, the simplicity of the instructions in advance directives belies the complexity of the case at hand. Advance directives often focus on the general, major conditions and symptoms that patients fear—such as vegetative state, coma, terminal illness, ventilator-dependency, pain, and dementia. They rarely go into detail about the various specific *ways* in which these conditions and symptoms can manifest. In general, any brief description of a scenario inevitably will leave out important details—real life is simply too complex to be captured in a relatively simply described case. Therefore, because that is what advance directives contain, there will be a significant question about whether instructions in advance directives even *apply* to particular cases that arise in the real world—despite *some* significant similarity between described cases and actual cases, there inevitably will be aspects of the real-life situation that are not discussed in the directive or that are mentioned in ambiguous terms; and the way those blanks are filled in might make all the difference when it comes to what the patient would want. Thus, when a surrogate is charged with implementing the patient's directive, there will be a problem of accurately interpreting and translating those instructions into directions that are indeed what the patient would want—if the directive is too general or insufficiently described to apply clearly to the case at hand, then there is a significant chance that such a translation will be inaccurate.

Research backs up this concern. In one important study, surrogates were asked to make decisions for their loved ones in hypothetical scenarios, and those results were compared with what the patients themselves said they would want.[15] Three different groups were compared—one in which the surrogates had no advance directive to follow, one in which they did have their loved ones' advance directives, and a third in which the surrogates both had the directive and discussed it with their loved ones. As it turned out, the accuracy of the surrogates' decisions (as compared with the patients' decisions) was statistically equivalent among the three groups—having advance directives, even when they were discussed with the patient, did not improve the accuracy of the surrogates' decision making. A plausible explanation is the problem with specificity mentioned above; advance directives simply are not detailed enough to meaningfully apply to the complex, context-sensitive cases that arise in the real world.

Of course, advance directives could be made more specific—they could describe various scenarios with a significant degree of detail, attempting to capture all the complexity of cases that might actually arise. The more specific the scenarios, however, the less likely they are to exist in real life—and it would be unworkable to describe so many cases so as to significantly alleviate that problem (such a document would be so onerous as to preclude its practical feasibility). The upshot is that any practically realistic advance directive either will be too general to provide meaningful, accurate instructions in real-life situations, or it will be too specific to be likely to apply to cases that actually occur. Thus, because of the nature of the documents themselves, in concert with certain human limitations, advance directives very often fail to accurately represent what the patient would want.

The Limited Usefulness of Advance Directives

Despite these significant problems, it could be suggested that advance directives are useful in a limited class of cases: those in which the patient has experience with the conditions and/or symptoms at issue, and about which the patient has issued specific, unambiguous instructions about the case at hand, such as might occur with a disease with a clear and predictable trajectory. Indeed, depending on the degree to which these sorts of factors pertain, it is likely that there would be a range of accuracy for advance directives, ranging from essentially useless (i.e., providing no significant evidence of what the patient would actually want) to highly accurate (i.e., providing very strong such evidence), even if, as their most staunch critics maintain, the majority of advance directives are close to the former end of the spectrum. At the very least, it is plausible that an advance directive can, at least sometimes, provide *some* evidence of what the patient would want, and are at least to *some* degree translatable and applicable to the situation that actually will come to pass. It will be suggested that it is these marginal cases—cases in which advance directives are neither useless nor highly accurate—that have significant ethical implications specifically for the use of ADEs.

Ethical Issues with Marginally Effective Advance Directives: Euthanasia versus Removing Life Support

The type of case that raises ethical problems for ADEs are cases in which a patient's advance instructions for euthanasia in certain future circumstances imply that the patient *probably* would want euthanasia in the real-world situation at issue, yet it is *not* the case that that probability is especially high. What follows shall address why such problems might present a *special* worry for ADEs—a worry that does not also apply to advance directives for the withdrawal of life support. First, however, this section addresses in more detail the type of case at issue and why such cases present problems with the use of ADEs. Suppose that (1) a patient has requested euthanasia should he or she be permanently ventilator dependent, unable to communicate, and be expected to die, with 90 percent probability or greater, with one month, (2) the patient has experienced being on a ventilator long term, and (3) the patient is clear and consistent in his or her instructions. Now suppose that the conditions outlined in the advance directive come to pass. Of course, there will be other features of the case that might not have been described in the directive. The patient might, for example, from time to time indicate some degree of joy via subtle facial cues, for example slight smiles (in which case the question arises whether that counts as "communication"—this would be an instance of problem with specificity and context sensitivity). And the patient might not have experienced the precise condition in question (e.g., terminal illness), even if he or she has experienced some of its aspects (e.g., long-term ventilation). Nevertheless, even taking into account the problems with affective forecasting and translation, it might be reasonable to think, in a case like this, that the directive for euthanasia is *somewhat* reliable, such that it raises the probability that the person would indeed want euthanasia to more than 50 percent, but it is not *highly* reliable due to the problems mentioned. Suppose, for instance, that in such a case the probability that the person would want euthanasia is 60 percent—more likely than not, but not particularly high. In that case, even though performing euthanasia has the greatest probability of honoring the patient's wishes, the argument can be made that surrogates should err on the side of life—that even though we are more likely to respect the person's autonomy by performing euthanasia than by not doing so, the price of being wrong is too high, and thus euthanasia ought not be performed. On this view, it would be *worse* to end someone's life when that's not what he or she would want than to *fail* to end someone's life when it *is* what he or she would want. There are various ways to argue for this view, none of which will be uncontroversial but all of which are at least somewhat plausible—such arguments are discussed below. First, however, it is instructive to consider in a bit more detail the general form of the argument under consideration: That in certain cases surrogates should err on the side of life even when someone *probably* wants euthanasia.

Such an argument is based on a calculation of the *expected value* of performing euthanasia in the type of case in question. The expected value of a decision with an uncertain outcome can be thought of as the average "return," positive or negative, that one can expect from that decision, taking into account the fact that various outcomes are possible. More precisely, the expected value of a decision is the average (mean) value of the outcomes of an infinite number of such decisions. Suppose, for example, that I decide to make a bet with you on the flip of a coin—you choose heads and I choose tails, and the loser pays the winner $10. The expected value of making such a bet is $0—if the flip were performed an infinite number of times, we should expect an equal number of heads and tails to come up, therefore we would each win $10 half the time and lose $10 half the time, thus breaking even. If, however, you were to win $20 if heads comes up and still lose only $10 if tails comes up, or alternatively, if the coin was biased such that heads comes up 75 percent of the time and tails 25 percent, then the expected value of the flip would be in your favor—it would be greater than $0 for you and less than $0 for me. In the first case you would win $20 half the time and lose $10 half the time, thus on average you would win $5 per flip; in the second case you would win $10 three times for every loss of $10, thus on average you would also win $5 per flip—the expected value of a flip in both cases would therefore be $5 for you and -$5 for me. (See below for a description of a more mathematically precise way of calculating expected value.)

If the expected value of a decision is greater than any alternative, then it is a good decision with respect to the value at issue, that is, it is the *best bet*; if not, then it is a bad decision, that is, *not* one's best bet. In the coin-flip case, the value at issue is *monetary* value; with regard to the ethics of ADEs, the relevant value is *moral* value. The argument under consideration is that expected moral value is maximized by *not* performing euthanasia when there is a modestly high probability (e.g., 60 percent) that the person would indeed want euthanasia performed in the case at issue. That will be the result given that it is significantly worse to perform euthanasia when a person would not want it than to fail to perform euthanasia when a person would want it. In that case, even though euthanasia *probably* is what the patient would want, performing euthanasia is not worth the risk, due to the fact that the "moral loss" of performing euthanasia when the patient actually *wouldn't* have wanted it would be so great—according to this argument, performing euthanasia given the uncertainty at issue would be a *bad bet*, morally speaking. We can represent this numerically as follows (Table 14.1).

In Table 14.1, the middle row represents the cases in which, in the first column, euthanasia is performed and the patient would prefer life, and in the second column, euthanasia is not performed and the patient would prefer death. As the argument under consideration has it, the moral (dis) value of the former case (represented here by the numerical value -10) is significantly worse (numerically lower) than the value of the latter case

Table 14.1

	Euthanasia Performed	Life Maintained
Would **prefer** this outcome	+5 (60%)	+10 (40%)
Would **not** prefer this outcome	−10 (40%)	−5 (60%)
Expected Value	−1	+1

(-5).The upper-left box represents the case in which the patient would prefer death and euthanasia is performed, and the upper-right box represents the case in which the patient would prefer life and euthanasia is *not* performed; the numerical values in those boxes are simply the positive analogs of the (dis)values of the middle two boxes. Finally, the lower two boxes show the expected values of each decision (performing euthanasia and maintaining life) and can be calculated as follows. For each of the two potential *outcomes* of each decision (either the patient prefers that decision or does not), the *value* of each outcome is multiplied by the *probability* of that outcome occurring. The results of that operation then are added together for each of the two potential outcomes, and the result is the expected value of the decision. Given, as the table represents, that it is significantly worse to perform euthanasia against the patient's will than to maintain the patient's life against his or her will, the expected value of maintaining life is greater than that of performing euthanasia.

But why might we think that euthanizing a patient against his or her will is worse than maintaining life against his or her will? One argument for such a view is that it seems to be a worse *autonomy violation* to end someone's life against her will than to keep a person alive against his or her will. In support of this, it could be argued that most people would—if given the choice between being kept alive against their will and being killed against their will—prefer the former case to the latter. A person generally desires *more strongly*, that is, that he or she is not killed against his or her will than that he or she is not kept alive against his or her will—and, plausibly, the degree of an autonomy violation is proportional to the strength of the desire that is thwarted by that violation.

Another argument for the claim that it is morally worse to end life against a person's will than to preserve life against a person's will is that, in the latter case, there is the opportunity to reevaluate the choice and correct it based on new information, but in the former case it is an irrevocable decision. Perhaps, that is, if we fail to end life when we're 60 percent sure that's what the patient would want, then new evidence will come to light that should make us highly confident about what the patient would indeed want, one way or the other.

For example, in the case of the terminal patient who is permanently ventilator dependent, even if we are 60 percent sure he or she would want his or her life ended, a caregiver might refrain from carrying out those wishes with an eye toward the possibility of new and relevant information (e.g., a clearer understanding of the patient's prior statements, preferences, and values; newly acquired medical evidence that more accurately describes the patient's current condition and prognosis), which might significantly alter our estimate of the probability to which the patient would want to live and would want to die. By failing to end the patient's life now, we leave open that possibility and thus have the option (if it should come to pass) of doing what the patient would want (and thus respecting his or her autonomy) with a far greater degree of certainty. Ending the patient's life forecloses that possibility, and thus, according to the argument under consideration, presents a strong prima facie reason to err on the side of life in such cases.

A final argument is based on the premise that life itself has at least some degree of intrinsic moral value, such that the preservation of human life per se (i.e., regardless of its quality or its bearer's desire to live) is an independent moral consideration in its own right. If that is correct, then there is necessarily a reason why it is worse to end a patient's life against her will, because there always is a prima facie moral reason to refrain from ending human life per se. And if the intrinsic value of preserving human life is great enough, it could provide the kind of significant moral reason at issue—the sort that would imply that we should preserve a patient's life even if doing so means *probably* doing something that the patient would not prefer, for at least some range of probabilities greater than 50 percent. This justification, unlike those discussed in the previous two paragraphs, would not be an *autonomy*-based reason to err on the side of life, but rather a reason based on the putatively distinct moral value of preserving human life itself.

Each of these considerations provides some basis for thinking it better to err on the side of life when ADEs have only a modestly greater than 50 percent chance of applying to the case at hand. Note, however, that those considerations apply to the use of advance directives for the withdrawal of life support just as they would to ADEs. In other words, the argument presented here, without some further explanation that would distinguish ADEs from advance directives for the withdrawal of life support, would appear to show that the latter sort of directive is just as problematic as the former in the type of cases at issue. Thus, it has not yet been shown that there is a problem with ADEs per se. Recall that the main issue here is not whether ADEs are morally illicit, but rather whether they are *specially* so, that is, whether there is something about ADEs that makes *them* morally illicit in particular. If the only way of showing that ADEs are morally problematic also shows that advance directives for the withdrawal of life support are equally problematic (and indeed, problematic for the same reasons), that is if the morally troubling feature of ADEs derives from a more *general* problem that applies to other sorts of advance directives as well, then it would not serve to distinguish ADEs in the relevant way.

With that in mind, the next section describes what the author takes to be the most promising way of setting ADEs apart from directives for the withdrawal of life support, such that there is indeed a special moral problem for ADEs. The relevant distinction relies on a fundamental difference between removal of life support and euthanasia—in the former case, the patient is *refusing treatment*, and in the latter case the patient is *requesting treatment*. The right to refuse treatment is widely considered to be stronger than the right to receive treatment. Indeed, the right to refuse treatment is thought to be more or less absolute—only in extremely rare cases involving significant harm to others would it be considered morally permissible to force-treat a competent patient, that is, to treat such a patient against his or her will, at least according to the prevailing view in medical ethics. Even granting the existence of a prima facie right to medical treatment, however, that right generally is thought to be relatively weak in comparison with the right to refuse treatment. For example, physicians who believe it is ethically inappropriate to provide treatment may refuse to do so—physicians are free to conscientiously refuse to provide treatment, at least in certain cases. However, it is widely thought that physicians are *never* (or almost never) free to conscientiously refuse to *withdraw* treatment at a competent patient's request—if a physician believes it is morally objectionable to withdraw treatment, then he or she nevertheless must comply with a competent patient's request to do so. To fail to accede to the patient's request would be a *bodily invasion* and a form of battery—unwanted touching—which is generally considered to be a particularly egregious sort of moral violation.

For the purposes here, there are two significant upshots of such a view. First, because the performance of euthanasia when a person prefers life *itself* involves bodily invasion, it provides an additional reason to believe that performing euthanasia when someone prefers to live is morally worse than failing to perform euthanasia when someone prefers to die. Second, and more importantly, it provides a basis for distinguishing

ADEs from advance directives for the removal of life support, in the sort of cases at issue. That is because the moral disvalue of bodily invasion must be included in the moral calculus when evaluating the use of marginally accurate advance directives. Even if it is morally right to err on the side of life with ADEs due to the considerations outlined above, when it comes to advance directives for removing life support the moral disvalue of bodily invasion might tip the ethical balance in the other direction, as that is an added moral negative involved in keeping someone on life support against his or her will. According to such an argument, the expected value calculations for removing life support and keeping it maintained would be as follows (Table 14.2).

Here, the calculation is the same as with euthanasia, except that the second column of the middle row—the case in which life support is maintained when it is *not* the patient's preference—has value 10 points less due to the moral disvalue of bodily invasion. On the argument in question, that disvalue is sufficient to change the expected value of maintaining the patient's life, that expected value is lower than the expected value of ending life. Thus, this is a plausible morally relevant difference between honoring a marginally accurate ADE and a marginally accurate advance directive for removing life support, such that the overall moral expected value of honoring the ADE is *worse* than not doing so, and the expected value of honoring the directive for removing life support is *better* than not doing so. The upshot, if this sort of argument succeeds, is that there is indeed a special moral problem with the use of ADEs, at least in certain cases.

Of course, this way of distinguishing ADEs from advance directives for withdrawing life support will be controversial to the extent to which it is controversial that ending life against a patient's will is worse than preserving life against the patient's will. The putative reasons described above that support such a view are not objection free. The autonomy-based reason—that people are in general more averse to having their lives end when that's not what they prefer than to being kept alive when that's not what they prefer—is plausible yet questionable; presumably, a full defense of such a premise would require an empirical justification.

Table 14.2

	Life Support Removed	Life Maintained
Would **prefer** this outcome	+5 (60%)	+10 (40%)
Would **not** prefer this outcome	-10 (40%)	-5 -10 = -15 (60%)
Expected Value	-1	-5

Further, it could be claimed that, even if correct, the implication for ADEs is just that we should *include* that issue in the directive. That is, we can ask people whether they have such a preference; indeed, we could even ask what they would prefer *given* the moderate probabilities at issue, for example we could find out what they would prefer in the case that we are 60 percent sure that they would want euthanasia. We also could ask these questions in light of the irrevocability issue—we could ask whether they would prefer that we hold off doing what they would *probably* want given the possibility of identifying in the future what they would *more* probably want. Giving patients such choices via the relevant sort of "meta-directive" seems to be the best way of respecting their autonomy, by providing for the greatest chance of doing what such patients prefer. The idea, then, is that ADEs do not present any *irresolvable* ethical problems, but simply call for an extra layer of moral support: they require a meta-directive.

It is important to note, however, that such a strategy itself will be susceptible to worries about translation and affective forecasting. The concern, then, is that meta-directives will not provide us with the certainty needed to avoid the kind of expected-value calculation that grounds the argument in question. Consider, once more, the case of the ventilator-dependent patient with an ADE that is moderately likely to apply to the case at hand, such that we can be 60 percent sure that the patient would indeed want euthanasia in that case. Now suppose that we also have a meta-directive from the patient that says that *if* we're 60 percent sure that the patient would want euthanasia based on the original directive then we should go ahead with the procedure. If the meta-directive is itself open to translation and affective forecasting problems, however, then it might provide only 60 percent confidence. Thus, the need for an expected value calculation reemerges. Additionally, even though the meta-directive provides *some* added evidence of what the patient would want in such circumstances, and thus even though it raises the probability that the patient would indeed want euthanasia (compared with just the original directive), it does not raise that probability to a particularly *high* level of certainty, due to its own merely modest probability of applying. Thus, in many such cases, the expected-value calculation still will end up in favor of erring on the side of life. That said, meta-directives might tip the balance in favor of euthanasia in *borderline* cases, that is, cases in which the expected value calculation without the meta-directive is only *barely* on the side of not performing euthanasia.

Let us take stock. This chapter has tried to show that there is a plausible argument (although by no means a conclusive one) against honoring ADEs when doing so is only moderately likely to result in a decision that the patient would want—a type of situation that would be likely to occur due to certain flaws with the use of advance directives in general. It has suggested that these arguments apply to ADEs per se (although not necessarily to *all* ADEs); in particular, they do not apply to the removal of life support due to a key difference between euthanasia and withdrawing life support—that the latter case, but not the former, involves *refusing* treatment.

An important question that remains at this point is what do these arguments mean for *policy*? In light of the concerns raised, should we, as a society, ban the use of ADEs, even if euthanasia should be permitted for competent patients? The answer to that question depends on the extent to which it is feasible to identify when an ADE is, in all likelihood, only marginally accurate and when it has a much higher chance of accuracy. If we can be confident in making such judgments then the use of ADEs could be restricted to the latter type of case, and we thus could be confident that ADEs are being permitted when their use stands to have a positive moral expected value. Such cases might involve situations in which the patient has a clearly and narrowly circumscribed path of illness; a simple, specific, and clear set of instructions for exactly when euthanasia is to be performed; and experience with, and a clear and strong memory of, the symptoms and other experiences that are to be expected as the illness progresses. It seems plausible that the probability of respecting the patient's autonomy in that sort of case by honoring the patient's ADE is quite high; and insofar as such cases can be distinguished from those in which ADEs only will be marginally accurate, the possibility exists of policy—good policy—that permits the use of ADEs.[16] Of course, whether such a policy is realistic depends on whether it will be practically feasible to implement the relevant regulatory regime, due to various political, social, institutional, and economic factors. Ethically, however, at least in principle, it seems that good policy is possible here—policy that distinguishes between ADEs of different levels of probable accuracy, and thus policy that allows for cases in which honoring an ADE indeed has a greater expected moral value than not doing so, and protects against the use of ADEs in other cases.

Advance Directives for Euthanasia and Severe Dementia

This section discusses a kind of case which, although not presenting any moral problems unique to ADEs (the same problems will apply to advance directives for withholding and withdrawing life-support), does warrant highlighting because it involves a type of situation in which ADEs, if permitted, stand to be relatively prevalent, and in which using ADEs is potentially highly morally problematic.

The type of case at issue involves *severe dementia*. Many people want to avoid such a state, even if it means living a shorter life, not simply because they fear the experiences that such a state entails, but also (perhaps primarily) because they desire to avoid what they perceive to be the indignity involved in dementia in its most serious forms. In particular, many people wish to avoid loss of connection to that which they used to value, including loved ones, and many people do not want to be remembered as a confused and dependent shell of their former self. Such people very well might opt for euthanasia in such circumstances, if given the choice, via advance directive. As it stands, such patients generally are within their legal rights to refuse life-sustaining treatment; but many people who suffer from severe dementia have no life-threatening condition that would provide the release they would want, thus euthanasia often will be the only way of achieving their goal. It is therefore reasonable to suppose that if ADEs are permitted, directives in which the condition for implementation is severe dementia, or the occurrence of particular symptoms characteristic of severe dementia, will be fairly common.

The problem, however, is that in many cases of severe dementia, death does not appear to be in the patient's best interests—in some cases, the life of the patient with dementia, as it is experienced by him or her, is decidedly worth living. For example, the patient might enjoy simple pleasures such as eating and watching TV, or interacting on some minimal level with nursing home staff and residents. Indeed, such a person might be happy, overall, and suffer from no major illnesses, physical disabilities, or pain that would seriously impair his or her quality of life. This type of case gives pause when it comes to honoring a directive that would result in the patient's death, such as withholding antibiotics for an easily curable but life-threatening infection. The same moral qualms apply to ADEs in this sort of case.

Various arguments have been proffered in support of the contention that there is something seriously immoral about allowing a happy and otherwise healthy patient to die in such cases. Some have argued that the patient, due to the extreme psychological differences between himself or herself now and his or her prior competent self, is literally a different person now than when her or she made the choice in the advance directive; and because one person's choice does not apply to a different person, the directive no would longer apply.[17] Others have claimed that paternalism could be justified in this sort of case, due to the degree of harm that would ensue by allowing the patient to die.[18] It is argued elsewhere that we do not respect a person's autonomy by honoring the desires and values he or she used to have, but only those that a person currently has—thus if the patient's dementia is so severe that he or she genuinely has lost the desires and values that prompted the choice against continued life, we do not respect the patient's autonomy by honoring that choice; in that case, other moral considerations, such as the patient's current happiness, will be dispositive.[19] The details and merits of these arguments shall not be addressed here. The point is this: *If* any of these arguments succeeds, and more generally if—despite an informed and accurate advance directive—it is immoral to allow patients to die in the type of case at issue, and thus (presumably) immoral to kill such patients, then permitting the use of ADEs in general will come with serious moral costs. That is because the prevailing legal regime supports the use of life-limiting advance directives in cases of severe dementia, via the refusal of treatment. It is therefore highly likely that if ADEs were permitted there would be no curb on their use in such cases, resulting in a proliferation of the sort of putative moral transgression at issue.

That said, the upshot for policy (i.e., the question of whether to permit ADEs) plausibly depends on how often ADEs will be used for severe dementia and must be balanced against the good that ADEs stand to do in other cases. That in part will be an empirical issue (just how prevalent use of such directives would be) and in part an ethical one (whether the value of ADEs in the right sort of case outweighs, morally speaking, the disvalue of their use in cases of happy dementia, taking into account the relative frequency of each type of case). That is a question that cannot be answered here. The point is that the potentially problematic use of ADEs for severe dementia is at least a serious moral consideration that should be taken into account in any analysis of the overall policy prospects for ADEs.

Conclusion

This chapter outlines what the author takes to be the most promising way of arguing that there is a particular compelling moral problem with the use of ADEs, at least in a significant class of cases—a problem that is compatible with the propriety of euthanasia for competent patients, does not impugn the appropriateness of advance directives in general (although it derives from concerns about the general accuracy of advance directives), and does not imply that it is morally problematic to use advance directives for the withdrawal of life support. Further, it is suggested that permitting the use of ADEs might be morally worrisome due to their probable extension to cases involving severe dementia. Although perhaps not a *special* problem for the use of ADEs (because the same concerns apply to refusal of life-sustaining treatment), it is a *pressing* problem, given the plausibility of the view that, prior wishes notwithstanding, it would be seriously immoral to kill a patient with severe dementia whose present life is decidedly worth living.

That said, the ultimate decision whether ADEs should be allowed (assuming that euthanasia otherwise about ought to be permitted) turns on various empirical issues that cannot be resolved here. With regard to the issue of severe dementia, even if it is wrong to euthanize happy dementia patients regardless of any advance directive, the consequence for ADE policy depends on (1) how many patients would author ADEs for severe dementia, (2) how many clinicians would be willing to implement such directives in the case of happy dementia patients, and (3) how many ADEs would be implemented in the *right* sort of cases (those in which the patient would indeed want to be euthanized). Perhaps the value of (3) will be greater than the relevant risks, especially if those risks are significantly mitigated by low numbers vis-à-vis (1) and (2). Similarly, regarding problems of accuracy, whether ADEs should be permitted in general given that they should *not* be permitted when they have only a marginally high likelihood of accurately representing a patient's wishes turns on the extent of the collective ability to identify *when* an ADE stands to be marginally accurate and when it stands to have a very high probability of accuracy. If that determination can be made, then ADEs can be permitted in the latter type of case and their use banned in the former type; if not, then we must decide whether to ban or permit *all* ADEs—something that would depend on the *overall* (society-wide) expected moral value of each option, based on the likely prevalence, as well as the expected moral value, of euthanasia being performed in each kind of case. Ethical analysis per se, therefore, only takes us so far—it can, perhaps, identify the sorts of cases in which implementing an ADE is morally permissible and the kinds of cases in which it is not; but policy recommendation also requires identifying how likely each sort of case is to occur in the real world. That is a task for social scientists, and thus any justified policy position, either for or against permitting the use of ADEs, must involve an interdisciplinary approach.

Notes

1. Throughout this chapter, the term "advance directive" refers to advance directive *forms* or *documents*, as opposed, for example, to advance *statements* made by the patient, even if such statements are recorded in the patient's medical record. Additionally, the sort of documents to which "advance directives" refers are *living wills*—specific instructions for treatment or lack of treatment in particular circumstances, and descriptions of general values and preferences that might apply

to various cases (e.g., the desire to prioritize lack of pain over mental lucidity), or a belief in the "sanctity of life." This is a common usage of "advance directive," although it is worth noting that the term is sometimes used to include verbal statements as well as *proxy designations* or *powers of attorney for health care*: documents that specify who is to be the patient's surrogate should he or she become incompetent to make her own medical decisions.

2. Likewise, the patient can indicate wishes *for* treatment. However, because treating is usually the default (both because treating is the modus operandi of physicians, and because family members often are reluctant to refuse treatment for their loved ones—especially life-saving treatment), most advance directives will *limit* care.

3. Thus, this chapter uses "euthanasia" to mean what some call "active euthanasia," as opposed to "passive euthanasia," which refers to withholding or withdrawing life-sustaining treatment. This chapter avoids that linguistic convention for several reasons. First, there is nothing "passive" about withdrawing life support—shutting off someone's ventilator, for example, is a decidedly "active" occurrence. Second, the way the term "euthanasia" and its cognates most often are used in English fails to support the convention. This is seen most clearly with the verb "*euthanize*."

Consider the claim that Bob was euthanized. Such a claim, in ordinary contexts, is not ambiguous between the claim that Bob was directly killed (for his own good or at his request) and the claim that life-sustaining treatment was withheld or withdrawn—it means the former. Indeed, it is simply an obvious misuse of language to say that a patient who was not given life-saving treatment was *euthanized* (Is every DNR order an order to *euthanize* patients who undergo cardiopulmonary arrest? Does a physician who refrains from giving a life-saving blood transfusion to a competent Jehovah's Witness *euthanize* such a person?). These sorts of considerations provide good reasons, in the author's view, to abandon use of the term "passive euthanasia" indeed, in bioethics the term is already somewhat passé. In short, this author thinks that the terminological convention of distinguishing between "passive" and "active" euthanasia is clumsy and unfitting; and refrains from using it, instead using "*euthanasia*" and "*withholding or withdrawing life-sustaining treatment.*"

4. For an overview of such problems, see Fagerlin & Schneider (2004).

5. Several authors have argued that the problems with advance directives in general (including the problems discussed in this section) make ADEs problematic. In this author's view, however, those other authors have not identified problems with ADEs per se, because the problems they identify would likewise apply to other sorts of advance directives, such as directives for the withdrawal of life support. See, e.g., Francis (1993), Otlowski (1997), and van Delden (2004). To identify a special problem with ADEs, what is needed is a plausible explanation of why ADEs are problematic in a way that does not apply to advance directives for other acts (especially, for the withdrawal of life-sustaining treatment); providing a potential such explanation is the central aim of this chapter.

6. Schwarz and Clore (1983).

7. Dutton and Aron (1974).

8. Schkade and Kahneman (1998), Wilson et al. (2000).

9. Read and Loewenstein (1995).

10. For an overview of various ways in which false self-theories result in defective affective forecasting, see Loewenstein & Schkade (1998).

11. Gilbert et al. (1998).

12. Sprangers and Aaronson (1992), Tang and McCorkle (2002), McPherson and Addington-Hall (2003).

13. Slevin et al. (1990).

14. Forrow (1994).

15. Ditto et al. (2001).

16. That said, if the moral disvalue of using euthanasia when the patient would not want it is great enough, then nothing short of virtual infallibility would justify allowing ADEs. On such a view, it is *so* bad to perform euthanasia when it is not what the patient would want that *any* realistic risk of that happening is not worth whatever moral good is to come from permitting ADEs (in particular, respecting the autonomy and promoting the welfare of many other patients). Thus, to justify the use of ADEs when it is not 100 percent certain that the patient would want euthanasia (which will probably be every case), even if we can be *highly confident* that the patient would want euthanasia, we must assume that the moral disvalue of "mistakenly" performing euthanasia is not so great as to make it unethical to take *any* realistic risk of doing so.

17. Dresser 1989; King 1996; Quante 1999.

18. Dresser 1992; Dresser and Robertson 1989.

19. Vogelstein 2016, forthcoming.

Bibliography

Ditto, Peter H.; Danks, Joseph H.; Smucker, William D.; Bookwala, Jamila; Coppola, Kristen M.; Dresser, Rebecca; Fagerlin, Angela; Gready, R. Mitchell; Houts, Renate M.; Lockhart, Lisa K.; and Zyzanski, Stephen (2001). "Advance Directives As Acts of Communication: A Randomized Controlled Trial." *Archives of Internal Medicine* 162: 421–30.

Dresser, R. (1989). "Advance Directives, Self-Determination, and Personal Identity. In *Advance Directives in Medicine* (155–70), C. Hackler, R. Moseley, and D. Vawter (eds.). New York: Praeger Publishers.

Dresser, R. (1992). "Autonomy Revisited: The Limits of Anticipatory Choices." In: *Dementia and Aging: Ethics, Values, and Policy Choices* (71–85), R. Binstock, S. Post, and P. Whitehouse (eds.). Baltimore: Johns Hopkins University Press.

Dresser, R., and J. Robertson (1989). Quality of Life and Non-Treatment Decisions for Incompetent Patients: A Critique of the Orthodox Approach." *Law, Medicine & Health Care* 17: 234–44.

Dutton, D. G., and A. P. Aaron (1974). "Some Evidence for Heightened Sexual Attraction Under Conditions of High Anxiety." *Journal of Personality and Social Psychology* 30: 510–17.

Fagerlin, A., and C. E. Schneider (2004). "Enough. The Failure of the Living Will." *Hastings Center Report* 34(2): 30–42.

Forrow, L. (1994). "The *Green Eggs and Ham* Phenomena." *Hastings Center Report* 24(6): S29–S32.

Francis, Leslie (1993). "Advance Directives for Voluntary Euthanasia: A Volatile Combination?" *Journal of Medicine and Philosophy* 18(3): 297–322.

Gilbert, D. T., E. C. Pinel, T. D. Wilson, S. J. Blumberg, & T. P. Wheatley (1998). "Immune Neglect: A Source of Durability Bias in Affective Forecasting." *Journal of Personality and Social Psychology* 75: 617–38.

King, N. M. P. (1996). *Making Sense of Advance Directives* (rev. ed.). Washington, DC: Georgetown University Press.

Loewenstein, G., and D. Schkade (1998). "Wouldn't It Be Nice? Predicting Future Feelings." In *Foundations of Hedonic Psychology: Scientific Perspectives on Enjoyment and Suffering*. E. Diener, N. Schwartz, and D. Kahneman (eds.). New York: Russell Sage Foundation.

McPherson. C. J., and J. M. Addington-Hall (2003). "Judging the Quality of Care at the End of Life: Can Proxies Provide Reliable Information." *Social Science & Medicine* 56: 95–109.

Otlowski, M. (1997). *Voluntary Euthanasia and the Common Law* (Oxford: Clarendon).

Quante, M. (1999). "Precedent Autonomy and Personal Identity." *Kennedy Institute of Ethics Journal* 9: 365–81.

Read, D., and G. Loewenstein. 1995. "Diversification Bias: Explaining the Discrepancy in Variety Seeking Between Combined and Separated Choices." *Journal of Experimental Psychology: Applied* 1: 34–49.

Schkade, David A., and Daniel Kahneman. 1998. "Does Living in California Make People Happy? A Focusing Illusion in Judgments of Life Satisfaction." *Psychological Science* 9(5): 340–46.

Schwarz, N., and G. L. Clore. 1983. "Mood, Misattribution, and Judgments of Well-Being: Informative and Directive Functions of Affective States." *Journal of Personality and Social Psychology* 45: 513–23.

Slevin M. L., L. Stubbs, H. J. Plant, P. Wilson, W. M. Gregory, P. J. Armes, and S. M. Downer. 1990. "Attitudes to Chemotherapy: Comparing Views of Patients with Cancer with Those of Doctors, Nurses, and General Public." *British Medical Journal* 300(6737):1458–60.

Sprangers, M. A., and N. K. Aaronson. (1992). "The Role of Health Care Providers and Significant Others in Evaluating the Quality of Life of Patients with Chronic Disease: A Review." *Journal of Clinical Epidemiology* 45: 743–60.

Tang, S. T., and R. McCorkle. 2002. "Use of Family Proxies in Quality of Life Research for Cancer Patients at the End of Life: A Literature Review." *Cancer Investigation* 20: 1086–104.

van Delden, J. J. M. 2004. "The Unfeasibility of Requests for Euthanasia in Advance Directives." *Journal of Medical Ethics* 30: 447–51.

Vogelstein, E. 2016. "Autonomy and the Moral Authority of Advance Directives." *Journal of Medicine and Philosophy* 41 (5): 500–520.

Vogelstein, E. (forthcoming 2016). "Deciding for the Incompetent." *Routledge Handbook of End-of-Life Ethics*. John Davis (ed.) (New York: Routledge).

Wilson, Timothy D., T. Wheatley, J. M. Meyers, D. T. Gilbert, and D. Axsom. 2000. "Focalism: A Source of Durability Bias in Affective Forecasting." *Journal of Personality and Social Psychology* 78(5): 821–36.

CHAPTER FIFTEEN

Pediatric Euthanasia

Jacob M. Appel

Few topics in contemporary bioethics are likely to generate as much controversy as the various practices lumped together under the collective heading of pediatric euthanasia. To contemporary physicians and philosophers, the distinction between these loosely related interventions are often apparent and well defined. Infanticide generally refers to the killing of a child younger than one year old, and neonaticide refers exclusively to the killing of an infant within 24 hours of birth. Less commonly discussed are pedocide (the act of killing any child or children) and filicide or prolicide (the act of killing one's own children).

Euthanasia refers "to the act of painlessly putting to death persons suffering from incurable conditions or diseases," and usually is limited to cases in which the goal is to serve the interests of the victim with the purpose of death being to end the physical, emotional, or existential pain and suffering of the subject.[1] Further distinction can be made with regard to whether the pediatric subject is able to assent to such a fate (or consent, in jurisdictions where the legal consent of minors is permitted under certain circumstances) or whether such an outcome is imposed at the judgment of a third party, such as a parent or doctor—a phenomenon analogous to "voluntary" and "nonvoluntary" euthanasia among adults. In the case of neonates and infants—such as those whose lives are terminated through the Groningen Protocol in the Netherlands—neither assent nor consent is obviously ever possible.[2] In contrast, some older minors are capable of making informed choices about when and how to end their lives; several jurisdictions, including Belgium and (to a degree) the Netherlands, allow them to do so. Lastly, a distinction must be made between actively ending life—such as through assisted suicide or aid-in-dying—and passively allowing a minor to die.[3]

These distinctions often are of relatively modern origin. As recently as the early 20th century, eugenicists and progressives conflated infanticide for the social good with euthanasia for the benefit of the subject. Distinctions between active and passive euthanasia only came to the fore of the bioethics literature in the 1970s and 1980s and remain fraught with controversy. What is clear is that when discussing "pediatric euthanasia" it must both clear and precise which practices one has in mind.

History

Infanticide in Pre-Modern Times

Contemporary Western culture places considerable value on the preservation of the lives of infants and children. As a corollary, Western nations either prohibit the active termination of the lives of minors or impose significant legal restrictions and ethical proscriptions upon the practice. These protections, however, reflect a rather new development in the history of humankind. Anthropological data suggest that infanticide has been widespread across cultures since Paleolithic times. According to Laila Williams, "infanticide has been practiced on every continent and by people on every level of cultural complexity, from hunters and gatherers to high civilizations, including our own ancestors."[4] Joseph Birdsell argued that "systematic infanticide has been a necessary procedure for spacing human children, presumably beginning after man's entry into the niche of bipedalism, and lasting until the development of advanced agriculture."[5] Estimates of infanticide rates among prehistoric humans are gross approximations: Williams places the figure at 15 percent to 20 percent, James Neel at 15 percent to 20 percent, and Birdsell at 15 percent to 50 percent. Infanticide remains a frequent practice in extant hunter-gatherer societies.[6] Edward Moffat Weyer noted significant gender imbalances among Eskimo populations attributable to the killing of newborn females.[7] Weyer argued these deaths represented part of a "population policy" to ensure tribal survival. Although many explanations exist for particular patterns of infanticide among prehistoric and contemporary hunter-gatherer peoples, Larry Milner has noted that, "If our forefathers had to practice infanticide, it was out of the hardness of their lives, not the hardness of their hearts."[8]

Many societies in classical antiquity embraced infanticide to varying degrees. According to W. K. Lacey, "there can be no doubt whatever that the exposure of surplus children was practiced throughout antiquity."[9] The Greek city-state of Sparta appears to have had a highly complex system of infanticide motivated by perceived communal welfare. The laws of Lycurgus dictated that the decision would be that of the authorities. "If they found [the infant] well-built and sturdy, they would order it reared."[10] In contrast, "if the infant was ill-born or deformed, they would order it brought to . . . the chasm at the foot of Mt. Taygetus, where it was abandoned or thrown off a cliff."[11] In Athens, where fathers—rather than the state—had the final say in determining whether an infant was permitted to live, infanticide appears to have been widely accepted. Plato seems to approve of infanticide in Book V of the *Republic*. Of his guardian class, he explains that "the best men must cohabit with the best women in as many cases as possible and the worst with the worst in the fewest, and that the offspring of the one must be reared and that of the other not."[12] In book VII of his *Politics*, Aristotle appears to endorse infanticide directly, writing, "As for the exposure and nurture of infants, let there be a law against nourishing those that are deformed."[13] The "majority of newborns that were killed by Greek parents were either disabled, illegitimate or born to parents who could not afford to raise them."[14]

Roman society also appears to have accepted infanticide. Like Athenian fathers, the fathers of Rome were granted absolute authority—the power of "*patriae potestas*"—over their legitimate offspring (but not, incidentally, over illegitimate children).[15] In contrast, mothers and the state generally were forbidden from engaging in child killing, although extralegal infanticide and abandonment was likely widespread.[16] In the second century CE, the Greek-born physician Soranus wrote in Book II of his *Gynecology* about "how to recognize the newborn that is worth rearing."[17] Among the factors to be consider, according to Soranus, were whether the infant had "been born at the due time, best at the end of nine months," "when put on the earth it immediately cries with proper vigor," "it is perfect in all its parts, members and senses," and "the natural functions of every member are neither sluggish nor weak."[18] Soranus in some ways anticipated the Apgar score used in contemporary medicine to predict newborn survival—with the exception that, in Rome, a father whose infant failed this test "would not raise the child and could legally dispose of the baby."[19] John Eastburn Boswell, however, has written convincingly that not all of these victims of "*expositio*" died, but that no legal protections prevented such an outcome.[20] Only after the conversion of Emperor Constantine to Christianity, which generally proscribed neonatal killing, did that Roman state ban the practice. Constantine wrote against infanticide in 319 CE; under subsequent emperors Valentinian, Valens, and Gratian, the act of killing a newborn became itself a crime punishable by death.[21]

Although infanticide was illegal in medieval Europe, data reveal that it was relatively commonplace.[22] Both Josiah Russell's research on England and Emily Coleman's on France suggest a gender-based component to the practice. Throughout the Middle Ages, those accused of infanticide in Catholic Europe were largely not tried before secular courts, but before Church courts where penalties proved lighter.[23] Acts of "overlaying" or smothering an unwanted infant—often occurring while the parents allegedly were drunk—frequently were tolerated. These killings generally required some form of penance, such as a diet of bread and water for one year, and "without wine or flesh" for two more years. Sometimes sexual intercourse between husband and wife also was prohibited during this period.[24] Historian Barbara Kellum notes that "the very commonality of infanticide and child murder . . . allowed them to be condoned even in court."[25]

Infanticide in the 18th and 19th Centuries

The 18th and 19th centuries saw a profound shift in attitudes toward both children and their being killed. French historian Philippe Ariès in his seminal and controversial text, *Centuries of Childhood: A Social History of Family Life* (1960), argues that medieval parenting was fundamentally different from that of succeeding centuries, as high infant-mortality rates in the earlier period led parents to a position of detached indifference. By the 17th and 18th centuries, and even more so in the Victorian era, infants and children became valued—and even cherished—for their unique characteristics. Widespread victimization of lower-class women by men in positions of power occurred during the 18th and 19th centuries, and many of these women turned unwanted infants over to midwives who would use "starvation or a dose of opiates" to "settle the child's fate in matter of days."[26] For the first time, however, large-scale efforts were conducted by both the state and professional organizations to curtail infanticide. Foundling hospitals were established across the continent. In Great Britain, physicians John Brendon Curgenven, the founder of the Infant Protection Society, and William Ryan, the author of "Infanticide in Medical-Legal Relations," demanded government action.[27] The passage of the Infant Life Protection Act (1872), which required the registration of infants, marked a considerable step toward the preservation of neonatal life.[28]

The Eugenics Movement

The last decades of the 19th century and the first of the 20th century witnessed the rise of a eugenics movement in both northern Europe and the United States. Among the central scientific tenets of this movement was the belief that "human mental, temperamental, and moral traits were determined by heredity."[29] The "problem of the 'differential birthrate'" between those of higher and lower socioeconomic status led eugenicists to fear "that society's best were being swamped by society's worst."[30] Often, the same activists who crusaded for Progressive social reforms advocated for measures to increase the population of the purportedly fit. Concomitantly, figures such as Lothrop Stoddard drew attention to high birthrates among the so-called feebleminded, and the subjects of Henry H. Goddard's eponymous *The Kalikak Family* (1912) became cultural shorthand—among the upper and middle classes—for the mentally defective and morally degenerate families who threatened the social order. Starting with Indiana in 1907, a majority of American states passed compulsory sterilization laws that resulted in at least 62,162 eugenic sterilizations by 1961—the majority of them performed on females.[31] The challenge to Virginia's eugenic statute by victim Carrie Buck led to the notorious *Buck v. Bell* (1927) decision in which Supreme Court Justice Oliver Wendell Homes justified the state's involuntary salpingectomy statue on the grounds that "three generations of imbeciles are enough."[32] Mandatory sterilization laws targeting alleged mental defectives also took hold in much of Protestant Europe including Germany (1933), Sweden (1934), Denmark (1934), Finland (1935), and Iceland (1938); Great Britain proved a notable exception.

Against this background, partisans of neonatal euthanasia gained sporadic traction. The most prominent early-20th-century advocate for withholding care from infants with poor mental or physical prognoses was Harry J. Haiselden (1870–1919), the chief surgeon at German-American Hospital in Chicago. Haiselden gained national prominence in 1915 when he refused to operate to correct deformities in an infant born to Allen and Anna Bollinger, knowing that failure to act would lead to the baby's death. Haiselden's refusal rested entirely on the grounds that the baby was likely to grow up to be mentally and physically impaired. Although in this case he did not actively kill the child, but rather allowed it to die, Haiselden generally failed to distinguish between active and passive forms of euthanasia and vocally favored both. Haiselden wrote, "It is our duty to defend ourselves and future generations against the mentally defective we allow to grow and suffer among us and to add to our burden and our problems."[33] He added that "farmers select the best stock for sowing. . . . Poor humans rely only upon chance and are as welcoming as any to enlarge families. Think of it."[34] The *Baby Bolinger* case became a national cause célèbre and the subject of considerable public debate. Among those supporting Haiselden's position were historian Charles Beard, suffragists Lillian Wald and Inez Milholland Boissevain, and disability-rights advocate Helen Keller.[35, 36] The position was endorsed by the Medico-Legal Society.[37] The story of Harry Haiselden and Baby Bollinger was disseminated to the lay public through a popular silent film, *The Black Stork* (1917), which advanced the eugenics/euthanasia cause. Although Haiselden himself later was stricken from the medical rolls by the Chicago Medical Board, he singlehandedly made the prospect of euthanizing infants a national issue.

Two aspects of the "Baby Bollinger" case are particularly noteworthy. One is the assertion by Haiselden—largely unchallenged—that allowing infants to die was a common practice in the United States during the early 20th century. He told the coroner's jury in the case that approximately one baby was allowed to die *daily* in Chicago alone.[38] What set the Bollinger case apart was the willingness of Haiselden to publicize the practice. Other cases drew national attention soon thereafter, including that of Grace Werder, an infant allowed to die by Dr. Jacob Faltermeyer on account of her hydrocephalus and lower-limb paralysis.[39] The second aspect of note was that two distinct factors motivated Haiselden. He expressed concerns for the welfare of society—noting his fear that the state would be burdened with responsibility for such children and that they might harm others—but he also justified his actions on the grounds that they would prevent the infants in these cases from leading lives of pain and suffering. This two-pronged justification defined the pediatric euthanasia movement in the pre–World War II era, largely distinguishing it from the more recent incarnation of the movement, which relies almost exclusively on the latter justification.

Although some aspects of the eugenicists' program gained widespread traction in the United States—most notably birth control and compulsory sterilization—advocates of euthanasia never saw the program enacted into law. Leading proponent Anna Hall managed to secure debate over a euthanasia bill in the Ohio state legislature in 1906, but the proposal was soundly defeated.[40] After that, interest flared up intermittently until the Second World War. Revelations during the Nuremberg trials about Nazi Germany's pediatric "mercy killing" program—which started in 1939 with the killing of "Child K"—however, turned public sympathies in the United States and the West more generally against both euthanasia and eugenics. In 1949, the Euthanasia Society of America unsuccessfully petitioned the State of New York to legalize euthanasia; after that, the voices of advocates for legalization largely fell silent for three decades.

After World War II

When debate about neonatal and pediatric euthanasia resurfaced in the 1970s and 1980s, much of the discussion focused on the withholding or withdrawal of care. Advances in life-prolonging technologies, particularly for premature infants and those born with birth defects, created both emotional and economic challenges for families and providers. Several widely publicized cases brought this debate into America's living rooms. In 1982, the parents of an Indiana infant with Down syndrome refused to permit surgery to repair a tracheoesophageal fistula, which prevented "Baby Doe" from receiving nutrition; a year later, in New York, the parents of an infant with spina bifida, "Baby Jane Doe," declined life-saving brain surgery that would have allowed the child to survive, but with severe impairments. These cases troubled senior figures in the conservative administration of President Ronald Reagan. Surgeon General C. Everett Koop pushed for congressional action, which ultimately resulted in the passage of the Baby Doe Law in 1984.[41] The regulations prevented any child from being "denied any form of medical care because of poor prognosis based on its predicted quality of life."[42] Although many ethicists joined *Chicago Tribune* columnist Joan Beck in asking, "Are some babies better off dead?" until the late 1970s nobody in mainstream medicine or bioethics dared suggest ending lives through active means.[43]

A pair of phenomena laid the groundwork for active pediatric euthanasia to reenter the public discourse at the end of the 20th century. The first was the decriminalization and ultimately legalization of adult euthanasia or "assisted suicide" in a number of nations. The revolution in patients' rights that started in the 1960s and shifted the emphasis in medical ethics from beneficence to autonomy, first witnessed the establishment of a "right to die" in many jurisdictions. High-profile right-to-die cases such as that of Anthony Bland in Great Britain and Nancy Cruzan in the United States drew further attention to the subject. The withdrawal or withholding of care for adults led to arguments in favor of permitting active voluntary euthanasia. In the Netherlands, adult euthanasia went unprosecuted by authorities throughout the 1990s, as long as certain guidelines were met, and ultimately was legalized by parliament with the passage on the Termination of Life on Request and Assisted Suicide Act in 2002. Belgium (2002) and Luxemburg (2008) soon followed, and Swiss laws permitting aid-in-dying gained renewed public attention through the efforts of the organization Dignitas, under the leadership of attorney Ludwig A. Minelli. Many, although not all, of the arguments that favored legalizing adult euthanasia—prevention of suffering, the preeminence of quality of life—also could be used to justify euthanasia in the neonatal or pediatric setting.

The second event was the publication of utilitarian philosopher Peter Singer's *Practical Ethics* (1979), which advanced ethical arguments for the nonvoluntary euthanasia of infants.[44] Although Singer was not the first contemporary philosopher to endorse this viewpoint, his prominence and advocacy drew both attention and credibility to the position. According to Singer, it was not "the fact that a being is a human being" that is "relevant to the wrongness of killing it," but rather, "characteristics like rationality, autonomy, and self-consciousness that make a difference."[45] Because "[i]nfants lack these characteristics," killing them "cannot be equated with killing normal human beings, or any other self-conscious beings."[46] Put in its starkest terms, "No infant—disabled or not—has as strong a claim to life as beings capable of seeing themselves as distinct entities, existing over time."[47] Singer acknowledged that killing disabled infants was a complex matter—requiring an assessment of parental attitudes and answers to such questions as whether the parents would have another child in the deceased infant's place. Yet, Singer's declaration that such killings are "[v]ery often . . . not wrong at all" opened the door for other philosophers and physicians to debate the question publically.[48] The backlash against Singer's book in Germany and Austria also attracted considerable pubic attention—likely having the paradoxical effect of increasing public awareness of these ideas and placing them within the realm of acceptable public debate.[49]

Increased public discourse ultimately led to two major legislative events in the Low Countries. Dutch physicians announced a program of legal, nonvoluntary euthanasia for neonates known as the Groningen Protocol (2005). Nearly a decade later, Belgian lawmakers embraced a system of voluntary euthanasia for pediatric patients (2014).

Contemporary Law and Practice

Neonatal Euthanasia in the Netherlands

During the mid-1990s, the Netherlands became to first modern Western nation effectively to decriminalize neonatal and infant euthanasia under limited circumstances. Two high-profile court cases laid the groundwork for this change. In 1993, Dr. Henk Prins ended the life of a three-day-old girl, Rianne Quirine Kunst, who suffered from a severe form of spina bifida. A year later, Dr. Gerhardus Kadijk terminated the life of a three-week-old baby born with Trisomy 13 (Patau syndrome). In both cases the children were expected to die within several months and were believed to be enduring "excruciating pain."[50] Although Dutch law at the time did not permit euthanasia for children younger than age 16, Prins and Kadijk each followed the guidelines for assisted suicide for patients 16 years of age and older (which had been decriminalized since 1985) including obtaining a second opinion from an outside physician and reporting the case to the local prosecutor's office. Both doctors also obtained consent from the infants' parents. Prins was convicted of murder, but the court found his actions to be justified and the prosecutor asked for no punishment.[51] In Kadijk's case, the court determined that prosecutors had proven the charges against him, but that the physician had "no choice but to end the infant's life" and dismissed the case.[52] Over the next decade, 22 similar cases arose—all involving advanced spina bifida—and no physicians were prosecuted for their actions.[53] Although in the wake of these court rulings the Dutch government repeatedly pledged to develop guidelines for the practice, it failed to do so.[54]

Against this background, Dutch pediatricians Eduard Verhagen and Pieter J. J. Sauer developed a protocol for the practice in their local community in 2002 and proposed formal codification of the decriminalization of infant euthanasia in 2005. Writing in the *New England Journal of Medicine*, Verhagen and Sauer reported on the ongoing practices at the University Medical Center in the northern Dutch city of Groningen, which had been developed in coordination with the medical staff and the local district attorney. After reviewing the rationale for permitting euthanasia for adults, the authors wrote, "The question under consideration now is whether deliberate life-ending procedures are also acceptable for newborns and infants, despite the fact that these patients cannot express their own will. Or must infants with disorders associated with severe and sustained suffering be kept alive when their suffering cannot be adequately reduced?"[55] The authors went on to assert that such procedures would be justified in three cases: When an infant had no chance of survival; when an infant's prognosis was poor and the infant depended on intensive care; and, most controversially, for "infants with a hopeless prognosis who experience what parents and medical experts deem to be unbearable suffering."[56] Verhagen and Sauer outlined specific requirements that might justify euthanasia in these cases: "[T]he parents must agree fully, on the basis of a thorough explanation of the condition and prognosis; a team of physicians, including at least one who is not directly involved in the care of the patient, must agree; and the condition and prognosis must be very well defined."[57] Additionally, "[a]fter the decision has been made and the child has died, an outside legal body should determine whether the decision was justified and all necessary procedures have been followed."[58] Known at the "Groningen Protocol," the principles have since been adopted throughout the Netherlands and were approved by the Dutch Pediatric Association in June 2005.[59] Although neonatal euthanasia technically remained illegal in Holland, because the minister of justice could in theory overrule the collective agreement of the Council of Attorneys General not to prosecute, current rules make it realistically improbable that any physician who follows the guidelines will be prosecuted.[60]

One of the principal concerns of Verhagen and his colleagues in developing the protocol was that euthanasia was occurring sub rosa. They estimated that, based on a national survey, 15 to 20 such cases arose in the Netherlands each year, and on average only three were reported.[61] The goal was to bring the practice into the open for public debate. Six months after the publication of Verhagen and Sauer's article, the Dutch government finally established an Advisory Committee on the Termination of Life of Neonates in November 2005.[62] The guidance to Parliament from the minister of justice and the secretary of state of health, welfare and sport, included the following requirements for neonatal euthanasia:

1. Diagnosis and prognosis must be certain, hopeless and unbearable suffering must be present, withdrawal of treatment must be acceptable according to current medical opinion.
2. Both parents have given informed consent.
3. Parents have been extensively informed about the diagnosis and prognosis and they have also concluded that reasonable alternatives are absent.
4. At least one independent physician was consulted, who examined the child and gave an opinion on the requirements mentioned here. Instead of consulting an independent physician, a multidisciplinary team can be consulted.
5. The termination of life must be performed in accordance with the accepted medical standard.[63]

The five years following the promulgation and acceptance of the Groningen Protocol in the Netherlands witnessed a surprising decline in the number of such cases reported.[64] The total number of nonvoluntary neonatal deaths reported over this period was two, and both were infants with lethal epidermolysis bullosa. Congenital malformations such as spina bifida, which accounted for 15 cases of euthanasia in the period prior to the protocol, declined to zero. The main mode of death in Dutch intensive care units remained withdrawal of life support (95 percent); about 60 percent of these cases occurred when the prognosis was terminal and about 40 percent were for quality-of-life reasons in infants who otherwise might have lived.[65] Much of that improvement can be attributable to improved prenatal screening techniques. Some ambiguity in the guidelines as to whether the administration of paralytic agents that hastened the dying process was reportable, however, also could have led to reduced numbers. A multidisciplinary task force reviewed this question and decided that although the "administration of paralytic medications is permitted if the aim is to stop prolonged gasping during ventilator withdrawal and to end a protracted dying process of several hours or more," in light of the controversy surrounding such practices, they should be reported for review.[66] Although these were not the cases that the Groningen Protocol was designed to address, such an approach might lead to higher case reports in future years.

Arguments Favoring the Groningen Protocol

The Groningen Protocol had the effect of bringing a long tabooed subject into the heart of public discourse. Nearly all of the arguments advanced in favor of neonatal euthanasia relied in some way upon the best interest of the child or of the child and her family. In the post-Nazi era, defenders of such a program no longer could rely upon claims to the overall welfare of society.

One of the most significant challenges these proponents faced in modern times was the widely held view that "the interest in continued existence is usually the most fundamental interest a person can possess."[67] Advocates of neonatal euthanasia were in essence arguing that, at times, death is preferable to life. One argument in favor of this position relied upon analogy to cases of competent adults seeking to end life-sustaining care. B. A. Manninen, for instance, wrote that

> [i]t is not that any type of life, even a life consisting of nothing more than intense pain, is better than no life at all. Indeed, because of the strong conviction that there are times when death is preferable to life, many people choose to cease life-sustaining treatment either for themselves or as a proxy for someone else.[68]

For severely ill adults, deciding whether to endure pain for some larger or future benefit—such as more time with one's family—might justify suffering. The cost and benefit of prolonged life is inherently personal. In contrast, Manninen explained,

> [I]nfants are not these sorts of creatures. All infants lack the cognitive ability to look forward to anything, to anticipate a future activity, to take comfort

in the fact that tomorrow they will be able to see their loved ones and spend more time with them. Infants are the types of beings that are locked in a perpetual state of present emotions and desires. The life of an infant in agony is nothing but perpetual existence in that agony.[69]

Lindemann and Verkerk note distinctive aspects of Dutch society and the Dutch health care system that might make the Groningen Protocol more palatable there than elsewhere.[70] These aspects include a much greater degree of trust between physicians and patients than found in other nations, such as the United States; in fact, such trust "is deliberately cultivated as a socially valuable good."[71] Dutch decision making often is consensus oriented. Lindemann and Verkerk argue that in the Netherlands "it is important to take parents' interests, wishes, and fears very seriously," in contrast to the United States and United Kingdom, where "refusal to countenance informal caregivers' concerns seems to be a permanent fixture of bioethics."[72] As a result, "[b]ecause parents feel that they are equal partners in the decision-making process, they seem content to let the final decision rest with the physicians who are directly responsible for their babies' care."[73] It could be argued that such a protocol is ethical, in part, because it is culturally acceptable to Dutch families or, conversely, that such a program would be unethical in a society in which the culture did not support such a practice. The latter sentiment was echoed by leading American bioethicist Arthur Caplan who, at the time the protocol was announced, told the *New York Times* that he could not see a similar regimen being adopted in the United States because "it's not acceptable to the culture."[74] This "situated analysis" has drawn criticism from those who object to the practice on universal grounds, such as the Hastings Center's Dan Callahan, who wrote, "That it is culturally feasible there hardly entails that it is moral. Are their babies different from ours?"[75]

Arguments Against Groningen Protocol

Neonatal euthanasia has not been without its critics. These included both tempered, reasoned objections from within the medical community, and more hostile assessments in conservative media that compared the Protocol to a "Hitleresque type of eugenics programme."[76] In *The Lancet*, bioethicist Eric Kodish of the Cleveland Clinic advocated for "resistance in the form of civil disobedience" in the hope that "[n]on-violent protest of the Groningen [P]rotocol could change the current practice."[77]

Shortly after the publication of Vergahen and Sauer's article, Israeli physicians Allan Joktowitz and Shimon Glick of Ben-Gurion University of the

Negev published a rebuttal in the *Journal of Medical Ethics* that summed up many of the opponents' arguments.[78] Although acknowledging that "the originators believe that they are acting in the best interests of the infant," Joktowitz and Glick outlined six serious objections to the practice. First, the "primary ethical justification for active euthanasia" in adult patients had been "autonomy," and Dutch law required "an absolute insistence on initiation of the request by a competent adult."[79] That was clearly not possible in the case of infants. The authors noted that surrogates cannot give informed consent for euthanasia in adults, and questioned the logic of permitting this for children.[80] In their thinking, the protocol manifested the enactment of the very slippery slopes that critics of legalizing aid-in-dying for adults had advanced during the 1980s.[81] Second, Joktowitz and Glick raised questions about the inherent quality of informed consent that parents could offer in these cases. Because "[t]he parents who agree to the decision are relying on experts to predict the future for them without having experienced it," they could lack a "true understanding of the situation."[82] Additionally, there is "clear potential for bias in the parents' decision making because of the emotional, physical, and financial hardships they face in the long-term care of a severely disabled child."[83] Third, the authors noted that physicians "tend to overestimate the importance of quality of life on a patient's desire to live" and inevitably bring their own personal biases about caring for a disabled child to the discussion.[84] Fourth, the state itself might have financial responsibility for the infant's long-term care, leading to a bias in favor of euthanasia.[85] Fifth, significant alternatives to euthanasia exist—such as palliative care—that can prevent the suffering feared in the protocol.[86] Finally, the authors raise a moral objection that the protocol ignores "human essence of the child."[87] The article concludes with a powerful salvo against the protocol: "The sole criterion for ending the life of these infants is their poor quality of life. Who gave physicians the right to determine quality of life and to practise euthanasia on that basis?"[88] In fact, critics of the Dutch policy who voice concerns about a slippery slope could take morbid solace in the Royal Dutch Medical Association's 2013 report on the protocol included the following among justifications for a lethal injection, "The period of gasping and dying persists and the inevitable death is prolonged, in spite of good preparation, and it causes severe suffering for the parents."[89]

Alexander Kon argues that the most significant difference between euthanasia in the adult and neonatal settings is that no meaningful mechanism exists to assess the suffering of infants.[90] To justify neonatal euthanasia on the grounds of beneficence, Kon believes that the question "Would this infant prefer to be dead than in this amount of discomfort?" must be

asked.[91] Because infants have no way to process this question or communicate an answer, their preferences are inherently unknowable.

Orlowski et al. have argued that increased emphasis on palliative care,
including improved pain control, symptom management, and psychosocial support would supplant the need for neonatal euthanasia.[92] They
argue that "the treatment of pain and discomfort in children is often sub-
optimal" and "that Dutch physicians do not receive enough training in
palliative care and pain control."[93] Chervenak et al. question the protocol's
conflation of pain and suffering, raising the possibility that infants might
experience only the former without the latter—or, in cases of spina bifida,
could experience no pain at all.[94] They write that

> [c]linicians typically understand suffering to be a complex psychosocial
> phenomenon in which an individual experiences the loss, to different
> degrees, of the ability to realize intentions, desires, and hopes for the future.
> Pain, by contrast, is a physiologic phenomenon: the awareness of reports of
> tissue damage or threat of tissue damage in the central nervous system. Pain
> may cause suffering, but not in all cases. Suffering can be accompanied by
> pain, but not in all cases. An infant with spina bifida cannot have and there-
> fore cannot have lost the ability to realize intentions, desires, and hopes for
> the future; it can feel pain but cannot "suffer" in the sense described above.[95]

By speaking of "unbearable suffering," Chervenak et al. argue that
Verhagen has invoked "parental response to their child's condition to be
included in the concept of unbearable suffering"; the result is that the
interests of the parents, rather than the child, are served.[96]

Special Considerations

One of the cornerstones of the Dutch policy is a requirement for two-
parent consent. This author has elsewhere questioned the logic of this
requirement.[97] Appel has argued that "although an emphasis on parental
agreement may make this practice more politically palatable, what is not at
all clear is why the preferences of family members—rather than solely the
medical condition of the infants—should be dispositive factors in determining whether to engage in active euthanasia."[98] Such an approach is
consistent with the general practice of favoring the neonatal or pediatric
patient's best interests, even when they run contrary to family wishes. As
the American Pediatric Association notes,

> providers have legal and ethical duties to their child patients to render com-
> petent medical care based on what the patient needs, not what someone

else expresses. Although impasses regarding the interests of minors and the expressed wishes of their parents or guardians are rare, the pediatrician's responsibilities to his or her patient exist independent of parental desires or proxy consent (*Informed Consent* 1995).[99]

Fortunately, parents and physicians agree in the vast majority of these tragic cases. If they do not, however, then what remains unclear is why the parental preference rather than the degree of the infant's suffering should prove dispositive. In fact, Dr. Henk Prins, one of the pioneers of the practice, implicitly questioned the parental role as early as 1995. He stated, "It is important that the parents agree, but it is not the basis of the decision. . . . The basis of the decision is the interests of the child."[100]

A second complexity arises in cases where the infant's injuries are not due to birth defects, but rather stem from injuries inflicted by the parents themselves. The cases occur not too infrequently in regard to the question of withdrawal of care in the United States.[101] To date, no similar case has been reported in the Netherlands. If and when such a case does arise, however, physicians will have to determine whether such cases permit a deviation from the two-parent consent rule, especially if one parent faces increased legal penalties in the case of infant death.

Pediatric Euthanasia in Belgium

Another form of pediatric euthanasia, and one equally fraught with controversy, is that of older minors who voluntarily seek to end their own lives in the face of terminal illness or extreme suffering. In the United States, the jurisdictions that permit aid-in-dying (Oregon, Washington, Montana, Vermont, and California) have limited the practice to individuals older than age 18. The Netherlands sets the cutoff at 16, but permits patients who are 12 to 16 years old to choose euthanasia under limited circumstances with parental consent. Luxemburg's code also limits the practice to "capable adults."[102] When Australia's Northern Territory approved the Rights of the Terminally Ill Act in 1995, briefly sanctioning assisted suicide, the statute restricted the practice to those over age 18.[103] Until 2014, no jurisdiction had permitted voluntary euthanasia for patients younger than age 12 with terminal illnesses.

Belgium legalized euthanasia for competent individuals 18 years of age and older in May 2002.[104] A 2007–2008 study found that a strong majority (69 percent) of Belgian physicians providing medically care to children who died favored expanding the law to include minors.[105] This support and concomitant support among the general public led in 2014 to changes to the 2002 euthanasia law that permitted voluntary pediatric euthanasia. According to the amendments, euthanasia was allowed for pediatric patients experiencing "constant and unbearable suffering."[106] Children with cognitive limitations or psychiatric illnesses were excluded. The Belgian protocol required a voluntary request by the child and formal consent by the parents. A multidisciplinary team then reviews the decision before deciding to proceed.

Arguments Favoring Belgian Law

Arguments in favor of the Belgium's law largely follow those favoring legalized assisted suicide for adults. These include respect of personal autonomy and increased dignity during the dying process. Many patients who ultimately do not choose to end their own lives still benefit from the solace of knowing that they could choose suicide if their suffering proved unbearable. Recent trends in medicine have attempted to increase the autonomy of children—such as the recognition of "mature minor" doctrines that permit informed pediatric patients the right to make their own medical decisions before full emancipation. If other medical decisions can be trusted to these patients, why not those pertaining to life and death?

One of the principal justifications in American law for withholding certain forms of decision-making authority from pediatric patients and their parents—such as the right of Jehovah's Witness children to reject life-saving blood transfusions—is that society wants these patients to live until they reach maturity, at which time they can make more informed decisions. In what might be the most well-known pronouncement on the subject, Supreme Court Justice Wiley Rutledge wrote, "Parents may be free to become martyrs themselves. But it does not follow they are free, in identical circumstances, to make martyrs of their children before they have reached the age of full and legal discretion when they can make that choice for themselves."[107] Yet such concerns seem ill-placed in circumstances in which a child is terminally ill. Barring some miracle cure, these children still will perish before reaching the age of maturity. The question is not whether or when they will die, but how. Supporters of the Belgian law note that, rather than being mutually exclusive, palliative care and legal euthanasia can work together to serve a pediatric patient's interests.[108]

Arguments Against Belgian Law

Much of the criticism of Belgium's policy comes from critics of adult euthanasia, who fear a slippery slope and a broadening of criteria for a practice they oppose under all circumstances. Other opponents, however, note distinctions between terminally ill adults and similarly situated children. Siegel et al. describe these differences as follows:

> What the law does not consider, however, is that adults choose euthanasia for reasons that go beyond pain. For adults, the decision to end their life can be based upon the fear of a loss of control, not wanting to burden others, or the desire not to spend their final days of life fully sedated. These desires might be supported by the experience they have had witnessing a loved one express a loss of dignity or because they understand what terminal sedation is and wish to refuse it. Children, however, lack the intellectual capacity to develop a sophisticated preference against palliative interventions of last resort. Instead, in the case of the new Belgian law, children seem to be asked to choose between unbearable suffering on the one hand and death on the other.[109]

Although children can experience pain, "concepts like loss of dignity or the fear of losing self-determination" are alien to them.[110] Under the circumstances, these critics argue, enhanced palliative care is preferable to euthanasia. Critics also note that spontaneous requests for euthanasia by pediatric patients are extremely rare and that palliative care generally is advocated for insufficiently in Belgium.[111]

Conclusions

Neither the Dutch model for neonatal euthanasia nor the Belgian system of pediatric euthanasia has yet extended beyond these nation's boundaries. Great Britain did briefly dabble with the decriminalization of neonatal euthanasia in a case highly reminiscent of the Dutch cases preceding the Groningen Protocol. A Scottish neonatologist, Michael Munro, delivered lethal doses of pancuronium, a muscle relaxant, "to hasten the deaths of two premature babies from whom treatment had been withdrawn" in 2005.[112] Although critics described the act as "tantamount to euthanasia," the UK General Medical Council in 2007 cleared Munro on the grounds that his "primary purpose had been to relieve suffering."[113] No further British cases have been reported, thus it remains unclear whether these two incidents suggest a trend toward decriminalization or are outliers reflecting the circumstances of particular patients. More recently, the Dutch Pediatric Association has endorsed adopting a voluntary euthanasia protocol for assenting minors under age 12, mirrored after the Belgian model.[114] Yet these are rare exceptions. On the whole, the world medical community has been reluctant to follow the lead of the Low Countries.

This author continues to believe that nonvoluntary euthanasia for neonates and voluntary euthanasia for pediatric patients should be safe, legal, and rare. Evidence from the ongoing policy laboratory of the Netherlands and Belgium suggests that few parents and children ultimately will opt for euthanasia. For example, although Dutch law permits children between the ages of 12 and 16 to choose euthanasia, only one minor younger than age 16 has done so in the 13 years since the practice was legalized.[115] Only 4 children between the ages of 16 and 18 took advantage of the law between 2002 and 2015.[116] Yet, much like adult euthanasia, pediatric and neonatal euthanasia offer children and families an escape hatch of last resort—the solace of knowing that, if all else fails, they no longer need to suffer.

Notes

1. Orlowski, James P., MD; Martin, L. Smith, STD; and Jan Van Zwienen, MD (1992). "Pediatric Euthanasia." *American Journal of Diseases in Children* 146(12):1440–46.

2. Ibid.

3. Ibid.

4. Williamson, Laila. 1978. "Infanticide: An Anthropological Analysis." In Marvin Kohl, *Infanticide and the Value of Life*. New York: Prometheus Books, 61–75, at 61.

5. Birdsell, Joseph, B. 1986. "Some Predictions for the Pleistocene Based on Equilibrium Systems Among Recent Hunter Gatherers." In Richard Lee and Irven DeVore, *Man the Hunter*. Aldine Publishing Co., 239.

6. Hill K., A. M. Hurtado, and R. S. Walker. 2007. "High Adult Mortality Among Hiwi Hunter-Gatherers: Implications for Human Evolution." *Journal of Human Evolution* 52: 443–54.

7. Weyer, Edward Moffatt. 1932. *The Eskimos: Their Environment and Folkways*. New Haven: The Yale University Press, 483.

8. Milner, Larry Stephen. 1998. *Hardness of Heart/Hardness of Life: The Stain of Human Infanticide*. University Press of America.

9. *The Family in Classical Greece* (London: Thames and Hudson, 1968), 164.

10. Ibid., 28.

11. Ibid.

12. *Plato's Republic*. 1935. Translated by Paul Shorey. Book V, Section, 459d.

13. Lu, Mathew. 2013. "Aristotle on Abortion and Infanticide." *International Philosophical Quarterly* 53(1) (March): 48.

14. Milner, Larry Stephen. 1998. *Hardness of Heart/Hardness of Life: The Stain of Human Infanticide*. University Press of America, 24 (Front Cover).

15. Ibid., 31.

16. Ibid.

17. Iceton, Shannon, William A. Whitelaw, Arty R. Coppes-Zantinga. 1999. "How to Recognize the Newborn That Is Worth Rearing." The American Pediatric Society and The Society for Pediatric Research. *Pediatric Research* 45: 126A.

18. Ibid.

19. Iceton, Shannon. 2001. "The Soranus Score." *Canadian Medical Association Journal* (March 6) 164(5): 674.

20. Boswell, John Eastburn. 1984. "Expositio and Oblatio: The Abandonment of Children and the Ancient and Medieval Family." *The American Historical Review* 89(1) (February), 10–33.

21. Carrick, P. "Medical Ethics in Antiquity." *Philosophical Perspectives on Abortion and Euthanasia*, Chapter 6, Footnote 7.

22. Kellum, Barbara. 1974. "Infanticide in England in the Later Middle Ages." *History of Childhood Quarterly* 1(3) (Winter): 367–88.

23. *Infanticide and Parental Care*. 1994. Edited by Stefano Parmigiani, and Frederick S. vom Saal. Chur, Switzerland: Harwood Academic Publishers, 111.

24. Kellum, Barbara. 1974. "Infanticide in England in the Later Middle Ages." *History of Childhood Quarterly* 1(3) (Winter): 367–88.

25. Ibid.

26. Langer, W. L. 1974. "Infanticide: A Historical Survey. *History of Childhood Quarterly* 1(3) (Winter): 353–66, 357.

27. Ibid., 361.

28. Ibid., 357.

29. Paul, Diane. 1995. *Controlling Human Heredity*. Humanity Books, 1.

30. Ibid., 7

31. Kluchin, Rebecca M. 2009. *Fit to Be Tied: Sterilization and Reproductive Rights in America, 1950–1980*. New Brunswick, NJ: Rutgers University Press, 17.

32. *Buck v. Bell*, 274 U.S. 200 (1927).

33. "Surgeon Who Would Not Save Life of Baby Is. . . : Coroner's Physician Upholds Statement of Surgeon That Child Would Have Been Defective for Life." *The Austin Statesman and Tribune* (1915–1916) [Austin, TX], November 18, 1915: 1.

34. Ibid.

35. Keller, Helen. 1915. "Physicians' Juries for Defective Babies." *The New Republic* (December 18).

36. "Defective Baby Divides Doctors: Clergymen United in Declaring Infant Should Have Been Saved Precedent a Peril, Professor Asserts Decision of the Mother Should Prevail, Declares Dr. Stechman—Scientists Disagree." *New York Tribune* (1911–1922) [New York], November 18 1915: 5.

37. Ibid.

38. "Baby a Day Allowed to Die: Dr. Haiselden Says Doctors Secretly Let Them Expire. Special to The Washington Post." *The Washington Post* (1877–1922), November 21, 1915. *ProQuest Historical Newspapers: The Washington Post*, p. 2.

39. "Lets Baby Die, Defies Society: Chicago Doctor Joins Haiselden in Demanding Showdown, and May Get It. Telegraph to the Tribune." *New York Tribune* (1911–1922) [New York] December 9 1915.

40. See Appel, J. M. 2004. "A Duty to Kill? A Duty to Die? Rethinking the Euthanasia Controversy of 1906." *Bulletin of the History of Medicine* 78(3): 618.

41. "Reagan Signs 'Baby Doe' Law on Infant Treatment." *Los Angeles Times* (October 9, 1984), A2.

42. Colen, B. D. 1986. "Case Stirs Debate on Baby Doe Law," *Newsday, Nassau Edition* (October 5).

43. Beck, Joan. 1981. "Are Some Babies Better Off Dead?" *Chicago Tribune* (May 22), p. 19.

44. Singer, Peter. 1993. *Practical Ethics*, 2nd ed. (Cambridge), 175–217.

45. Ibid.

46. Ibid.

47. Ibid.

48. Ibid.

49. Singer, Peter. 1991. "On Being Silenced in Germany." *New York Review of Books* (August 15). Some scenes from academic life in Germany and Austria today.

50. Corder, Mike. 1995. "Infant Mercy Killing Troubles Dutch." *Moscow Times* (December 7).

51. "Infants' Euthanasia Sets Off New Dutch Debate." *American Medical News* (January 1, 1996).

52. "Euthanasia Count Voided." *Tulsa World* (November 14, 1990).

53. Verhagen A. A., J. J. Sol, O. F. Brouwer, P. J. Sauer. 2005. "Deliberate Termination of Life in Newborns in The Netherlands; Review of All 22 Reported Cases Between 1997 and 2004." *Nederlands Tijdschrift voor Geneeskunde* 149(4) (January 22):183–88.

54. Verhagen, E. E. 2006. "End of Life Decisions in Newborns in The Netherlands: Medical and Legal Aspects of the Groningen Protocol." *Medicine and Law* (June): 406.

55. Verhagen, Eduard E., and Pieter J. J. Sauer. 2005. "The Groningen Protocol—Euthanasia in Severely Ill Newborns." *The New England Journal of Medicine* (March).

56. Ibid.

57. Ibid.

58. Ibid.

59. Verhagen, E. E. 2006. "End of Life Decisions in Newborns in The Netherlands: Medical and Legal Aspects of the Groningen Protocol." *Medicine and Law* (June): 405.

60. Ibid.

61. Verhagen, Eduard E., and Pieter J. J. Sauer. 2005. "The Groningen Protocol—Euthanasia in Severely Ill Newborns." *The New England Journal of Medicine* (March).

62. Verhagen, E. E. 2006. "End of Life Decisions in Newborns in The Netherlands: Medical and Legal Aspects of the Groningen Protocol." *Medicine and Law* (June): 407.

63. Ibid.

64. Eduard Verhagen. 2014. "Neonatal Euthanasia: Lessons from the Groningen Protocol." *Seminars in Fetal & Neonatal Medicine.*

65. Ibid.

66. Ibid.

67. Manninen, B. A. 2006. "A Case for Justified Non-Voluntary Active Euthanasia: Exploring the Ethics of the Groningen Protocol." *Journal of Medical Ethics* 32(11): 643–51 (Nov.).

68. Ibid.

69. Ibid.

70. Lindemann, H., and M. Verkerk. 2008. "Ending the Life of a Newborn: The Groningen Protocol." *Hastings Center Report* 38(1): 42–51 (Jan.-Feb.).

71. Ibid.

72. Ibid.

73. Ibid.

74. Schwartz, John. 2015. "When Torment Is Baby's Destiny, Euthanasia Is Defended." *New York Times* (March 10).

75. Callahan, D. 2008. "Are Their Babies Different from Ours?" *Dutch Culture and the Groningen Protocol. Hastings Center Report* 38(4) (July–August).

76. Manninen, B. A. 2006. "A Case for Justified Non-Voluntary Active Euthanasia: Exploring the Ethics of the Groningen Protocol." *Journal of Medical Ethics* 32(11) (November): 643–51.

77. Kodish, Eric. 2008. "Paediatric Ethics: A Repudiation of the Groningen Protocol." *The Lancet* (371) 9616, 892–93 (March 15).

78. Jotkowitz, A. B., and S. Glick. 2006. The Groningen Protocol: Another Perspective. *Journal of Medical Ethics.* 32(3) (March): 157–58.

79. Ibid.

80. Ibid.

81. Ibid.

82. Ibid.

83. Ibid.

84. Ibid.

85. Ibid.

86. Ibid.

87. Ibid.

88. Ibid.

89. Cook, Michael. Netherlands, "Belgium Racing to Okay Euthanasia for Disabled Children." *Life Site News* (June 14, 2013).

90. Kon, A. A. 2007. "Neonatal Euthanasia Is Unsupportable: The Groningen Protocol Should be Abandoned." *Theoretical Medicine & Bioethics* 28(5): 453–63.

91. Ibid.

92. Orlowski, James P., MD; Martin L. Smith, STD; Jan Van Zwienen, MD. 1992. "Pediatric Euthanasia." *American Journal of Diseased Children* 146(12): 1440–46.

93. Ibid.

94. Chervenak, F. A., L. B. McCullough, B. Arabin. 2006. "Why the Groningen Protocol Should Be Rejected." *Hastings Center Reports* 36(5) (September–October): 30–33.

95. Ibid.

96. Ibid.

97. Appel, Jacob M. 2009. "Neonatal Euthanasia: Why Require Parental Consent?" *Journal of Bioethical Inquiry* (December) (6)4: 477–82.

98. Ibid.

99. "Informed Consent, Parental Permission and Assent in Pediatric Practice." 1995. *Pediatrics* 95(2) (February): 314–17.

100. Corder, Mike. 1995. "Infant Mercy Killing Troubles Dutch." *Moscow Times* (December 7).

101. Appel, Jacob M. 2009. "Mixed Motives, Mixed Outcomes When Accused Parents Won't Agree to Withdraw Care." *Journal of Medical Ethics* 35: 635–37.

102. Loi du 16 mars 2009 sur l'euthanasie et l'assistance au suicide [Law of 16 March 2009 on euthanasia and assisted suicide].

103. Bradbury, Lisa W. "Euthanasia in the Netherlands: Recognizing Mature Minors in Euthanasia Legislation." 210 *New England Journal International and Comparative Law* 9(1): 231.

104. Siegel, Andrew M., Dominic A. Sisti, and Arthur L. Caplan. 2014. "Pediatric Euthanasia in Belgium: Disturbing Developments." *JAMA: The Journal of the American Medical Association* 311(19) (May): 1963–64.

105. Ibid.

106. Ibid.

107. *Prince v. Massachusetts*, 321 U.S. 158 (1944)

108. Hanson, S. S. 2015. "Pediatric Euthanasia and Palliative Care Can Work Together." *American Journal of Hospice and Palliative Care* (February 8).

109. Siegel, Andrew M., Dominic A. Sisti, and Arthur L. Caplan. 2014. "Pediatric Euthanasia in Belgium: Disturbing Developments." *JAMA: The Journal of the American Medical Association* 311(19) (May): 1963–64.

110. Ibid.

111. Francesca Giglio and Antonio G. Spagnolo. 2014. "Pediatric Euthanasia in Belgium: Some Ethical Considerations." *Journal of Medicine and the Person* (December) 12(3): 146–49.

112. Dyer, Owen. 2007. "Doctor Cleared of Act 'Tantamount to Euthanasia.' " *BMJ* (July 14) 335(7610): 67.

113. Ibid.

114. Huggler, Justin. 2015. "Give Children under 12 the Right to Die, Say Dutch Paediatricians." *The Telegraph* (June 19).

115. Ibid.

116. Ibid.

CHAPTER SIXTEEN

Traveling for Assisted Suicide

*I. Glenn Cohen**

Medical tourism—also known as "medical travel" and "cross-border health care consumption"—is a global multibillion dollar industry. For the purposes here it's defined as the travel of patients who are residents of one country (the "home country") to another country (the "destination country") for the primary purpose of receiving medical treatment. This definition, among other things, excludes individuals who receive health care incidental to other travel, such as when on vacation. After providing a brief primer on the phenomenon more generally and situation travel for assisted suicide within it, this chapter then turns to the sociological, legal, and ethical elements of this type of travel.

It starts with some nomenclature. The most frequently used term to describe what these patients undergo is "suicide tourism" or "assisted suicide tourism." This chapter employs the term "assisted suicide" for the kind of services sought by individuals who want to end their life, rather than using terms such as "aid in dying" or "assisted dying." The author

* Professor, Harvard Law School. Faculty Director, Petrie-Flom Center for Health Law Policy, Biotechnology, and Bioethics. Parts of this work are adapted from Cohen, I. G., *Patients with Passports* (New York: Oxford University Press, 2015). Chapter 8, Medical Tourism and Ending Life: Travel for Assisted Suicide and Abortion; Cohen, I. G., "Circumvention Tourism," *Cornell Law Review* (2012) 97: 1309–98; and Cohen, I. G., *Travel for Aid in Dying* (under review). I thank Roi Bachmutsky and Russell Spivak for excellent research assistance.

does not, however, intend this choice of term to connote any normative or other intellectual baggage. Instead, and for no other reason, this chapter relies upon it because it is the term more familiarly used in American legal discourse. Those who prefer another term can read it into the arguments presented.

The "tourism" terminology also is open to dispute as applied to this type of travel. This author has defended use of the term "medical tourism" in the contexts of travel for hip replacements, cardiac bypass, and other legal goods in part because many foreign providers really do couple the health care with tourism (e.g., a trip to the Taj Mahal), because the industry often sells "luxury" and wellness along with surgery, and because the industry often is promoted by not only by the health care ministry but also by its business development and tourism council.[1] These points do not fit as well for travel to end one's life, although one set of authors claims that "Dignitas, for example, offers their clients attractive packages which provide a day (or more) of enjoyment and relaxation before the assisted suicide takes place."[2] All in all, it seems that the better term, and the used in the rest of this chapter, is "travel for assisted suicide."

A Brief Primer on Medical Tourism

Medical tourism is part of a larger phenomenon of the globalization of health care that has been developing in the last several decades. The rationale for this globalization has its roots in David Ricardo, the *British Economist's* 1817 theory of comparative advantage, a fundamental argument in favor of free trade among countries and of specialization among individuals. Ricardo argued that there is mutual benefit from trade (or exchange) even if one party (e.g., resource-rich country, highly skilled artisan) is more productive in every possible area than its trading counterpart (e.g., resource-poor country, unskilled laborer), as long as each concentrates on the activities for which it has a relative productivity advantage.

This theory has been put to work in most aspects of daily life. The clothes people wear, the computers people type on, some of the food people eat, all have been made elsewhere. This allows countries such as Canada to focus on what it does best and not try to do everything. To be sure, there are winners and losers distributionally, but this global trade has reduced prices for many goods and services dramatically and made both recipients and the sending countries wealthier.

Until relatively recently, however, this same insight was not applied to health care. Health care primarily was obtained locally, not globally. That has begun to change. Medical tourism is one of a series of globalizing moves in health care. It sits alongside several others, including medical migration (also known as the "medical brain drain")—the movement of health care professionals, largely from the less-developed world to the more-developed world with concomitant savings for wealthier countries based on reduced training costs for less-developed countries; telemedicine—where the patients and providers stay put, but medical care is provided remotely, encompassing everything from the low technological (e.g., telepsychiatry), to the middle (e.g., teleradiology), to the very high technological (e.g., telerobotic surgery); and the globalization of research and development for drugs and other therapeutics—a significant portion of clinical trials, in particular, are conducted in the developing world to reduce cost, access treatment-naïve research participants, and for other reasons.

In its modern form, medical tourism is the newest of these instances of health care globalization. "Modern form" is said here because, in fact, medical tourism actually has ancient roots. Ancient Greeks traveled to spas known as "*asklepia*" in the Mediterranean for purification and spiritual healing; and for more than 2,000 years, foreign patients have traveled to the Aquae Sulis reservoir built by the Romans in what is now the British town of Bath.[3,4] These days, patients are more likely to travel to Thailand, Mexico, or India than were the travelers of old.

At the highest level, the modern version of medical tourism can be divided into three types, each of which raises ethical questions (which this author has outlined elsewhere). These types are (1) medical tourism for services that are illegal in both the patient's home and destination countries (such as organ purchase in the Philippines); (2) medical tourism for services that are illegal or unapproved in the patient's home country but legal in the destination country (such as travel for reproductive technologies, assisted suicide, experimental drug, and stem cell therapy); and (3) medical tourism for services legal in both the home and destination countries (such as travel for heart valve replacement, hip replacement, cosmetic surgery). The patients also can be divided based on who pays for their travel and health care, such as those who pay out of pocket; those whose care is paid for by a private health care insurer; and those whose care is paid for by a public insurer, such as through the EU health care Directive.

Travel for assisted suicide falls into the middle category of medical tourism for services that are illegal in the patient's home country, what elsewhere in this chapter is called "circumvention tourism"[5,6] because the patient is circumventing the prohibition on accessing that service in the home country and traveling to where it is permitted, the destination country. In terms of the payer type it falls into the first self-pay category. All forms of medical tourism raise a host of ethical issues—including concerns about the quality of care available to patients, how informed patients are about the conditions under which their care is delivered, difficulties in securing adequate follow-up care, the patients' ability to recover in medical malpractice for injuries that occur, and the effects on destination-country health care availability. This chapter, however, focuses on elements that are unique to this form of medical tourism.[7]

The Phenomenon of Travel for Assisted Suicide

When most people think of travel for assisted suicide, they think of the headline-grabbing English case of Daniel James. Mr. James was a rugby player for the England Youth teams and suffered a terrible injury during a training session in March 2007: a spinal compression leading to dislocation of two vertebrae that led to tetraplegia (paralysis from the chest down) and an inability to move his hands or fingers. He was determined to both prove that the diagnosis was incorrect and recover much of the function he had lost. James attempted rehabilitation but ultimately did not recover much of what he had lost.[8] He finally accepted his doctors' prognosis that significant improvement was unlikely and began to consider suicide as an option—expressing the wish that he had died in the accident, and in the words of his psychiatrist "he could not envisage a worthwhile future for himself now."[9] James unsuccessfully attempted suicide three times; he subsequently contacted the Swiss clinic, Dignitas, for assistance in dying, and at that point his story becomes one of travel for assisted suicide.[10,11]

Dignitas is a Swiss clinic founded in 1998 that claims to have "helped more than 1,700 people to end their lives gently, safely, without risk and usually in the presence of family members and/or friends."[12,13] It has a multistep process for requesting aid.

> The Dignitas protocol begins with the requester becoming a member of the organization and providing reasons for requesting an assisted suicide (with accompanying medical reports on diagnosis, prognosis, etc.). Dignitas then assesses the patient for compliance with its guidelines (i.e., the individual must be suffering from a fatal disease or have an unacceptable disability). If its criteria are met, Dignitas finds a collaborating physician who might be willing to write a prescription. That physician conducts a detailed medical assessment of the individual, and if satisfied that the patient is competent, has a firm desire to die, and meets other criteria, then the physician prescribes life-ending medication. During the final part of the process, typically two months from the prior step to allow time for the patient to reconsider, a volunteer from Dignitas is present and assists with the end of life. The

individual is asked again whether the individual still wishes to die and a declaration of suicide is signed. At this point the individual takes anti-vomiting medication, followed by Pentobarbital about half an hour later. A representative of Dignitas then contacts the police and informs them that an assisted suicide has occurred.[14]

The steps of this protocol were essentially followed in James's case. He contacted Dignitas and arranged for psychiatric evaluation. The psychiatrist found that he had full capacity, had clearly weighed the alternative, and that Mr. James reached his decision without pressure from family members or others. After repeated attempts to convince him to change his mind, James's parents eventually accepted their son's decision and helped him arrange the suicide abroad.[15] A family friend (still unnamed) who originally had offered to organize travel abroad to let James see specialists who might assist in his recovery in the end helped James's parents arrange a flight to Zurich. Mr. James signed a declaration on August 27, 2008, while in the United Kingdom. It was witnessed by his doctor, stating his wish to travel to Switzerland for assisted suicide and that his body be returned to England after he ended his life. On September 12, 2008, accompanied by his parents, James traveled to Zurich. There, in the presence of his parents, a doctor assisted him in ending his life—apparently, according to postmortem blood samples, using a fatal dose of a barbiturate.[16]

The plural of anecdote is not data. Although his story is compelling, how typical is James's narrative? How widespread is this practice? It is very hard to get comprehensive data on travel for assisted suicide, as one might expect from an act that is both extremely private and in some places illegal. For this author's recent book, *Patients with Passports: Medical Tourism, Ethics, and Law*, and again for this chapter, the author reviewed the available academic and medical literature, finding that it suggests that Switzerland remains the most common destination for travel for assisted suicide both in media and academic accounts. The main reason is that, unlike other countries (or states) that permit assisted suicide for residents, Switzerland permits a nonresident to end his or her life through this system as well.[17,18]

That said, there is some controversy in the literature about whether the Netherlands really does have a residency requirement and whether it is easily circumvented.[19,20] In the last several years there have been reports that the organization "Exit International has been providing information to interested individuals looking to legally purchase veterinary barbiturates from over-the-counter pet pharmacies in the northern parts of Mexico,"[21] which are easier to access by individuals from the United States.

In some countries there also could be interstate or interprovince differences in legal treatment facilitating medical tourism *within the country.* In a country such as the United States, for example, where some states do permit assisted suicide, there are suggestions in the literature that some citizens have relocated to permissive states and established residency there to obtain assisted suicide.[22]

Switzerland itself has considered imposing a residency requirement, and in May 2011 a draft bill that would have restricted access to those who lived in the Canton of Zurich for at least one year was rejected.[23,24] Although there are six official voluntary right-to-die organizations that operate in Switzerland, only four of the six offer their services to those who are neither Swiss citizens nor residents.[25]

In terms of the numbers, in a 2014 paper Gauthier et al. report that the six organizations that assist with suicide in Switzerland claim on their websites to collectively assist 600 suicides a year, including roughly 150 to 200 travelers. Dignitas is the main organization facilitating travel for assisted suicide.[26]

As a partial check on these claims (it is possible the organizations have incentives to over- or underreport) Gauthier et al. provide official numbers from Zurich's Institute of Legal Medicine for the period of 2008–2012. Although useful, these figures are from Zurich (the primary canton for travel for assisted suicide) only, so they also might somewhat undercount the total number of individuals traveling for assisted suicide.

Every time an assisted suicide is carried out in Switzerland there is a legal investigation undertaken by the Canton of Zurich. This enabled Gauthier and the coauthors to examine records from investigations and postmortem examinations carried out by the Institute of Legal Medicine in Zurich from January 1, 2008, to December 31, 2012. As far as this author is aware, this is the most complete data set relating to travel for assisted suicide in existence. The entire Gauthier paper is well worth a read, but the key findings are summarized below.

- **Number:** The number of patients traveling for assisted suicide varied considerably from year to year: 123 in 2008, 86 in 2009, 90 in 2010, 140 in 2011, and 172 in 2012, for a total of 611 cases on record. Dignitas assisted almost all of the travelers seeking assistance in suicide, and Exit International assisted four of them.

- **Gender:** In the sample, 58 people or 5 percent of those who received assisted suicide were women (though there were year-to-year fluctuations from a low of 54 percent to a high of 62 percent). Those traveling for assisted suicide ranged in age from 23 years old on the low end to 97 years old on the high end, with a median age of 69.

- **Reason:** The reasons given by each patient for the suicide varied significantly. The most common reasons provided were neurological disease (47 percent), followed by cancer (37 percent), and then rheumatic and cardiovascular diseases; 28 percent listed more than one reason for seeking assisted suicide.

- **Origin:** Travelers for assisted suicide came from 31 different countries but most were Europeans, with nearly half coming from Germany (43.9 percent), followed by the UK at 20.6 percent, and France at 10.8 percent. The United States had only 21 patients (34 percent of this population). Over the period studied, the countries that had the largest growth were Germany, Italy, France, the United Kingdom, and the United States, although in some cases original and final numbers are both small so it could be due to random fluctuation (the authors did not conduct tests of statistical significance). Still, Italy had a quite dramatic increase with 10 times as many suicide tourists in 2012 (22) as in 2008 (2).[27]

- **Changes over Time:** To generate a longer time series, Gauthier et al. also compare their findings to those of Bosshard et al.[28] (who studied the period 1990–2000), and Fischer et al.[29] (who studied 2000–2004). They found that the *total* number of assisted suicides in the Canton of Zurich increased from 331 to 421 to 950 in the three periods. The studies contained data on those who traveled for assisted suicide only in the latter two periods, which showed an increase from 255 in 2000–2004 to 611 in 2008–2012.[30,31]

In commenting on their findings, Gauthier et al. suggest that the decreased travel for assisted suicide from 2008 to 2009 and the significant increase from 2009 to 2012 could be explained by media attention in 2008 to four cases of assisted suicide involving helium inhalation (described as "excruciating"), as opposed to ingestion of sodium pentobarbital in all other cases.[32]

How much does assisted suicide cost? According to a report in the newspaper *The Mirror,* "[t]he price of a suicide at Dignitas is believed to be around £5,000. But the full service, including funerals, medical costs and official fees, can be as high as £7,000."[33] Another set of authors (themselves relying on the work of British journalists) wrote that the "cost of a simple suicide at Dignitas has risen from £1,800 in 2005 to £4,500 [in 2010],"[34,35] in addition to the travel and lodging costs of an individual medical traveler. The most recent version of the Dignitas website itself indicates a more detailed cost breakdown.[36] It appears as though these costs are paid by the patient seeking the suicide (perhaps with financing from their family), but the Dignitas website does not contain specific information on this aspect.

Travel for Assisted Suicide and the Law

Countries vary significantly on to what extent they permit assisted suicide, and this chapter does not seek to review here the details that are covered in other chapters in this volume. Instead, it discusses how home countries regulate the international *travel* of their citizens and residents for assisted suicide.

International Law

As a general rule, when a country passes a law it does *not* have "extraterritorial" application, that is the rule governs conduct by individuals *within* the territory but not *outside* of it. Under this general background rule, even home countries that criminalize assisted suicide in their territory will not criminalize assisting suicide in the destination country to which a patient travels.

That said, this is a *default rule*. Under international law a home country *may* extend its prohibition extraterritorially in some circumstances. To give but one example, the U.S. PROTECT Act ("Prosecutorial Remedies and Other Tools to End the Exploitation of Children Today") criminalizes child sex tourism abroad by U.S. citizens, and thus extends its criminal law extraterritorially.[37] Another good example is the way in which the United States prohibits "[a]ny citizen of the United States, wherever he may be," from conducting certain correspondence with foreign governments.[38]

Without going too far into fine legal distinctions, note that there are several different types of extraterritorial jurisdiction for domestic laws. Here the focus is on "jurisdiction to prescribe" or "prescriptive jurisdiction." Such jurisdiction consists of the power "to prescribe rules," for example, to make it a crime in the United Kingdom for a UK citizen to procure assisted suicide in Switzerland where the local territorial law does not make the act illegal. This form of jurisdiction is to be contrasted with "enforcement jurisdiction," for example, the ability of the United Kingdom in the same circumstance to violate Swiss sovereignty and arrest a Swiss citizen for performing acts that are criminal in the United Kingdom. Even when a country has and exercises its power to prescribe, it typically does not have jurisdiction to enforce and instead relies on extradition processes to get the offender back into the country's sovereign territory and custody.[39,40] Under international law, a home country's exercise of prescriptive jurisdiction often is given more deference than its enforcement jurisdiction, such that international law might permit a home country to declare an extraterritorial activity of its citizen a crime under its domestic law but *not* permit it to have jurisdiction to enforce the law by arresting its citizen in the foreign country. In the case of assisted suicide this is no great obstacle for home country regulation because, as in Daniel James' case, the friend or family member who travels abroad with the patient typically intends to return to the home country. Upon return to the United Kingdom, they could subsequently can be arrested or prosecuted.

To extend its prescriptive jurisdiction extraterritorially a home country must identify a valid basis for prescriptive jurisdiction under international law. The "Nationality Principle" permits a state to assert jurisdiction over the acts of its citizens wherever they take place, and will easily allow home countries to criminalize the activities of their citizens abroad in assisting a suicide.[41] Other bases of prescriptive jurisdiction also might support action here—"subjective territorial jurisdiction" comprehends crimes that are initiated in one's home territory but completed in another territory, and "passive personality" might provide a home country jurisdiction based on the fact that the victim (rather than perpetrator) is a citizen of the home country—but they are more complicated. This chapter does not delve further into these juridical weeds because the such factors likely only would come into play if the home country attempted to (prescriptively) criminalize the activity of destination country citizens rather than its own.[42]

Even when there is a jurisdictional basis for extraterritorial application of law, that basis usually is constrained by a "reasonableness" standard in its actual execution.[43] This limitation, discussed elsewhere, explains why, in the context of assisted suicide, a country that criminalizes the act at home likely will not be found to be unreasonable under this analysis if it criminalizes the same activity extraterritorially.[44,45] Importantly, this author believes that this conclusion will hold even if the destination country is one that legally permits the activity, as is true in the case of travel to Switzerland for assisted suicide.

Domestic Law and European Union Law: The Case of the United Kingdom

The fact that international law *permits* assertions of extraterritorial prescriptive jurisdiction in criminal matters, such as assisted suicide, does not itself *require* the home country to make that assertion. Indeed, the mere fact that *international* law permits it does not even itself answer the question of whether it is permitted, because one must look as well at domestic and supranational law, the latter being particularly important in the case of the European Union.

The country with the most developed jurisprudence on prosecuting individuals who assisted in travel for suicide is the United Kingdom, which has litigated several important cases. This perhaps is not surprising given that, based on the Gauthier et al. study discussed above, after Germany, UK citizens were the most common travelers to Switzerland for assisted suicide.

The most well-known case relating to assisted suicide came before the European Court of Human Rights (ECHR) and was decided by that court in 2002. It involved Dianne Pretty, who suffered from motor neuron disease, a degenerative illness that rendered her increasingly debilitated, and she sought assurances from the director of public prosecution (DPP) that her husband would not face prosecution were he to assist her in committing suicide by accompanying her to a Swiss clinic.[46,47] Pretty was concerned that her husband's activities would constitute a criminal offense The relevant criminal offense fell under the English Suicide Act of 1961, which stated that "[a] person who aids, abets, counsels or procures the suicide of another, or an attempt by another to commit suicide, shall be liable on conviction on indictment to imprisonment for a term not exceeding fourteen years."[48] The DPP refused to confirm that Pretty's husband would not be prosecuted, leading Pretty to argue before the House of Lords in 2001 and ultimately before the ECHR that this violated her rights under Article 8 of the European Convention to respect for private and family life.[49] Both bodies rejected this claim.[50,51] The ECHR also held that a blanket was not disproportionate to the aim of public protection because the history of attempts to carve out exceptions had suggested the potential for abuse of the exception, particularly in cases of vulnerable individuals.[52]

In a more recent case (decided in 2009), Deborah Purdy, who suffered from multiple sclerosis, anticipated a time when she would want to end her life. Purdy applied to the High Court seeking an order that the DPP issue guidance that declared that her husband would not face charges should he assist her travel to Switzerland to die.[53] The High Court refused to give her the relief she sought, prompting Purdy to take her case to the House of Lords.[54,55] The House of Lords upheld the general criminal prohibition on assisted suicide, but found a problem under the European Convention's Article 8 as to fair warning and consistency of application of the Code for Crown Prosecutors—the Code that specifies the principles under which prosecutors exercise their discretion as to whether to prosecute.[56,57] The Lords found it problematic that it could not be determined from the Code ahead of time whether helping a loved one commit suicide could lead to prosecution; that is, whether prosecutorial discretion would be exercised for or against the individual's prosecution.[58]

In response to this decision, in 2010 the DPP sought to cure this defect and issued final guidelines listing 16 factors in favor of prosecution and 6 against prosecution.

Public interest factors tending in favour of prosecution:

(1) The victim was under 18 years of age;
(2) The victim did not have the capacity (as defined by the Mental Capacity Act 2005) to reach an informed decision to commit suicide;

(3)   The victim had not reached a voluntary, clear, settled, and informed decision to commit suicide;

(4)   The victim had not clearly and unequivocally communicated his or her decision to commit suicide to the suspect;

(5)   The victim did not seek the encouragement or assistance of the suspect personally or on his or her own initiative;

(6)   The suspect was not wholly motivated by compassion; for example, the suspect was motivated by the prospect that he or she or a person closely connected to him or her stood to gain in some way from the death of the victim;

(7)   The suspect pressured the victim to commit suicide;

(8)   The suspect did not take reasonable steps to ensure that any other person had not pressured the victim to commit suicide;

(9)   The suspect had a history of violence or abuse against the victim;

(10) The victim was physically able to undertake the act that constituted the assistance him or herself;

(11) The suspect was unknown to the victim and encouraged or assisted the victim to commit suicide by providing specific information via, for example, a website or publication;

(12) The suspect gave encouragement or assistance to more than one victim who were not known to each other;

(13) The suspect was paid by the victim or those close to the victim for his or her encouragement or assistance;

(14) The suspect was acting in his or her capacity as a medical doctor, nurse, other health care professional, a professional carer [regardless of whether for payment], or as a person in authority, such as a prison officer, and the victim was in his or her care;

(15) The suspect was aware that the victim intended to commit suicide in a public place where it was reasonable to think that members of the public may be present;

(16) The suspect was acting in his or her capacity as a person involved in the management or as an employee (whether for payment or not) of an organisation or group, a purpose of which is to provide a physical environment (whether for payment or not) in which to allow another to commit suicide.

Public interest factors tending against prosecution:

(1)   The victim had reached a voluntary, clear, settled, and informed decision to commit suicide;

(2)   The suspect was wholly motivated by compassion;

(3)   The actions of the suspect, although sufficient to come within the definition of the offence, were of only minor encouragement or assistance;

(4) The suspect had sought to dissuade the victim from taking the course of action which resulted in his or her suicide;

(5) The actions of the suspect may be characterised as reluctant encouragement or assistance in the face of a determined wish on the part of the victim to commit suicide;

(6) The suspect reported the victim's suicide to the police and fully assisted them in their enquiries into the circumstances of the suicide or the attempt and his or her part in providing encouragement or assistance.[59]

The UK guidelines continue to prompt legal challenges, recently including the UK Supreme Court's decision in R. (Nicklinson and Lamb) v. Ministry of Justice and R. (AM) v. Director of Public Prosecutions of June 2014.[60] In this case, the UK Supreme Court (the highest court in the land, succeeding the House of Lords in this role) heard several challenges relating to the DPP guidelines: that the criminalization of assisted suicide was incompatible with Article 8 of the European Convention on Human Rights (respect for private life), that the DPP should clarify and modify the published policy for prosecutors, and that the DPP's policy was not sufficiently clear in its application to health professionals. The Supreme Court ultimately decided 7 to 2 against the challengers but did so through a series of separate opinions, many of which suggest that the U.K.'s criminalization of assisted suicide and the DPP policy could be in trouble in future litigation.

The Normative Question: How *Should* the Law Treat Travel for Assisted Suicide?

Thus far this chapter has dwelled on the legal question and has shown that, under international law, countries *may* exercise prescriptive jurisdiction to impose criminal penalties on home country citizens who assist other home country citizens in suicide, and that individual countries (such as the UK) have and will adopt laws or policies governing under what circumstances they *will* prosecute.

There is a very separate normative question: *Should* countries extend their criminal law extraterritorially to prosecute a home country citizen/resident who helps a patient travel from the home country to the destination country for assisted suicide? One way to go about answering this question is to make final ethical determination on the morality of assisted suicide. Perhaps other chapters in this book undertake that effort, but that is not the task of this chapter. Instead, it is interested in the following question: To the extent a home country *already has* determined to criminalize assisted suicide domestically, to what extent does it have a prerogative or obligation to criminalize the same conduct when performed by one of its citizens on one of its citizens abroad?

The argument that home countries should refrain from extending domestic prohibitions extraterritorially has as its most sophisticated proponent Professor Guido Pennings, who has advocated for a notion of "external tolerance" that he applies to (among other things) travel abroad for assisted suicide. According to Pennings, where "a certain norm is applicable and applied in society as wanted by the majority while simultaneously the members of the minority can still act according to their moral view by going abroad" the state has a moral duty to allow individuals to go abroad and travel for the service because it "demonstrates the absolute minimum of respect for their moral autonomy."[61] Pennings' approach permits a type of "*modus vivendi*," which "prevents a frontal clash of opinions which may jeopardise social peace."[62]

Richard Huxtable has applied this approach more directly to assisted suicide, writing that

> If we continue to presume that the originating state is broadly prohibitive, then that must constitute a considerable victory for opponents of the practice. Such a position necessarily excludes the proponents, including those who would themselves wish to take up the option if available. As assisted suicide is indeed available elsewhere (subject to the satisfaction of certain criteria) it seems unduly heavy-handed of the jurisdiction of origin to seek to prevent or penalise those who seek to take up the offer.[63]

This author is the chief proponent of the other view in the literature, a view that argues that the other approach yields too much to pluralism in some instances.[64] The author has spilled quite a lot of ink making this argument through a series of claims about political theory and through case studies and thought experiments, but in a small nutshell it can be summarized as: Criminal law is serious business. When a home country makes something a crime at home—especially in the face of a full-throated minority opposition—it has concluded that the interests worth protecting by criminalization outweigh the interests in accommodating pluralism.

Very often criminalizing conduct is motivated by the desire to prevent serious bodily harm or death; certainly, that is the view of countries that criminalize assisted suicide at home. Many of them do so because they do not view the consent of the "victim" as being enough to change the wrong-making nature of the killing act because they are dubious of the quality of that consent, or because they think that suicide itself is wrong even when voluntary.

Some readers might think that the home country is wrong to believe these claims about assisted suicide, but that is *not* the point. That would be a good argument for making the act of assisted suicide legally permitted at home. That is a debate worth having, but it is *not* the debate regarding *travel* for assisted suicide. Instead, here the question is whether having concluded that criminalization should not yield to pluralism at home, the home country can justifiably reach the opposite conclusion when patients travel abroad for the service.

Having concluded that assisting suicide is a grave crime that the criminal law should punish at home, it would be beyond strange to think that the location of the offending act matters in terms of what makes the act wrong. This author has argued that under social contractarian, communitarian, and other political theories, the state's interest in preventing one of its citizens from seriously harming another of its citizens is the key moral basis for establishing the sovereign's right to punish, much more so than the happenstance that the act in question occurred within its physical territory.

In terms of most of the perquisites of citizenship and the home country's obligations to its citizens, people carry their citizenship abroad with them when they travel and also should take with them the minimal duty not to harm fellow citizens in ways prescribed by the home country when the home country has extended the reach of its laws extraterritorially. Thus, the home country not only has the legal authority but also has the moral authority to prescriptively criminalize an act by one home-country citizen that causes serious bodily harm to another.

But what about the "victim's" consent? Does that make the case different from, for example, murder, female-genital cutting, or perhaps even abortion? This author thinks not. With assisted suicide, the consent is not one that the home country accepts as justified in making the act *lawful at home*, either because it thinks consent is irrelevant, it is suspicious of the quality of the consent,[65] or for some other reason. Unless there is a good argument as to why the home country views the consent given by someone *who travels abroad* as different from the consent of the person who *stays at home* and seeks help ending his or her life, it is hard to understand why the home country should treat the two cases differently when it is its own citizen who is assisting in the suicide of its own citizen.

If the underlying reason for rejecting consent is fear of pressure or manipulation, then the home country has good reason to criminalize the act abroad. Indeed, it could seem that assisted-suicide tourism is *worse* in this regard because the state cannot use its existing laws and regulations relating to the supervision of its physicians (including licensure and disciplinary rules for physicians) to protect against these undue influences.

The only argument that the author has seen provided to the contrary is an argument that he has offered—that time, expense, and preparation involved in traveling abroad give us more confidence that the person seeking assisted suicide demonstrates more self-reflection or seriousness of purpose than the one who seeks it at home.[66] Although possible, this author has seen no evidence and does not think this serves as a persuasive reason to distinguish engaging in the activity at home versus abroad. Therefore, for countries whose main reason for criminalizing assisted suicide at home is preventing harm to the patient who commits suicide, then they have a strong reason to extend that prohibition extraterritorially.

Of course, the criminalization of travel for assisted suicide is not *only* about serious bodily harm. In some instances, it is about maintaining particular mores about the value of life and avoiding corruption of the medical profession.[67] In these instances, to determine whether a home country that prohibits a particular act for *this* reason should also prohibit medical tourism for the engaging in the activity while abroad, we must ask whether the act is truly the same. The issue is discussed in much greater depth elsewhere, but for present purposes suffice to say that if fear of attitude-modification *at home* is the main reason for the criminalization, then the cases of travel for suicide abroad could be different than at home. The key question is empirical but ultimately is hard to answer: Is the fact that the activity takes place abroad likely to have as much of an attitude-modifying effect on home-country citizens as if it took place at home?

Thus the *reason* why the prohibition is in place at home partially determines whether the criminalization should be extended extraterritorially. In cases where there are multiple reasons why a domestic criminalization is in place the picture becomes quite complicated, making it difficult to determine which reasons are necessary and sufficient and how much each contributes as justification for the prohibition.

Even if under this analysis a home country does justifiably apply its prohibition on assisted suicide extraterritorially, as Srinivas has noted, that is not a magic bullet for deterrence. The threat of criminalizing assistance by family members or friends instead could lead patients to travel abroad for assisted suicide earlier in the course of their illness when they are able to make the trip without aid. It also could mean that those individuals who help loved ones might bank on the sympathy of the public or a lack of nerve on the part of prosecutors, and reason that they will not be charged or will be acquitted if prosecuted.[68] All that said, both of these arguments apply equally to prosecution for assisting suicide *within* the home country. This again suggests that a home country's position should be consistent wherever the assisted suicide takes place, at home or abroad.

Conclusion

Travel for assisted suicide is not going away. Indeed, the data suggest that it has increased over the last decade, with most of the travel being to Switzerland. Under international law, countries have the power to regulate the circumstances in which their citizens engage in this travel. Most home countries, however, have not done so; even those countries that have might face domestic or supranational legal challenges to that regulation. From a moral perspective, though, it is potentially problematic for a country to prohibit assisted suicide at home, create an incentive for circumvention tourism, and then look the other way when citizens travel for the very thing the country has outlawed.

Notes

1. See Cohen, G. 2015. *Patients with Passports*. New York: Oxford University Press. "Chapter 8, Medical Tourism and Ending Life: Travel for Assisted Suicide and Abortion," 315–18.

2. Miller, D. S., and C. Gonzalez. 2013. "When Death Is the Destination: The Business of Death Tourism—Despite Legal and Social Implications." *International Journal of Culture, Tourism, and Hospitality Research* 7 (3): 293–306. doi: 10.1108/IJCTHR-05-2012-0042.

3. See Howze, Kerrie S. 2007. "Note, Medical Tourism: Symptom or Cure?" 41 *Georgia Law Review* at 1015–16, n.18.

4. Cearley, Anne, and Penni Crabtree. 2006. "Alternative-Medicine Clinics in Baja Have History of Controversy." *San Diego Union Tribune* (February 1) at A8. http://www.sandiegouniontribune.com/uniontrib/20060201/news_1n1clinic.html (accessed July 5, 2016).

5. Cohen, *supra* note 1.

6. Cohen, I. G. "Circumvention Tourism." 2012. *Cornell Law Review* 97: 1309–98. http://www.ncbi.nlm.nih.gov/pubmed/23072007 (accessed July 5, 2016).

7. Cohen, *supra* note 1.

8. Hughes, M. 2008. "At 23, Daniel Chose to End His 'Second Class' Life." *The Independent* (October 18). http://www.independent.co.uk/news/uk/home-news/at-23-daniel-chose-to-end-his-second-class-life-965447.html (accessed August 25, 2016).

9. Crown Prosecution Service, "Decision on Prosecution—The Death by Suicide of Daniel James," (September 12, 2008), section 6. http://www.cps.gov.uk/news/articles/death_by_suicide_of_daniel_james/ (accessed September 24, 2016).

10. Mullock, A. 2009. "Commentary: Prosecutors Making (Bad) Law?" *Medical Law Review* 17: 290–93. doi: 10.1093/medlaw/fwp009.

11. Cohen, *supra* note 1.

12. DIGNITAS. 2014. *How DIGNITAS Works, On What Philosophical Principles are the Activities of This Organization Based? Dignitas* 3(2) (May): 1–28. http://www.dignitas.ch/images/stories/pdf/so-funktioniert-dignitas-e.pdf (accessed August 25, 2016).

13. Miller, *supra* note 2

14. Ost, S. 2010. "The De-Medicalisation of Assisted Dying: Is a Less Medicalised Model the Way Forward?" *Medical Law Review* 18(497): 521–22. doi:10.1093/medlaw/fwq025.

15. Mullock, *supra* note 10.

16. Ibid.

17. Cohen, *supra* note 1.

18. Smith, S. 2007. "Some Realism About End of Life: The Current Prohibition and the Euthanasia Underground." *American Journal of Law & Medicine* 33: 55,70. http://www.ncbi.nlm.nih.gov/pubmed/17547355 (accessed July 5, 2016).

19. Safyan, A. 2011. "A Call for International Regulation of the Thriving 'Industry' of Death Tourism." *Loyola of Los Angeles International and Comparative Law Review* 33(2) (January 1): 287, 304. http://digitalcommons.lmu.edu/cgi/viewcontent.cgi?article=1665&context=ilr (accessed July 5, 2016).

20. Bix, B. 2003. "Physician Assisted Suicide and Federalism." *Notre Dame Law Journal of Ethics & Public Policy* 17: 53, 60. http://scholarship.law.nd.edu/cgi/viewcontent.cgi?article=1263&context=ndjlepp (accessed July 5, 2016).

21. Higginbotham, G. 2011. "Assisted-Suicide Tourism: Is it Tourism?" *Tourismos: An International Multidisciplinary Journal of Tourism* 6(2): 178.

22. Slotnik, D., and Brittany Maynard. 2014. " 'Death with Dignity' Ally, Dies at 29." *New York Times* (November 3). http://www.nytimes.com/2014/11/04/us/brittany-maynard-death-with-dignity-ally-dies-at-29.html (accessed April 24, 2015).

23. Miller, *supra* note 13.

24. Gauthier, S., J. Mausbach, T. Reisch, and C. Bartsch. 2014. "Suicide Tourism: A Pilot Study on the Swiss Phenomenon." *Journal of Medical Ethics* (August 20): 1–7. doi:10.1136/medethics-2014-102091 (accessed April 24, 2015).

25. Ibid.

26. Ibid.

27. Although the authors note various law changes or proposed law changes in these countries that might be related to these fluctuations, it is hard to tell a clean causal story about why these changes (many of which actually represent liberalization) led to increases in travel for assisted suicide. One answer, though speculative, is that it is the media *attention* to these potential law changes, which increases the rates, rather than the law changes themselves. As to Italy, the authors suggest (with appropriate caution) that the increase might be due to a well-publicized political debate in the country about a single case that sent a message that liberalization was unlikely to occur within Italy in the foreseeable future.

28. Bosshard, G., E. Ulrich, and W. Bär. 2003. "748 Cases of Suicide Assisted by a Swiss Right-to-Die Organisation. *Swiss Medicine Weekly* 133: 310–17. doi: 2003/21/smw-10212.

29. Fischer, S., C. A. Huber, L. Imhof, R. Mahrer Imhof, M. Furter, S. J. Ziegler, G. Bosshard. 2008. "Suicide Assisted by Two Right-to-Die Organisations." *Journal of Medical Ethics* 34: 310–17. doi:10.1136/jme.2007.023887.

30. Gauthier, *supra* note 24.

31. Bosshard, *supra* note 28.

32. Gauthier, *supra* note 24.

33. Gregory, A. 2013. "Dignitas Suicide: British Man Ends His Life at Swiss Clinic As He Could Not Face Dementia. *Mirror* (May 30). http://www .mirror.co.uk/news/uk-news/dignitas-suicide-british-man-ends-1920713 (accessed August 25, 2016).

34. "Dignitas Founder Is a Millionaire." 2010. *The Telegraph* (June 24). http:// www.telegraph.co.uk/news/worldnews/europe/switzerland/7851615/Dignitas-fo under-is-millionaire.html (accessed August 25, 2016).

35. See Miller, *supra* note 13.

36. According to the Dignitas website the costs of an assisted suicide are broken down into four distinct fees: the administrative preparation, a required doctor's consultation, the funeral and registry service, and the suicide itself. The administrative expenses incurred cost the individual 3,000 Swiss Francs, or approximately £2,400, or U.S. $3,600. To fulfill the requirement that a Swiss medical doctor, in cooperation with Dignitas, must meet with the individual and prescribe the necessary drug costs approximately 1,000 Swiss Francs, or GBP £800, or U.S. $1,200. The funeral and registry costs are the most flexible, with the basic services of a funeral director and cremation beginning at 2,000 Swiss Francs, and Dignitas offers to take care of registry costs for the family for an additional fee of 1,500 Francs. Lastly, the suicide itself compels a contribution of another 3,000 Swiss Francs, or approximately GBP £2,400, or U.S. $3,600. In total, if Dignitas is not handling the administrative work, then the total cost is 7,000 Francs, GBP £5,600, or U.S. $8,400. If Dignitas is handling the administrative work, then the total cost is 10,500 Francs, GBP £8,400, or U.S. $12,600. DIGNITAS. *Dignitas* (information brochure). http://www.dignitas.ch/images/stories/pdf/informations -broschuere-dignitas-e.pdf (accessed July 5, 2016).

37. The PROTECT Act of 2003, 18 U.S.C. § 2252(B)(b).

38. 18 U.S.C. § 953 (2006).

39. Lowe, V. 2006. "Jurisdiction." In Evans, M. D. ed. *International Law*. Oxford: Oxford University Press, 335–60.

40. Cohen, *supra* note 5.40. Lowe, *supra* note 37.

41. Lowe, *supra* note 39.

42. Ibid.

43. *Restatement (Third) of the Foreign Relations Law of the United States* § 402(1) (a) (1987).

44. Cohen, *supra* note 1.

45. Cohen, *supra* note 7.

46. *Pretty v. United Kingdom*, 2002-III Eur. Ct. H.R. 155, 161.

47. Mullock, *supra* note 9.

48. Suicide Act. 1961. 10 Eliz. 2, c. 60, § 2 (Eng.).

49. See R. (Pretty) v. Dir. of Pub. Prosecutions, [2001] UKHL 61, [2002] 1 A.C. 800 (H.L.) (appeal taken from Eng.).

50. Ibid.

51. Pretty v. United Kingdom, 2002-III Eur. Ct. H.R. 155, 161.

52. Ibid.

53. R. (Purdy) v. Dir. of Pub. Prosecutions, [2009] EWCA (Civ) 92, [4]–[6] (Eng.).

54. Ibid.

55. Greasley, K. 2010. "R. (Purdy) v. DPP and the Case for Wilful Blindness." *Oxford Journal of Legal Studies* 30: 301, 305.

56. R. (Purdy), EWCA (Civ) 92, at [4]–[6].

57. Greasley, *supra* note 53.

58. R. (Purdy), EWCA (Civ) 92, at [4]–[6].

59. Mullock, *supra* note 8.

60. R (Nicklinson and Lamb) v. Ministry of Justice, R. (AM) v. Dir. of Pub. Prosecutions, [2014] UKSC 38 (appeal taken from Eng.)

61. Pennings, G. 2008. "Reproductive Tourism As Moral Pluralism in Motion." *Journal of Medical Ethics* 28(6): 340. doi:10.1136/jme.28.6.337.

62. Ibid.

63. Huxtable, R. 2009. "The Suicide Tourist Trap: Compromise Across Boundaries." *Bioethical Inquiry* 6: 334. doi: 10.1007/s11673-009-9170-5.

64. Cohen, *supra* note 1.

65. Stewart, C., C. Peisah, and B. Draper. 2011. "A Test for Mental Capacity to Request Assisted Suicide." *Journal of Medical Ethics* 37: 36. doi:10.1136/jme.2010.037564.

66. Cohen, *supra* note 1.

67. Ibid.

68. Srinivas, R. 2009. "Exploring the Potential for American Death Tourism." *MSU Journal of Medicine and Law* 13: 91–122.

About the Editor and Contributors

Editor

Michael J. Cholbi (PhD) is a professor of philosophy at California State Polytechnic University, Pomona. He received his doctorate from the University of Virginia. Dr. Cholbi has published many articles on ethical issues relating to suicide and the right to die, including articles in the *Journal of Moral Philosophy, Journal of Ethics, History of Philosophy Quarterly, Journal of Applied Philosophy, Bioethics*, and the *Journal of Medical Ethics*. He also is the author of the entries on suicide in the *Stanford Encyclopedia of Philosophy*, the *International Encyclopedia of Ethics*, and *Oxford Bibliographies Online*. His 2011 book, *Suicide: The Philosophical Dimensions* (Broadview Press), was named a CHOICE Outstanding Academic Title. He is the editor (with Jukka Varelius) of a collection of papers titled *New Directions in the Ethics of Assisted Suicide and Euthanasia*, published by Springer in 2015. Dr. Cholbi has lectured on five continents and has given many interviews to local, national, and global press outlets on suicide and other ethical controversies.

Contributors

Asunción Álvarez del Río (MA, PhD) holds a master's degree in psychology and a doctorate in bioethics. She is a professor and researcher at the Department of Psychiatry and Mental Health, Faculty of Medicine, UNAM (Mexico), vice president of the Colegio de Bioética, and a board member of For the Right to Die with Dignity, Mexico. Álvarez del Río also published *Euthanasia. Practice and Ethics* (2005) (ebook, 2014) (in Spanish).

Jacob M. Appel is a novelist and fiction writer, a licensed attorney, and a bioethicist. He holds advanced degrees from Brown University, Columbia

University, Alden March Bioethics Institute, Harvard Law School, and New York University.

Julieta Gómez Avalos (MD) is a general physician and graduated from the National Autonomous University of Mexico (UNAM). She has done research stays on bioethics at the Department of Psychiatry and Mental Health, Faculty of Medicine, UNAM, where she currently is performing research on the subject of medical education in end-of-life care.

Brett Barleyman (MA) earned his master's degree in Buddhist Studies at Komazawa University, Tokyo. He has conducted further research at Komazawa University for three years, working toward his doctoral degree which he is completing through Waikato University, New Zealand, in the field of Religious Studies. Additionally, Mr. Barleyman has practiced Zen under Harada Tangen Roshi in Fukui Prefecture and Gudo Wafu Nishijima Sensei in Tokyo.

Tuba Erkoç Baydar (MA) graduated from Uludag University Faculty of Theology with minor in Social Sciences in 2009. She completed her master's degree at Istanbul University, Faculty of Theology, in 2011. In the same year, Ms. Baydar started working as a research assistant at Medeniyet University. In 2011, her doctorate studies started at Marmara University in the field of Islamic Law, and she currently is working as a research assistant at the same department.

Joseph Boyle was a professor of philosophy at the University of Toronto. He was a leading scholar in bioethics, particularly on the doctrine of double effect.

Courtney S. Campbell is the Hundere Professor in Religion and Culture at Oregon State University and the former director of its Program for Ethics, Science, and the Environment. Mr. Campbell previously was a research associate at the Hastings Center and has written widely about the legalization of assisted suicide, particularly Oregon's Death with Dignity Act.

I. Glenn Cohen is a professor at Harvard Law School, as well as the faculty director of the Petrie-Flom Center for Health Law Policy, Biotechnology, and Bioethics. He has published more than 80 scholarly articles and chapters, and comments on bioethical issues regularly in both the print and electronic media.

Raphael Cohen-Almagor (D. Phil., Oxon) is an educator, researcher, and human rights activist. Cohen-Almagor also holds a chair in politics at the University of Hull, United Kingdom. His publications include *The Right to Die with Dignity: An Argument in Ethics, Law, and Medicine* (2001), and *Euthanasia in the Netherlands: The Policy and Practice of Mercy Killing* (2004).

Colin Gavaghan is an associate professor in the Faculty of Law at the University of Otago. He directs that institution's Centre for Law and Policy in Emerging Technologies.

Isaac González Huerta is a general physician who graduated from the University of Guadalajara. Dr. Huerta has done research on bioethics at the UCSC in Rome, Italy, and at the National Autonomous University of Mexico (UNAM), where he is currently conducting an interdisciplinary research project on medical decisions at the end of life of patients with dementia. He is a founding member of INRED México (National Institute of Human Duties and Responsibilities).

Ilhan Ilkilic (MD, PhD), has studied medicine, philosophy, Islamic science, and oriental philology in Istanbul, Bochum, and Tübingen (Germany). Dr. Ilkilic is currently professor and chair of the Department of History of Medicine and Ethics at the Istanbul University Faculty of Medicine. He has been a member of the German Ethics Council since 2012 and directs the Institute of Health Sciences at the Istanbul University in Turkey.

Paul T. Menzel is professor emeritus of philosophy at Pacific Lutheran University and an affiliate professor in the Department of Bioethics and Humanities at the University of Washington School of Medicine. He has published extensively on many topics in the medical ethics field.

Ben A. Rich (JD, PhD) is an emeritus professor and Alumni Association Endowed Chair in the Bioethics Program at the University of California, Davis. He has written widely on legal issues related to bioethics, including palliation, respect for patient autonomy, and end-of-life care.

Jack Simmons (PhD) received his doctoral degree from Tulane University and now is an associate professor of philosophy at Armstrong State University. Dr. Simmons has written widely on topics in medicine and education from a Continental perspective.

Lloyd Steffen is a professor of religion studies and University Chaplain at Lehigh University. He is also director of the Dialogue Center and the Lehigh Prison Project. He is the author of *The Ethics of Death: Religious and Philosophical Perspectives in Dialogue* (2014) and *New Perspectives on the End of Life: Essays on Care and the Intimacy of Dying* (2013).

Arthur G. Svenson (PhD) received his doctoral degree from the University of California, Santa Barbara, and is David Boies Professor of government at the University of Redlands. Dr. Svenson is the coauthor of *Physician-Assisted Suicide: The Anatomy of a Constitutional Law Issue* (2003).

Eric Vogelstein (PhD) received his doctoral degree from the University of Texas at Austin and is currently an assistant professor at Duquesne University with joint appointments in philosophy and the School of Nursing. Dr. Vogelstein has written on several issues related to medical decision making, including competence and advance directives.

Robert Young is a research associate at La Trobe University. He has written extensively on moral and legal issues related to assisted dying, including "Voluntary Euthanasia" (*Stanford Encyclopedia of Philosophy*) and *Medically Assisted Death* (Cambridge, 2007).

Index